T0306190

INDIAN BUSINESS

The Indian economy is projected to become the world's fourth largest by 2020 and it is central to global economic performance. In a period of rapid change, understanding the business environment is a challenge. This book highlights the unique mix of challenges and opportunities for investors and organizations in India.

Indian Business brings together a wide range of experts to present a comprehensive insight into doing business in India. It draws on research-based evidence and expert coverage of the emerging political, legal and social frameworks. It is divided into three parts: the Indian business context, conducting business in India, and emerging practices relevant for foreign investors. Each chapter outlines the context and justification for study, along with an analysis of the present situation and future options. Useful features include a case study with questions for analysis, and links to useful web resources.

This book provides business practitioners and students with a thorough understanding of how to start and grow successful organizations in India.

Pawan S. Budhwar is Professor of International HRM at Aston Business School, Birmingham, UK. He is the Associate Pro-Vice Chancellor International (India) of Aston University, the Joint-Director of the Aston India Centre for Applied Research and Co-Editor-in-Chief of the *British Journal of Management*.

Arup Varma is Professor of Management at Loyola University Chicago, USA. His research interests include performance appraisal and expatriate issues. He has published articles in leading journals, including the *Academy of Management Journal*, *Personnel Psychology*, and the *Journal of Applied Psychology*.

Rajesh Kumar is currently the Principal of International Strategic Consultants (www.internationalstrategicconsulting.com), an international business advisory consultancy. Prior to this, he was Professor of International Business at Menlo College, CA, USA. His expertise lies in the area of managing strategic partnerships, negotiating across cultures and managing in emerging markets.

INDIAN BUSINESS

Understanding a Rapidly Emerging Economy

Edited by Pawan S. Budhwar, Arup Varma and Rajesh Kumar

Routledge
Taylor & Francis Group

LONDON AND NEW YORK

First published 2019
by Routledge
2 Park Square, Milton Park, Abingdon, Oxon OX14 4RN

and by Routledge
52 Vanderbilt Avenue, New York, NY 10017

Routledge is an imprint of the Taylor & Francis Group, an informa business

British Library Cataloguing in Publication Data
A catalogue record for this book is available from the British Library

Library of Congress Cataloging-in-Publication Data
Names: Budhwar, Pawan S., editor. | Varma, Arup, editor. |
Kumar, Rajesh, 1954- editor.
Title: Indian business : understanding a rapidly emerging economy / edited by Pawan S. Budhwar, Arup Varma and Rajesh Kumar.
Description: Abingdon, Oxon ; New York, NY : Routledge, 2019. |
Includes bibliographical references and index.
Identifiers: LCCN 2018060713 (print) | LCCN 2019004389 (ebook) |
ISBN 9781315268422 (eBook) | ISBN 9781138286498 (hardback : alk. paper) |
ISBN 9781138286504 (pbk. : alk. paper)
Subjects: LCSH: Business enterprises--India. | Management--India. |
India--Commerce. | India--Economic conditions.
Classification: LCC HF3786.5 (ebook) | LCC HF3786.5 .I5234 2019 (print) |
DDC 338.0954--dc23
LC record available at https://lccn.loc.gov/2018060713

ISBN: 978-1-138-28649-8 (hbk)
ISBN: 978-1-138-28650-4 (pbk)
ISBN: 978-1-315-26842-2 (ebk)

Typeset in Bembo
by Taylor & Francis Books

To Laxmi and Gaurav, for all their love and support – PB.

To my mother, Leela Wati – AV.

To my mother, Dharmvati Kumar, for all her inspiration and support – RK.

To those who have an interest in doing business in India.

CONTENTS

ILLUSTRATIONS

Figures

Tables

Case studies

CONTRIBUTORS

Bimal Arora is a Lecturer at Aston Business School, Birmingham, UK.

Vidu Badigannavar is a Senior Lecturer in Human Resource Management at Aston Business School, Birmingham, UK.

Sudeshna Bhattacharya is a Teaching Fellow at Aston Business School, Birmingham, UK.

Dharm Prakash Sharma Bhawuk is Professor of Management and Culture and Community Psychology, University of Hawaii at Manoa, USA.

Pawan S. Budhwar is Professor of International HRM at Aston Business School and the Joint Director of Aston India Centre for Applied Research and an Associate Pro-Vice-Chancellor International (India), Aston University, Birmingham, UK.

Rajesh Chandwani is an Assistant Professor of Human Resource Management at the Indian Institute of Management, Ahmedabad, India.

Bhaskar Dasgupta is the Managing Director and Chief Operating Officer, UK Export Finance, London, UK.

Debashree De is a doctoral researcher at Aston Business School, Birmingham, UK.

Soumen De is Professor of Finance and Director of the Asia Research Center at Menlo College, Atherton, California, USA.

Prasanta Dey is Professor in Operations Management at Aston Business School, Birmingham, UK.

Hoa Do is an Assistant Professor in Management at the PDP Education Center, Musashi University, Japan.

Tony Fang is a Professor of Business Administration at Stockholm Business School of Stockholm University, Sweden.

Rajen K. Gupta served as a Professor of Organizational Behaviour at the Management Development Institute, Gurgaon, India.

Sam Hariharan is a Senior Lecturer in Strategy and Global Business, Management Division at Babson College, Wellesley, MA, USA.

Divya Jyoti is a doctoral researcher at Aston Business School, Birmingham, UK.

Naresh Khatri is an Associate Professor of HR in the Health Management and Informatics Department at the University of Missouri, Columbia, Missouri, USA.

Devendra G. Kodwani is Professor of Financial Management and Corporate Governance at the Open University Business School and Executive Dean of Faculty of Business and Law, the Open University, Milton Keynes, UK.

Kunal Kamal Kumar is an Assistant Professor of Organizational Behaviour and Human Resource Management at the Indian Institute of Management, Udaipur, India.

Rajesh Kumar is a Principal with Global Advisory Consulting and a Visiting Professor at the Auckland Institute of Technology, New Zealand.

S.N.V. Siva Kumar is Professor and Area Chairperson of Economics at K.J. Somaiya Institute of Management Studies and Research, Mumbai, India.

Upam Pushpak Makhecha is an Associate Professor of OB & HRM at the Indian Institute of Management, Trichy, India.

Sushanta Kumar Mishra is Professor of Organizational Behaviour at the Indian Institute of Management, Indore, India.

Claudia Müller is a Principal of CIM Consulting and an Associate Professor for Intercultural Leadership at ESCP Europe's Berlin Campus, Berlin, Germany.

Surender Munjal is an Associate Professor of International Business and Strategy and the Director of James E. Lynch India and South Asia Business Centre at the University of Leeds, UK.

Peter Norlander is an Assistant Professor of Human Resources and Industrial Relations at the Quinlan School of Business, Loyola University Chicago, USA.

Abinash Panda is an Associate Professor of Organizational Behaviour at the Management Development Institute, Gurgaon, India.

Raja P. Pappu is a serial entrepreneur, researcher and start-up mentor and Professor of International Business Strategy at GITAM School of International Business, GITAM University, Visakhapatnam, India.

B.C. Pradhan is a career diplomat and presently the Consul General of India at Birgunj, Nepal.

U. Srinivasa Rangan is Professor of Strategy and Global Business and Luksic Chair Professor of Global Studies at Babson College, Wellesley, MA, USA.

Indu Rao is an Associate Professor of Human Resource Management at the Institute of Management, Nirma University, Ahmedabad, India.

Debi S. Saini is an Emeritus Professor of HRM at the Indian Institute of Management, Ranchi, India.

Sanjoy Sen is the Global Head of Research and Eminence for Deloitte's Extended Enterprise Risk Management Group and a doctoral researcher at Aston Business School, Birmingham, UK.

Vivek Shabi is a revenue recognition controller, Nokia, Gurgaon, India.

Ravi Shanker is Professor of Marketing and Chairperson, International Collaborations and Capacity Development Division at the Indian Institute of Foreign Trade, New Delhi, India.

C.K. Sharma is the Director of DS Group: Dharampal Satyapal Ltd, Noida, U.P., India.

Vivek Soni is a management professional, researcher and academic consultant, New Delhi, India.

Rajiv M. Srivastava is ex-Professor of Finance, Indian Institute of Foreign Trade, New Delhi, India.

Arup Varma is Professor of Management at the Quinlan School of Business, Loyola University Chicago, USA.

ACKNOWLEDGEMENTS

Since we wrote the *Doing Business in India* volume in 2011, a number of significant changes have taken place in the Indian business context. This is particularly the case since the present government came to power in 2014. Hence, we believe this volume is both timely and unique in many ways – in terms of up-to-date content, research-based evidence, chapter case studies and clear takeaway points.

Book projects such as this are the result of the efforts of a number of dedicated scholars. Given both the spread of topics covered in this volume and the scarcity of reliable information, it was imperative that we invited leading scholars in the field in order to deliver a quality product. The majority of the contributions to this volume are original and have been specifically written at our request. We would like to thank all the contributors for being responsive to our demands, and revising their chapters as per our suggestions.

We would also like to thank all those who have helped us in various capacities, often behind the scenes, to bring this project to fruition. Our special thanks to Routledge for giving us the opportunity to develop this volume and also giving us the freedom to choose its contents and features. Finally, we would like to thank Terry Clague, Izzy Fitzharris, Judith Lorton, Lucy McClune and Matthew Ranscombe at Routledge for their help and assistance at various stages of the production of this volume.

Pawan S. Budhwar
Aston India Centre for Applied Research
Aston University, Birmingham, UK
Arup Varma
Loyola University Chicago, USA
Rajesh Kumar
Global Advisory Consulting

FOREWORD

When I take visitors on a tour around Parliament, I always stop to show them the mural at St Stephen's Hall depicting Sir Thomas Rowe – Britain's first Ambassador to India – presenting his credentials to the Mughal Emperor Jahangir in 1614.

Today, the UK's relationship with India spans over 400 years – a long and, at times, tempestuous history – and today, more than ever, the UK and India need to look to each other for economic support and collaboration on trade. Since liberalization in 1991, the Indian economy has opened up and created a thriving culture of entrepreneurship, creativity and global collaboration. Mutual respect between the two nations, the UK and India, is at an all-time high.

Increasingly, other international trading partners have looked to India as an emerging market brimming with innovation and vitality. India is the world's second most populous country, home to almost 1.3 billion people. Its economy is growing quickly; its middle class is increasing in size; and it has an increasing reputation for ease of doing-business, with English regarded as the language of business by many who trade there. India will be one of the top two or three leading economies of the world over the coming decade or more, and this book makes clear the consequences of India's rapid emergence.

Yet there is already a strong basis of collaboration between UK and India for us to build on. India invests more in the UK than it does in all the other EU countries put together. The UK is the largest investor in India of all of the G20 nations. More than 800 Indian-owned businesses are already thriving in the UK, employing more than 110,000 people, according to Grant Thornton's 2018 India Tracker report.

Despite the scale of capital flows and the huge size and diversity of India's market – comprising 29 states and seven union territories – the CBI reports that UK trade with India totalled just £16.3bn in 2015, less than the UK's trade with Belgium, a country barely a tenth the size.

How can we bridge this trading gap? Global India is searching for trading partners that match its bold, international ambitions. The freight giant Maersk recently reported a 16 per cent rise in Indian-made retail and lifestyle goods, showing that India can excel in the most competitive global markets where previously it had not. India's export growth has been led in part by its manufacturing powerhouse: Prime Minister Narendra Modi wants to expand the manufacturing sector from 16 to 25 per cent of GDP by 2025 and has drawn up valuable plans to modernize the Indian manufacturing sector and open it up to the global market. We should have a counterpart to the 'Make in India' strategy in the UK. Moreover, we should collaborate with India to share expertise and innovative technology, such as the expertise in digital technologies that can make the UK-India partnership a global force in the Fourth Industrial Revolution.

Along with these opportunities, however, there are challenges in doing business with India. Businesses who want to export will require research; they will need an appreciation of India's political system and its leaders' agenda. India is a federal system consisting of 29 states and seven union territories, each of which has law-making powers; each of these states requires handling differently. This book underlines the challenges that come with managing business relationships with India with pragmatism and optimism and serves as an important guide to doing business in India for the first time – a valuable tool.

More than ever, UK lawmakers must also use their vital influence to elevate the UK-India partnership. Trade agreements are not just about goods and tariffs, they are also about the movement of people, as Prime Minister Modi made clear to Prime Minister Theresa May on her first international visit, to India, in 2016. We need to bring an end to the UK's hostile and economically illiterate immigration policies, which have proved a deterrent to investors, entrepreneurs and international students, if we are going to agree more trade deals with India.

The UK Government needs to accept higher levels of mobility between India and the UK, including tourists, business visitors, skilled workers and especially international students. I am the third generation of my family to have been educated in the UK and I have grown a business, Cobra Beer, in the UK, benefiting from its remarkable environment for doing business and trade around the world. Cobra Beer is now sold in 45 countries around the world and we have three breweries in India along with our Joint Venture partners, Molson Coors.

Books like this are essential in highlighting India as an economic powerhouse – one that is transforming business around the world. India is becoming a major economic force and global centre for business. Now, India is gaining ground and has overtaken the UK as the fifth largest economy in the world. The UK must celebrate India's success and seize its historic opportunity once more to show it is India's greatest world partner.

Lord Karan Billimoria, CBE, DL, FCA
Founder and Chairman, Cobra Beer
Chancellor, University of Birmingham, UK

ABBREVIATIONS

AAI	Airports Authority of India
ADRs	American Depositary Receipts
ARPU	average revenue per user
ASEAN	Association of South-East Asian Nations
AWS	Alliance for Water Stewardship
BA	Bharti Airtel
BF	Bharat Forge
BFSI	banking, financial services and insurance
BIS	Bureau of Indian Standards
BJP	Bharatiya Janata Party
BMS	Bharitya Mazdoor Sangh
BO	Branch Office
BOC	boards of conciliation
BOGOF	buy one, get one free
BOT	build, operate and transfer
BPM	business process management
BPO	business process outsourcing
CAGR	compound annual growth rate
CAR	capital adequacy ratio
CDP	Carbon Disclosure Project
CGST	Central Goods and Services Tax
CITU	Communist Trade Union Federation
CLA	Contract Labour (Regulation & Abolition) Act
CLARA	Child Labour (Abolition and Regulation) Act
CO	conciliation officer
COP	Conference of Parties
CPI	Communist Party of India

CPSE	Central Public Sector Enterprises
CRBP	Child Rights and Business Principles
CRW	Corporate Responsibility Watch
CSO	Central Statistical Office
DB	design-build
DIPP	Department of Industrial Policy and Promotion
DISCOMs	state distribution companies
DPE	Department of Public Enterprises
DPP	Defence Procurement Policy
DPSU	defence public sector unit
ECA	Employees' Compensation Act, 1923
EPFA	Employees Provident Funds (and Miscellaneous Provisions) Act, 1952
EPFS	Employees' Provident Fund Scheme
EPS	Earnings per share
ERA	Equal Remuneration Act, 1976
ERP	enterprise resource planning
ESIA	Employees' State Insurance Act, 1948
ESIC	Employees State Insurance Corporation
ESIS	employee state insurance scheme
FCCBs	Foreign Currency Convertible Bonds
FDI	foreign direct investment
FICCI	Federation of Indian Chambers of Commerce and Industry
FII	foreign financial institutions
FIPB	Foreign Investment Promotion Board
FMCG	fast-moving consumer goods
FMRAI	Federation of Medical and Sales Representatives Association of India
FSC	Forest Stewardship Council
FVTOCI	Fair Value through Other Comprehensive Income
GAAP	Generally Accepted Accounting Principles
GDCF	gross domestic capital formation
GDP	gross domestic product
GDRs	global depositary receipts
GFI	Global Reporting Initiative
GIWB	gross impersonalized work behaviour
GNP	gross national product
GoI	Government of India
GPWB	gross personalized work behaviour
GSCs	global supply chains
GST	Goods and Services Tax
GVA	gross value added
GVCs	global value chains
GW	gigawatt

HR	human resources
HRD	human resource development
HRM	human resource management
IASB	International Accounting Standard Board
IASC	International Accounting Standard Committee
IBEF	India Brand Equity Foundation
ICAI	Institute of Chartered Accountants of India
IDA	Industrial Disputes Act, 1947
IEC	Importer Exporter Code
IESOA	Industrial Employment (Standing Orders) Act, 1946
IFC	International Finance Corporation
IFRS	International Financial Reporting Standards
IGST	integrated GST
IIPM	Indian Institute of Personnel Management
IMF	International Monetary Fund
Ind AS	Indian Accounting Standards
IPR	intellectual property rights
IR	industrial relations
IRBI	India Responsible Business Index
ISMWA	Inter-State Migrant Workmen (Regulation of Employment & Conditions of Service) Act
ISRO	Indian Space Research Organization
IT	information technology
ITC	International Trade Centre
ITUC	International Trade Union Congress
JLR	Jaguar Land Rover
LLP	limited liability partnership
LO	Liaison Office
MBA	Maternity Benefit Act, 1961
MCA	Ministry of Corporate Affairs
MMTPA	million metric tons per annum
MNC	multinational company
MSIL	Maruti-Suzuki India Ltd
MSIs	multi-stakeholder initiatives
MSMEs	micro, small and medium-sized enterprises
MUDRA	Micro Units Development and Refinance Agency
MW	megawatt
MWA	Minimum Wages Act, 1948
MWB	Mixed Work Behaviour
NASSCOM	National Association for Software and Service Companies
NDA	National Democratic Alliance
NGO	non-governmental organisation
NIGF	new Indian global firm
NILM	National Institute of Labour Management

NIPM	National Institute of Personnel Management
NPA	non-performing assets
NTL	nurturant-task leadership
NVGs	National Voluntary Guidelines
NWPs	non-work practices
OCI	other comprehensive income
OECD	Organisation for Economic Co-operation and Development
OEMs	original equipment manufacturers
PAN	permanent account number
PCNNP	per capita national net product
PGA	Payment of Gratuity Act, 1972
PLA	Plantations Labour Act, 1951
PMO	project management office
PO	project office
POBA	Payment of Bonus Act, 1965
PPP	public-private partnership
PWA	Payment of Wages Act, 1936
RBI	Reserve Bank of India
RSS	Rashtriya Swayamsevak Sangh
SA8000	Social Accountability 8000
SBI	State Bank of India
SBR	standard benefit rate
SC/ST	scheduled caste/tribe
SDGs	United Nations Sustainable Development Goals
SEBI	Securities Exchange Board of India
SGST	State GST
SIWB	subtle impersonalized work behaviour
SOE	state-owned enterprise
SPWB	subtle personalized work behaviour
TAN	tax deduction account number
TDS	tax deducted at source
TM	Tata Motors
TRAI	Telecom Regulatory Authority of India
TUA	Trade Unions Act
UNCTAD	United Nations Conference on Trade and Development
UNFSS	United Nations Forum on Sustainability Standards
UNGC	United Nations Global Compact
UNGP	United Nations Guiding Principles on Human Rights
UNI	Global Union Network International
UPA	United Progressive Alliance
UT	Union Territory
UTGST	Union Territory GST
VSS	Voluntary Sustainability Standards
WTO	World Trade Organisation

PART I

The Indian business context

1

INTRODUCTION

The Indian business context

Pawan S. Budhwar, Arup Varma, Rajesh Kumar and Hoa Do

Aims of this chapter are to:

- Provide insights into the Indian socio-cultural, historical, political and economic context
- Highlight the uniqueness of the socio-cultural, political and economic issues that foreign investors need to carefully understand when doing business in India
- Present an overview of the structure of the book

Introduction

Since the liberalisation of its economy in 1991, India has emerged as a major player on the global economic front. The World Bank and other bodies have regularly projected that India is likely to sustain its economic growth over the coming decade and more and is likely to become the second or third leading economy of the world. Also, during most of the 2000s, it was acknowledged that, after China, India was preferred for foreign direct investment (FDI), even ahead of developed countries like the USA. In 2011, this was the case, despite the worldwide economic slowdown and the fact that India's infrastructure is well recognised as less developed than that of most Western nations (UN, 2017). In order to sustain economic development, the present Indian government, which came to power in June 2014, has initiated a number of meaningful initiatives, such as 100 Smart Cities, major infrastructure projects, 'Swachh Bharat' (Clean India), 'Make in India', among others. As per the latest United Nations report (UN WESP, 2017), India is projected to remain the fastest-growing large developing economy, on the back of robust private consumption and significant domestic reforms gradually being implemented by the government. Further, investment demand is expected to pick up and sustain, helped by the easing of monetary restrictions, government efforts towards infrastructure investments and public-private partnerships, and the implementation of domestic reforms such as the demonetisation in November 2016 and the introduction of the Goods and Services Tax (GST) Bill. Not surprisingly, such developments have led to a renewed interest in India, and foreign investors have been making a beeline to enter the lucrative Indian market.

Accordingly, since 1991, the number of academic and other publications related to India has increased. These cover topics like the rapid economic developments in India (e.g., Tharoor, 2007; Kumar et al., 2009; Arevalo and Aravind, 2011; UN WESP, 2017); comparing India and China (e.g., Cappelli et al., 2010; Cooke and Budhwar, 2015), management in India (e.g., Budhwar and Bhatnagar, 2009; Venkatesan, 2013; Budhwar et al., 2016), areas of further development (e.g., Singh et al., 2012; Thite et al., 2016), and how to do business in India (see Kumar and Sethi, 2005; Budhwar and Varma, 2011; Nair, 2017).

Nevertheless, given the dynamic nature of the Indian business environment, which is changing rapidly on most fronts, there is still a paucity of research-based evidence regarding available and emerging opportunities for foreign investors, and the key challenges they might face in doing business in India. Indeed, potential investors would be well served by publications directed towards addressing the issues they might face, as well as suggestions on how to successfully navigate these. As the Indian economy grows at a rapid pace, businesses are facing numerous critical issues, such as:

- expanding competition;
- increasing pressures to attract and retain talent;
- pressure for further reforms in different sectors;
- developments and deficiencies in infrastructure;
- finding relevant Indian-based partners;
- divestments in the public sector;
- bureaucratic delays in the approval of proposals of foreign direct investments, etc.

In addition, foreign investors would likely have to deal with other issues, such as:

- corruption;
- limited infrastructure (power, transport);
- outdated labour legislation;
- challenging stakeholders, including union policies and practices that are sometimes counter to progressive business.

While millions of Indian students graduate from high schools and colleges each year, many of them lack employable skills, and need further training.

Finally, India's geography offers both advantages and disadvantages. With thousands of miles of coast, and a diverse topography, India is indeed a land of opportunities for potential investors. However, it is also a nation bordered by unstable neighbouring countries and suffers from poor border controls, resulting in regular insurgencies and a continuous in-flow of illegal immigrants (see Budhwar and

Varma, 2011). Thus, potential investors would need to devise project plans and strategies that incorporate more than simple 'business-oriented' steps. A more detailed presentation of the complex, uncertain and challenging aspects of the Indian business environment and ways of dealing with them is the focus of this volume.

Table 1.1 presents the ranking of India by the World Bank (2018) on various parameters on the 'ease of doing business' in a comparison of 190 economies. The figures in Table 1.1 are telling, and indeed, discouraging; however, given the opportunities India offers to foreign operators, the potential is immense, and those that make the effort are likely to be rewarded handsomely in terms of their bottom line. The key to success in India, however, lies not only in their own competencies, but also more importantly on how best they understand the Indian business context and efficiently function in it.

The importance of understanding a given 'context', and developing appropriate management systems as a prerequisite for success, is now well acknowledged in the literature (e.g., Budhwar et al., 2016). If those foreign operators developing strategies for their Indian implementation fail to carefully understand the Indian business context, the potential for mistakes and eventual failure can be high. This volume is specifically designed to provide information, which should prove extremely useful for multinational companies (MNCs) and their decision-makers, as they formulate their strategies for doing business in India.

We started by noting some of the shortcomings of the Indian business environment, and the potential pitfalls that foreign investors might face. We now address some of the tremendous strengths and related opportunities that are available in the Indian business landscape. These include cheap resources, a pool of reasonably skilled talent, a massive national market (a population of 1.25 billion or so), a rapidly growing middle class (over 350 million) with increasingly stronger purchasing power, and one of the youngest populations in the world. In addition,

TABLE 1.1 India's ranking on ease of doing business 2018 (against 190 economies)

Parameters of ease of doing business	Doing business 2018 rank
Starting a business	156
Dealing with construction permits	181
Getting electricity	29
Registering property	154
Getting credit	29
Protecting minority investors	4
Paying taxes	119
Trading across borders	146
Enforcing contracts	164
Resolving insolvency	103

Source: World Bank (2018).

India boasts one of the most diverse populations in the world, with a democratic political set-up, a free press, and a reasonably reliable judicial system, which though slow, is known to be robust. Further, Indians are known for their entrepreneurial abilities, and the willingness to learn, adapt and integrate into the global business systems. In addition, time and again India has shown the capacity to absorb global economic/financial crisis-related ripples.

Due to its uniqueness in many ways, the economic development model pursued by India is considerably different from other emerging markets, which perhaps minimises the impact of global events, such as the different economic crises in the past couple of decades. Broadly speaking, it is characterised by:

- the strengthening and enhanced contribution of the private sector;
- indigenous entrepreneurship;
- the presence of massive local and national markets;
- increased support to encourage FDI – both inward and outward – and the entry of multinational companies to India;
- massive contributions from non-resident Indians to India's foreign reserves in the form of remittances sent from overseas;
- the growth of the Indian multinational companies;
- increasing global leadership of specific sectors (such as information technology, software, business process outsourcing, knowledge process outsourcing, pharmaceuticals, research and development, animation, among many others).

Most aspects of the Indian economic model are strongly ingrained into the unique socio-cultural, political, legal and economic milieu of India; as a result, the challenges regarding developing a good understanding of the Indian business context and how to successfully operate in it can be both complex and demanding for foreign investors. An attempt has been made in this volume to address such issues. This should contribute to better practice development. We believe this information will be useful to a variety of readers, including top managers, researchers, consultants, students and academics. This volume then provides latest research-based evidence and consolidates it in a single source of information which helps to address questions pertaining to the 'what', 'why', 'how' and 'when' of doing business in India.

The structure of the book

The majority of the contributors are Indian and have been conducting research in their respective fields for a number of years. We believe this helps to minimise the 'Western bias' for this project and this has enabled us to present a more realistic picture of the key issues facing foreign investors in India. The contributors were given a framework to develop their respective chapters:

- key points to take away from the chapter;
- why the chapter topic is critical to successfully operating in India;

- any historical background about the topic and changes that have taken place since the 1991 economic reforms;
- the present state of affairs;
- the present and future challenges, and the way forward;
- a short case study and a list of useful web resources.

This volume is divided into three Parts: Part I, The Indian business context; Part II, Conducting business in India; and Part III, Emerging practices.

In Chapter 2, Pradhan and Kumar start off the volume by highlighting the scenario related to the Indian economic environment, including both the growth achieved historically and particularly since the liberalisation of the Indian economy in 1991 and the key constraints on the same. They also provide an overview of the key reforms and initiatives pursued by India since 2014 (when the present government came to power). They close the chapter by discussing the advantages India presently holds for economic growth, and emerging growth opportunities and challenges for doing business in India.

In Chapter 3, Saini analyses the Indian political and legal frameworks influencing employment. In particular, he focuses on the provisions of the main labour laws (i.e. relating to working conditions, the law of industrial relations, laws relating to wages and monetary benefits, and the law of social security). He also covers issues relating to the structure and functioning of various branches of Indian employment law and assesses the obstacles that the Indian labour law framework poses to the smooth conduct of business. Saini summarises his chapter by highlighting the precautions employers should take when complying with Indian labour laws.

In Chapter 4, Kumar, Mishra and Fang discuss the cultural paradox in the form of India's contradictory identities and value systems. They use the concept of *Ardhanarishvara* (a Sanskrit word which represents the synthesis of masculine and feminine energies of the universe, believed to have been represented only by Lord Shiva) to explain and appreciate a variety of cultural Indian paradoxes. They also the highlight the usefulness of the *Ardhanarishvara* perspective to better understand the cultural considerations crucial for fostering business relations in India.

Badigannavar highlights the critical role played by trade unions in the various spheres of organisation in India in Chapter 5. He starts by providing background information on trade unions in India, then discusses the main reasons for the continued increase in trade union membership in India, and finally makes suggestions regarding how to manage trade unions in India.

Khatri and Varma cover the sensitive and challenging topic of corruption and cronyism in India in Chapter 6. Given the common understanding that both corruption and cronyism are seriously ingrained in the Indian business environment, Khatri and Varma discuss the types of cronyism and corruption prevalent in India and their impact on businesses. They then reveal the role played by political parties in the promotion of such practices. Finally, they provide guidance to managers and policy-makers regarding how to minimise the influence of both corruption and cronyism in their organisations.

In Chapter 7, Panda and Gupta unravel the Indian mindset and present a comprehensive understanding of the way Indians behave. They make a number of suggestions regarding how business leaders can craft culturally appropriate ecosystems to productively leverage the Indian mind-set.

Pappu in Chapter 8 highlights the challenges faced by an entrepreneur in India. He provides an overview of the key operational challenges and opportunities offered by the business ecosystem in India, linking it with past and present changes in the legislation and their effect on businesses. He later provides a number of suggestions to set up a successful venture in India.

In Chapter 9, Kodwani discusses various aspects of the infrastructure industries in India. He starts with a brief overview of recent developments in the Indian economy and dwells on the present policy framework for private and multinational investors in the infrastructure industries in India. He also highlights the emerging trend in private sector and foreign investment in the infrastructure industries and the evolving business and consumer-friendly regulatory institutional framework. Finally, he presents a list of opportunities for investment in energy, transportation and the telecommunication industries and tips for both the users and investors in the Indian infrastructure.

In Chapter 10, Munjal discusses and critically analyses the dynamics associated with the entry mode options available to foreign investors. He presents a framework for the selection of entry modes in India and also provides key contact details useful for foreign investors.

In Chapter 11, Shanker and Sharma analyse the evolving consumer markets in India, and highlight the need for customisation due to the complex diversity existing in India along with complex consumer behaviour. They attempt to decode Indian culture to better understand the consumer and highlight the dilemma experienced by decision-makers regarding the selection of distribution channels. They also emphasise the need to understand the Indian rural market and in particular the topics of affordability and pricing in order to successfully drive growth in India.

De, in Chapter 12, highlights the challenges of accessing finance in India and makes a number of useful recommendations to tackle this problem.

In Chapter 13, Srivastava and Shabi analyse the accounting systems prevalent in India. Their analysis reveals the changes taking place in the Indian accounting standards in light of the historical developments in the Indian accounting systems. They also highlight how the Indian accounting standards are converging with global standards.

Dey, De and Soni present information about project management for the Indian context in Chapter 14. They start by identifying the risk factors involved in project management in India by carrying out a risk analysis. They then detail project planning, covering the scope, schedule, budget, quality, human resources, procurement, communication, and risks, and how this should be assessed before implementation. They also highlight the usefulness of keeping the project plan flexible to adopt the necessary changes in projects as one proceeds. Finally, they emphasise the necessity of dynamic evaluation of projects to track their progress and make quicker decisions in order to remain on time and within budget.

In Chapter 15, Budhwar, Varma, Rao and Bhattacharya present core issues related to the management of human resources (HR) in India. Initially, they explore the evolution of the HR function in the Indian context, followed by a discussion of the key factors determining human resource management (HRM) policies and practices in firms operating in India. They also discuss the nature of HRM systems prevalent in foreign firms operating in India and provide a list of key suggestions for MNCs on developing HRM policies and practices appropriate to the Indian context.

Building on the theme of HR, in Chapter 16, Chandwani and Makhecha highlight the complex mix of traditions and modern perspectives contributing to the creation and practice of context-specific HRM systems in India. They also emphasise the significance of being aware of the sources of such a confluence in order to leverage one's design and the implementation of HRM systems.

In Chapter 17, Müller and Kumar cover the important topic of alliances. They cover the need to understand the different types of ambiguity that an alliance is subject to and highlight the significant cultural gap between the mindset of the foreign investor and the potential Indian partner and how this cultural gap must be navigated to minimise misunderstanding. They also discuss the significance of effective communication and flexibility between the partners to overcome the challenge of ambiguity during the implementation of the alliance.

Chapter 18 is devoted to risk management and governance in the outsourcing and offshoring sector. Sen highlights how risk management and (corporate) governance around outsourcing initiatives can help achieve wider strategic benefits. He also reveals the changing perceptions of risk management and governance and the emergence of risk management as a 'matter of choice' rather than a 'matter of chance' with companies' boards. He also emphasises the utility of addressing a chain of related areas with equal rigour in order to implement good governance and risk management.

In Chapter 19, Varma, Dasgupta, Budhwar and Norlander present information that should prove extremely valuable to foreign managers in connection with adjusting, working and living in India. They cover important topics, such as food habits, availability of global cuisine, religion, festivals, housing, shopping, medical care, transport and insurance, as well as dealing with etiquette and dos and don'ts of living in India.

In Chapter 20, Hariharan and Rangan introduce the new Indian global firm and describe how foreign investors can learn from them. They highlight the features of such a firm and present a framework of entrepreneurial globalisation and challenges and opportunities highlighted by this firm for foreign investors.

Bhawuk, in Chapter 21, covers the complex topic of spirituality and its significance in the Indian context. He portrays the importance of understanding the significance of spirituality as an integral part of Indian life. His analysis advises the international managers not to lose sight of how people balance spirituality and material progress in order to better understand the rationale behind their various actions and behaviours. International managers can also use their experience in

India for their own personal spiritual growth by exploring various practices of spirituality, including yoga and meditation.

Finally, Arora and Jyoti, in Chapter 22, present the scenario of corporate social responsibility (CSR) in the Indian context and also introduce the emerging voluntary sustainable standards (VSS). They then reveal how to make CSR and VSS effective in India and also discuss the usefulness of aligning CSR and VSS with the firms' mission, core processes and operations.

Useful websites

Livemint www.livemint.com/Opinion/hn43udHIaCiaQiO8HH5xvJ/Doing-business-in-India-myths-and-realities.html

The Diplomat https://thediplomat.com/2017/11/the-ease-of-doing-business-in -india/ money.cnn.com/2017/10/31/news/economy/india-ease-of-doing-business/index.html

The Hindu Business Line www.thehindubusinessline.com/economy/policy/india -makes-it-to-top-100in-ease-of-doing-business/article9935450.ece

UK India Business Council www.ukibc.com/india-guide/how-india/

The World Bank www.doingbusiness.org/data/exploreeconomies/india

The World Bank www.worldbank.org/en/news/press-release/2017/10/31/doing-business-2018-fact-sheet-india

References

Arevalo, J.A. and Aravind, D. (2011) Corporate social responsibility practices in India: Approach, drivers, and barriers. *Corporate Governance: The International Journal of Business in Society*, 11(4): 399–414.

Budhwar, P. and Bhatnagar, J. (eds) (2009) *The Changing Face of People Management in India*. London: Routledge.

Budhwar, P. and Varma, A. (eds) (2011) *Doing Business in India*. London: Routledge.

Budhwar, P., Varma, A. and Patel, C. (2016) Convergence-divergence of HRM in Asia: Context-specific analysis and future research agenda. *Human Resource Management Review*, 26(December): 311–326.

Cappelli, P., Singh, H., Singh, J. and Useem, M. (2010) The India way: Lessons for the US. *Academy of Management Perspectives*, 24(2): 6–24.

Cooke, F.L. and Budhwar, P. (2015) Human resource management in China and India. In F. Horwitz and P. Budhwar (eds) *Handbook of HRM in Emerging Markets*. Cheltenham: Edward Elgar, pp. 337–356.

Kumar, N., Mohapatra, P.K. and Chandrasekhar, S. (2009) *India's Global Powerhouses: How They Are Taking on the World*. Boston: Harvard Business Press.

Kumar, R.K. and Sethi, A.K. (2005) *Doing Business in India*. Basingstoke: Palgrave Macmillan.

Nair, D.P. (2017) 7 hiring trends we'll see in 2017. *The Hindu Business Line*, 2 January 2017. Available at: www.thehindubusinessline.com/specials/7-hiring-trends-well-see-in-17/article9459549.ece

Singh, P., Bhandarker, A. and Rai, S. (2012) *Millennials and the Workplace: Challenges for Architecting the Organizations of Tomorrow*. New Delhi: Sage Publications India.

Tharoor, S. (2007) *The Elephant, the Tiger and the Cell Phone: Reflections on India, the Emerging 21st-century Power*. New Delhi: Viking Penguin.

Thite, M., Wilkinson, A. and Budhwar, P. (eds) (2016) *Indian Multinationals: Taking India to the World*. Oxford: Oxford University Press.

United Nations (2017) Report. Available at: http://economictimes.indiatimes.com/article show/56629889.cms?utm_source=contentofinterest&utm_medium=text&utm_campa ign=cppst (accessed 30 August 2017).

UNWESP (United Nations World Economic Situation and Prospects) (2017) Report. Available at: www.un.org/en/development/desa/policy/wesp/index.shtml (accessed 30 August 2017).

Venkatesan, R. (2013) *Conquering the Chaos: Win in India, Win Everywhere*. Boston: Harvard Business Review Press.

World Bank (2018) Doing business. Available at: www.doingbusiness.org/data/explor eeconomies/india

2

THE ECONOMIC ENVIRONMENT

Facts and initiatives

B.C. Pradhan and S.N.V. Siva Kumar

Aims of this chapter are to:

- Understand the growth and constraints during the first phase of the Indian economy post-independence, 1947–1990
- Explain the economic reforms in 1991
- Describe the Indian business environment between 1991–2014
- Present policy initiatives, post 2014
- Explain doing business in India: the India advantage
- Outline challenges and opportunities for doing business in India

Introduction

The latest report of the World Bank 'Doing Business' (World Bank, 2018) reveals that India's rank in ease of doing business has moved up by 31 places from 131 in the 2017 to 100 in 2018. There is a significant upward move due to the recent reforms undertaken by the Government of India (GoI), which came to power in 2014, to attract foreign direct investment (FDI). India now fares well in the areas of starting a business, getting electricity, and protecting the interest of minority investors.

India also has a federal structure and has 29 states and the laws in the various states differ significantly. External investors need to be aware of which states in India implement business-friendly reforms in letter and spirit. Metros like Chennai, Mumbai and Kolkata and other state capitals like Hyderabad or Bengaluru have shown visible improvements, which need to be replicated in the other states and in the smaller metro cities. Another feature is that the newly formed states show greater flexibility and faster implementation of online approvals, based on a set of rules and process guidelines. Chhattisgarh, Andhra Pradesh and Telangana States come into this category.

Indian economic growth has been in the range of 8 per cent annually during 2004–2012 with increased contribution of services sector. The economic growth trend for the last five years is depicted in Table 2.1.

Gross Value Added (GVA) is a term that refers to the computation of national income, taking into account the intermediate consumption. In other words, output minus intermediate consumption provides a derived GVA. Gross National Product (GNP) refers to gross domestic product plus or minus net income earned from abroad. Per capita national net product (PCNNP) refers to the national product divided by the population. Gross domestic capital formation (GDCF) refers to the level of investment in the economy.

It can be observed that there was a slowdown in GVA in the year 2012–2013 due to high inflation, the depreciating rupee and a persistent current account deficit. However, with the change in political leadership and optimistic business expectations, economic growth accelerated to 7.2 per cent and 7.9 per cent during 2014–2015 and 2015–2016, respectively, making India the fastest-growing economy in the world. However, one can observe a slowdown again in 2016–2017 due to both domestic and global concerns.

Two important policy measures were implemented in India, namely, demonetization on 8 November 2016 and the introduction of GST (Goods and Sales Tax) on 1 July 2017. These two major policy measures have resulted in immediate short-term negative effects, coupled with decreasing exports, including services sector exports.

Per capita national product has been following an increasing trend from 2012 onwards from 3.3 per cent to 6.8 per cent in 2015–2016 and fell slightly in 2017 to 5.7 per cent. The level of investment (GDCF), which was at 39 per cent during 2012, started falling from 2015 onwards, reaching a low of 35.4 per cent, and this is cause for concern as it results in slow growth in GVA.

Historical background of Indian economy

Post-independence in 1947, India adopted a mixed economy method of growth, where features of both socialism and capitalism were incorporated. Five-year plans were designed and implemented by the Planning Commission (1951–2014), and the NITI Aayog (Policy Commission) implemented in the latter half of the twelfth Five-Year Plan

TABLE 2.1 Select Indian macroeconomic indicators

Year	GVA	GNP	PCNNP	GDCF
2012–2013	5.4	5.1	3.3	39.5
2013–2014	6.1	6.0	4.6	35.2
2014–2015	7.2	7.3	6.3	35.5
2015–2016	7.9	7.9	6.8	35.4
2016–2017	6.6	6.5	5.7	–

Source: Central Statistical Office (CSO), Ministry of Statistics and Programme Implementation, India.

Note: All figures are in percentages and at constant prices with base year, 2011–2012.

for the period 2015–2017. Protectionism of centralized planning, import substitution, large state-owned public sector companies, elaborate regulation of labour, financial markets and businesses became the core focus of the Indian economic policies between 1947 and 1991. Industrial policies, the 'Licence Raj' restricting the economy to the 'Hindu Rate of Growth', saddled by red tape, made inefficient use of capital and labour. A high population and low-income growth led to the perpetuation of poverty and underdevelopment.

Economic reforms of 1991

Faced with a severe budget deficit and balance of payments crises in 1991, the Indian economy embarked upon market reforms to open up the economy to trade and investment, private sector enterprise and competition. The rupee was devalued, high tariff barriers were gradually reduced, foreign direct investments (FDI) were allowed in many sectors and markets were deregulated. The reform process continued despite over two decades of coalition politics although the pace of reforms was often hindered by vested political interests.

Consistent reforms pushed economic growth and unleashed entrepreneurial forces. This was complemented by FDI flows, trade expansion and improvements in the balance of payments. Economic growth rate registered more than 6 per cent in the early 1990s. The central government's policy initiatives in the Telecommunication and Information Technology sectors emerged and these have been the new growth centres of the Indian economy since the beginning of the new millennium. The adoption of innovative financing models for the ambitious National Highway Development programme and Pradhan Mantri Gramya Sadak Yojana (the PM's Rural Road Construction Programme) fuelled a nation-wide demand for steel, cement, labour and economic growth. The initial positive impact of the liberalization measures led to increased economic growth rates, a reduction in budget and current account deficits, thus managing inflation and interest rates to facilitate the growth process during 1995–2004.

Government initiatives, 2014 onwards

After 25 years of political instability and weak coalition politics, a stable and majority government assumed power in 2014. Consequently, the decision-making became faster by speeding up the pace of economic reforms. The new government made important institutional changes, the impacts of which are altering the dynamics of macroeconomic policies and economic growth. As a consequence of actions taken by the incumbent GoI and regulators, growth became robust, the current account deficit has narrowed down significantly, the fiscal deficit is on a consolidation path, and inflation has decreased considerably.

Given the fact that India is constituted as federal structure and not much can be achieved without the majority support of the state and local governments, one has to appreciate and have patience and give reasonable and sufficient time to the new government to understand the ground realities and address the challenges one by one.

There have been debates on what the government needs to do:

- take short-term or long-term measures;
- address the industry lobby or the mass population;
- attend to poverty or reduce income inequalities.

The only practical approach for the GoI is to involve all the 29 states and the 7 Union Territories as far as is feasible, and ensure that the policy decisions are implemented in letter and spirit. At the broader level, below are some of the important policy initiatives taken by the GoI and the progress made since 2016.

The Mudra Bank

The Government and the Reserve Bank of India (RBI) have taken various measures to facilitate easy access to finance for micro, small and medium-sized enterprises (MSMEs). These measures include launching a Credit Guarantee Fund Scheme for micro and small enterprises, issuing guidelines to banks regarding collateral requirements and setting up a Micro Units Development and Refinance Agency (MUDRA). The Mudra Bank envisages providing financial assistance to vendors and businesses. Some 61 per cent of these beneficiaries belong to the socially backward sections of society. In the absence of such financial assistance, they end up paying huge interest sums to moneylenders, which makes them debt-prone and also leaves no savings.

The Swachh Bharat Mission

This is aimed at keeping the public places and surroundings neat and clean and aimed to do the following:

- Eliminate open defecation by constructing toilets for households and communities;
- Eradicate manual scavenging;
- Introduce modern and scientific municipal solid waste management practices;
- Enable private sector participation in operating the sanitation system;
- Change people's attitudes to sanitation and create awareness of what is correct etiquette.

The programme plans to construct 12 crore (120 million) toilets in rural India by October 2019, at a projected cost of Rs. 1.96 lakh crore. The poorer sections of society will gain the most advantage from this project as they fall sick due to poor maintenance of their living environments. Expenditure on avoidable diseases forces them to save huge sums of their hard-earned income to pay for medicine bills.

Skill Development for Youths

In July 2015, through a policy-driven approach, the GoI started to wage a war against poverty. The Prime Minister stated: 'This mission is not limited to skill; the government has linked entrepreneurship to it.' It is estimated that over the next decade India will have a surplus manpower of four to five crore, and there is an urgent need to provide this cohort of youthful manpower with the skills and ability to tackle global challenges. The government has called for constant updating of training programmes and syllabi to ensure that the young people are exposed to the latest technology and industry environment. Skill building would not only sustain India's high growth rate, but also would improve labour productivity, which is the hallmark of a typically developed economy.

Make in India

This programme includes major new initiatives designed to facilitate investment, foster innovation, protect intellectual property rights, and build a best-in-class manufacturing infrastructure. Under this policy, doing business in India became easier through new delicensing and deregulation measures to reduce complexity, and significantly increase speed and transparency. The process of applying for an industrial licence and an industrial entrepreneur memorandum now can be done online on 24/7 basis through the eBiz portal. The validity of the industrial licence has been extended to three years.

Digital India

The GOI decided to provide all the major government services electronically to the citizens through the Digital India initiative. To enable this, the introduction of broadband to 2.5 lakh villages in the countryside is being undertaken in a very short time span. Digi-lockers, attendance of government employees on a real-time basis, engaging all the citizens of the country through My Government in governance and development are some of the objectives of this programme. This programme is aimed at transforming India into a digitally empowered society and knowledge economy. The classic examples of getting a passport, processing rail tickets online and also banking transactions through payment gateways show the power of Digital India. The new initiatives include creating a digital locker system (my.gov.in), an e-sign framework, online registration of hospitals (eHospital), a national scholarship portal, Bharat Net, and Deity (digitized India platform for large-scale digitizing of land records). The implementation of the digital roll-out is expected to reduce corruption to a large extent and also enhance the country's ranking in related indices. Small measures and steps like setting-up CCTV cameras will reduce the instances of glaring corruption on the streets; reduce road accidents and help catch the culprit responsible for road accidents. The Aadhaar card issuance to over one billion users has the potential to reduce errors in the public distribution system and in distribution of subsidies to needy people.

Smart Cities

The current situation of overflowing Indian cities with perennial intense traffic congestion, pollution, scarcity of drinking water and inefficient electric supply calls for more urbanization of the second tier cities that has been pending for a long time. Well-connected and self-contained cities with all the possible amenities will make the working population safer and enhance productivity in terms of reducing time to travel from home to workplace and other related problems. Inter-connectivity through web conferencing, and conducting meetings or interviews online will reduce the travel costs to the companies and the time spent on travelling. India needs 25 more cities like Chandigarh, which is a well-planned city. It is heartening to note that the GoI has announced 90 proposals for smart cities out of the total 100 envisaged for India.

Start-ups

The GOI launched the 'Start-up India' initiative and unveiled the Start-up Action Plan to build a strong eco-system to nurture and empower innovation and start-ups in the country. The programme includes the creation of a dedicated start-up fund worth Rs 10,000 crore (US$1.47 billion), as well as other incentives, such as no tax on profits for the first three years and relaxed labour laws, a simple compliance regime based on self-certification, legal support and a fast-tracking patent examination at reduced cost, and relaxed norms of public procurement for start-ups and faster exit.

In the technology-driven start-ups, India has moved up to third position with the USA occupying the top position with more than 47,000 and the UK with over 4,500. India's tech start-ups numbered around 4,200 up to 2015. In terms of total number of start-ups, comprising both tech and non-tech areas, India again figured among the five largest hosts in the world, along with China (10,000 each). Ola, Flipcart, Snapdeal are a few examples of up-and-coming multi-billion entities in the next five to six years.

Defence: indigenous production

India is the fourth largest defence spender (US$50.7 billion in 2016–2017) and the largest importer of armaments, and the GoI has raised the FDI limit in the sector up to 49 per cent, allowing foreign companies to own as much as 100 per cent equity in the local defence sector through the government approval route, in cases where it is likely to result in access to modern technology. India's defence expenditure is estimated to reach US$64 billion by 2020.

The Indian Ministry of Defence has been focusing on encouraging the procurement of defence equipment from indigenous manufacturers. It initiated the process of signing various contracts with the private sector under the Buy-Make category of the DPP (Defence Procurement Policy). New equipment and technology in the coming years, along with a massive upgrade programme, have opened up a huge market for all global original equipment manufacturers (OEMs), defence public sector units (DPSUs) and private sector players. The key procurements by the Indian government include medium multi-role combat aircraft, artillery guns in the 155 mm category and light combat aircraft.

The defence-offset obligation will provide more than US$10 billion as an investment opportunity in five years. The 36 fighter jets that were acquired by India recently were purchased for almost 8 billion euros and came with a 50 per cent offset clause: this offset clause ensures that 50 per cent of the deal's amount needs to be invested in the Indian defence eco-system.

Introduction of the Goods and Services Tax (GST)

India's tax to GDP ratio of 16.6 per cent is much lower than the average of emerging market economies of 21 per cent and the OECD (Organisation for Economic Co-operation and Development) average of 34 per cent. Only 5.5 per cent of those individuals earning are in the tax net and tax evasion is pervasive. To address the complex and inefficient tax infrastructure, India finally passed the long-awaited GST Reform Act in August 2017. It is viewed as India's biggest tax reform in 70 years, which will replace some 17 central and state taxes and bring them into than one unified tax regime. The GST is expected to create a unified market and facilitate the seamless movement of goods across states and reduce the transaction costs of business. It will also bring down the overall cost of goods and services, broaden the tax base, incentivize tax compliance, and will accelerate economic growth by 1 to 2 per cent.

Foreign Direct Investment (FDI)

India has emerged as the number one FDI destination in the world. The FDI policies have been radically liberalized in the past two years and India is now considered the most open economy in the world for FDI. Major FDI policy reforms have been made in the following areas:

- defence
- insurance
- railways
- construction development
- the pension sector
- single brand retail trading
- the manufacturing sector
- limited liability partnerships
- civil aviation
- the broadcasting sector
- plantations

- credit information companies
- satellites: establishment and operation
- asset reconstruction companies.

The foreign investment limit has been increased in some of these sectors, easing conditions for others and putting many on the automatic route for approval. FDI in the railway infrastructure, excluding operations, has been allowed. Although foreign firms are not allowed to operate trains, the new policy allows them to invest in areas, such as creating the network and supplying trains for bullet trains.

Measures undertaken by the government have resulted in increased FDI inflows of US$55.46 billion in the financial year 2015–2016, as against US$36.04 billion during the financial year 2013–2014. This is the highest ever FDI inflow for a particular financial year. According to fDi Intelligence, a unit of the *Financial Times* group, India was the top destination for FDI in 2015, ahead of China, which was top for many years, with US$63 billion worth of foreign investment. Liberalization, the simplification of processes and raising the sectoral limits for FDI in vital sectors, namely, the BFSI (banking, financial services and insurance), IT/ITES (information technology enabled services), pharmaceuticals, automobiles, civil aviation, telecommunication, retail and infrastructure sectors have led to increased FDI flows, which currently stand at US$60.08 billion in 2016–2017, a new all-time high.

Current status of Indian business environment

Besides the above, the NDA (National Democratic Alliance) government at the centre has also signed treaties and accords with major countries, such as the USA, the UK, Germany, France, Australia, China, Saudi Arabia and many more. These agreements include the construction of the bullet train between Mumbai and Ahmedabad and subsequently to Delhi with an initial investment of Rs 98,000 crores of Japanese developmental assistance and technical know-how of 50 years of successful monitoring of over 300 bullet trains in Japan. The loan is for a period of 50 years with a moratorium of 15 years, at a very nominal interest rate of 0.1 per cent. India has also been receiving global support and appreciation for its initiative on climate change commitment, combating terrorism, the development of new and renewable energy, smart cities, etc.

Thus, India's macroeconomic framework has been radically transformed if one takes into account major global dynamics. Monetary and fiscal policies have been made more robust by bringing in rule-based prudence. The economy, which had traditionally been agrarian for the first four decades since independence in 1947, has been transformed today into a services sector-driven economy with significant private sector participation. The banking and financial sectors, along with infrastructure growth using the public-private partnership (PPP) model, have grown spectacularly during the past two decades. Foreign institutional investment (portfolio) norms have also been gradually simplified and limits raised, which led to greater inflows into Indian equity and debt markets.

With the above major initiatives, the macroeconomic scene of India is poised for a great positive change in the coming years. More savings, more investment (domestic and FDI), transparency in sectors like real estate, the reduction or elimination of corruption through the Direct Benefit Transfer scheme, access to institutional loans under the Jan Dhan Yojana, the involvement of the poor people in development, these are some of the ways through which the economy stands to benefit from the above initiatives of the Government of India.

Challenges ahead

India needs to address the twin balance sheet problems: the over-indebted corporate sector and the public sector banks, which are burdened with bad loans, to re-establish private investment as the major driver of growth. Gross NPA (non-performing assets) climbed to almost 12 per cent of gross advances for public sector banks at the end of September 2016. At this level, India's NPA ratio is higher than any other major emerging market, with the exception of Russia. Credit growth to crucial sectors, especially to industry and medium and small-scale enterprises, has reduced to levels unseen over the past two decades. Indian banks and companies face short-term downside risks due to the cash crunch, arising from the government's decision to invalidate the old high-value currency notes, but the move will be beneficial for the Indian economy in the long run, according to the global rating agency, S&P.

Indian companies struggle when facing a set of common challenges related to logistics, labour regulations and disadvantages emanating from the international trading environment compared to competitor countries. India needs to bring in the desired reforms.

The infrastructure sector has been grappling with many policy-related problems that are pending at the centre and state levels, some actions taken by the centre have been visible. Getting consensus on the political front, the allocation of resources, the prioritization of projects, all require a lot of effort to get all the stakeholders to be on one platform and carry on the reforms process. While the government efforts so far seem to be in the right direction, it will require some time to get the results on the ground.

The way forward

India's high growth rate in recent years has come under adverse conditions: the worst drought for two consecutive years, a global slowdown and contraction of exports by more than 16 per cent over 18 consecutive months, high interest rates and the high cost of capital, a serious credit crunch and slack in private sector investment and an inadequate infrastructure. Fast-paced reforms of the economy and the decision-making process have strengthened the macro-economic fundamentals and stepped up economic growth. Increased digitalization, greater tax compliance and a reduction in real estate prices could increase the long-run tax revenue collections and GDP growth. India is on the right track in consolidating and unifying its market, strengthening its human resources and creating an enabling policy framework to lead the economy on a long-term and sustainable path of high growth and build a new engine of growth for the global economy.

CASE STUDY: INDIA 2030

The Indian economy has been transforming itself from that of a developing nation to an emerging economy in order to get into the list of top five countries in the world. Despite all the constraints and challenges, the various economic reform measures implemented have been delivering the expected outcomes. The Niti Aayog (the new planning agency) released its vision, the India 2031–32 statement, in line with the UN Sustainable Development Goals, that clearly laid out its 15-year vision: a 7-year strategy and a 3-year action plan to achieve the goals.

A snapshot of the current status, goals, action plan and transformation to become one of the top five economies by 2030 is briefly explained below:

- India is the fastest-growing economy in the year 2017–2018 in terms of GDP growth and has become a US$2.5 trillion economy now.
- It has achieved 7.5 per cent real GDP growth in the last three years.
- External debt to GDP in the year 2015 has been 23.5 per cent as a percentage of gross national income.
- Savings as a percentage of GDP stood at 32.46 per cent for 2015.
- The services sector as a percentage of GDP stood at 52.93 in 2015 and is expected to rise.

India has been climbing upwards in the global rankings in terms of ease of doing business, due to the conscious efforts of the government to reform sectors, such as FDI in retail and infrastructure. Governance and stable political leadership have resulted in increased capital inflows into the economy.

The Indian private sector has been supplementing government initiatives in the form of public-private partnerships in various sectors, including railways, telecommunications, manufacturing and infrastructure, roads and waterways. The Digital India initiative has been transforming India's banking and financial services sector by bringing the informal sector into the mainstream of finance and economic growth process. The GST, aimed at increasing the indirect tax pool and streamlining the process of tax filing, will make India achieve a robust tax collection system once it is fully implemented.

With reference to the Make in India initiative, it can be observed that the states in India, which have fallen behind with regard to industrialization, have now decided to close the gap with renewed vigour. The more interesting reflection that has emerged is that the larger Indian states, like Uttar Pradesh, Madhya Pradesh and Bihar, are going all out to attract more investment. It follows that there could be job creation and an increase in the income levels of the people in these highly populated states.

Here is a five-point agenda to focus on in the next three years:

1. Consolidate the various initiatives and review the cost benefits of each policy measure and focus on a few policies on a priority basis.
2. Invest in the manufacturing sector through the Make in India initiative that is expected to create new jobs.
3. Focus on the real estate sector that has multiplier effects on other sectors and also is critical to higher economic growth.
4. Encourage domestic private investment by providing a sustainable policy framework.
5. Focus on growth from the informal sector to generate employment through various skill development initiatives.

Useful websites

Export to India www.export.gov/article?id=India-Market-Overview
Invest India www.investindia.gov.in/
Make in India www.makeinindia.com/home
Ministry of Corporate Affairs www.mca.gov.in/MinistryV2/easeofdoingbusiness.html
UK India Business Council www.ukibc.com/india-guide/how-india/

References

Ministry of Statistics and Programme Implementation Available at: www.mospi.gov.in/
World Bank (2018) Doing business. Available at: www.doingbusiness.org/data/explor eeconomies/india

3

POLITICAL AND LEGAL FRAMEWORKS AND HURDLES IN INDIA

Debi S. Saini

Aims of this chapter are to:

- Explain the key objectives of Indian labour laws
- Present the structure of the labour laws in the Indian political context
- Provide the basic frameworks and their key provisions
- Give an overview of the obligations of the employers
- Describe the working of labour laws
- Present the precautions that employers need to take to comply with the labour laws

Introduction

The Indian labour and employment law model has been built on a socialist pattern of society that was envisaged by the Congress Government after attaining independence in 1947. In furtherance of this broad goal, the government built a comprehensive framework of employment legislation, aimed at providing social justice to the working classes. This chapter seeks to analyse the structure of Indian employment law and its framework for employers in view of the changing needs of the global economy. The terms labour law and employment law are used interchangeably in this chapter.

Political context of employment legislation

The contents of most labour laws in India are rooted in the constitutional obligation of the Indian state to dispense social, economic and political justice. The Constitution came into force with effect on 26 January 1950 and it envisaged a fundamental right for children below the age of 14 years whereby it was now illegal for them to work in factories and hazardous employment. Chapter IV of the

Constitution contains the Directive Principles of State Policy, most labour laws have their source in these directives.

During the 1950s and the 1960s, the government took measures to further strengthen the socialist edifice of nation-building. The most notable employment legislation then was the inclusion of the requirement for the provision of government permission for every case of retrenchment (redundancy), closure, and layoffs by larger factories, plantations and mines, i.e., those which employed 300 or more workers. This provision was introduced during the internal emergency declared in June 1975 (the emergency lasted 19 months) in the key industrial relations (IR) legislation in India entitled the Industrial Disputes Act 1947 (IDA). Most surprisingly, this limit of 300 workers was reduced to 100 in the 1982 amendment of the IDA.

Key areas of labour and employment law

For the sake of convenience, the various pieces of Indian labour legislation can be divided into four categories: (1) the law relating to conditions of work; (2) the law of industrial relations; (3) the law of wages and monetary benefits; and (4) the social security law. The basic scheme of the Constitution is to confer law-making power on both the federal (central) as well as the 29 state legislatures. Consequently, India has about 50 pieces of central labour legislation and nearly 200 pieces of state labour legislation (for details, see Saini, 2008; Saini and Budhwar, 2007).

The law related to working conditions

The main pieces of legislation regulating working conditions for different sets of employers include the following:

- the Factories Act, 1948
- shops and establishment legislation
- the Mines Act, 1952
- the Plantations Labour Act, 1951
- the Contract Labour (Regulation & Abolition) Act (CLA), 1970
- the Inter-State Migrant Workmen (Regulation of Employment & Conditions of Service) Act (ISMWA), 1979
- Child Labour (Abolition and Regulation) Act (CLARA), 1985

The Factories Act, 1948

This was one of the first pieces of labour legislation enacted after independence. Factories fall under the organized sector in India. The principal definition under the Act is of the term 'factory'; it means premises or precincts where a manufacturing process is carried out with the use of power by 10 or more persons or by 20 or more persons without the use of power. The term 'manufacturing process' also has a very wide connotation. It even includes the pumping of water, oil, repair workshops, etc. besides the conversion of raw materials into a finished product for use, sale or otherwise disposal. Similarly, the term 'worker' under this Act has a wide definition. It means a person employed in the manufacturing process and includes even those persons who are employed by or through a contractor in the principal employer's factory.

The main provisions of the Factories Act are those related to:

- health, welfare, and the safety of workers;
- the conditions under which women work;
- the working hours for adults and children;
- leave with wages for workers;
- protection against hazardous operations;
- payment of overtime;
- inspection of the work in factories by inspectors;
- the role of other authorities under this law.

The Act obliges every employer to register their factory and obtain a licence from the state government before they can seek to set up a factory. The Act also provides for certain obligations of every occupier before the factory starts operating.

Provision has been made for a certain amount of annual leave with wages for workers, depending on the number of days worked. A factory worker can be asked to work for a maximum of 9 hours per day, for 48 hours per week and a rest interval of half an hour after every five hours of work has to be provided. The total spread over of work in a day cannot exceed 10½ hours. Employers wanting the workers to work overtime must pay double the normal rate. Every employer must provide a weekly day off to all workers.

The provisions relating to the health of factory workers include certain requirements as to: rest, waste disposal, handling of dust and fumes, ventilation, artificial humidification, provision of drinking water, provision of latrines and urinals, and avoidance of overcrowding. The Act also provides for certain welfare facilities, such as washing and drying of clothes, providing the facility of seating to workers in certain cases, shelters, canteens, lunch rooms, first aid appliances, and crèches for the children below 6 years of age of women workers.

Under the safety provisions, this Act provides for detailed specifications regarding the space to be provided to every person working in a factory; the installation of machines, their fencing and working space; installation and maintenance of hoists, lifts, chains, ropes, lifting machines, etc.; opening in floors, pits and sumps; precautions in case of fire; and the maximum weight that a worker can be asked to carry. This Act was substantially amended in 1987 as a consequence of the Bhopal gas disaster. The amendment was carried out to Chapter IV-A to tighten the provisions related to hazardous processes (see Sections 41-A to 41-H in this regard). Section 111-A of the Act gives workers the right to ask for information related to their health and safety at work. The amended Act substantially enhanced the penalties to be inflicted on persons responsible for its violation. After the amendment, imprisonment has been increased up to two years and a fine of 100,000 rupees can be applied for certain violations of the Act.

The legislation related to shops and establishments

The shops and establishments legislation in India is not a central legislation, rather, each state legislature has the power to enact a law in this regard. The establishments which do not fall under the definition of the factory, as per the Factories Act 1948, as they employ fewer number of workers are covered under the shops and establishments law. The term also includes those establishments (small or large) which do not carry out any manufacturing processes. Most such pieces of state legislation have made provisions related to the compulsory registration of shops and establishments. They have also made provisions related to the hours of work per day, spread over work, rest interval, opening and closing hours, days on which the shops/establishments must be closed, provision of national and religious holidays, provision of overtime, etc.

The Mines Act, 1952

This Act provides for health, safety and welfare of workers employed in mines. They include, among others, the supply of drinking water, medical appliances and conservancy. There is also a provision for giving notice to the appropriate authorities if any accident takes place or a worker catches any disease. The overtime rate is also provided at a rate twice the daily wages that a worker receives. This is for both workers working above ground and workers working below ground. Women and those under the age of 18 are prohibited from working below ground. However, there is a provision that apprentices and trainees who are not below the age of 16 years can be allowed to work below ground, provided they are under proper supervision of the manager. The mine workers are entitled to annual leave with wages. These leave provisions have to be calculated at the rate of one day's leave for every 15 days of work.

The Plantations Labour Act, 1951

The Plantations Labour Act 1951 (PLA) applies to plantations of coffee, rubber, and cinchona. All plantations are required to be registered with a registration officer appointed under the Act. The provisions of the PLA mainly deal with health and welfare measures, such as drinking water, medical facilities, crèches, recreational facilities, educational facilities, housing for workers and their families, supply of umbrellas, blankets and raincoats. The Act envisages that employers shall provide and maintain necessary housing accommodation for every worker, including his or her family residing in the plantation; and for everyone residing outside the plantation if he or she has put in six months of continuous service in the plantation and desires to reside in the plantation. Among others, the Act regulated working hours, weekly holiday and leave with wages. The employer has to provide free educational facilities for workers' children who are between the ages of 6 and 12 years.

The Contract Labour (Regulation & Abolition) Act (CLA), 1970

According to the CLA, all employers employing contract labour are required to register with the registrar appointed by the appropriate government concerned. And the contractor working for the principal employers must obtain a licence from the appropriate licensing authorities. One of the principal provisions of the Act relates to the payment of wages to the contract workers in the presence of the principal employer's representative. Such a representative has to certify that wages were paid to the workers concerned in their presence. It is also important that the employer should employ contract labour in a way that is permissible under the law.

The Act lays out certain health and welfare measures for contract labour, in its Chapter V. Among others, a canteen is to be provided by the contractor if 100 or more contract workers are employed. If the contract labour has to work at night, the contractor is to provide restrooms for them. The Act also states that first aid facilities must be readily made available for contract workers. Among others, the welfare facilities to be provided by the contractor include: wholesome drinking water; latrines and urinals; and washing facilities. Under the Act, if any of these facilities is not provided by the contractor, then it is the duty of the principal employer to provide them. Of course, they are entitled to recover the money so spent from the contractor concerned while paying the bills of the contractor.

The Inter-State Migrant Workmen (Regulation of Employment & Conditions of Service) Act (ISMWA), 1979

Indian industries employ a good number of inter-state migrant workers. The conditions of work of these workers are regulated by the Inter-State Migrant Workmen (Regulation of Employment and Conditions of Service) Act (ISMWA), 1979. This Act was enacted with a view to protecting the migrant workers from exploitation. The Act seeks to provide them with certain minimum conditions of employment. It applies to every establishment and the contractor who employs five or more interstate migrant workmen. Among others, the Act provides for compulsory registration of the principal employer and the licensing of the contractor concerned. It is also envisaged that all the liabilities of migrant workers shall be extinguished after the completion of the contract of employment.

The Act dictates issuing a passbook to every inter-state migrant worker, which shall contain full details about their employment, payment of displacement allowance, payment of journey allowance and payment of wages during the period of the journey, suitable residential accommodation and medical facilities, protective clothing, and equal pay for equal work irrespective of sex, etc. The responsibility for payment of wages to the contract workers is that of the contractor, which they are supposed to do in the presence of a representative of the principal employer.

Child Labour (Abolition and Regulation) Act (CLARA), 1985

It is believed that the highest number of child workers in the world is found in India. This law prohibits the employment of children below the age of 14 years in factories and hazardous employment. Such employment, among others, includes making glass and glassware, fireworks and matchmaking, and carpet weaving. In those cases where children are allowed to work, the Act regulates their employment. The working hours for children have also been fixed, i.e., not to exceed six hours and provision is made for a weekly holiday. Health and safety measures are to be provided for all children as per the Act. Stringent punishment follows violation of the Act.

The law regulating employee relations

The Indian labour law system lays out three principal industrial relations laws, which seek to regulate employer-employee relations:

- the Trade Unions Act (TUA), 1926
- the Industrial Employment (Standing Orders) Act (IESOA), 1946
- the Industrial Disputes Act (IDA), 1947.

The Trade Unions Act (TUA), 1926

This Act seeks to provide for registration of trade unions, and thus to create a countervailing power in favour of the working class in the game of industrial relations. Interestingly, this Act provides that all employees employed in industry, including managers, can become members of trade unions. It even makes it possible to have a trade union in which workers, managers and employers are members. However, in reality, mostly it is the workers who become members of a trade union and any seven or more members can register a trade union. But this is subject to a minimum of 10 per cent of the workers who are employed in the industry or 100, whichever is less. When a trade union is registered, it acquires a corporate status or what may be called a legal personification through the act of incorporation under the TUA. Among others, the law lays down the rights and liabilities of a registered trade union, including the immunities it enjoys from certain civil and criminal wrongs that amount to conspiracy under the Indian Penal Code, and are committed in the furtherance of a trade dispute. The Act also provides that a certain number of outsiders can become members of a trade union. These are called special members, who are members of the executive of a trade union. Recognition of a trade union is purely a discretionary matter for the employer; the employer can refuse to recognize a union or unions without any legal consequences. The TUA does not contain any provisions for recognition.

The Industrial Employment (Standing Orders) Act (IESOA), 1946

The objective of this Act is to define with sufficient precision the conditions of work for different categories of workers and to make them known to them so that they develop some awareness of their employment rights. This Act applies to industrial units that employ 100 or more workers. But many state governments have extended its applicability to establishments employing fewer workers. The term workman has the same meaning as in the Industrial Disputes Act 1947. This legislation envisages a certifying officer appointed by the appropriate government, whose job is to receive draft standing orders from the employers, making them known to the union concerned or to workers if there is no union, to hear both sides, and eventually certifying the standing orders that they consider just and fair for both sides. The matters about which the standing orders can be certified have been provided in the Schedule to the IESOA. Various matters are found in this Schedule, among others: classification of workmen, disciplinary rules, shift working, workers' attendance and late-coming, conditions for applying for leave, disciplinary action and termination of employment, and means of grievance redress. If a worker is suspended for committing misconduct, they have to be paid a suspension allowance as per the provisions of the Act. The Act also provides for suspension allowance to be paid to a worker while they remain suspended for disciplinary action. After certification, each of the standing orders is deemed to be written in the contract of employment of the worker concerned.

The Industrial Disputes Act (IDA), 1947

Perhaps the most important of all the labour laws in India is believed to be the IDA. The hallmark of this Act is the statutory machinery for dispute processing and resolution. This machinery envisages conciliation, adjudication and arbitration as the key methods of resolving industrial disputes if mutual negotiation fails. The machinery contemplated in the IDA applies to individual as well as collective rights and interest rights issues. The IDA provides for seven forums for dealing with disputes or matters related to them. Works committees are to be appointed by every employer who employs 100 or more workers in an industry. The provision of conciliation relates to the appointment by the appropriate government of a conciliation officer (CO) and the constitution of boards of conciliation (BOC). The COs are normally appointed for different regions to handle industrial disputes in their region. They are government officers, who are expected to facilitate the dispute process between the disputants. A BOC is not a standing body like a CO; it has to be appointed as per the demands of a particular dispute.

If a dispute is not resolved through the mediation of the conciliation machinery, it can go for adjudication. Three adjudicatory bodies have been envisaged in the IDA: labour courts, industrial tribunals, and national tribunals. They all have different jurisdictions, which are provided in the Second Schedule and the Third Schedule of the Act. The former contains rights matters that fall under the jurisdiction of labour courts and the latter enumerates interest matters that can be processed only by an industrial tribunal. However, industrial tribunals can even decide rights matters contained in the Second Schedule. Unlike civil courts, adjudicatory bodies under the IDA cannot be activated by the parties themselves. An industrial dispute can be processed and decided by an adjudicatory body only if it has been referred to it by the appropriate government in its discretion. However, a 2010 amendment to the Act provides that in relation to an individual termination dispute, the worker may directly approach the labour court for adjudication, and no reference is needed for that. The adjudicatory bodies are not strictly judicial in nature, but are only quasi-judicial. They deliver awards that bind the disputant parties.

The IDA also makes provision for arbitration of industrial disputes by a mutually agreed arbitrator. The arbitrator under the IDA is selected by the disputant parties. But they have to approach the appropriate government to publicize the arbitration agreement in the government's gazette. The arbitrator is expected to process the dispute with fewer legal formalities and can also be quicker in delivering their decision.

Wages and monetary benefits legislation

The following four pieces of legislation are worth mentioning in the category of the law relating to wages and monetary benefits:

- the Minimum Wages Act (MWA), 1948
- the Payment of Wages Act (PDWA), 1936
- the Payment of Bonus Act (POBA), 1965
- the Equal Remuneration Act (ERA), 1976

The Minimum Wages Act (MWA), 1948

This Act aims to fix minimum wages for workers in the employments listed in the two schedules attached to it; these consist of Parts I and II. Part I contains among others, the following industries: wool carpet making, rice mill, flour mill, municipality, public motor transport, construction and maintenance of roads, docks and ports, and most mines. State governments have amended the schedule to this Act to add additional industries. Part II includes employments that are mostly related to agricultural operations. The minimum wage is fixed by the appropriate government, which can be the central as well as the state government in their respective jurisdictions.

The MWA envisages two methods of minimum wage fixation: (1) the committee method, and (2) the gazette notification method. The minimum wages under the Act can be fixed in the form of a time rate or a piece rate (with a guaranteed time rate) and an overtime rate. Wage rates under the Act can be fixed per hour or per day or per month or even for any longer period.

The Payment of Wages Act (PWA), 1936

The objective of the PWA is to ensure that the employer actually pays wages to the worker on time, pays them in the current coin, and does not make non-permissible deductions from them. The Act applies to factories, railways and other establishments. Every employer is obliged to fix a wage period, which cannot exceed one month. If an employer employs fewer than 1,000 workers, they must normally pay wages before the expiry of the seventh day from the last day in the wage period. In other cases, they must be paid before the expiry of the tenth day from the last day in the wage period.

The Act contains detailed provisions listing permissible deductions that the employer can make from the worker's wages. Some of these include: fines; absence from duty; damage or loss of goods entrusted to employed person; accommodation and service; recovery of advance; recovery of loans; income tax, etc. Employers are obliged to maintain registers and records, which help in facilitating inspection of these books and registers.

The Payment of Bonus Act (POBA), 1965

This Act envisages a scheme of sharing the gains of industry between the employer and the employee in a specified way. The Act applies to all factories defined under the Factories Act, 1948 and all establishments wherein 20 or more persons are employed on any day during the accounting year. The Act sets out certain conditions according to which the employee is entitled to receive a bonus under this Act. These conditions include that the employee must have worked for at least 30 days in a year. If an employee was dismissed for any fraud or riotous behaviour while on the premises; or for theft, misappropriation or sabotage of any property of the establishment; they may be disqualified from receiving a bonus. The POBA talks of payment by every covered employer of minimum annual bonus, even in situations of losses. It is for this reason that the minimum bonus in India is treated as a deferred wage. But in the initial five years of the existence of the establishment, the bonus will be payable only if the employer has a surplus that is allocated, calculated as per the scheme of this Act.

The Equal Remuneration Act (ERA), 1976

The ERA applies to all establishments, whether in the public or the private sector. It envisages a duty on the part of all employers to pay equal remuneration to men and women for doing the same work or work of similar nature. Broadly speaking, in determining whether the work done is the same or of a similar nature, it is important to see skill, efforts and responsibilities of the employees concerned. The Act prohibits discrimination between men and women even in matters related to recruitment for doing the same work or work of a similar nature.

The social security law

Social security in India is treated as part of labour law. There are two known social protection mechanisms: social insurance and social assistance. So far as the organized sector workers in India are concerned, social security can be divided into three categories: (1) the state's creation of statutory unilateral liability of the employer in case of certain specific contingencies; (2) social insurance schemes; and (3) provident funds. So far as the employer's unilateral liability is concerned, four main laws fall into this category. They are: the Employees' Compensation Act (ECA), 1923; the Maternity Benefit Act (MBA), 1961; the Payment of Gratuity Act (PGA), 1972; and some parts of the Industrial Disputes Act (IDA), 1947. In the second category falls the main social insurance law of India, i.e., the Employees' State Insurance Act (ESIA), 1948. Some countries in South Asia provide social security to the organized sector workers through some special funds called provident funds. In India, this fund is envisaged under the Employees Provident Funds (and Miscellaneous Provisions) Act (EPFA), 1952.

The Employees' Compensation Act (ECA), 1923

The ECA is one of the earliest labour laws in India. It fixes a unilateral liability on an employer for any injury or death resulting from an accident that takes place in the course of employment and arises out of their employment duties. In case of injury, compensation is payable to the injured worker himself or herself, in case of death, it is payable to his or her dependants. Apart from injuries resulting from accidents, protection has also been given in case of occupational disease occurring in certain circumstances. The employments that are covered in this Act include factories, mines, plantations, railways, construction, electricity generation, cinemas, and the circus. Many other categories of employment that are considered hazardous have also been included in the coverage (see Schedule II of the ECA). Normally, persons employed in a clerical capacity are excluded, though not in all situations. Also, if a person is covered under the Employees' State Insurance Act 1948 (ESIA), they cannot claim any benefit under the ECA.

Compensation is determined with reference to a worker's wages and a relevant factor appropriate to the worker concerned (which depends on the age of the worker). Younger workers have a higher relevant factor. Compensation is payable in four types of situations: (1) death; (2) permanent total disablement (100 per cent); (3) permanent partial disablement; and (4) temporary disablement. All workers are covered under the Act despite their wages; but a notional ceiling of Rs. 4,000 per month is set by the Act for the purpose of calculation of compensation.

The Employees' State Insurance Act (ESIA), 1948

The ESIA is the principal social insurance law in India. The hallmark of this law is an employee state insurance scheme (ESIS) that is administered by the Employees State Insurance Corporation (ESIC). In order to obtain the benefits envisaged, the employees must have paid contributions as per the scheme of the Act. The contributions are payable by the employer as well as the worker. Presently the rates of contribution made by the employer for each employee are 4.75 per cent of the employee's monthly wages. The employee has to contribute 1.75 per cent of their monthly wages. The employer is responsible for making the payment for their own as well as their contractor's workers. Of course, they can recover it from the contractor while paying the contractor's bills or otherwise.

The ESIA initially covered factories employing 20 or more persons. Later on, its application was extended to other power-using factories, which employ between 10–19 persons, shops, hotels and restaurants, and cinemas. It covers employees receiving a salary up to Rs 21,000 per month. Unlike most other labour laws, the ESIA covers all employees irrespective of their designation, provided their salary is below the specified wage limit. Unlike the other unilateral liability laws, the ESIS envisages making available a number of benefits to the employees covered. The amount of benefit that an employee beneficiary gets under this Act is proportionate to the average daily wage that the employee concerned receives.

The employer has to deposit the ESI contribution in the ESI Fund. This fund is administered by the ESI Corporation (ESIC) and the benefits provided under the ESIS are sickness and extended sickness benefit, maternity benefit, disablement benefit, dependants' benefit, reimbursement of funeral expenses, and medical benefit. Sickness benefit is payable when an employee produces a certificate to that effect. It is payable at the standard benefit rate (SBR). Roughly, this rate is about 50 per cent of the employee's wages. In order to discover one's SBR, one has to look at the Standard Benefit Rate table. The ESIC runs and manages its own hospitals and dispensaries throughout India, which make medical treatment available to the beneficiary employees.

The Employees' Provident Fund (and Miscellaneous Provisions) Act (EPFA), 1952

Two of the key pieces of legislation that deal with the provision of social security are ESIA and the EPF Act. The EPF Act applies to factories related to any of the industries that are specified in Schedule I of this Act, provided 20 or more persons are employed in it; and to other establishments employing 20 or more persons that may be specified by the central government through a notification. The Act covers employees whose salaries do not exceed Rs 1,500 per month. It is believed that this limit is soon going to be raised to Rs 25,000 per month. However, voluntary coverage is permitted; and employers wanting to cover their employees are free to do so. Three important schemes are envisaged under the EPF Act: (1) the Provident Fund Scheme; (2) the Deposit-linked Insurance Scheme; and (3) the Employee Pension Scheme.

The main scheme of this Act is the Employees' Provident Fund Scheme (EPFS). This is a savings scheme in which both the employees and employer make a regular contribution to a fund. Both these contributions are credited to the account of the employee concerned. Normally, the employer deducts the employee's contribution from their monthly salary and the employer makes a matching contribution. The rate of contribution is 12 per cent of wages for employees employed in the notified industries (where the wages are known to be better than the others) where the number of persons employed is 50 or more. Other establishments have to contribute 10 per cent of the employee's salary as the employer's contribution with matching contribution from the employee.

The Maternity Benefit Act (MBA), 1961

The MBA aims to protect the earnings of women employees in relation to pregnancy and childbirth-related issues. This Act regulates women workers' employment in certain establishments for certain specified periods before and after childbirth. The benefit under this Act is payable in three situations: (1) childbirth; (2) miscarriage; or (3) sickness arising out of pregnancy. Like some of the other social security laws, the MBA also imposes a unilateral responsibility on the employer to pay maternity benefit to the women employees covered. The Act applies to those factories, mines, circuses, plantations, and shops and establishments, which employ 10 or more persons. But if a woman employee is covered under the ESIA, she will not be entitled to benefit under the MBA.

The MBA provides the maximum period for which the maternity benefit is allowed under this Act. It is 26 weeks in case of childbirth. The Act also provides that every establishment with 50 or more employees shall provide crèche facilities for the children of women workers. Leave with wages at the rate of maternity benefit for a period of six weeks immediately following the day of her miscarriage is payable to the woman concerned in the case of miscarriage. For illness arising out of pregnancy, delivery, premature birth of a child or miscarriage, the rate of maternity benefit is the admissible maximum for a period of one month. This Act provides a fast track method of maternity benefit payment in case of any dispute.

The Payment of Gratuity Act (PGA), 1972

Gratuity is a benefit that is payable by the employer to the employee on termination of the employee's service and is regulated by the PGA. It is a unique protection prevalent in the Indian organized sector. It involves payment of money in a lump sum to a person covered who has delivered more than five years of continuous service to the employer. The Act applies to factories, mines, oilfields, plantations, ports, railway companies, shops and other establishments, which employ 10 or more persons.

Though mostly it is paid at the time of termination of service of the employee due to superannuation, or retirement, it is also payable in situations of resignation, death or disablement caused by any accident or disease. The rate of gratuity is 15 days' wages for every completed year of service or part thereof, in excess of seven months. Interestingly, under the PGA, there is no wage ceiling for coverage. The maximum amount of gratuity payable under the Act is Rs 1,000,000.

The PGA also makes provision for the forfeiture of the gratuity wholly or in part. This can be done if the service of an employee is terminated by the employer for any act or wilful omission or negligence that has caused any damage or loss to the employer's property. The employer can also refuse to pay the gratuity if an employee indulges in any riotous or disorderly conduct or other act of violence or for moral turpitude in the course of employment and the employer has terminated their services on account of that.

Key problems and caveats

Indian labour law is known to be proving harsh to some employers in many situations. Among others, problems are faced when an employer wants to close their operations or lay off or retrench workers so as to carry out a re-engineering programme. The requisite permission from the government is sometimes difficult to obtain. The relevant part of the IDA in this regard is Chapter V–B. It has been found that this legal process has led to unnecessary harassment of many genuine employers. It is a sad reality that in many cases arbitrariness is often exercised in handling the permission issues. Sometimes, decisions are made by government officials on extraneous considerations and many organizations that are perennially sick have been denied permission.

Another area that requires the government's attention is Section 9-A of the IDA. This section envisages the 21-days' notice that an employer must give to union/workmen if they want to make any change to the workers' service conditions. If this has not been done, the workers can instigate an industrial dispute because of the change, and many times employers miss some critical opportunities to make their competitive position better. This tends to be the biggest stumbling block in managing change.

Further, the multiplicity of labour laws in India is a big hurdle for employers. This has made the system very complex for ordinary managers as well as workers. Many of the problems in this regard relate to the applicability of these laws; the definitions of the various terms like worker/employee; who is the appropriate government; wages; different administrative structure for enforcement of these laws; and the creation of special dispute resolution bodies, etc. This leads to an excessive role for lawyers, which should be avoided so as to promote a greater degree of voluntarism in industrial relations.

A plethora of case law has been delivered by the judiciary to clarify these complexities. Many of these decisions are not easy to comprehend which adds to the existing confusion of the employers. This has made understanding the labour laws a very complex affair. In fact, labour law complexity tends to convert union leaders into full-time pleaders, who have set up labour law practice as a vocation.

However, there are some silver linings for the employers so far as their competitive position vis-à-vis workers are concerned. Some of these recent labour judgments reflect the belief that the judiciary is more sympathetic to the employers' predicament. The number of strikes resorted to by workers is declining and employers have successfully used lockouts to fight the union power. More dismissal decisions of employers are being upheld by the higher judiciary so as to make the employers' position in the game of industrial relations stronger.

Points to note

- All employees in multinational companies (MNCs) operating in India, whether citizens of India or outsiders, are covered by Indian employment laws and with regard to the applicability of these laws, no discrimination is done on the basis of citizenship of a worker employed in an MNC.
- Labour law is treated as a distinct branch of law in India. For most labour and employment matters, the jurisdiction of the civil courts is barred and quasi-judicial bodies have been created under different pieces of labour legislation to settle different types of labour disputes.
- Prior approval of the state government for the particular site and construction plans of a factory premises is required before starting any manufacturing operations in India.
- It is not obligatory on the part of an employer to recognize a trade union except in states such as Maharashtra and Madhya Pradesh, where a recognition issue can be taken for adjudication by a labour court.
- Labour courts and industrial tribunals in India have the power to reinstate a worker if they feel that they were wrongfully dismissed by an employer.
- An employer wanting to make any change in any service conditions of their workers must give at least 21-days' notice as per the requirements of the IDA before effecting such a change.
- It is lawful for employers to lay off and retrench workers, or to close the business operations, as per the provisions of the IDA; however, in certain situations, as envisaged in Chapters V-A and V-B of the IDA, they require the permission of the government to do so.
- If an employer runs a factory, plantation or a mine and employs 100 or more workers, and wants to lay off or retrench some workers or wants to close the establishment, they have to obtain permission from the appropriate government to do so. But there is no requirement to obtain such permission if the employer employs such number of workers in, say, an airline or a travel agency or a software company, etc., i.e., establishments that do not fall under the category of a factory, plantation or mine.
- Workers employed by an employer through a contractor are not workmen under the IDA; so they cannot raise any industrial dispute against the principal employer. Their concern should be mainly with the contractor only. But they are considered as workers under the Factories Act. This simply implies that these workers must be allowed to work in the factory subject to the same health, welfare and safety conditions as are available to the workers directly employed by the principal employer.

- An employer can enter into a settlement with workers or a union privately without involving the conciliation officer, but it is better to involve the conciliation officer as a conciliated settlement under the IDA has wider applicability on all present and future workers.
- The employers covered are supposed to pay minimum wages to their workers. They are also required to pay the minimum bonus as per the Payment of Bonus Act, 1965 to their workers, even in situations when they are suffering losses unless they are in the infancy period of the initial five years.
- The Indian system of social security in the organized sector can be divided into three broad types, namely: (1) the creation of employer's unilateral liability through legislation like the ECA, PGA, MBA, etc.; (2) social insurance legislation like the ESI Scheme; and (3) creation of provident fund under the EPF Act.
- Different pieces of employment legislation in India have different applicability. While some Acts apply to all workers/employees (e.g. the MBA or PGA or TUA), others apply to only non-managerial employees (e.g. the IDA, IESOA).

CASE STUDY: MARUTI-SUZUKI INDIA LTD

Maruti-Suzuki India Ltd (MSIL) is India's largest car maker. It started production in is Gurgaon plant in 1984 and added another one in 2007 in Manesar (in the same state of Haryana). It had a major power struggle with its trade union during 2000–2001. The union lost that battle; state agencies played a major role in the union's defeat. Since then the union has cooperated with the management.

Around May 2011, some Manesar plant workers decided to form and register a separate trade union. Management resisted as it wanted them to become members of the Gurgaon plant union. The workers refused and went on strike three times during June to October 2011 on this and related issues. The management initiated disciplinary action against many workers for acts of misconduct. As per a settlement, the company took back most of the dismissed/suspended employees, except for 12 key union activists who were retired from the company in return for a hefty secret payment. Interestingly, the workers succeeded in registering an independent union in February 2012.

On 18 July 2012, union and management talks got deadlocked on the issue of suspension of a Manesar worker who had assaulted a supervisor. A violent crowd of workers ruthlessly beat managers, and set some offices on fire. Dev, the HR chief of the Manesar plant, was burnt to death in this incident. Those injured included 96 MSIL executives. Management declared a lockout of the factory that lasted for 34 days, causing production losses of Rs 25 billion. MSIL terminated the services of about 500 core workers, by way of 'discharge' for participating in the 18 July violence. The police arrested 147 workers and union leaders for the violence and put them on trial for murder and violence, and they have remained in jail since July 2012 facing criminal prosecution.

Two years after the violent incident, the parent company Suzuki tightened its control on MSIL and removed executive powers from its three top Indian executives, whom it held responsible for the July 2012 fiasco. It re-designated them chief mentors, without any real responsibility. The new Managing Director of MSIL now pays surprise visits to different departments in both plants. The MD frequently meets the union people at Manesar, and has monthly communication meeting with them. In March 2017, the trial court sentenced a dozen union leaders to life imprisonment for Dev's murder, and set free more than 100 workers who were facing charges of violence and other charges. The union appealed against the convictions in the state High Court. The discharged workers have been contesting their termination cases in a Gurgaon labour court. The union was also asking for the reinstatement of those workers who were set free by the trial court. The company has refused to take them back, which has led to further complexity. MSIL was eagerly searching for sustainable ways to manage the issues so that it will stay ahead of competition in future.

1.   What are the key HR and employment law issues in this case, and why have they come up?
2.   What employment law problems is MSIL facing, which may prove to be problems for it in the era of intense competition?

Useful websites

Chief Labour Commissioner (Central) http://clc.gov.in/clc/
Complete Indian Labour Laws www.citehr.com/108238-complete-indian-labour-laws.html
Comply4HR: the Indian labour law encyclopaedia www.comply4hr.com/
Global legal insights www.globallegalinsights.com/practice-areas/employment-and-labour-law/global-legal-insights—employment-and-labour-law-2017-5th-ed./india
Government of India, Ministry of Labour http://labour.gov.in/
Indian labour law https://en.wikipedia.org/wiki/Indian_labour_law
Indian Law Institute www.ili.ac.in/
Labour law in India www.lawyersclubindia.com/forum/Websites-for-labour-law-in-india-2638.asp
Labour Law Reporter www.labourlawreporter.com/

References

Saini, D.S. (2008) Labour law in India: Structure and working. In P. Budhwar and J. Bhatnagar (eds) *The Changing Face of HRM in India*. London: Routledge.
Saini, D.S. and Budhwar, P. (2007) HRM in India. In R.S. Schuler and S.E. Jackson (eds) *Strategic Human Resource Management*. 2nd edn. Oxford: Blackwell.

4

THE INDIAN CULTURAL PARADOX

Kunal Kamal Kumar, Sushanta Kumar Mishra and Tony Fang

Aims of this chapter are to:

- Highlight the contradicting identities and value systems that Indians follow and the rationale behind the same
- Discuss the concept of Ardhanarishvara in India, and yin and yang in China and how they help others appreciate the paradoxes of the East
- Highlight how the Ardhanarishvara perspective provides a better understanding of the cultural considerations crucial to fostering business relations in India

Introduction

The emphasis of this chapter is on the cultural history of India. We highlight the paradoxical value systems that govern the Indian mindset and their impact on business behaviour. Our arguments are based on the assumption that value systems govern the individual, group and institutional norms and behaviours. Therefore, to successfully undertake business activities in a country, we need to understand its value systems. The chapter is structured in the following way: first, the cultural history of India is given. Next, we highlight the multiple identities and value systems that govern the Indian mindset. We stress that because of its diverse cultural roots, the Indian mind is capable of managing seemingly opposite values which might seem paradoxical to a Western mind. We introduce the 'Ardhanarishvara' perspective to accentuate our arguments that the Indian mind is capable of handling seemingly opposing values at any given time. We extend the argument to another non-Western cultural setting, i.e., China, and discuss the yin and yang perspective which emphasizes balancing apparently opposite ends, the quintessence of the more generic Eastern mind. The chapter concludes with the argument that the ability to manage paradoxes is what makes the Indian businesses unique, and successful in their home turf. Finally, a brief case study is presented.

The birth of a civilization

It started with a love story that would enthral even the most objective reader. Dushyanta, a king of Puru scion and a ruler whose kingdom spread across a large part of modern-day India, Pakistan, Bangladesh and Afghanistan, was captivated by the beauty of a girl, named Shakuntala. He married the girl through the Gandharva form of marriage (of a wishful woman with a man of sensual desire), citing its legitimacy in the context in which both found themselves: he a lovelorn Kshatriya (warrior clan) king and she the courted one. Their union took place once it was promised that their son would be the heir to the throne. Subsequently, the king returned to his kingdom and Shakuntala gave birth to a boy. As the boy grew, Shakuntala went to the palace of King Dushyanta. Surprisingly, the king refused to acknowledge Shakuntala as his wife and cursed her, calling her a born liar of lower birth. Upset and deeply wounded, when Shakuntala was about to leave the palace, a heavenly message was heard, pronouncing the legitimacy of Shakuntala's union with the king. The heavenly voice also named the child 'Bharata' and graced the child with heavenly blessings. As time passed, Bharata not only proved his mettle by becoming the ruler of the world (read Indian subcontinent) but also gave his name to the people he served – modern-day India has two official names: India (in English) and Bharata, its ancient name and the one used in its national anthem. Knowing the story, the simple question that comes to the mind of a reader is: what rationale had the king in starting an argument about the 'lower birth' of Shakuntala? Why did he refute the marriage in front of a large audience in the royal palace? A lovelorn king calling his love 'a born liar' – what a paradox!

Let us picture the situation: a royal palace with the king attending to the daily activities of the court; suddenly a woman and a child enter: the woman claims she is the legal wife of the king and the child is their legitimate child. Decoding some of the facts surrounding this situation (i.e. decoding the context): the populace understand that their king is yet to find a suitable bride; a hermit woman suddenly enters the palace and states that she is the virtuous queen and her son the worthy heir to the throne and hence their future ruler. The people are confused: is Shakuntala worthy of the king, and is the boy born out of their union? Let us roll back time (this will help us decode the values that govern the situation): hundreds of years back into unrecorded history, when the great war of Mahabharata was yet to be fought, the values of the time dictated that a Kshatriya king must marry someone of equal stature. The king engages in an argument to prove that the hermit woman is worthy of being a queen; the subsequent interference by the heavenly voice further certifies her worth and provides legitimacy to the child as being born of their wedlock and as being the virtuous crown prince.

King Dushyanta, admired for his high moral character, humility, truthfulness, and goodness, would suddenly seem vile, arrogant, untruthful, and evil if we uproot his actions from their unique situation, context and time. The ancient

Indian stories are full of such paradoxes: they seem paradoxical to us because of our inability to decode their unique *situation, context*, and *time*. As time determines the values that govern a situation and context in which the situation is embedded, historical understanding is not only important but a prerequisite to comprehend paradoxes. Since this chapter is concerned with the cultural considerations of India and as cultural values are embedded in time, let us now present a brief history of India.

The ancient land

While the evidence of human settlement in the Indian subcontinent stretches far back in the history of human civilization, the first settlements that took the form of urban civilization were arguably around the fertile land along the three rivers: Indus, Ghaggar-Hakra, and the now extinct Saraswati (Stein, 1942). It might be noted that the Old Persians pronounced Indus as Hindhu and used the word 'Hindhu' to denote all those who lived near it; subsequently, the philosophy/religion of these people was termed 'Hindu'. On a similar note, when the Greeks came to India, they pronounced the name of the River Indus as Indos: Indos through subsequent phonetic changes became India (Avari, 2007, p. 1).

While the civilization flourished for hundreds of years starting in 7000 BCE, it reached its maturity during the period 2600–1900 BCE, subsequently entering a phase of decline (McIntosh, 2008, pp. 83–108). Around the same time, to the east of the declining urban settlements, a new settlement had already started: the new settlement was across the valleys of the rivers Yamuna and Ganga (Avari, 2007, p. 54). The four Vedas that would become the most revered scriptures of Hindu philosophy and would set the framework of the future religions of India (Renou and Spratt, 1971, p. 136) were largely composed during this period. Towards the end of the Vedic period, the two epics, the *Ramayanas* and the *Mahabharata* were composed as well. Both epics demonstrate paradoxes ranging from the individual level to the societal level.

A land of religions

The Vedic period saw its decline towards the end of 600 BCE. Around the same period, Buddhism was founded. Aside from Buddhism, several other philosophies also emerged during this period; one of the most prominent being Jainism. Mahavira, the founder of Jainism, preached extreme austerity and complete abstinence from any form of violence. For the next few centuries the two major religions (i.e. Hinduism and Buddhism) survived side by side, mutually influencing one another (Monier-Williams, 1889, p. 2). This period saw the immense growth of science and mathematics: India became a centre of education, establishing the first university of ancient times (Robinson et al., 2005, p. 101).

Through the conquests of Alexander the Great, India was exposed to Greek values and culture; the Greeks were influenced by the prevalent Indian culture as well. The art and architecture of the times suggest an amalgamation of Greek,

Buddhist, and Hindu culture. Many of the Greek warriors soon accepted one of the Indian religions. To further their assimilation and as a sign of respect, they were included as honoured members of society (Rawlinson, 1912, pp. 137–138; McEvilley, 2002, pp. 372–379). After the Greeks, India encountered two major religions of the world: Christianity and Islam. Christian ideas spread in India well before they could spread extensively in Europe. As in the case of Christianity, Islam flourished in India a long time before it could proliferate in the Middle Eastern countries. A major impact of these religions spreading in India before their spread in Europe or the Middle East was the way both Christianity and Islam adapted to regional influences. Islam dominated the Indian culture for more than 500 years (late twelfth century to the early eighteenth century) and thus contributed to the spread of Islamic art, architecture and culture in the Indian subcontinent. One important cultural revolution in this period was the rise of a new philosophy in the early fifteenth century, that of Sikhism.

The birth of a nation

Starting in the nineteenth century, most of India was under the colonial control of the British. The first British to arrive in India were the traders who soon established themselves in small colonies located in the port cities. The British were, however, not the only European traders to settle on Indian land: they had to face intense competition from rival European traders, namely, the Portuguese, the Dutch, the Danes, and the French (Lach and Van Kley, 1965, pp. 105–117). While the Dutch and Danish colonies became part of the British colonies by the mid-nineteenth century, the Portuguese and the French maintained their colonies even after the British left India; subsequently these colonies became part of independent India. India gained its independence from British rule on 15 August 1947.

A land of multiple identities

As this exposition shows, the history of India is marked by continual contact with countless cultures of the world. In the history of the ages, empire builders from all over the world have targeted its lands and its people, sometimes assailing it so that it learns from the attacks, and occasionally settling here to leave deep imprints on Indian culture. For its part, the great empire builders in India expanded its boundaries, successively disseminating its culture to far-off places, in effect, furthering the process of the coalescence of cultures.

Through such cultural amalgamations, the Indian mind has developed an all-embracing attitude. When faced with a situation in which they have to choose between x and y, they do not go for an either-or approach, rather, they adopt a both-and approach, choosing both x and y. This is reflected best in the way Indians embrace the gods – they choose not one over the other, rather, they choose to worship many. To Indians, it is the context which determines which god will be worshipped, in what way, at what time. No wonder, when the Western mind looks at India, it is astounded by the number of gods and goddesses who are worshipped. Even in the assignment of gender to the supreme god, Indians follow a both-and approach. It may be noted that in the Indian tradition, the supreme god is considered genderless. In cases where gender is assigned, it is often in the form of dual gender. Take, for example, the Ardhanarishvara perspective in Hindu philosophy that states that God is half-man and half-woman (ardh = half, nari = woman, ishwara = god).

Similarly, when it comes to identities, an Indian mind can embrace multiple identities, namely, linguistic, caste, or religious identity. The Indian mind does not trade one identity for the other, rather they apply the both-and perspective. Thus, Indians can be both scientific and superstitious. This is illustrated when the top science institute ISRO (Indian Space Research Organization) launched its most sophisticated rocket after doing rigorous scientific calculations, yet it did not forget to seek the blessings of the almighty (*The Hindu*, 2005).

Living with paradoxes

The both-and approach that we highlight in this chapter is not unique to the Indian mind, rather, it is a quintessential part of many non-Western cultures, such as China. We have taken a leaf from Faure and Fang (2008), who highlighted pairs of paradoxical values to show how contemporary China balances seemingly opposite values. In this chapter, we highlight a similar set of paradoxical values to show their relevance in the Indian context. In doing so, we indicate the commonality between two major Eastern cultural systems: India and China. While the dominant Western thought looks at the end of the values spectrum, quite often classifying things as being fixed on a bipolar continuum, Indian and Chinese cultures focus on a fluid identity, wherein one can simultaneously be at both ends of the continuum. Such cultural systems have traditionally been more inclusive in nature and therefore demand our attention in today's world, which is undergoing complex and huge cultural amalgamations. A pragmatic reason lies in the sheer population figures: together, the Indian and Chinese cultures account for more than one-third of the world's population. It thus makes both philosophical as well as practical sense to look at the new perspectives.

Characteristics of the Indian mind

The personal and professional approach

In India, personalized networks are often dictated by caste or linguistic similarities (Vissa, 2011) that help in business growth. Similarly, in China, executives develop personal connections called *guanxi* for their businesses growth (Xin and Pearce, 1996). On the contrary, Indian business people often go beyond their personal networks and develop professional networks that are based on complementarities of skills rather than demographic similarities. Despite the importance of caste and linguistic ties, Indians follow the ancient saying that a person who is skilled should be revered by all. Such professionalism has been appreciated since time immemorial and its reflection could be seen even in ancient religious texts of the Indian sub-continent, most of which were compiled by people who are revered, despite belonging to lowly castes in the caste hierarchy.

Thrift and materialism

The Indian mind balances thrift and materialism by valuing both. While the religious scriptures talk about leading a plain and simple life, they also paint the goddess Lakshmi (the goddess of wealth) as having a flighty character: she does not stay with one person for long. The ancient teaching says that one should not hoard wealth for long, rather one should spend whatever wealth one has. The Indian scriptures talk about kings who lived in lavish palaces but at the same time were totally answerable to their populace. The key to ruling well is to balance grandeur with simplicity. One of the ancient folktales tells of the grandiosity of the Palace of Krishna and his behaviour towards his friend, poor Sudama, who has come to see him after a long time. While Sudama is intimidated by the grandeur of the palace and decides to turn away, the king breaks all traditions and runs barefoot to greet his friend. For a moment, the king becomes a commoner.

Leading a serene life marked by simplicity is highly valued in the Indian tradition. However, in recent years, there has been a rise in materialism and ostentatious consumption (Gupta, 2011). With the rise in the number of millionaires, there has been a significant change in the lifestyle of the urban population. The entertainment media has lately been showing images of a successful person as one who has the power to spend huge amounts of money on luxuries (Sengupta, 1996). On the other hand, the mass media has always projected in a positive light the people who are austere in their lifestyle and who prefer thrift to ostentatious consumption. With a quarter of the population living below the poverty line, ostentatious behaviour is seen as unethical by many; Indians who lead a serene life, despite being able to afford the luxuries, have long been idolized by the masses and are considered national heroes.

Group orientation and individuation

The notion of 'face' is important in the Indian business scene as people have strong relations with their community members. Indians have a strong sense of communal identity wherein the community could be formed based on different attributes, such as kinship ties, village ancestry, or caste bonds. For example, being a caste-based society, Indians have a strong group orientation which makes them committed to group values and they develop a sense of group orientation (Srinivas, 2002). India's business scene is also dominated by caste consciousness wherein both the flow of capital and the organization of labour are based on caste lines (Kumar and Mishra, 2014). However, the same Indians are also guided by the philosophy of *samsara* (the concept of reincarnation and cyclic existence) and *maya* (the illusionary nature of existence), which drive an individual towards developing one's true-self to gain freedom from social bonds. Further, while Indian cultures focus on the social aspect, they also emphasize individuality: Indian religions project salvation as an individual process (Sinha, 1988). This continued balancing of individualism and group orientation is characteristic of Indians who view their life as a story of balancing seemingly opposing forces.

Aversion to law and respect for legal practices

While, on the one hand, Indians can be observed showing disrespect to civil and criminal laws, on the other, they do have a high regard for the judiciary. In the context of business, the judicial process is also very slow in the Indian context which makes it easy for business organizations to treat their contractual relationships with disrespect (Chemin, 2012). Nonetheless, while corporations often indulge in bribing officials for short-term gains, companies that have made a name for themselves for pursuing ethical conduct, for example, the Tata Group companies, are seen in a positive light by Indians (Sivakumar, 2008).

Respect for etiquette, age and hierarchy and respect for simplicity, creativity and competence

Bow to grey hairs, respect authority, and remember that the boss is always right: these are some of the common feelings that most Indians share. Indians have great respect for their age-old traditions; they prefer to give respect on the basis of age and approve of the social and organizational hierarchy (Gesteland, 2010). Nonetheless, Indians have always had high regard for those who lead a simple and serene life. In business organizations, it is expected that older employees are treated with respect by the younger employees even though the latter might be superior in the organizational hierarchy. In formal situations while business etiquettes are expected to be followed, they are not important if the people have known one another for a long time.

Long-term and short-term orientation

Because of their philosophy of life, whereby time has a fleeting nature but the soul is everlasting and permanent, most Indians have both a long-term as well as a short-term orientation to different aspects of life. Consequently, Indians can display long-term as well as short-term orientation in business situations as well. Take, for instance, the case of bargaining: Indians are widely believed to be experts at bazaar haggling and can be involved in a continuous and prolonged bargaining process (Druckman et al., 1976); they try to get the best bargain and would push the other party to their final limit, as if they were only interested in short-term gains and not building a long-lasting relationship. However, the same people could be observed maintaining long-term relationships. The negotiating parties build enough fat in the opening position itself so that, even after a period of harsh bargaining, there is something for each party to gain, and profit is not made at the cost of personal relationships (Metcalf et al., 2006).

Traditional creeds and modern approaches

Traditions are very important in Indian society; respect for tradition and culture is deep-rooted, and it is expected of people that they follow the traditions (Gesteland, 2010). For instance, many Indians believe that there are auspicious periods for business dealings; Indian stock traders even follow *muhurat* trading practices in which there is nearly an hour of the trading window that is considered auspicious, according to astrological calculations (Manian, 2007, p. 57). However, the same age-old traditions are respected by traders who engage in the scientific analysis of stock prices. The way Indians embrace modern approaches alongside respecting traditional beliefs provides a quintessential example of balancing opposing ends.

Discussion

The preceding discussion has emphasized the paradox present in Indian cultures. Indians live with these paradoxes as they do not look at things with an either-or mindset but rather with a both-and mindset. They look at the context and determine what best to do – what they do in one context could be totally different from another context, so much so that an external observer may find it paradoxical. To further illustrate our point, we present a brief case study, that of Christian Fabre, a Frenchman who came to India in search of two seemingly opposing aims: business and spirituality. In addition, Christian Fabre, a Naga Sadhu (naked monks who worship Lord Shiva) is also a successful CEO, who sells all kinds of fashion garments but would not wear them himself. The focus of the case study is to show how an understanding of the dynamic nature of Indian culture helps individuals be successful in their home turf while balancing what may seem opposing ends. The case is based on in-depth, face-to-face interviews with the CEO and other employees of the organization. Apart from the interviews, secondary information was also analysed.

CASE STUDY: CHRISTIAN FABRE TEXTILES

Christian Fabre, a Frenchman, came to Madras in the early 1970s. He was a businessman and had an interest in spirituality – he thought he had come to the land of opportunities. He wanted to succeed in business while being spiritual. He wanted both and he got neither. He failed to balance the seemingly opposing worlds of spirituality and international business. He became destitute and lost everything: he had no money, no family, and no personal belongings. He had lost everything but his desire: the desire to be able to balance what seemed opposing ends to a Western mind – spirituality and materialism.

Having nothing more to lose, he wanted to understand India and its values. He was ready to lead a second life and tried to understand the complex world of Indian tradition and values. He soon joined the Guru-Shisya *parampara* (a teacher-disciple lineage). Under the guidance of his guru, Swami Sarveswara, he followed a new path. He wanted to experience the God Shiva. While the concept of Ardhanarishvara fascinated him (Pranavananda, 2011, p. 71), his Cartesian mind resisted, often telling him that all this was completely wrong! His spirit kept him going.

To understand the infinite world of Ardhanarishvara, he started a new journey. He became a seeker of Shiva; he wanted to experience God. As time passed, with proper guidance from his guru and with his forceful will, he began to comprehend the meaning of Ardhanarishvara. As the Guru-Shisya *parampara* goes, he was ready for *Sannyas Diksha* (initiation of the disciple by the guru towards consciousness). Finally, he came to know that what he was searching for outside was to be found within – Shiva was within him, he was the god whom he was searching for. His search had ended, and he was ready to lead a new life. His old identity was dead; he was re-born as Swami Pranavananda Brahmendra Avadhuta (the Liberated One).

He restarted his entrepreneurial journey with Fashions International in 1988 in the field of international business (exporting fashion garments). He headed the company with a new identity i.e., as Swami Pranavananda Brahmendra Avadhuta. However, when it came to choosing a brand name, his colleagues suggested his old identity: Christian Fabre. Fashions International was thus renamed Christian Fabre Textiles Pvt Ltd. He was now a Swami who made garments his business but he wore just two pieces of ochre cloth. As the tradition goes, the cloth had to be simple, non-ornate and should not be sewn.

The company has been successfully engaged in garment manufacturing and outsourcing for the past 40 years. It takes care of its employees as if they are family members. To gauge the requirement of its customers, the company's fashion designers regularly visit international fairs and prestigious fashion events in Europe. A proper balance is made to cater to the needs of customers while at the same time leading a path of spirituality. When asked how he manages the opposing world of business and spirituality, Fabre said: 'There is no opposition.' He finds both to be one and the same. Through business, he helps society; he does not see business activity as a force that takes him away from his duties. Rather, doing business is his duty, and in doing his duty, he serves God, the God within.

Conclusion

Paradoxical complexities in Indian culture can best be understood through a 'both-and' perspective. In this chapter, we used the Ardhanarishvara perspective to understand the nature of paradoxes. Further, Christian Fabre's case underlined that such Eastern perspectives have been the guiding force of leaders who often find themselves in situations where an either-or choice is analysed through a both-and perspective. By writing this chapter, we would like to emphasize that people who wish to understand the cultural considerations in the Indian context would be better guided if they look at the paradoxes through the lens of a perspective that is all-inclusive and thus better suited to address the paradoxes of Indian culture.

Useful websites

Centre for Cultural Resources and Training http://ccrtindia.gov.in/ One of the premier institutions working in the field of linking education with culture.
Culture of India https://en.wikipedia.org/wiki/Culture_of_India
Deccan Herald www.deccanherald.com/content/367580/superstitions-beliefs-indian- spa ce-scientists.html An article on the superstitions and beliefs of Indian space scientists.
Financial Times www.ft.com/content/dd68d7ca-fb0d-11e4-84f3-00144feab7de An article reaffirming Cambridge economist Joan Robinson's quote: 'Whatever you can rightly say about India, the opposite is also true.'
Indian government project http://knowindia.gov.in/knowindia/culture_heritage. php Project focused on showcasing India's cultural heritage.
Ministry of Culture, Government of India www.indiaculture.nic.in/
Ramakrishna Math and Ramakrishna Mission www.sriramakrishna.org/ The core of the Vedanta Movement, which aims at the harmony of the religions of the East and the West.
Society for the Promotion of Indian Classical Music and Culture Among Youth www.spicmacay.com/
USA Today www.usatoday.com/story/opinion/2017/01/29/health-care-surger y-india-america-disruption-column/97056938/ An article on Indian leaders' ability to balance both 'quality' as well as 'cost'.

References

Avari, B. (2007) *India: The Ancient Past: A History of the Indian Sub-Continent from c. 7000 BC to AD 1200.* New York: Routledge.
Chemin, M. (2012) Does court speed shape economic activity? Evidence from a court reform in India. *Journal of Law, Economics, and Organization*, 28(3): 460–485.
Druckman, D., Benton, A.A., Ali, F. and Bagur, J.S. (1976) Cultural differences in bargaining behavior: India, Argentina, and the United States. *Journal of Conflict Resolution*, 20(3): 413–452.
Faure, G.O. and Fang, T. (2008) Changing Chinese values: Keeping up with paradoxes. *International Business Review*, 17(2): 194–207.
Gesteland, R.R. and Gesteland, M.C. (2010) *India: Cross-Cultural Business Behavior: For Business People, Expatriates and Scholars.* Køge: Copenhagen Business School Press.
Gupta, N. (2011) Globalization does lead to change in consumer behavior: An empirical evidence of impact of globalization on changing materialistic values in Indian consumers and its aftereffects. *Asia Pacific Journal of Marketing and Logistics*, 23(3): 251–269.

Kumar, K.K. and Mishra, S.K. (2014) Capitalism in the Indian social environment: An ethnic perspective.In H. Kazeroony and A. Stachowicz-Stanusch (eds) *Capitalism and the Social Relationship: An Organizational Perspective*. Basingstoke: Palgrave Macmillan.

Lach, D.F. and Van Kley, E.J. (1965) *Asia in the Making of Europe*. Chicago: University of Chicago Press.

Manian, R. (2007) *Doing Business in India for Dummies*. Hoboken, NJ: John Wiley & Sons, Inc.

McEvilley, T. (2002) *The Shape of Ancient Thought: Comparative Studies in Greek and Indian Philosophies*. New York: Allworth Press.

McIntosh, J. (2008) *The Ancient Indus Valley: New Perspectives*. Santa Barbara, CA: ABC-CLIO.

Metcalf, L.E., Bird, A., Shankarmahesh, M., Aycan, Z., Larimo, J. and Valdelamar, D.D. (2006) Cultural tendencies in negotiation: A comparison of Finland, India, Mexico, Turkey, and the United States. *Journal of World Business*, 41(4): 382–394.

Monier-Williams, M. (1889) *Buddhism, in its Connexion with Brāhmanism and Hinduāism*. London: John Murray.

Pranavananda (2011) *The Holy CEO: An Autobiography*. Ahmedabad: Jaico Publishing House.

Rawlinson, H.G. (1912) *Bactria: The History of a Forgotten Empire*. London: Probsthain & Co.

Renou, L. and Spratt, P. (1971) *Vedic India*. Delhi: Indological Book House.

Robinson, R.H., Johnson, W.L. and Thanissaro, B. (2005) *Buddhist Religions: A Historical Introduction*. Belmont, CA: Wadsworth/Thomson.

Sengupta, S. (1996) Understanding consumption-related values from advertising: A content analysis of television commercials from India and the United States. *International Communication Gazette*, 57(2): 81–96.

Sinha, D. (1988) Basic Indian values and behaviour dispositions in the context of national development: An appraisal. In D. Sinha and H.S.R. Kao (eds) *Social Values and Development: Asian Perspectives*. Thousand Oaks, CA: Sage, pp. 29–55.

Sivakumar, N. (2008) The business ethics of Jamsetji Nusserwanji Tata: A forerunner in promoting stakeholder welfare. *Journal of Business Ethics*, 83(2): 353–361.

Srinivas, M.N. (2002) *Collected Essays*. New York: Oxford University Press.

Stein, A. (1942) A survey of ancient sites along the 'lost' Sarasvati River. *The Geographical Journal*, 99(4): 173–182.

The Hindu (2005) A prayer before the launch of every ISRO satellite, 24 December. Available at: www.thehindu.com/2005/12/24/stories/2005122400250200.htm

Vissa, B. (2011) A matching theory of entrepreneurs' tie formation intentions and initiation of economic exchange. *Academy of Management Journal*, 54(1): 137–158.

Xin, K.K. and Pearce, J.L. (1996) Guanxi: Connections as substitutes for formal institutional support. *Academy of Management Journal*, 39(6): 1641–1658.

5

TRADE UNIONS IN INDIA

Prospects and challenges

Vidu Badigannavar

Aims of this chapter are to:

- Present the background information on trade unions in India
- Provide the reasons for the increase in trade union membership in India
- Explain management's dealings with trade unions in India

Introduction

Trade unions globally are facing difficult challenges and Indian trade unions are no exception. Historically, union membership levels and density have typically been high in the social democratic countries like Sweden, Finland and Denmark and reasonably high in the coordinated market economies like Germany, the Netherlands and Japan. However, Organisation for Economic Co-operation and Development (OECD) figures indicate that even in the Scandinavian countries and those classified as coordinated market economies, unions are facing a decline in their fortunes. However, trade union membership in India was about 35 million workers in 2007–2008 which has increased to about 110 million workers in 2013 (Menon, 2013). This too is likely to be an underestimate as it only captures the union membership of the 10 largest national union federations in India, which are affiliated to various political parties, and does not include the membership of several thousand enterprise-level unions that are politically independent (Government of India, 2018). Trade union density in India is about 34.13 per cent nationally (Pal, 2008) which is substantially higher than the OECD average of 16.7 per cent (OECD, 2018). Some analysts suggest that aggregate union membership and density are likely to grow in India as by 2021 nearly 64 per cent of the population will be the working population (Desai, 2015). This rise in working population is likely to increase the pool of potential members for trade unions that are actively organizing in both the formal and the informal sectors of the economy. Hence, judging by the aggregate rise in union membership levels and the union density figures, it would not be prudent for either domestic businesses or foreign investors to simply write off Indian trade unions as a spent force.

What explains the rise in union membership in India?

It is worth noting that the aggregate union membership levels in India rose between 2008 to 2013, a period that coincides with the global financial crisis. It is equally worth noting that this period is marked with a remarkable rise in strike actions across India, with about 11 nation-wide general strikes being called by national union federations, with the two most recent strikes in September 2015 and September 2016, when nearly 150 million workers across India went on strike. *The Guardian* newspaper in the UK reported this strike as the 'world's largest ever industrial action' that cost the Indian economy nearly £2 billion (Safi, 2016).

Conventional wisdom would dictate that workers are less likely to join trade unions or engage in collective actions, such as strikes when the economy and businesses are struggling. There are several potential risks for workers in doing so. First, the risk of employer reprisal is very high. Second, there are few alternative employment options available if they were to lose their current jobs. Third, the prospects of securing employment security or wage rises through union actions are relatively weak in an economy which has fallen on its knees and when employers are facing a crisis of profitability. While the Indian economy has certainly not fallen on its knees, the global financial crisis did have a substantial slowing-down effect on private investments, gross domestic product (GDP) and job creation. However, the mobilization theory (Kelly, 1998) offers a more nuanced view on unionization and collective actions which may explain the Indian conundrum. According to the mobilization theory, workers are more likely to join unions and engage in collective actions when certain conditions are met. First, workers must harbour a strong sense of injustice, which is deeply felt and widely shared. The sense of injustice must be about serious breaches of promises made by the employers or the state, or both. Workers come to share their grievances through social interactions both within and outside their workplace. Unions offer these avenues for social interactions through workplace and community meetings. Second, workers must attribute the blame for their grievances to a particular agency, e.g., employers/the state and believe that the agent has the ability to redress their grievances. If, on the other hand, workers attribute blame to amorphous factors like 'globalization', then they are unlikely to engage in collective actions. Here again, union leaders play a pivotal role in 'framing' issues that collectivize grievances and attribute blame to specific target agents.

Third, workers engage in cost-benefit calculations. The costs largely relate to issues like lost income due to going on strike, potential employer/state reprisal, the extent to which the legal framework protects striking workers and their unions, etc. The benefits could be perceived as both short to medium term and long term. Short-term benefits could be wage rises or job protection whereas long-term benefits could be changes in state and employer policies resulting in overall improvements in employment conditions and welfare provisions. If workers perceive the potential benefits as outweighing the costs, then they are more likely to join unions and engage in collective forms of resistance. Finally, the very nature of the industrial action may alter the power resources available to parties involved in the dispute, i.e., the state, employers, workers and unions.

The conditions set out by the mobilization theory seem to apply to the Indian context. Successive governments in India since 1991 have pursued the policies of economic liberalization and privatization which seem to have resulted in GDP growth but at the same time have resulted in increased employment insecurity for millions of workers in the formal sector of the economy with growing casualization of work (Shyam Sundar, 2010). Even the public sector, which was hitherto protected in the pre-liberalization era, has witnessed large-scale job cuts through early retirement schemes and outsourcing, alongside recruitment freezes, resulting in both increased workloads and rising employment insecurity. The pace of economic reforms gained momentum during the second United Progressive Alliance (UPA) government led by the Congress Party (2009–2014) and subsequently, under the Bharatiya Janata Party (BJP) government since May 2014 onwards. Despite its 'socialist' face, India has always been an unequal society but income inequality in the post-1991 economic reforms period has steadily risen and rigorous studies have found that the share of wages in GDP has consistently fallen while the share of profits in GDP has exponentially risen. This is the case even in firms which are profitable, where employers can afford to pay higher wages and are not facing a crisis of profitability (Sen and Dasgupta, 2009). It is suggested that even the ostensibly independent judiciary under pressure from the state has tilted the balance of power squarely in favour of employers to support the investment-friendly de-regulation agenda (Cox, 2012). The cumulative hardship, caused by public sector reforms, the de-regulation of labour markets, weak protection of workers both in the formal and informal sectors of the economy and a welfare system that is conspicuous by its absence, has generated a deeply felt and widely shared sense of grievance across the Indian workforce.

The Indian workforce constitutes about 400 million workers, of which nearly 93 per cent are employed in the informal sector of the economy with very little protection under the labour and welfare laws. Of the remaining 7 per cent (i.e. 28 million workers) nearly 10 million are employed in the public sector. Hitherto, unions had concentrated their efforts on recruiting and representing workers in the formal sector enterprises and had at times treated casual and contract workers hired within formal sector enterprises as enemies within (Badigannavar, 2013). However, with the rising tide of contract workers now being hired in the formal sectors and the diminishing proportion of permanent regular employment in this sector, Indian unions have been forced to reorganize and recruit these casual or contract workers and bargain on their behalf (Monteiro, 2012). Likewise, with shrinking employment in the public sector and the formal sector generally, unions in India have been making a concerted effort to recruit unorganized workers employed in the informal sector of the economy, such as agriculture and agro-based industries, construction, transport, those employed on rural employment schemes, and the retail industry.

Unions in India have been forging alliances with international trade union federations such as Union Network International (UNI Global) and the International Trade Union Congress (ITUC) to recruit and organize workers in the so-called 'sunshine' industries like IT and IT-enabled services with some remarkable success. This is indicative of the rising level of grievance among workers in India, even in the formal sectors, and the way in which trade unions have mobilized workers around these grievances. What it also indicates is that just as private corporations in India have gone multinational, so have trade unions with international alliances and joint actions.

Trade unions in India have offered a counter-narrative to the conventional state and employer 'speak' of globalization and its benefits to the working classes. For example, in a recent interview, Dr Vivek Monteiro,[1] the National Secretary of the Communist Trade Union Federation (CITU), argued that the state policy of private sector investment, based on indiscriminate loans being offered to large businesses through public sector banks under political pressure, has resulted in an escalation of bad loans (also known as non-performing assets) on the books of these banks. Consequently, public sector banks are now forced to cut jobs, freeze recruitment and wages and cause hardship to their employees who were not responsible for these bad loans in the first place. Likewise, the de-regulation of the energy sector has resulted in the increased cost of electricity and energy for consumers and has resulted in closures of small and medium-scale enterprises which are unable to sustain large energy bills. Firm closures have in turn fuelled unemployment in the economy. This counter-narrative is also reflected in the charter of demands that were put forward by national trade union federations to the government, prior to the nation-wide general strikes. The demands are not restricted to wages and bonuses for formal sector workers but encompass wider concerns of the working population, such as rising fuel costs, food price inflation, poor health provision in public hospitals and demand for social security for unorganized workers in the informal sector of the economy. The counter-narrative of the unions enables workers to attribute blame to a specific agency, i.e., the state/ employers/businesses. Likewise, the broadening of the agenda also allows unions to reach out to the wider community and civil society organizations representing workers in the formal and informal sectors.

Professional workers' unions have also shown a significant increase in their membership and mobilization capacity. As mentioned above, union organizing campaigns in the IT and IT-enabled sector have recorded a reasonable degree of success. Another such white-collar professional union is the Federation of Medical and Sales Representatives Association of India (FMRAI), which represents sales professionals largely in the pharmaceutical industry but also in the retail industry. Like other national union federations, FMRAI also has broadened its agenda to raise issues such as corruption and the nexus between pharma companies and doctors, the unaffordable costs of branded medicines and drugs as well as surgical products like cardiac stents, which can cost several thousand US dollars, even in a developing country like India (www.fmrai.org). These issues have resonated well with the general public, earning the union public sympathy and support. On 18 April 2017, the Central Government of India declared its intentions to bring in legislation to force doctors to prescribe generic drugs and has made pharma companies reconsider their position. The public pressure created by FMRAI campaigns and demonstrations seems to have contributed to this policy shift by the central government.

Management's dealings with trade unions in India

Broadly speaking, employers can deal with unions in potentially two ways. First, actively pursue an anti-union strategy, which would entail either union busting or preventing trade unions from getting a foothold in the firm, if the firm happens to be non-union. Second, employers can work in cooperation with unions (where they are present) or with employee groups (in non-union establishments) and engage in what is known as a 'social partnership' model (Kelly, 2004; Badiganna-var, 2016a). Employers also need to consider the position of the state vis-à-vis trade unions when deciding how best to deal with them.

Let us discuss this last point first, i.e., the role of the state vis-à-vis trade unions in India. Going by the popular media coverage on labour law reforms, it would appear that the present government is determined to weaken trade unions through labour law reforms and by doing so, aims to create an investor-friendly environment. The Industrial Relations Bill 2015, which is under consideration in the Parliament, will (if passed in its current form) bring in reforms that will make it difficult for unions to organize workers in the formal sector or to engage in strike action. However, one has to take into account the political exigencies for the state. All national political parties in India have their own affiliate trade union federations. For instance, the largest trade union federation in India, namely, the Bharitya Mazdoor Sangh (BMS), with a membership of 33 million workers nationally, is affiliated to the Bhartiya Janata Party (BJP), which was elected to power in May 2014. The BMS is closely linked with the Rashtriya Swayamsevak Sangh (RSS), the parent organization of the BJP. Likewise, the Indian National Trade Union Congress (INTUC), with a membership of about 30 million workers, is affiliated to the Congress Party, and the All India Trade Union Congress, with a national membership of 14 million workers, is affiliated to the Communist Party of India (CPI).

In India, trade union federations have historically worked as captive vote banks for the political parties they are affiliated to. The union federations work as campaigning machines at the grassroots level, along with the party functionaries and help parties secure votes and win elections. In return, unions secure favourable treatment from their political parties in the form of pro-worker policies, union recognition agreements and collective bargaining deals with employers by virtue of their political clout. Even in times of economic reforms which put a strain on the relationship between political parties and union leadership, it is unlikely that any political party in India would go full throttle to antagonize its affiliated unions and risk losing elections. The current BJP government has already experienced this electoral loss in the federal state of Rajasthan, which is also BJP-ruled. Rajasthan was at the forefront of weakening the Industrial Disputes Act 1947, which allegedly offers disproportionate powers to workers and unions at the expense of employers.

Let us now consider the options available for employers when dealing with trade unions, i.e., union avoidance and social partnership. What are the factors that are likely to influence an employer's choice of industrial relations policy? Among several factors that may come into play, the two most important factors are product market strategy or production arrangements and labour market conditions. The state of the economy and the competitive position of the business in the market will also impinge on these policy choices. First, if the economy is doing well and the business is doing well too in terms of financial returns, then the cost of resistance to the business in the form of worker or union strikes and agitations is likely to be high. If workers strike or engage in other forms of collective or individual resistance, such as work-to-rule policies, go-slow policies, overtime bans or sabotage and theft, it is likely to hit the business harder in times of economic prosperity. Worker resistance in such times will make it difficult for the firm to deliver a timely and quality service and products to its customers and firms may find themselves undercut by their competitors. On the other hand, when the economy is sluggish and businesses are facing a crisis of profitability, then management is more likely to dig in their heels and engage in a protracted battle with the unions. With higher levels of unemployment in the labour market during economic downturns, workers and unions too may take a more considered view of engaging in antagonistic actions.

The level of competition in the product market and the favourability of the labour market are also important considerations for management when deciding on their industrial relations policies. If the product market is highly competitive, i.e., there are many other players in the market who sell the same products or services and, if the labour market is not very favourable to the firm, i.e., management cannot easily replace its existing stock of employees with other employees from the external labour market at the right time, in the right numbers with the right skill profile and at the right price (wage levels), then the situation demands a careful consideration of a social partnership approach with workers and unions. On the other hand, if the firm enjoys a virtual monopoly or oligopoly position in the product market and can easily hire and fire workers or replace its existing workforce with new workers from the external market, then there is very little incentive for the firm to engage in a social partnership with its workers and unions.

In India, it appears that employer hostility and anti-unionism rather than labour militancy have been the major causes of industrial conflict. Industrial conflict in the form of worker strikes and employer lock-outs is on the rise. If this means anything at all, longitudinal data taken from official government sources and primary studies suggest that employer lock-outs in India far outnumber worker/union strikes in terms of number of working days lost and number of workers affected (Shyam Sundar, 2010; Badigannavar and Kelly, 2012). The conventional logic of product-market strategy does not neatly apply to the Indian scenario. Even multinational firms like Suzuki, Hyundai and BOSCH, which are known internationally to be pursuing a strategy of innovation and quality, operate robust anti-union policies in their Indian subsidiaries (Shyam Sundar, 2010). What can explain this phenomenon? Research on the role of the judiciary in India offers some explanation. It is argued that since the launch of the economic reforms policies in 1991, the judiciary, i.e., industrial tribunals as well as High Courts and the Supreme Court, have delivered judgments which are employer-friendly and tilt the balance of power squarely in favour of employers. Judicial verdicts on employment of contract or casual labour have sub-stantially weakened the position of such workers who find themselves deprived of job security and facing increased exploitation by employers (Cox, 2012). Thus although the existing labour law framework in India appears to be pro-worker, the judicial interpretations of those laws have weakened the position of labour in the post-eco-nomic reforms period. This has perhaps emboldened employers to engage in anti-union strategies rather than engage in cooperative industrial relations with workers and unions. Pro-employer policies of the state further strengthen the position of employers who see little merit in engaging with their employees or unions. Employers in India historically have used lock-outs as a means to proxy firm closures and job cuts. During lock-outs, employers are not required to pay wages to workers and a prolonged lock-out wears down the will of the workers and their unions to engage in a protracted dispute. Employers use such opportunities to impose job cuts and inferior terms and conditions on employees and to discredit or bust unions (Badigannavar, 2013). This is unfortunately a very short-sighted approach to industrial relations.

Despite this rather grim picture, some 'green shoots' of social partnership have been witnessed in India. For instance, in a recent interview, Mr Arvind Shrouti,[2] an industrial relations consultant, reported that he had facilitated trust-based agreements between unions and management in companies in Pune, Maharashtra. The unique feature of these settlement deals were that they were signed without the unions submitting a 'charter of demands' to the management. Instead the unions submitted a 'productivity increase proposal' to management. The proposal offered an increase in productivity by 72 per cent through improvements in pro-duct quality, reduced rejection rates, reduction in wastage of raw materials and lower energy usage. In return, the management agreed to raise wages by around 20 per cent. All productivity-related issues were discussed jointly between manage-ment and the unions and the wage agreement was signed without any formal negotiations. Both the politically affiliated (e.g. BMS) and the non-affiliated unions were involved in this innovative consensus-based settlement. The jury is still out on the sustainability of these productivity-linked agreements as several exogenous factors can influence the financial viability of the firm.

Another such progressive industrial relations approach was recorded in a Mumbai-based company called Kamani Oil Industries Private Ltd,[3] which is a joint venture with a Swedish company, AAK. The company offered secure permanent employment to all of its 234 temporary contract workers. The HR department and the union representing the workers jointly discussed the proposal and concluded that offering permanency of employment would result in higher employee productivity. The senior management and the Swedish joint venture partner agreed with the proposal and offered permanent contracts to all casual workers employed in the firm with all the associated benefits that come along with permanent contracts. These are remarkable developments in union-management relations in India in recent years and offer a glimmer of hope. It is interesting, however, to note that in all these cooperative industrial relations ventures, the unions were in a relatively strong position with high membership levels and a history of strikes in the past.

Another important socio-cultural feature that plays into labour markets is the 'caste system' in India. Businesses need to take due cognizance of this issue for two reasons. First, in 2011–2012, the government of India published its preferential procurement policy along the lines of similar policies in developed countries like the USA, Germany and Canada. The policy entails that micro and small and medium-sized enterprises (MSMEs) should be given preference in all procurement and purchase of goods/services in the public sector. In India, the policy also stipulates that at least 20 per cent of such procurement should be from MSMEs owned or managed by individuals belonging to Scheduled Castes/Tribes (SC/ST). Second, the past decade has witnessed a rise in caste-based trade unions in India representing SC/ST workers largely in the public sector but increasingly in the private sector. These unions in most cases are not affiliated to political parties but, given that caste is a major electoral issue in India, these unions tend to enjoy a degree of political clout and are able to negotiate favourable deals with employers and government (Badigannavar, 2016b). The current BJP administration toyed with the idea of bringing in affirmative action policies (i.e., job reservations) for SC/ST individuals in the private sector. Such affirmative action policies have been in force in the public sector for the past six decades. Employer federations, such as the Federation of Indian Chambers of Commerce and Industry (FICCI), however, have opposed such statutory policies for the private sector and have instead come up with their own voluntary codes for social inclusion and diversity (see http://ficci.in/affirmative-action.asp). Trade unions representing SC/ST workers have welcomed such initiatives and are drawing up measures to monitor the implementation of such voluntary codes. However, mere lip service on the part of private sector employers to social inclusion and equal opportunities may not bode well with these caste-based unions and may result in industrial disputes and litigation.

Conclusion

Trade unions in India are facing challenges of labour reforms and de-regulation, however, they are far from a spent force. Aggregate union membership in India has increased nearly four-fold since 2008 and union density in the country outstrips that of many developed economies. This is an indicator that Indian trade unions are rising up to face the challenges of state reforms to labour markets, by engaging in concerted campaigns to recruit unorganized workers in the informal sector of the economy as well as casual and contract labour in the formal sector enterprises.

Businesses investing in India should be cognizant of the close links that national trade union federations have with various political parties ruling in the centre as well as the federal states. These political links do provide a degree of bargaining leverage to the unions as no political party can realistically afford to antagonize their union affiliates and risk losing elections. Trade unions in India have demonstrated their ability to mobilize mass support and win public sympathy by broadening their agenda and challenging government reforms through nation-wide strike calls. Even professional workers, such as those employed in IT and IT-enabled services, retail and the pharmaceutical industries, now appear to be more amenable to joining unions. Their efforts are bolstered through international collaborations with global unions like the Union Network International (UNI Global) and the International Trade Union Confederation (ITUC).

Industrial disputes have been on the rise in India since the launch of economic reforms in 1991. While employer-imposed lock-outs outnumber union strikes, either of the two are inimical to the financial interests of the enterprise. Labour-management cooperation, on the other hand, seems to offer greater promise of mutually beneficial outcomes, i.e. higher productivity for employers and better terms and conditions for workers than the traditional trench warfare approaches to industrial relations.

CASE STUDY: INDUSTRIAL RELATIONS AT VICEROY HOTELS

Workers for Viceroy Hotels in India have a union. The employees used to get 75 days holiday per year. The management wanted to reduce this to 25 days holidays, due to some managerial issues.

As this news spread among the workers, they readily and strongly opposed the proposal. They approached the union to resolve the issue. After a meeting, the union proposed to management that they were ready to convince the workers but in return the management had to pay 30 days extra salary in the month of December. The management agreed. The workers were also content and agreed to the proposal. Now the workers eagerly wait every year for the month of December to come so that they can get a good salary.

In the Viceroy hotels, frequent theft and pilfering of various items used to take place, such as shirts, towels, tissues, napkins, stationery, etc. So the hotel chain, in order to maintain its reputation and goodwill in the industry, used to replace the stolen items for its customers, for which the hotel had to make extra provision of Rs 50 lakhs (5 million) to satisfy the customers and thus it had to bear losses up to Rs 50 lakhs.

After some time a meeting was arranged between the management and the secretary of the union to solve the problem through a survey and thus find the proper solution to this problem. Through the survey it was found that the account statement of the hotel on one side showed the profit of Rs 1 crores and, on the other side, there was a loss of Rs 50 lakhs. Thus, management asked the union find the reasons for this discrepancy, and after further examination it was discovered that:

- of three supplied oil tankers ordered by the hotel, only one oil tanker had actually been received by the hotel, whereas the other two supplied oil tankers were found to be missing;
- of the 4,000 bulk products sent by Chennai Dyeing, only 2,500 products were actually received by the hotel, whereas the remaining 1,500 items were found to be missing.

After a further investigation was made by the union, it was found that two employees of the hotel were responsible for this theft.

The above examples show that a supportive role by unions can significantly help the company to manage peaceful industrial relations and enhance profits.

Useful websites

Centre of Indian Trade Unions www.citucentre.org/
Labour Bureau http://labourbureau.nic.in
New trade union initiative www.ntui.org.in/
Trade Unions, Statistical Yearbook http://mospi.nic.in/statistical-year-book-india/2017/210

Notes

1 Interview recorded by Mr Vivek Patwardhan and available to download from Vivek's World at: vivekvsp.com.
2 Author interview with INTUC official, December 2016.
3 Interview recorded by Mr Vivek Patwardhan and available to download from Vivek's World at: vivekvsp.com.

References

Badigannavar, V. (2013) Employment regulation in national contexts: India. In C. Frege and J. Kelly (eds) *Comparative Employment Relations in the Global Economy*. London: Routledge, pp. 305–323.
Badigannavar, V. (2016a) Is social partnership the way forward for Indian trade unions? Evidence from public services in India. *International Labour Review*. Available at: http://onlinelibrary.wiley.com/doi/10.1111/ilr.12028/full
Badigannavar, V. (2016b) Caste, class and trade unionism in India. Paper presented at the 28th Annual Meeting of Society for the Advancement of Socio-Economics, University of California, Berkeley, 24–26 June. Badigannavar, V. and Kelly, J. (2012) Do labour laws

protect labour in India? Union experiences of workplace employment regulations in Maharashtra, India. *Industrial Law Journal*, 41(4): 439–470.

Cox, J. (2012) With eyes wide open: Recent trends in Supreme Court labour and industrial judgements. In K.R. Shyam Sundar (ed.) *Contract Labour in India: Issues and Perspectives*. New Delhi: Dannish Books.

Desai, N. (2015) India: Trade unions and collective bargaining. Available at: www.nishith desai.com (accessed 5 April 2017).

Government of India (2018) Ministry of Labour and Employment report. Available at: www.labour.nic.in/

Kelly, J. (1998) *Rethinking Industrial Relations: Mobilization, Collectivism and Long Waves*. London: Routledge.

Kelly, J. (2004) Industrial relations approaches to the employment relationship. In J.A-M. Coyle-Shapiroet al. (eds) *The Employment Relationship: Examining Psychological and Contextual Perspectives*. Oxford: Oxford University Press.

Menon, S. (2013) Indian trade unions are getting bigger, coinciding with slowdown. *Business Standard News*, 6 April.

Monteiro, V.C. (2012) Trade unions and contract labour: Need to reaffirm the directive principles of the Constitution of India. In K.R. Shyam Sundar (ed.) *Contract Labour in India: Issues and Perspectives*. New Delhi: Dannish Books.

OECD (Organisation for Economic Co-operation and Development) (2018) Trade union density. Available at: https://stats.oecd.org/Index.aspx?DataSetCode=UN_DEN (accessed 5 April 2017).

Pal, R. (2008) Estimating the probability of trade union membership in India: Impact of Communist parties, personal attributes and industrial characteristics. Working Paper no. 2008-015. Mumbai: Indira Gandhi Institute of Development Research.

Safi, M. (2016) Tens of millions of Indian workers strike in fight for higher wages. *The Guardian*, 2 September.

Sen, S. and Dasgupta, B. (2009) *Unfreedom and Waged Work: Labour in India's Manufacturing Industry*. New Delhi: SAGE Publications India Ltd.

Shyam Sundar, K.R. (2010) *Industrial Conflict in India: Is the Sleeping Giant Waking Up?*New Delhi: Bookwell.

6

DYNAMICS OF CORRUPTION AND CRONYISM IN INDIA

Naresh Khatri and Arup Varma

Aims of this chapter are to:

- Understand the impact of corruption and cronyism on societies around the world
- Learn about the crucial differences between the related concepts of corruption and cronyism
- Explore how corruption and cronyism have affected business and society in India
- Understand how the economic liberalization and its resultant growth can help reduce corruption and cronyism

Introduction

The aim of this chapter is to paint a broad picture of corruption and cronyism in India. Although the average Indian probably faces, and talks about, corruption on a daily basis, systematic research and writing on the topic are limited. However, as we will see in this chapter, corruption and cronyism have severely affected India's economic growth and the well-being of its large populace (e.g., Khatri, 2016; Varma et al., 2016). Thus, it is fitting to examine the major factors that underlie cronyism and corruption in India.

This chapter is divided into three sections. In the first section, the concepts of corruption and cronyism are defined and distinguished from each other. The second section discusses the dynamics of corruption and cronyism in India. The final section derives implications for managers and policy-makers.

Corruption and cronyism: definitions and distinction

One of the most common definitions of corruption relates to the use of public office for private gain (Caiden, 2001; Larmour and Grabosky, 2001; White, 2001).

In virtually every society, historians and anthropologists have found that public affairs are distinguished by their exceptional privileges and trappings, and the activities most prone to corruption include bidding on public contracts, the use of public funds, the handling of property, tax assessment and collection, zoning and land use, the legislative and elective processes, law enforcement, and the administration of public services prone to political exploitation (Caiden, 2001; White, 2001; Barnett et al., 2013).

Cronyism usually gets lumped in with corruption but it has its own dynamics and patterns. The fundamental distinction between cronyism and corruption is that cronyism is based on a tie or a connection or relationship between actors and involves implicit, unspecified, and reciprocal transactions with no stipulation of a time period during which favours must be returned (Khatri et al., 2006). Unlike corrupt exchanges, cronyistic exchanges, more often than not, are based on trust, loyalty, and long-standing friendship.

In this chapter, we use the two terms of corruption and cronyism interchangeably, although our emphasis is on the systematic features of these phenomena, thus making the treatment closer to cronyism than corruption. The most basic definition or meaning of the word "cronyism" is preferential treatment shown to old friends and associates, without regard to their qualifications (Khatri and Tsang, 2003). Cronyism can occur in two basic forms: instrumental and relational (ibid.; Khatri et al., 2006; Pearce, 2015). Instrumental cronyism is motivated primarily by task, utilitarian, and self-interest considerations. Relational cronyism, on the other hand, has relationship, affection, and loyalty at its core, and is long-term in its orientation.

Dynamics of corruption and cronyism in India

Corruption is too vague a term and covers too much ground to be a useful tool for analysing and predicting acts of malfeasance. Indeed, different kinds of acts under the general rubric of corruption exhibit different dynamics, so linking them all together unnecessarily limits our analytic powers (Johnston, 2008). Appropriate reforms require an understanding of the deeper, long-term forces shaping and sustaining corruption, their links to observable local characteristics and contrasts, and careful thought as to how corruption control might function in a given context (ibid.; Jones and Stout, 2015). Based on *participation* (in the way people pursue, use, and exchange wealth and power) and *institutions* (economic, political, and social laws, systems, institutions), Johnston (2008) identified four syndromes of "Asian corruption" that capture important variations that can be traced to trends in the development of specific societies. Specifically, Johnston proposes the following syndromes of corruption: (1) *influence market corruption*, which is typical of well-developed economies, such as Japan, Germany, and the USA; (2) *elite cartel corruption*, which is found in Hong Kong, Korea, and Singapore, (3) *oligarch and clan corruption*, which is reminiscent of corruption in India, Malaysia, Sri Lanka, and Thailand; and (4) *official mogul corruption*, which is commonly observed in China, the Philippines, Pakistan, Indonesia, and Myanmar (see Ford et al., 2016). These four syndromes are discussed briefly next.

Influence market corruption deals in access to decision-makers and policy implementers within strong state institutions; often politicians serve as middlemen, trading connections for contributions both legal and otherwise. In elite cartel corruption, politics and markets are more competitive, but institutions are relatively weak. The oligarchic/clan corruption consists of a disorderly, sometimes violent scramble among contending oligarchs/clans seeking to parlay personal resources (e.g., mass following, a business, a bureaucratic chief, judicial or organized crime connections, or a powerful family) into wealth and power. In the official mogul corruption, institutions are weak, politics remain undemocratic or opening up only slowly, but the economy is being liberalized at least to a degree, and civil society is weak or non-existent.

Economic performance and corruption

An interesting question that puzzles scholars is whether corruption and cronyism can co-exist with fast economic growth. China and India both suffered from stagnant economies when they pursued the statist-nationalist economic strategy. However, since liberalization, the economies of both countries have exploded, despite the fact that the Corruption Perception Indices by Transparency International still rank them high in corruption. In India, to a large extent, the statist-nationalist philosophy reflected mainstream thinking among economists in the 1960s, as it did among development economists in many countries – especially in Latin America. It also coincided with India's early post-independence interest in Soviet planning models and with socialist thinking in the Congress Party (Lankester, 2004).

Democracy and corruption

The arguments pointing to the efficacy of elections in a democracy to curb corruption are intuitively appealing. The lower the cost to citizens of expelling non-performing officials, the more one would expect officials to act in the interests of citizens. In practice, however, electoral markets are often highly imperfect, disrupting electoral accountability and the ability of the citizens to sanction governments that allow poor governance outcomes to persist (Keefer, 2006). One key political market imperfection is uninformed citizens. If citizens cannot draw a connection between public policy and their own welfare, neither elections nor other, non-electoral, means of expelling politicians easily limit abuses by government officials. The dominance of the Congress Party and its dynastic rule beginning since the independence of the country in 1947 until mid-1985 resulted in a culture of cronyism and patronage, because the party faced no credible threat from the opposition parties.

Role of societal culture in corruption/cronyism

Although societal culture has been shown to be a key variable in understanding human behavior (Hofstede, 2001), policy-making institutions such as the World

Bank and the International Monetary Fund (IMF) are still dominated by economics and other related fields such as finance and political science. Only recently have scholars begun to realize that, perhaps, culture has a greater explanatory power than macroeconomic and financial variables (Steidlmeier, 1999; Waldron, 2002). In general terms, *"cultural logic* underscores the numerous socio-cultural values and beliefs that are embedded within organizations and function as a sort of internal gyroscope, which governs the social behavior of people" (Steidlmeier, 1999, p. 121). Khatri, Tsang, and Begley (2006) proposed four types of cronyism across the two major cultural dimensions: vertical and horizontal and individualism and collectivism (see Figure 6.1). Vertical cultures assume that people are different from one another, take hierarchy as a given, and accent status differences as well as respect for authority. Horizontal cultures value equality, see people as similar to one another, therefore as interchangeable, and minimize status and authority distinctions. In individualist cultures, individual beliefs, values, attitudes, and interests drive social behavior, and personal goals take priority over group goals. Individualists seek task achievement at the expense of relationships. On the other hand, the behavior of collectivists is driven by social norms, duties, and obligations, and collectivists tend to subordinate personal goals to group goals. Collectivists value harmonious relationships even at the expense of task accomplishment. Indian culture is high on vertical collectivism, thus making it prone to a high level of cronyism since vertical collectivist cultures are suggested to have the highest level of cronyism, followed by vertical individualist, horizontal collectivist, and horizontal individualist cultures, respectively (ibid.). The Corruption Perception Index of Transparency International corroborates Khatri et al.'s typology. Most of the countries

	Individualist culture	Collectivist culture
Vertical culture	Vertical Individualists (e.g., France, the UK, the USA) Highest level of instrumental cronyism	Vertical Collectivists (e.g., Asian, African, Latin American, East European countries; India, Brazil, Egypt, Hungary) Highest level of relational cronyism
Horizontal culture	Horizontal Individualists (Scandinavian Countries;Sweden, Denmark, Norway) None or low level of instrumental cronyism	Horizontal Collectivists (Israeli Kibbutz, New Zealand) None or low level of relational cronyism

FIGURE 6.1 Cultural dimensions and cronyism in India

on the higher end of the corruption index are vertical collectivists and most of the countries on the lower end of the corruption index are horizontal individualists. A collectivist culture like India values in-group relationships based frequently on kinship or other ascriptive ties. Thus, the members of a particular group feel obliged to take care of one another and feel duty-bound to allocate rewards more generously to in-group than to out-group members, otherwise they may face group sanctions. In India, strong boundaries between in-groups and out-groups are drawn, based on caste, religion, and region.

Although some think that the Asian countries, including India, are becoming westernized rather rapidly, the truth is that the changes presently taking place in these nations and societies, are mostly superficial and cosmetic in nature.

Indian political culture and corruption

The Indian National Congress has ruled India for most of the time since independence. The administrative systems and social, economic, and political institutions that exist in India today show the deep imprint of the Congress Party's philosophy and policies. As Luce noted:

> The Indian state was partly a creation of Nehru. But Nehru's motivations were ideological and they were in tune with broader international fashion at the time. Sixty years later, the persistence of the unreformed state can no longer be attributed to ideology. We have to look deeper to discover why India's state is still permitted to operate in its radical form. Some of the reasons are to be found in the habits and character of the Congress Party.
>
> *(2008, p. 197)*

A good example of cronyism rampant in the central government was reported in the Indian newspaper, The Economic Times (2007). The government forced all the independent directors – including directors elected by minority shareholders – of public sector banks to step down and appointed party workers and loyalists in their place. These supposedly 'independent' directors included at least five secretaries of the All India Congress Committee, as well as many senior members from the All India Mahila Congress and Sewa Dal. In general, institutional directors, who are appointed by the central government, sit as mute witnesses to various acts of corporate malfeasance and poor governance, stirring only when they receive directions from the government. And the government officials routinely used these directors as pawns in a complex game of favoritism and cronyism (ibid.).

Indian civil services and corruption

India has long practiced economic planning or command capitalism through extensive state regulative controls on industry and cumbersome licensing schemes, partly due to political and bureaucratic corruption (Das, 2001). *Netas* (politicians) and *babus* (bureaucrats) have run the show and strangled the tremendous human potential, creativity, and entrepreneurship of Indians. In general, Indian politicians have not taken kindly to administrative reforms that separate policy-making from policy implementation because doing so strips them of their ability to shower favoritism on their cronies. Similarly, the elite civil service has been in the vanguard of resistance to any attempt to change the status quo and have largely been successful because of the political leadership's undue dependence on them.

Not surprisingly, the civil service has also been shown to be corrupt and served the interests of patrimonial politics (ibid.). The present system has worked well only in coordinating rents and sharing them across both the official and political realms. Day-to-day administration provides ample opportunities for money-making, such as transfers and postings of civil servants, awarding of major contracts and concessions, and the provision of goods and services free or below market prices (ibid.). As the implementing body for all government policies, state laws and regulations, the civil service is at the heart of the governance problems in India (ibid.; Nikomborirak, 2007).

Oligarchic family control and corruption

Firms controlled by oligarchic families are generally adept rent-seekers who thrive in societies with low trust levels and corruption (Fogel, 2006). India has the second-highest number of billionaires per trillion dollars of GDP, after Russia (The Economic Times, 2008a). While Russia has 87 billionaires for the $1.3 trillion of GDP it generates, India has 55 for the $1.1 trillion of GDP. Three factors – land, natural resources, and government contracts – are the predominant resources of the wealth of Indian billionaires and all these features come from the government. Too many people in India have become rich based on their proximity to the government. A mutually reinforcing relationship exists in which poor institutions lead to the rise of concentrated economic power and the oligarchies in turn use their economic might to reap political advantages and shape the institutional development most favorable to their interests (Fogel, 2006).

Corruption and red-tape procedures, partly as a consequence of oligarchic control, are the major barriers to the growth of entrepreneurship in India, a government study has found. The study on entrepreneurship, conducted by the National Knowledge Commission and reported in The Economic Times (2008a) is based on interviews with 155 entrepreneurs from across the country. Entrepreneurs were found to face difficulty and delays in meeting various government requirements, such as the registration of the company, obtaining licenses, and registering the property. The study also quoted the World Bank report "Doing Business in South Asia 2007" to point out the inordinate delay of 35–52 days to start a business in India. The official costs of starting a business were noted to be high and the process quite complex, involving no less than 13 procedures (The Economic Times, 2008b).

While in the pre-reforms era, corruption used to be about sale of permits, reforms have created new sources of rents for the establishment. Land can be expropriated from those who do not have connections or formal title. Public land can always be disposed of to favored parties. Contracts can be assigned to chosen friends despite a sham of public bidding. The rents are shared by the politicians and corrupt businessmen (The Economic Times, 2008c).

Deterioration of institutions

At independence, India inherited a fairly corruption-free, robust administrative system. Individuals heading various central government bodies (for example, the chief of the army staff, the judges to the Supreme Court and High Courts, the vice-chancellors of universities, etc.) were chosen based on merit. Nehru, the first Prime Minister of India from 1947 to 1964, did not interfere in important appointments and the Indian administrative system remained a decent one. Since then, because of the interference of the government in appointments, the Indian administrative system and institutions have unravelled, and most central govern-ment departments and institutions and state government departments have become politicized and corrupt. The Indian judicial system was free from political inter-ference for many decades after independence, but became deeply politicized and corrupt over time. According to Transparency International's (2006) survey, 77 per cent of the Indian respondents described the judicial system as corrupt. About 36 per cent of the people paid bribes to the judiciary. The average amount of money paid by a household in India to the judiciary was the highest compared to other sectors. As of October 2017, the Supreme Court has 58,438 pending cases, the 24 High Courts had 4.15 million pending cases, while the subordinate courts have over 270 million pending cases (*The Indian Express*, 2017). Given that all court systems are short-staffed, it is anyone's guess when all these cases might see the light of day, or be settled.

Conclusion

What does it all mean for firms that want to do business in India? India's major undoing, more than anything else, was to rely on the socialist philosophy and its statist-nationalist economic strategy. Lack of economic freedom has been suggested to account for 71 per cent of corruption in a society (Wikipedia, 2009). There are so many examples of Asian countries that have prospered economically despite ubiquitous cronyism and corruption. But there is none that has grown rapidly using the statist-nationalist economy. Even the "Indian pseudo-intellectuals" who backed the socialist economic model in the past have understood the root cause of India's economic problems. Now, finally, the genie is out of the bottle and the Indian bandwagon is rolling; it is as hard to stop it now as it was to start it. Of course, there are many strong forces propelling India forward. First, the liberal economy is allowing Indian entrepreneurs to flex their muscles. Although presently the wealth is concentrated in a few hands, over time, new entrepreneurs, the likes of Narayana Murthy of Infosys, will keep appearing on the horizon. The Indian people have been constrained for too long. They are hungry and they are restless. They have waited for too long and seen many economies go past them. Second, India's democracy has matured and shown tremendous resilience. It is as vibrant a democracy as there can be. Democracy, in combination with its liberal economic strategy and its massive size, makes India the place to be. India's free and vigorous press is its third major strength. It will be a huge force in bringing more transparency and curbing corruption and cronyism in India. It has shown its calibre by bringing to light so many high profile corruption scandals, which might not have been possible in most other countries. The fourth Indian strength lies in the Indian people and professionals. Indian institutions and systems are already compatible with the Western economies and there is a large pool of British-educated people. Indian professionals and businessmen have already proved their acumen and brilliance all over the globe. As one British historian rightly noted: "There is not a thought that is being thought in the West or the East that is not active in some Indian mind."

One interesting and critical change has been the change of government at the centre. In 2014, an overwhelming majority elected the Bharatiya Janata Party, led by Prime Minister Narendra Modi. The Prime Minister and his team have undertaken many steps toward providing a clean and corruption-free government at all levels. For example, in November 2016, Mr Modi announced a major move whereby currency notes of Rs 500 and Rs 1000 denomination were taken out of circulation. The demonetization was designed to flush out the "black" money from private vaults and bring it back into circulation after taxes were paid on those funds. While the true extent of the impact of this and other such initiatives of the government will be judged by history, what is clear is that the image of India has started to improve substantially. Leading world bodies like the International Monetary Fund (IMF) applauded the government's move. At the same time, Moody's has upgraded India's ratings, and the country is rising on many global indices, including "ease of doing business."

Of course, there are historical forces that should not be underestimated that may resist the forces of change and once more knock India off track. Indian politicians (netas) and bureaucrats (babus) in tandem have perpetuated a highly cronyistic system. A recent survey ranked India's "suffocating bureaucracy" as the worst in Asia and suggested that it wields tremendous power at both the national and state levels (The Times of India, 2009). The survey also noted that the Indian civil service is extremely resistant to reform. The elite civil servants have become used to power and are not likely to give it up easily. The answer to neutralizing both netas and babus lies in a bigger and relatively unfettered private sector that can become an engine of Indian growth and prosperity. Netas and babus can keep getting their rents in the government/public sector.

The other major negative force to contend with is the concentration of wealth in the hands of a few families. These families want to protect their empires from upstarts. They want to continue to plunder rents in collaboration with the politicians and bureaucrats. Thus, they keep putting obstacles in the way of meaningful institutional reforms. Still another major obstacle in the way of India's growth and prosperity is the caste-based social system. The political parties keep reinforcing the caste system and, as a result, India remains a divided society.

As noted earlier, corruption in India is of two types: elite and petty. Indian society is very hierarchic and elitist. As a result, the elites, including international managers and companies, are not affected by the day-to-day corruption that the common Indians face. International managers and companies get into trouble only by showing arrogance and lacking cultural sensitivities but not because they are strangers or outsiders.

CASE STUDY: CRONYISM AND CORRUPTION: NAVIGATING THE MAZE

As Joanne's flight landed at New Delhi airport, she was filled with a whole host of emotions. Joanne had spent time in India in the late 2000s and had become quite comfortable with the way things worked in India. She enjoyed the spicy food, the long walks with her friends in the park near her apartment in Greater Kailash, and the late-night "paratha" runs to Moolchand. She had become very comfortable with the traffic, and had even learned to tolerate the incessant honking of the vehicles. She especially enjoyed being able to take the metro to almost every part of Delhi and even to the neighboring suburbs of Gurgaon and Noida. She was looking forward to meeting up with all her friends and enjoying some *chhole-bhaturey* and *lassi* at Lajpat Nagar market.

However, as she stepped off the plane, she was reminded of a couple of thing that had bothered her during her stay in India, and she wondered if she would be able to handle those things this time around. The first thing that bothered her a lot was how most people seemed to nonchalantly throw garbage just about anywhere. She was quite taken aback by this habit, as every single family home she visited was kept spotlessly clean inside, though even some of these very same friends and neighbors did not seem to think twice before throwing garbage out of their cars or from their balconies!

The other thing that had seemed rather odd to her was the subtle request for *bakhsheesh* (bribe) almost every time she had to deal with the government. Indeed, this was a common topic of discussion at most parties – how much someone had to pay to get their passport issued, how much someone had to pay to get their house registered, and so on. She was quite surprised at how casually people seemed to accept such transactions as part of life, or a "necessary evil," as one of her friends described it. But what really surprised her was how many of her friends and acquaintances seemed to take pride in 'knowing' the right people so they could get their work done at government offices. At one party, one of her neighbors was boasting how his daughter got her driving license without ever stepping foot in a transport office. "In fact," he boasted, "the license was delivered to our home!" When she inquired how much he had to pay to get this special treatment, the neighbor replied with a huge smile, "Not a single rupee! I know the Director there – he owes me many favors!"

As Joanne got into her classic Ambassador taxi (she loved these cars), she wondered how much things had changed since her last stay in India. Would the average person, without connections to politicians and bureaucrats, or loads of money, be able to get the services they rightfully deserved as a citizen? Or, would they still be given the run-around? Once she reached her hotel, her driver helped offload her bags, and when she asked him how much she owed him, he responded, "Madam, Rs 482.55." She gave him a crisp new Rs 500 note and started to walk off, but he called out, saying "Madam, your change!" and gave her Rs 17.45. Joanne stood there scratching her head at the irony: back in Chicago, her cab driver would have insisted on a much higher tip!

1. It is well known that many societies suffer from the evils of cronyism and corruption, in your opinion, what is at the heart of such behavior? How might societies try to eradicate such behavior?
2. Some scholars have argued that poverty is at the root of corruption, while others argue that greed leads to such behavior. What do you think? Please justify your responses.

Useful websites

Central Vigilance Commission www.cvc.nic.in/
Overseas business risk in India www.gov.uk/government/publications/overseas-business-risk-india/overseas-business-risk-india
Transparency International www.transparency.org/

References

Barnett, A., Yandle, B., and Naufal, G. (2013) Regulation, trust, and cronyism in Middle Eastern societies: The simple economics of "waste." *The Journal of Socio-Economics*, 44: 41–46.

Caiden, G.E. (2001) Corruption and governance. In G.E. Caiden, O.P. Dwivedi, and J. Jabbra (Eds.) *Where Corruption Lives*. Bloomfield, CT: Kumarian Press, pp. 15–37.

Das, S.K. (2001) *Public Office, Private Interest: Bureaucracy and Corruption in India*. New Delhi: Oxford University Press.

Fogel, K. (2006) Oligarchic family control, social economic outcomes, and the quality of government. *Journal of International Business Studies*, 37: 603–622.

Ford, M., Gillan, M., and Thein, H.H. (2016) From cronyism to oligarchy? Privatisation and business elites in Myanmar. *Journal of Contemporary Asia*, 46(1): 18–41.

Hofstede, G. (2001) *Culture's Consequences: Comparing Values, Behaviors, Institutions and Organizations across Nations*. Thousand Oaks, CA: Sage.

Johnston, M. (2008) Japan, Korea, the Philippines, China: Four syndromes of corruption. *Crime, Law, and Social Change*, 49: 205–223.

Jones, R.G. and Stout, T. (2015) Policing nepotism and cronyism without losing the value of social connection. *Industrial and Organizational Psychology*, 8(1): 2–12.

Keefer, P. (2006) *Governance and Economic Growth in China and India*. Washington, DC: World Bank Development Research Group.

Khatri, N. (2016) Definitions of cronyism, corruption, and crony capitalism. In N. Khatri and A. Ohja (Eds.) *Crony Capitalism in India*. London: Palgrave Macmillan, pp. 3–7.

Khatri, N., Tsang, E.W.K., and Begley, T. (2006) Cronyism: A cross-cultural analysis. *Journal of International Business Studies*, 37(1): 61–75.

Lankester, T. (2004) "Asian drama": The pursuit of modernization in India and Indonesia. *Asian Affairs*, XXXV: 291–304.

Larmour, P. and Grabosky, P. (2001) Corruption in Australia: Its prevention and control. In G.E. Caiden, O.P. Dwivedi, and J. Jabbra (Eds.) *Where Corruption Lives*. Bloomfield, CT: Kumarian Press, pp. 175–188.

Luce, E. (2008) *In Spite of the Gods: The Rise of Modern India*. New York: Anchor Books.

Nikomborirak, D. (2007) Civil service reforms and the quest for better governance: The Thai experience. *TDRI Quarterly Review*, 22(1): 3–8.

Pearce, J.L. (2015) Cronyism and nepotism are bad for everyone: The research evidence. *Industrial and Organizational Psychology*, 8(1): 41–44.

Steidlmeier, P. (1999) Gift giving, bribery, and corruption: Ethical management of business relationships in China. *Journal of Business Ethics*, 20(2): 121–132.

The Economic Times (2007) Good biz, poor governance. May 14.

The Economic Times (2008a) Political influence in businesses a concern. September 12.

The Economic Times (2008b) Corruption, red-tapism affect entrepreneurship in India: Study. July 7.

The Indian Express (2017) Pending cases go down in Supreme Court, High Courts; but see upward swing in lower courts. October 1.

The Times of India (2009) Indian bureaucracy ranked worst in Asia: Survey. June 3.

Varma, A., Hu, B. and Bloomquist, L. (2016) Crony capitalism and family oligarchies in India. In N. Khatri and A. Ojha (Eds.) *Crony Capitalism in India*. London: Palgrave Macmillan, pp. 159–176.

Waldron, J. (2002) One law for all: The logic of cultural accommodation. *Washington & Lee Law Review*, 59: 3–34.

White, R.D., Jr. (2001) Corruption in the United States. In G.E. Caiden, O.P. Dwivedi, and J. Jabbra (Eds.) *Where Corruption Lives*. Bloomfield, CT: Kumarian Press, pp. 39–55.

Wikipedia (2009) Political corruption. Available at: http://en.wikipedia.org/wiki/political_corruption (accessed 20 March 2009).

7

UNRAVELLING AND HARNESSING THE INDIAN MINDSET

Implications for organizations

Abinash Panda and Rajen K. Gupta

Aims of this chapter are to:

- Present a comprehensive understanding of the way Indians behave
- Unravel the Indian mindset
- Suggest how organization leaders should craft a culturally appropriate ecosystem to productively leverage the Indian mindset

Introduction

This chapter is intended to help corporate leaders of multinational companies (MNCs) and expatriate chief executive officers (CEOs) gain a relevant understanding of India, the Indian societal culture and organizations in India. It focuses on formal business organizations in India and is organized into six sections. The first section briefly discusses the pan-Indian cultural characteristics. The second delves into the work behaviour of Indians. It also describes the unique aspects of the Indian way of thinking and unpacks the 'Indian mindset'. Context sensitivity, discrepancy and duplicity are at the core of the Indian mindset. The third section deconstructs the context-sensitive nature of Indians' behaviour. The fourth delineates the working conditions that motivate Indians. The fifth section discusses nurturant task leadership and familial organization as the most effective and culturally aligned organizational form and leadership style in the Indian context. The sixth section presents the conditions and challenges for organization leaders in crafting an enabling ecosystem that can harness the creative potential of the Indian mindset. The final section concludes the chapter with a summary of the key takeaway points.

Pan-Indian cultural characteristics

The business and management culture in India reflects the complexity and diversity that characterize the country. Dheer, Lenartowicz and Peterson (2015) have identified nine sub-cultural divisions of India with distinct socio-cultural attributes. The nine regions are North-western India, Western India, North-central India, North-eastern India, Central India, Eastern India, Far-east India, South-western India, and Southern India. Despite such diversity in multiple aspects, Panda and Gupta (2004) identified six pan-Indian cultural characteristics: (1) a collectivist orientation; (2) respect for power and status; (3) the primacy of a personal relationship; (4) the desire to belong to an in-group; (5) a family focus; and (6) context-sensitive or situational behaviour.

Indians are socialized in their family relationships: (1) to develop a sense of helplessness; and (2) to attach importance to personal relationships and family, leading to a family-centric work ethic (Kanungo, 1990, p. 802). A sense of helplessness and lack of proactivity make Indians seek a hierarchical dependent relationship with others and respond to external situations in a passive manner, rather than trying to change events. They tend to believe that external factors are given, and one must accept that and respond prudently, depending on the situation, which also makes their behaviour highly context-sensitive. Consequently, Indians tend to be fatalistic too.

Indian society attaches great importance to the collectivistic tendency with a respect for power and status (respect for hierarchy). Indians also exhibit a desire to belong in their preferred in-groups. The nature of Indians, embedded in a group culture, encourages them to identify themselves strongly with family, caste or community.

Saliency of family and familial personal relationship

Family is found to be the most basic in-group (Sinha and Verma, 1987). Indians are motivated to achieve not for the sake of achievement itself, but for the enhancement of their family status. Indians are socialized to attach saliency to personal relationships with emotional intimacy, dependency and symbiotic reciprocity (Sinha et al., 2001).

Respect for status and hierarchy

Indians tend to be comfortable with the unequal distribution of status and power in both society and organizatios (Roland, 1980). The superior-subordinate relationship is characterized by a great degree of dependence of subordinates on their superiors. No employee can imagine an organizational role without a designation. This aspect of Indian culture is further highlighted in the following example. Michael Thiemann, CEO of ThyssenKrupp India, tried to demolish hierarchies in his company and distribute responsibilities according to capabilities, like they do in

Germany. The result, he says, was chaos. Thiemann then called in his senior colleagues to rework things. 'We developed the concept of team work with an Indian flavour, taking care of the hidden rules of the Indian working culture,' he says (Philip and Ganguly, 2014).

General pattern of work behaviour in Indian organizations

The work behaviour of the employees in organizations in India is shaped by how employees generally respond to the conflict between the social values they are socialized into and the rationale and values imposed on them through formal organizations. Indians who are socialized to attach importance to personal relationships and suppress their own feelings, are also expected to demonstrate suitable behaviour that is formally espoused by the organization. Consequently, they become victims of a 'double bind' (Garg and Parikh, 1995, p. 14), which implies a process where contradictory messages converge on the individual from both of the two distinct sources.

The traditional ethos is rooted in a traditional agrarian familial ethos, emphasizing personalized relationships. On the other hand, behaviour mandated by formal organizations is based on a Western industrial ethos, which is rooted in the Anglo-Saxon rationale that encourages employees to demonstrate a transactional relationship with colleagues and be guided by self-interest, independence and individual autonomy. It attaches importance to equality, equity and positional authority. In Indian organizations, both traditional and Western management systems co-exist. The general pattern of work behaviour reflects context sensitivity, and a tendency towards balance by integrating pluralistic considerations (Sinha and Kanungo, 1997, p. 100). Indians prefer authoritative and hierarchical forms of management. They respond favourably to close supervision (Roland, 1980) and prefer clear and direct orders from superiors. They value the personal relationships they have with their reporting managers, while demonstrating reverence and respect towards them. Leaders, in return, offer protection and support and express concern for subordinates (Sinha and Kanungo, 1997).

The Indian way of thinking

This context-sensitive way of behaving equips Indians to act differently in different contexts. In the organizational context, the natural pattern of behaviour, which is guided by an agrarian-familial worldview, tends to become dormant, whereas the rational Anglo-Saxon worldview is activated. The reverse is true in informal social set-ups. Because of the high context orientation and partly due to the complex way they conceive of and respond to a situation, it is found that 'Indians tend to demonstrate both individualistic and collectivistic tendencies depending on the situation. Indians combine both individualistic and collectivistic orientations in a more complex way' (Panda and Gupta, 2016, p. 191). Second, Indians, compared to Westerners, can more comfortably deal with the dissonance between a behaviour and the intention behind it (Bharati, 1985).

The Indian mindset

Equipped with both these worldviews, Indians can 'selectively draw paradoxical cultural frames, pick up discrete and even contradictory cognitions, and organize them into a novel but internally inconsistent set that is uniquely relevant to a particular situation or appropriate for dealing with a person of significance' (Sinha, 2014, p. 174). The findings of a select few studies on the Indian mindset reveal the following.

- 'Duplicity', which is understood to mean that 'people profess to believe and prefer what they consider to be desirable but tend to behave in contrary ways due to realistic compulsions' (Sinha et al., 2010, p. 12), is one of the dominant attributes of the Indian mindset (Sinha, 2014).
- Indians manifest high discrepancy in their beliefs, preferences, action orientations and high sensitivity to contextual cues (Sinha et al., 2010).

Indians rarely demonstrate a purely individualist pattern of behaviour and intention. Their behavioural response depends on the situational characteristics (Sinha et al., 2002). Indians also operate from different mindsets in different situations. For instance, they may demonstrate a materialistic mindset in international organizations, whereas they tend to exhibit dependence-prone or a collectivistic mindset in family-owned, bureaucratic or traditional organizations, depending on whether they value an easy-going life or a stable relationship, respectively (Sinha and Pandey, 2007).

Panda and Gupta (2012) deconstructed the context-sensitive nature of Indian behaviour using an 'interactional' framework and presented a behavioural taxonomy, which suggests how Indians tend to behave in various work contexts (family-owned, government and MNCs of Western origin). They identified three ideal-types of Indians: (1) westernized individualist; (2) hybrid; and (3) traditional collectivist. The taxonomy identifies five patterns of behaviour, namely:

1. Gross Personalized Work Behaviour (GPWB), marked by parochial, paternalistic and ingratiating tendencies.
2. Subtle Personalized Work Behaviour (SPWB), marked by covert parochial/paternalistic tendencies.
3. Mixed Work Behaviour (MWB).
4. Subtle Impersonalized Work Behaviour (SIWB), marked by subtle familial or relational orientation.
5. Gross Impersonalized Work Behaviour (GIWB), marked by contractual or transactional relationships.

Table 7.1 presents probable behavioural patterns as exhibited by the three ideal-types of Indians in three distinct work contexts. Some of these behavioural patterns are variants of the five generic behavioural patterns mentioned above.

TABLE 7.1 Behavioural patterns of Indians in different settings

	Western MNO	*Government organizations*	*Family-owned organizations*
Traditional collectivist Indian	Covert/parochial/paternalistic (subtle personalized) work behaviour	Mixed work behaviour	Parochial/paternalistic/ ingratiating (gross personalized) work behaviour
Hybrid Indian	Mixed work behaviour	Mixed work behaviour	Mixed work behaviour
Westernized individualist Indian	Gross impersonal work behaviour	Judicious/ cautious (subtle) impersonal work behaviour	Judicious/cautious (subtle) impersonal work behaviour

Creating an enabling context: motivating Indians to perform

Sinha (1990) identified two dominant work cultures prevalent in Indian organizations, namely, 'soft' and 'synergistic' work cultures. The soft work culture, where 'profit and productivity yield to familial ethic and in-group considerations' (Sinha and Kanungo, 1997, p. 102), seems to foster the 'GPWB pattern', whereas the synergistic work culture, where 'the organizations have been able to set up the objective of self-reliance, developed strong work-related norms, unequivocal performance standards and a generous reward system, all supported by people-oriented management' (ibid.), may foster a 'GIWB pattern'.

Sinha et al. (2010) found that Indians working under an 'enabling' reporting manager tend to be motivated to perform, come up with innovative ideas and share these with the team, be transparent and open with respect to sharing feelings and views with the reporting manager and colleagues. An enabling manager believes in empowerment, and, hence, involves subordinates by making them participate in discussing ideas, encouraging team members to contribute and nurtures them by offering help and guidance, supporting ideas.

Indians, when led by such enabling leaders, tend to be sensitive to the needs of their peer group without losing sight of the goals. They try to achieve a balance both by working diligently, availing themselves of challenging opportunities and remaining optimistic even in adverse situations.

On the other hand, employees working under 'disabling' reporting managers tend to carefully evaluate how they can serve their self-interests. They may say what people in the position of authority (powerful, in that sense) want to hear. 'Disabling' reporting managers tend to be 'autocratic', expecting personal loyalty, sycophancy and compliance from the subordinates. Such a manager is driven by the need for power.

Truly familial organization

Given Indians' preference for familial, personalized relationships and a family-like work environment, Gupta (1999) proposed the idea of 'truly familial organizations' in an Indian context, which are aligned to the Indian cultural milieu. Hence, such an organization may encourage employees to identify with the organization and its goals, Gupta proposed that the imaginary boundary of the organization should be extended to include the employees' family members emotionally. The survey on India's best companies to work for in 2017,[1] conducted by *The Economic Times* revealed that organizations that have employed structured methods to thank employees' families and involve peers in welcoming new employees to the organization not only enjoy a high positive perception as a caring employer, but have two and four times, respectively, a higher chance of breaking into the league of the 100 Best Companies to Work for in India (ET Bureau, 2017).

Nurturant task leadership: effective in the Indian context

A review of scholarly works on effective leadership in Indian context indicates the following:

1. There is a strong preference for an authoritative leader, who is strict, demanding but also caring and nurturing, very much like the *karta*-paternalistic role in a family.
2. The leader is nurturing in the sense of functioning as a benevolent guide to the subordinates and taking a personal interest in their well-being and growth.
3. There is a complementary tendency among the subordinates to idealize the leader and consider the leader the repository of virtues, deserving loyalty and respect. The leader is thus a role model with many facets: high integrity, system builder, humane father/mother figure.
4. There is a high preference for a personalized mode of relating to each other.

Effective leaders in the Indian context then emphasize both nurturing subordinates and task performance. The Nurturant Task Leadership (NTL) (Sinha, 1980) has been found to be effective in the Indian context and is also congruent with Indian cultural values and behaviour dispositions and draws heavily on patterns of interaction typifying family dynamics in India (Sinha, 1999).

In the Indian context, patronizing is associated with taking care of subordinates, which is viewed positively. Decisions about children's career choice, marriage, etc., are made by their parents. Indians having grown up with such a psyche are likely to expect patronizing behaviour from their bosses.

Kalra (2004) made a case for a consultative-style leadership, given the average Indian psyche, which is dependence-prone, feels comfortable in hierarchical structures, looks for support/approval from superiors, and even being heard by the boss gives the subordinate a feeling of acceptance.

An effective leader in Indian context should do the following:

- nurture and mentor subordinates;
- be mildly prescriptive, and task-oriented;
- show an interest in subordinates' growth and well-being;
- involve subordinates in organizational activities.

Performance orientation and problem-solving approach of effective leaders

Kalra and Gupta (1999) argue that an effective leader in the Indian context tends to be focused on problem solving and be mildly prescriptive, while dealing with subordinates, as nurturing and patronizing may at times be ineffective in ensuring desired performance.

In such situations, leaders may opt for a more systematic approach of imposing a work discipline, and thereby ensuring the desired performance. Such an approach includes quantifying the problem, establishing norms, sharing the problem perspective widely, identifying individual acts of violation, acting kindly but firmly on each violation, and, finally, zeroing in on hard-core offenders for disciplinary action. S.R. Mahesh, then Vice President, HR, of Indian Hotels brought unauthorized absenteeism down to the desired level and enhanced performance by adopting a systematic approach to problem solving (Mahesh, 1988). He leveraged personal communication and counselling techniques to deal with offenders. When this did not yield desired outcomes in a few cases, he took punitive measures, including legal recourse to get rid of them.

A leader, in order to be effective in the Indian context, must balance performance orientation and being patronizing and nurturing. Too much nurture without a performance focus or too much task obsession without a patronizing approach may not be effective in the Indian context. Further, an effective leader in the Indian context should be compassionate and caring towards subordinates. Anil K. Khandelwal has demonstrated a leadership style, which is marked by being tough on performance while being compassionate with the employees. He calls it 'tough love'.

The challenges of India for foreign MNCs and expat CEOs

India is culturally complex and diverse. Employees in any organization come from different ethnic and religious identities. They identify with different regions in India, harbouring different beliefs, values and preferences. The basis for their social identification tends to be narrow, which could be their *jati* (caste/ethnicity), language, region or religion. They tend to identify less with their employing organizations. Further, though the collectivist orientation augurs well for teamwork, the community *jati*-based social identity makes it difficult for Indians to work in a team. Given that, organization leaders should be cautious when and how to use teams.

Second, a leader is acceptable to the followers only if they understand and respond to their culturally specific psychological needs. Since Indian workers expect an attitude of paternal care from their bosses, the bosses will have to be nurturant with the subordinates with a tinge of personal relationship. The purely rational relationship, which is transactional in nature, may not be effective in the Indian cultural context. Hence, leaders, like fathers in the family, should act as a facilitator, mentor or a coach to the subordinates. When a leader acts like a father in a family, the subordinates feel psychologically safe seeking performance feedback from the leaders. Subordinates may find their jobs meaningful. A pure authoritarian leadership style may not be optimally effective.

Third, the situational nature of behaviour of Indians makes it tricky for organizations to motivate employees to perform. If Indians find the context and the leader enabling, they will be committed to organizational goals and perform well. On the other hand, if they find the context otherwise, they may not perform up to their potential. They are adept in demonstrating either self-seeking calculative or goal-driven achievement-seeking behaviour, depending on the context. Moreover, an Indian employee is more likely to shift to a more positive behaviour if they realize that the disabling situation has changed into an enabling one.

Creating an enabling eco-system to harness the Indian mindset: what organization leaders need to do

Based on what has been presented so far, organization leaders need to do the following to craft an enabling ecosystem to harness the Indian mindset productively:

1. Create a family-like work environment.
2. Demonstrate leadership that mentors subordinates.
3. Ensure performance without being task-obsessed.
4. Show leadership that engages the subordinates beyond work boundaries to create a truly familial organization in spirit.

Create a family-like work environment

Employees in India generally seek out meaningful working relationships. Devoid of meaningful personal relationships, employees may become disengaged and resort to social loafing. Hence, the same employees are found to be diligent in some situations but loafers in some others.

In a family-like work environment, the leader is like the head of the family (*karta*). If the leader-subordinate relationship is marked by relationship of *sneh* (affection) and *shradha* (deference), subordinates would do their best for their paternal superior to get the work done. Indian employees generally feel anxious and insecure if their superiors maintain a contractual/professional relationship. Such a relationship may demotivate and alienate employees.

By implication, organization leaders may effectively elicit productive behaviour from Indian employees, by judiciously lubricating the task relationship with emotional reciprocity and compassion. The work culture needs to be based on 'emotional reciprocity 'and 'trust', as in a typical Indian family. If organization leaders can recreate a family-like environment, employees may exhibit a sense of belonging and emotional connect with the organization. If employees can develop a sense of belonging, they will be productive.

Demonstrate leadership that mentors subordinates

Organization leaders should nurture subordinates through appreciation, guidance, recognition and develop them through empowerment. First, organization leaders need to address the deep urge for appreciation and recognition of their employees. People should be appreciated for the work they do. Take the example of Marico. It has a social recognition platform called Maricognize that allows peer recognition.

> Marico, the FMCG major has a social recognition platform called Maricognize that allows employees to appreciate others through an easily accessible platform. Awards are both monetary and non-monetary and categories include Applause, Spotlight, Gem of a Person, You Make a Difference and I Value You. For example, Spotlight is an on-the-spot individual award which can be given anytime by a supervisor to team members for efforts taken in cost leadership, people leadership and sustainable growth.
>
> (The Economic Times, 2017)

Second, Indian employees tend to be more productive and effective under a leader, who empowers them and includes them in the organizational decision-making. Take the example of Dr Khandelwal, who involved all branch heads when the management decided for extending the banking hours. He empowered them to come up with ideas and an implementation roadmap. Similarly, Jagdish Khattar, as Managing Director of MUL, empowered the employees to come up with suggestions and take full credit for the suggestions. In the process, he was grooming subordinates through empowerment and keeping them motivated by offering recognition.

Anil Khandelwal's leadership style may be effective in the Indian context. His leadership style focuses both on performance and relationship. Leadership based on 'tough love' (Khandelwal, 2011) balances both task orientation and nurture. Employees working under such a leader tend to be motivated to perform, come up with innovative ideas and share their ideas with the team, being transparent and open with respect to sharing feelings.

Organization leaders should also ensure that subordinates' self-efficacy is enhanced through job performance by ensuring that bureaucratic and other organizational constraints do not become roadblocks for task performance and that the employees develop the necessary capabilities required to execute the job effectively, through appropriate learning and developmental intervention.

Ensuring performance without being task-obsessed

As mentioned earlier, effective leaders in India, as perceived by their subordinates, tend to be patronizing along with being supportive, normative, and oriented towards problem solving. They also tend to be innovative, confronting/assertive and respectful. Hence, patronizing as a leadership style is not considered ineffective in the Indian context if it is combined with a problem-solving approach. The leaders must focus on the achievement of performance. Nurture should be made conditional, contingent upon task performance. The leader, for their part, should refrain from being task-obsessed. Such a task-obsessed approach may not be effective in the Indian context.

The work culture must be meritocratic with unambiguous articulation of performance norms and expectations and merit-centric organizational systems and processes. Along with stringent performance criteria, organization leaders should express confidence in the ability of their subordinates. The leaders may use punitive measures such as disciplinary actions to ensure performance and curb undesirable work behaviour, as mentioned above.

Leadership that engages subordinates beyond work boundaries

Finally, organization leaders should participate in non-work practices (NWPs) (Awasthy and Gupta, 2011), that include three kinds of activities. The first kind includes individual celebrations such as birthday celebrations, family function of employees, religious celebrations with employee family members. The second kind includes all those activities facilitated through the organization, such as picnics, to understand and connect with employees at a personal level. Finally, the third kind include activities where the superior is personally involved with juniors, such as superiors' participation with juniors in recreational activities, or visiting subordinates for marriages or festivals, etc., in their subordinates' homes.

When possible, organization leaders should voluntarily participate in such NWPs and the personal involvement of the leaders may enhance the employees' commitment. Employees may willingly come up with innovative ideas. Moreover, it is consistent with the principles of participative management, and the idea that employees prefer work environments where they can contribute to work they find meaningful.

Participating in religious festivities and family celebrations of employees may also encourage employees to accept organization leaders as one of the family members. The employees may feel personally obliged to the leader. Involvement of leaders in NWPs is significant in the Indian context as it fosters the spirit of truly familial organization.

Conclusion

This chapter has reviewed research conducted to understand the Indian mindset and the way Indians behave. The context-sensitive mode makes Indian behaviour highly unpredictable. Indians are found to be adept in demonstrating either self-seeking calculative or goal-driven achievement-seeking behaviour, depending on the context. If the context is enabling, the demonstrated behaviour is more likely to be functional and effective, whereas if the context is disabling, the demonstrated behaviour is more likely to be dysfunctional. To create an enabling context, organization leaders should: (1) create a family-like work environment; (2) mentor subordinates; and (3) engage employees beyond work boundaries (by participating in various non-work practices) to create a truly familial organization in spirit.

CASE STUDY: TATA MOTORS

Recently Tata Motors was in the news as its attempt to get rid of designations was faced with employees' resistance, which forced the company to scrap the idea of making the organization designation-free.

In June 2017, Tata Motors decided to do away with the system of hierarchy for its 10,000-plus employees in an effort to create a flat organization. The new business card of employees would have their name followed by the function/responsibility, for instance, 'Sales – Medium and Heavy Commercial Vehicles'.

This, according to Gajendra Chandel, CHRO Tata Motors, was supposed to reinforce the individual's responsibility and made the performance tracking process transparent. A person heading a team will simply be called 'Head' followed by the function, whether it is in the Jamshedpur Plant or the Paint Shop in Pune. For those who operate solo, their function/area of specialization would have been their calling card. The idea was to make people more accountable. The Executive Committee, comprising Günter Butschek, Managing Director, and his leadership team of some 10 people, will be the only ones to continue with their designations.

It was perhaps the first time that such a radical corporate hierarchical transformation had been attempted in India. 'This was a challenging task and we had a lot of debate on how people would react to the move,' admitted Chandel (Gopalan, 2017a). This move came only a couple of months after the company put in place a new structure with five reporting layers (reduced from 14).

The initiative faced resistance from its employees. Hence, in July 2017, the company decided to do away with the 'no designations' policy. Designations such as 'manager', 'general manager', were back within six weeks.

A company spokesperson admitted:

> It was earlier decided to do away with the designations of the employees, across the five management levels. However, given the current situation of a business turnaround and after reviewing the feedback received from employees across locations, we have decided to continue the designations … in the time being.

> (Gopalan, 2017b)

Acknowledgements

The authors are grateful to Dr J.B.P. Sinha for his comments and suggestions.

Note

1 *The Economic Times* survey, Decoding Trust in Organizations: Blueprint for a HIGH-Trust HIGH-Performance Cultures, India's Best Companies to Work for 2017, 10th edn. Available at: www.greatplacetowork.in

References

Awasthy, R. and Gupta, R. (2011) Do non-work practices in MNCs operating in India impact organizational commitment? *Organizations and Markets in Emerging Economies*, 2(4): 28–52.

Bharati, A. (1985) The self in Hindu thought and action. In A.I. Marsella, G. DeVos and F. L.K. Hsu (eds), *Culture and Self: Asian and Western Perspectives*. New York: Tavistock Publications, pp. 185–230.

Dheer, R.J.S., Lenartowicz, T. and Peterson, M.F. (2015) Mapping India's regional subcultures: Implications for international management. *Journal of International Business Studies*, 46: 443–467.

ET Bureau (2017) India's best companies to work for, 2017: The complete list. 3 July. Available at: http://economictimes.indiatimes.com/news/company/corporate-trends/indias-best-companies-to-work-for-2017-the-complete-list/articleshow/59419981.cms?utm_source=contentofinterest&utm_medium=text&utm_campaign=cppst

Garg, P. and Parikh, I. (1995) *Crossroads of Culture*. New Delhi: Sage.

Gopalan, M. (2017a) Tata Motors junks employee designations. *The Hindu Businessline*, 8 June. Available at: www.thehindubusinessline.com/companies/tata-motors-junks-employee-designations/article9723061.ece

Gopalan, M. (2017b) Flat response: Tata Motors brings back designations. *The Hindu Businessline*, 27 July. Available at: www.thehindubusinessline.com/companies/flat-response-tata-motors-brings-back-designations/article9791248.ece

Gupta, R. (1999) The truly familial organization: Extending the organizational boundary to include employees' families. In H.S.R. Kao, D. Sinha and N. Sek-Hong (eds) *Management and Cultural Values*. New Delhi: Sage Publications, pp. 102–120.

Kalra, S.K. (2004) Consultative managerial leadership style in India: A viable alternative. In C. Sengupta and P.N. Mukherji (eds) *Indigeneity and Universality in Social Science: A South Asian Response*. New Delhi: Sage, pp. 407–428.

Kalra, S.K. and Gupta, R.K. (1999) Some behavioural dimensions of effective managerial style in an Indian context. In H.S.R. Kao, D. Sinha and B. Wilpert (eds) *Management and Cultural Values: The Indigenization of Organizations in Asia*. New Delhi: Sage, pp. 287–296.

Kanungo, R.. (1990) Culture and work alienation: Western models and eastern realities. *International Journal of Psychology*, 25: 795–812.

Khandelwal, A.K. (2011) *Dare to Lead: The Transformation of Bank of Baroda*. New Delhi: Sage.

Mahesh, V.S. (1988) Managing discipline: A systematic approach. *Vikalpa*, 13(3): 17–22.

Panda, A. and Gupta, R. (2004) Mapping cultural diversity within India: A meta-analysis of some recent studies. *Global Business Review*, 5(1): 27–49.

Panda, A. and Gupta, R. (2012) Deconstructing context-sensitive nature of Indians' behaviour: A preliminary attempt to develop a taxonomy for three work contexts. *International Journal of Indian Culture and Business Management*, 5(6): 696–733.

Panda, A. and Gupta, R. (2016) Methodological approaches and challenges to studying Indian culture. In A. Malik and V. Pereira (eds) *Indian Culture and Work Organisations in Transition*. New Delhi:Routledge, pp. 182–219.

Philip, L. and Ganguly, D. (2014) Argumentative & too emotional: Are Indians tough to work with? *The Economic Times*, 26 December. Available at: http://economictimes.india times.com/magazines/corporate-dossier/argumentative-too-emotional-are-india ns-tough-to-work-with/articleshow/45638709.cms

Roland, A. (1980) Towards a psychoanalytic psychology of hierarchical relationships in Hindu India. Paper presented at the Indian Psychoanalytic Society, Bombay.

Sinha, D. (1999) Approaches to indigenous management. In H.S.R. Kao, D. Sinha and N. Sek-Hong (eds) *Management and Cultural Values*. New Delhi: Sage, pp. 43–52.

Sinha, J.B.P. (1980) *The Nurturant Task Leadership*. New Delhi: Concept Publishing.

Sinha, J.B.P. (1990) *Work Cultures in an Indian Context*. New Delhi: Sage.

Sinha, J.B.P. (2014) *Psycho-Social Analysis of the Indian Mindset*. New Delhi: Springer.

Sinha, J.B.P. and Kanungo, R.N. (1997) Context sensitivity and balancing in organizational behaviour. *International Journal of Psychology*, 32: 93–105.

Sinha, J.B.P. and Pandey, A. (2007) Indians' mindsets and the conditions that evoke them. *National Academy of Psychology*, 52(1): 1–13.

Sinha, J.B.P., Singh, S., Gupta, P., et al. (2010) An exploration of the Indian mindset. *Psychological Studies*, 55: 3–17.

Sinha, J.B.P., Sinha, T.N., Verma, J. and Sinha, R.B.N. (2001) Collectivism coexisting with individualism: An Indian scenario. *Asian Journal of Social Psychology*, 4(2): 133–145.

Sinha, J.B.P. and Verma, J. (1987) Structure of collectivism. In C. Kagitçibasi (ed.) *Growth and Progress in Cross-cultural Psychology*. Lisse, The Netherlands: Swets and Zetlinger, pp. 123–129.

Sinha, J.B.P., Vohra, N., Singhal, S., et al. (2002) Normative predictions of collectivist-individualist intentions and behaviour of Indians. *International Journal of Psychology*, 37: 309–319.

The Economic Times (2017) Decoding trust in organizations: Blueprint for a HIGH-Trust HIGH-performance cultures, India's best companies to work for 2017: Survey. 10th edn. Available at: www.greatplacetowork.in

8

THE CHALLENGES OF DOING BUSINESS IN INDIA

An entrepreneur's perspective

Raja P. Pappu

Aims of this chapter are to:

- Provide an overview of the key challenges in the business ecosystem in India
- Describe past and present changes in the legislation and their effect on business
- Outline the operational challenges and guidelines to tackle them
- Help in preparing well in advance, to set up a successful venture

Introduction

The aim of this chapter is to give the reader, especially the foreign businesses who want to invest in India, an overview of the existing challenges of doing business there, and to help them understand the potential barriers that can arise during the setting up and in continuing business in India. This chapter is divided into three main sections. The first section gives a brief overview of the overall performance of India in various aspects of business in comparison to global economies. The remaining sections focus on core issues that arise due to the government legislation, the prevailing economic, legal and social issues and challenges, and how an understanding of such information can help businesses operate better. The implications of the recent reforms in tax regulations, which have replaced the long-standing multi taxation system, and its impact are also discussed. This will benefit businesses by giving them an understanding of the Indian business environment and provide them with the necessary background information required to formulate and plan well ahead.

Background

By 2020, the population of India is projected to be close to 1.35 billion, of which the working-age population will be approximately 906 million. To make India's growth sustainable it is important to generate jobs for these 906 million people and this is only possible by achieving growth in the manufacturing and service sectors in India and attracting more private investment (Department of Industrial Policy and Promotion [DIPP], 2015). And to do so, the business environment in India needs to be made attractive and business-friendly. The regulatory framework that has existed for the past 60 years after independence needs to be restructured and that is already being considered. Recently many regulatory barriers have been removed but formidable challenges still remain for foreign investors to do business in India.

As stated in Chapter 1 and Chapter 2, according to the World Bank's Doing Business 2018 report (World Bank, 2018), India ranks 100 out of 190 economies, in ease of doing business, and has jumped up 30 places since 2017. On getting credit and protecting minority investors, India is ranked 29th and 4th respectively and ranks 156th in starting a business. Figure 8.1 shows the rankings of doing business topics from the World Bank report of 2018. *The Global Competitiveness Report, 2016–2017* (Schwab and Sala i Martin, 2016) ranks India as 39 out of 138 economies.

The Financial Times reported that India attracted US$55 billion in foreign direct investment (FDI) in the financial year 2015–2016, in comparison to US$19 billion two years earlier (Kazmin and Mundy, 2016). The *World Investment Report, 2016* (UNCTAD, 2016) ranks India third in both prospective top investing economies and prospective top destinations and it is lagging behind only the USA and China.

Post the May 2014 elections and the formation of the new government; India has been on a growth accelerator. The new government is determined to make India an investment hub and through its initiatives such as 'Make in India', it aims to make India a flexible, easy and simple place to do business. All the major sectors have been opened to FDI, making India the world's most open economy (Ernst & Young, 2015).

Though improving the basic regulatory framework is the primary need to attract more investment, there are still many prevailing problems, such as bribery, politics, infrastructure, legal frameworks, processing times, difficult tax laws, along with labour laws, foreign exchange control, etc. posing a major hurdle in the development of India. The IFC (International Finance Corporation, 2014) ranks bribery and corruption as the main constraints to growth, followed by electricity supply,

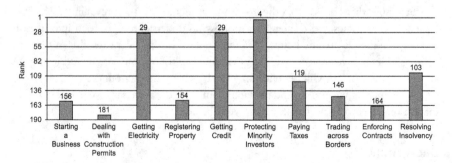

FIGURE 8.1 Rankings on doing business topics in India
Source: World Bank (2018).

taxation, etc. These formidable challenges need to be addressed before inviting further investments (Chandra, 2008).

Next, the main current key challenges are identified that can be a deterrent to operating in India and suggestions are made to tackle them.

Legislative challenges

The government framework

Since 2014, the Government of India has aggressively taken measures to make reforms in the regulatory framework and make it easy to do business in India by creating a business-friendly environment. The formation of a company was a very complex procedure in India, and with a very distributed framework, it was very difficult for foreign companies to understand the set-up. The new government has recognised this problem and has started helping foreign companies through its 'Make in India' initiative, where guidance and help are provided to foreign companies in setting up their business in India. The Indian Embassies and Consulate Generals in foreign countries are also playing an important role in this and are helping by providing the initial platform by arranging meetings with the bureaucrats and making connections to the relevant officials in India.

To simplify the compliance governed by the Companies Act, the Companies Law Committee was formed that proposed more than 100 amendments. Incorporation of a company can be done in one day, unlike 10 days formerly in the past, and procedures such as the requirement of common company seal have been removed. Most of the processes such as Name Availability, Director Identification Number and Incorporation of Company are integrated into one. Many processes have been digitised and provisions are underway to make the entire procedure paperless. India is working towards a new insolvency law that would create one of the world's most efficient and fastest bankruptcy systems, which are currently very sluggish (*Financial Times*, 2017). Although there are still many areas which need to be considered, such as creating an efficient credit report system that will help businesses to make a decision on the creditworthiness of their clients or suppliers, but at the same time reducing the overall procedure of incorporation to a more efficient and easy to understand process.

The *Doing Business* index mentions that the procedures involved in company formation can be discouraging for new businesses. There are still 12 procedures to complete in the incorporation of a business, which can cost a fortune, and the average time to complete the transactions is 30 days whereas the Organisation for Economic Co-operation and Development (OECD) average is 8.5 days. Businesses have to set themselves up as Private Limited companies to start doing business in India and to access funding from various state governments and the central government. Manufacturing units will require to spend a lot of time procuring construction permits, registration of the property and getting an electricity connection, which can take ages. The cost of getting construction permits can be outrageous and it involves 37 procedures and requires 194 days for completion. The government is committed to reducing the barriers in setting up businesses but as of now, there is still a lot that needs to be done to attract foreign businesses and give them confidence in a smooth and streamlined operation. A lot of information can be found on portals, such as www.makeinindia.com and www.doingbusiness.org which can help a potential business to assess the prospects, contact the relevant officials, prepare and then start working towards setting up a business in India.

The Indian legal system

The current legal system in India is based on common law that was introduced by the British (Balakrishnan, 2008). The Supreme Court is the apex body and has 24 High Courts, followed by numerous District Courts providing adequate protection for the execution of property and contractual rights. But the biggest challenges that foreign businesses face in India is the delay in settlement of the cases. According to data made available by the High Courts in India, there are more than 33 million pending cases in the High Courts and District and Subordinate Courts (Debroy, 2016). India ranks 164 out of 190 countries on the ease of enforcing contracts. India has a poor ranking in the quality of judicial processes, court structure and proceedings, case management, court automation and alternative dispute resolution.

There are alternative dispute resolution methods, such as arbitration, that comprehensively cover international and commercial arbitration and domestic arbitration and conciliation as well. This process is efficient but could potentially carry the risk of delay at the first level of dispute resolution because of the interference of the courts. India was one of the first members to sign the New York Convention, which recommends international arbitration as an alternative dispute resolution method, but still arbitration in India is not on a par with international best practices. This dispute resolution process has a huge impact on doing business in India. According to data collected by the *Doing Business 2016* report, India takes close to 1,420 days and 39.6 per cent of the claim value for dispute resolution (World Bank, 2016).

Currently in India, the arbitration process is conducted in an unstructured way and, according to the 246th report of the Law Commission of India (2014), the ad hoc arbitrations normally devolve into court hearings with regular adjournments and even lawyers do not help to complete the arbitration proceedings, rather, they are happy to attend the proceedings (ibid.). It is very important to have a reliable and stable dispute resolution process for a growing economy like India and to make it attractive to foreign businesses. With a huge backlog of pending cases in Indian courts, foreign businesses would aim for a quick resolution and turn-around time and arbitration can help the businesses do so.

Labour and employment law

Labour law provides a framework for fundamental principles and rights at work, which employers, workers and their representatives need to comply with. India has the a huge pool of surplus manpower available and employment is governed by several labour laws which are formulated by the central government, and many states in India also have their own set of special labour regulations and have made necessary amendments to the central laws to suit the business conditions of that particular state (see http://labour.gov.in/initiatives-state-government). Foreign investors should understand the labour laws of India and should obtain the appropriate registration and should maintain registers and notices, that are required under the Indian labour laws, to remain compliant with them. The current central government plans to make amendments in the labour and employment laws to make them industry-friendly and reduce the burden of compliance for the private sector.

Non-competition and non-solicitation clauses cannot be enforced beyond the length of the contract and it is a hassle to take the legal route to resolve disputes that arise from these situations. Indian law has strict regulations in place for the use of contract workers, and businesses have to register as 'principal employer' and need to have an appropriate licence to hire contractors. Reforms should be brought in for some laws, such as the Industrial Disputes Act, where any factory that employs more than 100 workers cannot lay off employees without approval from the appropriate state authorities. This discourages companies from keeping employees on a permanent basis and employers engage contractors on a requirements basis as necessary. Such contractors are paid less and are not eligible for any benefits offered. A 30–90 days' notice period is applicable while terminating any employee and non-performance cannot be considered the reason for termination. Foreign investors should be aware of the relevant labour laws and their consequences when dismissing workers or terminating employment.

Intellectual property rights (IPR)

In India, the IPR such as patents, trademarks, copyrights, designs and geographical indications are administered by the Patents Act 1970 & (Amendment) 2005, 2006 and Patent Rules 2003, Trademarks Act 1999 and the Trademarks Rules 2002, Indian Copyrights Act, 1957, Design Act 2000 and Rules 2001, and the Geographical Indications of Goods (Registration & Protection) Act, 1999 and the Geographical Indications of Goods (Registration & Protection) Rules 2002, respectively (FICCI, 2015). These laws are very well structured and are comparable to the European IP laws. However, there are some serious concerns over the IP implementation due to bureaucratic delays and concerns about transparency at the local level. It takes several months to register patents, trademarks, copyrights, etc. due to considerable backlogs at the IP registry (UK Department of International Trade, 2015).

Foreign investors should be aware that the IP protection is jurisdiction-specific and they must register the IP rights in India, even if they are protected elsewhere. They must take enough measures to protect their IPR from potential breach and misappropriation. They should plan well ahead and should have an IP management strategy in place, and particularly take advice from Indian IP rights experts and check with stakeholders on what is the best way to safeguard the rights. Piracy and plagiarism are very prevalent and measures should be taken to deal with them.

Social challenges

Corruption in India

Corruption is rampant in India and is the biggest obstacle while doing business in India. According to the Transparency International's Corruption Perceptions Index, 2016, India ranks 79th out of 176 countries in a study that measures the corruption level in the public sector (Transparency International, 2016). Bureaucrats, politicians, businessmen and criminals are the main players involved in corruption and cronyism. A lack of a transparent system, red tape, lack of powers given to the judicial system, low wages and the increasing cost of living, lack of unity among people and unhealthy competition are a few of the main reasons contributing to the prevalence of corruption.

Foreign investors face challenges from the inception of their company to acquiring land and acquiring appropriate licences and have to deal with bureaucracy at multiple levels at the local and state government levels. They can be exposed to a higher risk, such as delay in approvals and implementation of projects, if they are investing in sectors that require continuous interaction with the regulatory authorities and if this affects their profitability at the same time, many businesses tend to shut down their operations. It is strongly advised that the foreign investors should avoid violating the anti-corruption laws as this can adversely affect the business. They should do a proper risk assessment and due diligence and should examine the potential areas where they can be exposed to bribery. They should avoid dealing with third parties or anybody who can be potentially risky and a threat to the company's image.

India does have anti-corruption laws and legislation such as the Prevention of Corruption Act 1988, the Indian Penal Code 1960, the Prevention of Money Laundering Act, 2002, the Right to Information Act, 2005, the Benami Transactions (Prohibition) Act, 1988 and the Central Vigilance Act, 2003, etc. In order to promote good governance and stamp out corruption, India has taken a number of initiatives, including the recent 'demonetisation drive' to curb the black money flow, and has proposed amendments to the Prevention of Corruption Act (Proposed amendments as per Prevention of Corruption [Amendment] Bill 2013 and recommendations of Standing Committee and Law Commission on Bill).

The government of India executed a major change by demonetising the high value currency notes of Rs 500 and Rs 1000 denominations, which ceased to be legal tender from the midnight of 8 November 2016. The gradual replacement with a new set of notes happened in parallel and people were given the opportunity to exchange or deposit the old currency. Cash transactions were regulated and limits were placed on amounts that can be withdrawn. This move was aimed at curbing the black money flow, controlling the counterfeit notes and stopping illegal transactions and bribes (Bommakanti, 2016).

The amendments in the Prevention of Corruption Act ratified the UN Convention and made a bribe, given directly or indirectly, a punishable offence, and bribery of foreign officials to gain a business advantage is also covered (Rao, 2016).

Economic challenges

The Goods and Services Tax (GST)

In one of the biggest post-independence economic reforms, the government of India implemented the new Goods and Services Tax (GST) on 1 July 2017. It replaced the long-standing complex, indirect tax structure, that was comprised of various central and state taxes, such as Value Added Tax, Central Sales Tax, Entry Tax, Excise Duty, Service Tax, Entertainment Tax, Purchase Tax, Luxury Tax, Swachch Bharat Tax, state surcharges, etc., that were becoming a major barrier to India's aggressive growth plans and competitiveness. The GST has four tax rates – 5 per cent, 12 per cent, 18 per cent and 28 per cent – and will raise taxes on the basis of inter-state and intra-state supplies. The GST levied on intra-state supplies is classified into Central GST (CGST) and State GST (SGST or UTGST, in the case of Union Territory; UT) and is collected by the central government and the respective state or UT. In case of inter-state supplies, an integrated GST (IGST) is levied which is collected by the centre (Central Board of Excise and Customs, 2017).

All the states, except Jammu and Kashmir, have ratified the state GST laws, and the Union Territories with legislatures, such as Delhi and Pondicherry, also adopted the State GST Act (Ernst & Young, 2017). Other Union Territories have adopted the UTGST Act. It is expected that the manufacturing sector will get a big boost from this change as it removes the complex tax system and creates a single base for computing tax for both central and state governments, making it attractive to business. The 'One Nation and One Tax' market is beneficial to business and makes India a common market, eventually opening up multiple opportunities and boosting the economy by 1–2 per cent. The government is encouraging and pushing businesses to process their tax returns, and payments through the Digital Goods and Service Tax Network platform. This is the backbone of the entire roll-out as it aims to reduce the black money flow and tax evasion.

Such major implementations come with some immediate challenges. The existing businesses were given the deadline of 1 July 2017 to move to the new tax system. The existing enterprise resource planning (ERP) systems, invoicing systems, accounting packages, etc. have to be customised and tweaked to accommodate the new tax laws. The banking systems and industrial systems were not ready for these changes and more than 50 per cent of businesses were not aware of the GST implications and changes (*Hindustan Times*, 2017). Having a uniform tax system is definitely a welcome move but its implementation and getting the businesses on board are key to the success of this reform. The new tax system is definitely easier to understand for new businesses investing in India, although they should make themselves aware of these changes, analyse its impact and should take proper consultation from the accounting firms who are helping consumers with the implementation of GST.

Foreign direct investment (FDI)

According to UNCTAD (2016), India is the third most-favoured investment destination, and in 2016 the FDI inflow in India increased by 27.8 per cent to an estimated US$44.2 billion. The 'Make in India' initiative, launched in 2016, has secured investment commitments worth US$250 billion (*The Economic Times*, 2016). To attract new businesses, the Indian government has eased the foreign investment regulations and policies, allowing foreign investors to invest directly in most sectors without the requirement of obtaining prior approvals from the government or the Reserve Bank of India. There are few sectors such as banking, defence, etc. where foreign investors still need government approval and such investment requests are handled by the Foreign Investment Promotion Board (FIPB), which is part of the Department of Economic Affairs within the Ministry of Finance. Most of the states in India are attracting new businesses by offering lots of perks and discounted prices on land, electricity, water, etc. In the recent Pravasi Bharatiya Conference 2017 proceedings, the Chief Ministers of various states showcased their development forecasts and invited the companies to come and invest in their states. However, it can be a daunting task to convince the government of the feasibility and vision of the project and this is a major hurdle for foreign investors. There are still sectors like tobacco, real estate, gambling, etc. where FDI is not yet open. Khan and Khan (2015) studied the trends and issues associated with FDI in the Indian economy. There are many advantages to the recent FDI reforms but there are quite a few challenges also facing larger FDIs in India. In this regard, resource, equity, political and federal challenges are the root problems. India has abundant yet unexplored resources, available in urban and rural regions. India needs to invest US$150 billion to overcome the resource challenge by investing in infrastructure development. There is a tremendous amount of development in urban regions and this needs to be translated into rural regions to create a balanced and organic development, thus curbing the equity challenge. Foreign investors need the support of the political structure in India and this can open up investment opportunities and at the same time increase the reforms in FDI. India needs to speed up implementing FDI-friendly policies and regulations and states also need to ratify them to attract investments.

The infrastructure

Infrastructure is one of the key aspects to attract businesses to India. At present, India has an inadequate infrastructure in place, with unpaved roads, inadequate water and energy supply, and under-developed airports and ports. Such inefficiencies cause the manufacturing businesses to significantly invest more if they want to set up their businesses. However, the high-tech industry has grown massively in the last few years. It has a low dependency on the road infrastructure but still needs uninterrupted power to operate. Most of the companies in this sector were able to successfully set up their businesses in India, as their requirements are quite different from those of manufacturing firms.

India is investing heavily in infrastructure development and needs US$454.83 billion over the next five years, with 70 per cent of funds needed for power, roads and urban infrastructure segments. The power sector in India has a potential investment opportunity of US$250 billion in the next 4–5 years, providing immense opportunities in power generation, distribution, transmission and equipment. India has an ambitious plan for solar power generation and it aims to expand the total solar capacity from the current 3 megawatts (MW) to a reported 20 gigawatts (GW) by 2020 and 200 GW by 2050 (Costa, 2016). According to the Department of Industrial Policy and Promotion (DIPP), India has received FDI of $24.19 billion in construction development. The Airports Authority of India (AAI) plans to partner with private players to build the infrastructure near 13 regional airports to boost its revenues. The Indian government also intends to build 50 new regional airports in the next three years, making internal connectivity more efficient. The government also plans to develop 100 smart cities with a vision to enhance the infrastructure with world-class, self-sustainable habitats with minimal pollution levels, maximum recycling, optimised energy supplies and efficient public transportation (Tolan, 2014). This will certainly attract the foreign businesses to invest in India in and around these smart cities.

There are multiple challenges in infrastructure development causing severe delays in the implementation or sometimes even forcing a halt, such as issues pertaining to land acquisition, a delay in regulatory and environmental clearance, funding constraints, etc. In the past, many companies have faced these challenges. A few years ago, Tata Motors started construction of factory to manufacture the world's cheapest car in Singur, West Bengal, but had to stop in the middle due to issues in land acquisition (Chandra, 2008). Better governance and a straightforward framework will make it easy to avoi such mishaps.

Conclusion

It is clear that India want to attract foreign businesses to increase job opportunities and is pursuing a number of initiatives, and making changes in the existing framework. For example, the initiative to produce 20 GW solar power by 2020 and making India a power-surplus nation is the vision of the current government and they are working towards it. However, delays in projects due to bureaucratic interventions cannot be ruled out, but initiatives like a complete digital framework are being introduced and interactions between local authorities and bureaucrats are helping the initiatives move ahead. The Make in India programme has initiated multiple reforms and the government is moving at a fast pace to implement changes and make India an investment-friendly zone. Businesses should understand the dynamically changing government policies and framework, the market opportunities and the associated risks and challenges. It is also important to gain local knowledge and have the right local people who can help in navigating and dealing with local challenges and in turn help the businesses to explore India's enormous economic landscape. Getting local accounting and legal firms on board is also vital; otherwise it can be a daunting task to establish a business in India. The challenges mentioned in this chapter have existed for many years, yet many businesses have gone to India due to the economic reforms of 1991, and have been hugely successful. These and other challenges have been identified by the current government. and through its push to resolve, reframe and ease them, and make India an attractive investment for manufacturing firms is helping a lot of organisations to look to India as a possible destination to do business.

CASE STUDY: WAL-MART IN INDIA

Wal-Mart attempted a joint venture with Bharti Enterprises to open up retail stores across India in 2007. In 2012, the government opened FDI in the retail sector. This gave Wal-Mart an opportunity to set up superstores directly in India. While the government had to relax many regulations which were in place for foreign brands investing in India, such as retail companies had to buy 30 per cent of their stock from local companies every year, they can only set up stores in cities with a population over one million, etc. The government took measures to relax these regulations and gave a five-year period to reach targets of 30 per cent sourcing. The government had faced a lot of resistance from the local retailers and trade unions, as they anticipated that it would eventually close their businesses. However, Wal-Mart was unable to reach the targets in five years and moreover the Indian government started investigating a loan that was given to Bharti by Wal-Mart, which potentially breached the foreign investment rules and the US government was also investigating at the same time bribery allegations against Wal-Mart in India and Mexico. These things eventually slowed the plans of Wal-Mart to do business in India.

In the past, the German auto manufacturer Volkswagen has also been involved in bribery and cheating charges when a senior executive from VW cheated the Government of Andhra Pradesh out of two million Euros with a promise to set up a plant in the state.

There have been many cases of bribery in defence deals, power sector deals, etc. in India and corruption is treated as the main challenge for foreign businesses. At the same time, many businesses have found success in India by pursuing a consistent and patient policy.

In the newspapers

The Economic Times Is doing business in India really easier now? https://economictimes.indiatimes.com/news/economy/indicators/is-doing-bus iness-in-india-really-easier-now/articleshow/61542423.cms

The Economic Times French companies take up business challenges with government officials
https://economictimes.indiatimes.com/news/economy/foreign-trade/french-compa
nies-take-up-business-challenges-with-government-officials/articleshow/61497088.cms
The Economic Times GST rollout: How businesses and consumers coped with India's biggest tax reform
https://economictimes.indiatimes.com/news/economy/policy/gst-rollout-how-busi
nesses-consumers-coped-with-indias-biggest-tax-reform/articleshow/59402920.cms
The Hindu India moves up 30 spots in WB's ease of business ranking
www.thehindu.com/business/india-moves-up-in-wbs-ease-of-business-ranking
/article19956459.ece
The Hindu Foreign defence companies paid huge bribes to alleged Indian arms dealer
www.thehindu.com/news/national/'Foreign-defence-companies-paid-huge-bri
bes-to-alleged-Indian-arms-dealer'/article16086789.ece
The Hindu Businessline $83.5 billion and counting: How Invest India keeps FDI rolling in
www.thehindubusinessline.com/economy/835-billion-and-counting-how-invest-
india-keeps-fdi-rolling-in/article9928334.ece

Useful websites

Entry India http://entryindia.com
Invest India http://investindia.gov.in
Make in India www.makeinindia.com/homeUK India Business Council www.
ukibc.com
US India Business Council www.usibc.com

References

Balakrishnan, K.G. (2008) An overview of the Indian justice delivery mechanism. Paper presented at the International Conference of the Presidents of the Supreme Courts of the World, Abu Dhabi, 23–24 March, pp. 1–12.
Bommakanti, U. (2016) Fake currencies, black money, and terrorism: Modi's ban on Rs 500, Rs 1,000 can stop them all. *The New Indian Express*, 8 November.
Central Board of Excise and Customs (2017) GST – CONCEPT & STATUS – As on 5th April, 2017. Available at: www.cbec.gov.in/resources//htdocs-cbec/gst/gst-concept-sta
tus-ason05Apr2017.pdf (accessed 16 July 2017).
Chandra, N.K. (2008) Tata Motors in Singur: A step towards industrialisation or pauperisa-tion? *Economic & Political Weekly*, 13 December, pp. 36–51.
Costa, A.D. (2016) India announces groundbreaking solar plan. Available at: www.worldwa
tch.org/node/6220 (accessed 20 January 2017).
Debroy, B. (2016) Start from the top: To set an example for the judiciary, the Supreme Court must address its own backlog of cases. *Indian Express*. Available at: http://indianexp

ress.com/article/opinion/columns/supreme-court-pending-cases-justice-t-s-thakur-judge s-appointment-njac-4366873/ (accessed 22 January 2017).

Department of Industrial Policy and Promotion (DIPP) (2015) Assessment of state implementation of business reforms. New Delhi: Ministry of Commerce and Industry, Government of India.

Ernst & Young (2015) EY's attractiveness survey India, 2015: Ready, set, grow. Available at: www.ey.com (accessed 14 July 2017).

Ernst & Young (2017) GST implementation in India. Available at: www.ey.com/in/en/ser vices/ey-goods-and-services-tax-gst (accessed 14 July 2017).

FICCI (2015) IPR-related issues in India. Available at: http://ficci.in/sector/24/Project_ docs/IPR-profile.pdf

Financial Times (2017) India moves to unblock sluggish bankruptcy process. Available at: www.ft.com/content/d63d1e60-5d45-11e7-9bc8-8055f264aa8b (accessed 30 July 2017).

Hindustan Times (2017) GST rollout from July 1: A list of challenges threatening implementation. Available at: www.hindustantimes.com/business-news/gst-rollout-from-july-1-a -list-of-challenges-threatening-implementation/story-E4OQCVVdppdNdZ0YcNpEbJ.htm l (accessed 13 July 2017).

International Finance Corporation (2014) *India Country Profile, 2014.* Washington, DC: The World Bank.

Kazmin, A. and Mundy, S. (2016) Is India really the most open economy for FDI? Available at: www.ft.com/content/bacdacee-3780-11e6-a780-b48ed7b6126f (accessed 20 January 2017).

Khan, M.S. and Khan, A.M. (2015) FDI and the Indian economy: Issues, challenges and prospects in India. *Paripex: Indian Journal of Research,* 4(12): 44–47.

Law Commission of India (2014) Report No. 246: Amendments to the Arbitration and Conciliation Act 1996. New Delhi: Law Commission of India.

Make in India (2013) Make in India. Available at: www.makeinindia.com/home (accessed 20 January 2017).

Rao, P. (2016) The Prevention of Corruption (Amendment) Bill, 2013 and proposed 2015 amendments. Available at: www.prsindia.org/uploads/media/Corruption/LB-%20Preven tion%20of%20Corruption%20(A)%20Bill%202013%20-%202015%20amendments.pdf (accessed 21 January 2017).

Schwab, K. and Sala i Martin, X. (2016) *The Global Competitiveness Report 2016–2017.* Geneva: World Economic Forum.

Sehrawat, M. and Dhanda, U. (2015) GST in India: A key tax reform. *International Journal of Research, Granthaalayah,* 3(12): 133–141.

The Economic Times (2016) 'Make in India Week' gets Rs 15.2 lakh crore investment commitment. Available at: http://economictimes.indiatimes.com/news/economy/p olicy/make-in-india-week-gets-rs-15-2-lakh-crore-investment-commitments/article show/51040369.cms (accessed 22 January 2017).

Tolan, C. (2014) Cities of the future? Indian PM pushes plan for 100 'smart cities'. Available at: http://edition.cnn.com/2014/07/18/world/asia/india-modi-smart-cities/index.html (accessed 20 January 2017).

Transparency International (2016) Corruption Perceptions Index 2016. Available at: www.transparency.org/news/feature/corruption_perceptions_index_2016 (accessed 22 January 2017).

UK Department of International Trade (2015) Overseas Business Risk – India. Available at: www.gov.uk/government/publications/overseas-business-risk-india/overseas-busi ness-risk-india (accessed 22 January 2017).

UNCTAD (2016) *World Investment Report, 2016: Investor Nationality: Policy Challenges*. New York: United Nations.

World Bank (2016) *Doing Business 2016: Measuring Regulatory Quality and Efficiency*. Washington, DC: International Bank for Reconstruction and Development/The World Bank.

World Bank (2017) *Doing Business 2017: Equal Opportunity for All*. Washington, DC: World Bank.

World Bank (2018) *Doing Business 2018: Reforming to Create Jobs*. Washington, DC: World Bank.

PART II

Conducting business in India

9

THE INFRASTRUCTURE IN INDIA

Challenges and opportunities

Devendra G. Kodwani

Aims of this chapter are to:

- Present government policy framework for private and multinational investors in infrastructure industries
- Indicate trends in private sector and foreign investment in infrastructure industries
- Describe how a business and consumer-friendly regulatory institutional framework is evolving
- Reveal opportunities for investment in energy, transportation and the telecommunication industries

Introduction

Since the launch of the economic reforms in 1991, the federal and provincial (states) governments have implemented policy reforms in infrastructure services to advance India's competitive advantage. The benefits of the improved infrastructure in roads, telecommunications and liberalised markets in energy have begun to make India a major destination for doing business.

There has been a concerted effort to improve the business environment through regulatory and legislative changes raising India's World Bank ranking for ease of doing business by 30 places in one year from 130th to 100th in 2017. India is the only large country to have recorded this shift so fast. Since 2003, India has adopted 37 reforms and half of these have been implemented in the past four years. Some of the specific reforms to make it easy to do business in India include:

- the simplification of the procedures to start up a business;
- the protection of minority investors;

- a drastic reduction in the number of permits required for construction;
- an improvement in import and export regulation implementation;
- the introduction of the National Judicial Data Grid which has allowed speedy enforcement of contracts, and the introduction of insolvency and bankruptcy codes.[1]

Why does the infrastructure matter?

Meeting the rising expectations of a better standard of living for the 1.25 billion-strong population of India presents a challenging opportunity. The provision of basic amenities at an affordable price and of acceptable quality to all citizens depends critically on the development of the infrastructure (Haque, 2016). Added to affordable access and quality is the expectation of environmental sustainability that Indian policy-makers need to bear in mind. Power, transportation and water infrastructure services illustrate this triple challenge but at the same time these present an opportunity to innovate both institutionally and technically.

The current low infrastructure index offers opportunity for investment in India compared to other Association of South-East Asian Nations (ASEAN) countries, such as China and Malaysia (Mishra et al., 2016). The government of India has taken major steps to streamline permissions, to make compliance easier and to reduce barriers to entry and exit.

This chapter has three main objectives. First, to discuss the status of and expected developments in infrastructure services that support business in India. Second, to argue why multinational and other business enterprises should consider investing in Indian infrastructure sectors. Finally, to discuss the issues that investors in infrastructure should understand when implementing their business plans in infrastructure services in India.

The chapter is organised as following. The next section explains what infrastructure means in the Indian policy framework. The scope of infrastructure services is described and services are grouped into three categories, namely, *energy, telecommunications, and transportation.* This is followed by a discussion of the business opportunities and challenges faced in each of these groups. Next, the salient features and uses of PPP (public-private partnership) in India are discussed. The users' perspective is discussed in the following section before concluding the chapter with summary of opportunities and challenges.

Infrastructure services in the Indian economy: the big picture

The scope of discussion in this chapter is restricted to the three groups of industries and the construction industry. These are the ones which the central government's advisory committee on infrastructure considers to be the infrastructure industries.

Energy industries: suppliers' perspective

A 30-year forecast by the central government think tank Niti Ayog suggests that rapid and significant investment is required in the energy industries in India, however, the import dependence of India for energy is still likely to be high and increasing over coming 20 years, as shown in Figure 9.1. The ambitious target of renewable power generation capacity of 175 gigawatt (GW) by 2021–2022 presents opportunities for suppliers of solar, wind, bio-energy and hydro technologies.

Electricity supply chain

Electricity markets and the energy policy have witnessed major changes since 1991. The present market structure is characterised by government-owned utilities dominating in all three segments of the industry (generation, transmission and distribution). The government's policy objective of ensuring reliable electricity access for all Indians requires a financially sustainable power supply chain. Thus, 100 per cent private and foreign direct investment is permitted in the generation sector, along with fiscal incentives. Recent years have seen an increase in private sector participation in the generation sector. Between 2012 and 2017, the additional capacity of 92,423 megawatt (MW) has been added (Government of India, 2017a, p. 14). Incentives offered to provide a supply of clean energy have attracted investment from foreign and domestic companies, including Vestas (Danish), Enercon (German), Gamesa (Spanish) and GE Wind Energy (US), who have invested in wind energy in India. Currently about 18 per cent of the total generation capacity for power comes from renewable sources of energy[2] and this has grown rapidly. Of the renewable sources, wind energy constitutes about 63 per cent, as of March 2016.

To mitigate the risk of dependence on monopolistic state-owned collieries, electricity generators are now allowed to import coal. The state governments have also tried to address the concerns of the private sector to enter generation business by providing guarantees regarding the obligations of state-owned

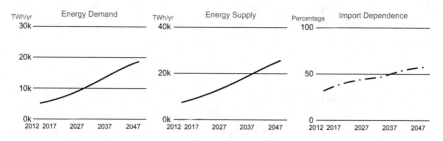

FIGURE 9.1 An estimate of energy demand and supply: the Niti Ayog view
Source: Niti Ayog (2017).

distribution companies who buy power from private generators. As of March 2018, 45 per cent of installed generation capacity is owned by the private sector.[3]

For the transmission segment, the focus of central government is on developing the transmission network for inter-state transmission of power, to enable the development of competitive wholesale electricity markets. So far, this segment has been owned and managed by a central government-owned National Grid Corporation, but with the establishment of power trading platforms and appropriate regulatory institutions, the market for inter-state trading in power has become more active.

Petroleum and natural gas

The petroleum and natural gas supply industry, comprising the transportation, refining and marketing of petroleum products, constituted about 15 per cent of India's Gross Domestic Product. India's oil demand is expected to grow by 3.6 per cent per annum until 2040. Between 2000 and 2017, about US$6.9 billion foreign direct investment was made in the oil and gas industries. According to government estimates, investment opportunities in these industries are spread across the supply chain in oil and gas exploration, production, installation of distribution networks in the cities, and building liquid cargo terminals at major ports for the import of crude oil and gas. Prospecting for natural gas in deep waters is likely to create opportunities for investment over the next decade (Government of India, 2017b). Thus, 100 per cent private and foreign capital is allowed in the sector.

Major multinational firms now operate in the Indian oil and gas industries. Petrol and diesel prices still are determined by the government but competition based on service quality has been increasing in the distribution segment of this industry. To further streamline the regulatory and market structure in oil and gas, the government of India has set up the Petroleum and Natural Gas Regulatory Board. In June 2017, the government control on the retail price of petrol and diesel was removed. This is a big step towards making the market more competitive. Gas exploration and laying of gas distribution networks are likely to remain huge investment opportunities for private investors. In conclusion, the following key messages are worth noting regarding the energy industries in India.

- Electricity:
  - The electricity markets are now segmented into generation, transmission and distribution.
  - The generation markets are opened up for inter-state supply, creating an opportunity for competitive markets.
  - A sound regulatory system is in place in most of the states.

- The central government has initiated steps to improve the financial position of state distribution companies (DISCOMs).

- Petroleum and natural gas:

  - Oil and gas exploration policy has been liberalised, 100 per cent FDI is permitted in most of the supply chain.
  - Government control of retail prices of petrol and diesel has been removed.
  - A regulatory board has been set up.
  - Private sector participation in exploration and development has increased.

Telecom: Connecting India and investing in the convergence revolution

India is the second largest telecom services market in the world with turnover likely to touch US$37 billion in 2017 as estimated by IBEF (2017a). Table 9.1 shows the dramatic growth in the tele-density (number of landline phones for every 100 people) in urban areas in India. However, it can also be seen that there is big difference between the urban and rural tele-density figures, creating opportunities beyond major cities and towns into villages.

As of September 2016, there were 1.05 billion wireless subscribers and 24.4 million wire-lines connections as shown in Table 9.1 (TRAI, 2016). Connections provided by private sector companies which include multinational companies such as Vodafone and Hutchison have increased from 75 per cent in 2009 to over 90 per cent in 2016 (Figure 9.2).

Combined with basic telephone services, there is going to be big demand for network expansion and modernisation, as the demand for broadband increases. The convergence of voice-video communication, broadcasting and e-platform businesses, such as Amazon, is likely to increase and to create demand for supporting technologies, data and digital payment services. Between 2000 and 2016, foreign direct investment in the sector was US$23.92 billion (IBEF, 2017a). The Telecom Regulatory Authority of India (TRAI) regulates the prices, quality standards and encourages competition in the sector. The revenue streams are not distorted by subsidies although there is universal service obligation applicable to basic telephone service providers. The following key messages emerging from the above discussion of telecommunications show a promising start and a bright future for Indian telecommunications.

- Sources of sustained demand:
  - Telecommunications are the backbone of the knowledge-based industries which are going to grow in India.
  - Expansion and modernisation of networks.
  - Broadcasting and entertainment industries will expand.
  - Increasing role of internet-based commerce.
  - Digitalisation of commerce and payments systems.
  - Stable and transparent regulatory environment.
  - Private sector and multinational companies encouraged to invest.

TABLE 9.1 Increasing connectivity and tele-density in India

Particulars of subscribers (millions)	Wireless	Monthly growth rate (%)	Wireline	Monthly growth rate (%)	Total (wireless + wireline)	Monthly growth rate (%)
Total telephone subscribers	1049.75		24.49		1074.24	
Net addition in September, 2016	20.86	2.03	-0.02	-0.07	20.84	1.98
Urban telephone subscribers	603.80		20.57		624.38	
Net addition in September, 2016	17.91	3.06	0.01	0.03	17.92	2.95
Rural telephone subscribers	445.94		3.92		449.86	
Net addition in September, 2016	2.95	0.67	-0.02	-0.56	2.92	0.65
Overall tele-density	82.17		1.92		84.09	
Urban tele-density	151.10		5015		156.24	
Rural tele-density	50.80		0.45		51.24	
Share of urban subscribers (%)	57.52		83.99		58.12	
Share of rural subscribers (%)	42.48		16.01		41.88	
Broadband subscribers	174.47		17.84		192.30	

Source: TRAI (2016).

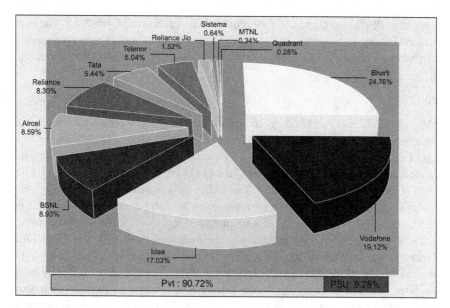

FIGURE 9.2 Highly competitive and private sector-driven telecom market in India
Note: PSU means Public Sector Units.
Source: TRAI (2016).

Transportation: Removing bottlenecks and supporting trade

The transport sector contributes 6 per cent of India's GDP, of which nearly 70 per cent is contributed by road transport. Bringing down the costs, improving efficiency and the quality of the transport infrastructure are the key policy objectives of the government of India. We consider below the scope and business environment in each of these infrastructure services.

Roads

India has the second largest road network in the world with 3.3 million km, and over 60 per cent of freight and 90 per cent of passenger traffic is carried on the roads (Make in India, 2016a). There has been rapid growth in the length of the National Highways from 91,287 km on 31 March 2014 to 1,01,010 km in 2016. The primary mode of road network development has been through the use of public-private partnership (PPP). The government of India has set an ambitious target of nearly doubling the national highways network to 200,000 km over the next five years and also has ambitious plans for making the existing highways into four-lane roads.

The government of India encourages private investment in the road sector by allowing 100 per cent private and foreign investment in the sector. There has been a significant increase in the private sector investment in the road sector with 113 completed PPP projects and 136 PPP projects in progress as of March 2016. The main business model used involves the award of a construction contract to private companies. who are contracted to build, operate and transfer (BOT) under PPP schemes.

Ports

More than 200 major and other ports in India handle nearly 1 billion tonnes of cargo per annum. By 2025, this is likely to grow to 2.5 billion tonnes. India has over 7500 km of coastline but cargo transportation by coastal and inland waterways is only 6 per cent compared to China's (47 per cent), Japan's (34 per cent) and the USA's (12.4 per cent) (Government of India, 2015). The Indian government aims to raise the contribution of coastal and waterways transportation from 6 per cent to 10 per cent by 2020, hence significant opportunities are presented for private sector involvement.

There are 12 major ports in India that are managed by Port Trusts. The Tariff Authority fixes the tariffs for major ports. Major ports handle 70 per cent of the volume of cargo and 187 minor ports manage the rest of the cargo. Recently there has been a policy shift to encourage private participation in port development. Some of the big investments on a BOT basis have been made by Maersk (Mumbai port), Dubai Ports International (Mumbai, Chennai, Vizag and Kochi), P&O (Mundra Adani port). The Ports Project involving investment of over US$10 billion has been identified for award during the next five years. The policy allows 100 per cent FDI and 100 per cent income tax exemption for a period of 10 years. The bulk of the development of minor ports in the coastal states of Gujarat, Andhra Pradesh and Tamil Nadu is envisaged to be financed by private sources, again using PPP as an organisational vehicle.

To improve the productivity of the ports requires the construction of new berths, including those capable of handling large container ships, investing in the mechanisation of the port operations and the computerisation of procedures. In addition, investment is required for the construction of storage space and providing road and rail connectivity to the hinterland.

Railways

The Indian railway system is the third largest rail system in the world with the route length of 66,030 km. Cargo movement through containers is the key link to improving the logistics efficiency. Long-term plans of the government include the construction of six high-capacity, high-speed dedicated freight corridors along the Golden Quadrilateral and its diagonals (Make in India, 2016b).

Fourteen private companies have been granted a licence to run container trains. There are plans to create a dedicated rail network for cargo movement. The Dedicated Freight Corridor Corporation of India Limited, a special purpose entity for the development of dedicated rail network for cargo movement has been set up (Planning Commission, 2009). Along the dedicated freight corridors, special economic zones are being developed where multi-modal logistics parks will be developed. Private sector companies have opportunities to participate in all these projects to enhance the quality and quantity of the transportation capacity of the Indian railway network system.

Airports

There are 454 airports and airstrips in India and 16 designated international airports. Passenger traffic and air cargo business are expected to grow with the economic development. The domestic passenger traffic is likely to cross the 100 million mark in 2017 (IBEF, 2017b). Most of the airports in India are owned by the central government through a public enterprise, the Airports Authority of India. But there have been a few major privatisation decisions whereby international airports at Delhi, Mumbai and Bengaluru are now privately managed. This development is significant, as it has enabled bringing the best global practices in the airport services and providing performance benchmarks for other airports. During the 2000–2016 period, the FDI in this sector was US $931 million (Government of India, 2017c).

Opportunities are more likely to be in greenfield projects and in acquiring airports through privatisation transactions. The government of India wants to improve air connectivity in the country by developing 50 new airports by 2020 (ibid.). The business model to be used is going to be PPP in most cases.

Below is a summary of the Indian transportation sector:

- Roads, railways, ports, and airports all need to expand capacity and improve the quality of their services.
- Investment in transportation projects is of a long-term nature with typical project life being 20–30 years.
- A supportive institutional framework will be required.
- Fiscal benefits include tax holidays.
- 100 per cent foreign direct investment is allowed.
- Government is conscious of risks involved and willing to share the operating risks.
- Viability Gap Funding and other financial support will be available.

Making PPP work in India

As a developer of infrastructure over a long period of time, PPP projects typically spanning over 20–30 years face the risk of losing bargaining power related to tariffs and other matters, if there are abrupt changes in the economic or policy environment, which are beyond the control of developers. To minimise these risks, a committee recommended setting up an independent regulatory body and ring-fencing contracts to protect against risk of future changes to policy/political framework (Kelkar, 2015).

In 2016, the government of India issued a guidance book for practitioners involved in PPP contracts.[4] Table 9.2 provides details of the prevalent models for public-private partnerships in India described in the *PPP Practitioners Guide*.

Infrastructure services: the users' perspective

For the businesses that use infrastructure services, the following industry-specific observations may be useful.

Electricity

There are two specific aspects of policy that are user-oriented. Increased choice for bulk electricity consumers to buy electricity at competitive prices. Second, large users with capacity to invest in captive power plants can do so. These policy measures thus empower the large electricity consumers.

In the past few years, a number of cement and steel manufacturers have set up captive power plants.

TABLE 9.2 Prevalent PPP models

- *User fee-based BOT models*: Medium to large-scale PPPs have been awarded mainly in the energy and transport sub-sectors (roads, ports and airports). Although there are variations in approaches, over the years, the PPP model has been veering towards competitively bid concessions where costs are recovered mainly through user charges (in some cases partly through Viability Gap Funding from the government).
- *Annuity-based BOT models:* These models are seen in sectors/projects not amenable to sizeable cost recovery through user charges, owing to socio-political affordability considerations. Typically, the rural, urban, health and education sectors are the ones where these factors are an issue. In this model, the government harnesses private sector efficiencies through contracts based on availability/performance payments. Implementing the Annuity-Based BOT model will require the necessary framework conditions, such as a payment guarantee mechanism made available through multi-year budgetary support, a dedicated fund, or a letter of credit, etc. The government may consider setting up a separate window of assistance to encourage annuity-based PPP projects. A variant of this approach could be for the government to make a larger upfront payment (say, 40 per cent of the project cost) during the construction period.
- *Performance-based management/maintenance contracts*: In an environment of constrained economic resources, PPPs that improve efficiency or involve performance-based management or maintenance contracts of existing assets are very relevant. Sectors amenable to such models include water supply, sanitation, solid waste management, road maintenance, etc.
- *Modified design-build (turnkey) contracts*: In traditional Design-Build (DB) contracts, the private contractor is engaged for a fixed-fee payment on completion. The primary benefits of DB contracts include time and cost savings, efficient risk-sharing and improved quality. The government may consider a turnkey DB approach with the payments linked to the achievement of tangible intermediate construction milestones (instead of a lump-sum payment on completion) and short period maintenance/repair responsibilities. Penalties/incentives for delays/early completion and performance guarantees (warranty) from the private partner may also be incorporated. Subsequently, as market sentiment turns around, these projects could be offered to the private sector through operation-maintenance tolling concessions.

Petroleum and natural gas

In 2017, the government control on the retail price of petrol and diesel was removed. This is a big step towards making the market more competitive. This allows users of petroleum products choice in procurement.

Telecommunications

In terms of quality, access and cost, the Indian telecommunications services are globally competitive. But, as noted above, much of the growth has been in urban areas. Most of the software and IT-exporting businesses have developed clusters of companies around a few major cities in India. This has introduced a geographical imbalance in the growth of telecommunication networks. This further influences the choice of industrial locations where IT and the internet are likely to be key requirements.

The telecom industry will need to provide affordable access to high bandwidth internet connectivity to such users who at the moment are restricted to only a few pockets in the country. Digitalisation of commerce and financial transactions is further likely to create opportunities in telecommunications services.

Transportation

The transportation costs in India will decrease and service quality will improve significantly over the next few years.

Key points

Below, the key messages from the users' perspective are presented:

- Large electricity users can choose their suppliers and even set up their own captive power plants to secure the supply of electricity.
- Gas markets are liberalised and becoming more competitive which should benefit the users of gas.
- World-class telecommunication facilities exist in big cities and the surrounding satellite towns like Gurgaon near New Delhi.
- Huge improvements in the capacity and quality of transport infrastructure services are underway.
- Opportunity to participate in the development of 50 new airports by 2020.

Summary

At present, the infrastructure industries need substantial improvements and capacity expansion, hence significant long-term business opportunities for investment in infrastructure do exist.

- *Understand institutional and market environment:* From the investors' perspective, doing business in India means the same as doing business anywhere, i.e., dealing with people and organisations in a given institutional environment. As a constitutional federal structure democracy, the institutional environment varies across the states in some industries. Hence, it is important to understand the nuanced context of doing business in India.

  - There are policy intentions and instruments in place to create competitive markets in the generation and supply of electricity, petroleum and gas.
  - In telecommunications, the institutional structure, regulation and markets seem to be working well and the scene is set for increasing competition.
  - In the transport sector, railways, aviation and highways have all witnessed significant institutional development to remove barriers to entry and doing business.
  - A regulatory framework has been set up to facilitate competition, the rationalisation of tariffs and to provide consumer protection in most of the infrastructure industries.

- *Understand opportunities:*

  - Opportunities in the infrastructure industries are in long-term projects requiring large capital investments.
  - Public-private partnerships are going to be the preferred mode of joint ventures between the government and the private sector.
  - Significant long-term tax benefits and other incentives are on offer.
  - Although telecommunications have reached most urban parts of India, there still remain opportunities to expand access and tele-density.
  - In addition, there are opportunities to upgrade the telecommunication networks to increase the capacity to handle increasing traffic on the internet and also to manage the convergence of the telecommunications, media and entertainment industries.
  - With arrival of major e-platforms, businesses, such as Amazon, digital payment systems, or mobile phones, are likely to drive demand for telecom infrastructure further.

- *Managing challenges:* The policy framework in most of these sectors is still evolving and is directed towards encouragement of private investment but rapid progress has been made in the past few years. It was argued that the two biggest challenges for any investors in this sector are in the external environment for business:

  - Mobilising the finance for huge projects from Indian and international investors.
  - In some sectors, like road development, the government of India has reformed the administrative procedures for land acquisition at the centre but at state level this may be variable challenge.

Most states have created an institutional framework and streamlined administrative procedures to support the private sector interested in investing in infrastructure services.

CASE STUDY: INVESTING IN THE RAILWAY INFRASTRUCTURE

Indian railways are the eighth largest employer in the world with 1.4 million employees and US$25 billion annual turnover in 2015–2016. The government has plans to set up the first dedicated railways university in India to meet the demand for skilled manpower in the railways.[5]

The government of India allowed 100 per cent foreign direct investment in construction, operation and maintenance of railway infrastructure in November 2014. Since then until December 2016, FDI of US$282 million has been attracted to the manufacturing of railway wagons, coaches, mechanical and electro-mechanical signalling systems and safety and traffic control systems. Table 9.3 details some of these investments.

TABLE 9.3 Investments by multinational companies in Indian railway infrastructure

Foreign collaborator	Country	Indian company	FDI inflows (US$ million)
ALSTOM Transport Holdings B.V.	The Netherlands	ALSTOM Transport India Ltd.	85.2
BOMBARDIER Transportation Holdings	Singapore	BOMBARDIER Transportation India Pvt. Ltd.	39.50
ANSALDO STS Australia Pty Ltd.	Australia	ANSALDO STS Transportation Systems India	21.52
GE Capital International	Mauritius	TITAGARH Wagons Ltd.	14.73
INVERSIONES EN Concessiones	Spain	CAF India Pvt. Ltd.	11.57

Source: www.makeinindia.com/documents/10281/114126/Railways+Sector+-+Achievement+Report. pdf, p. 4.

CASE STUDY: REDUCING THE CARBON FOOTPRINT IN THE AVIATION INDUSTRY: THE SUCCESSFUL CASE OF COCHIN INTERNATIONAL AIRPORT

The tension between industrialisation-led economic growth and its impact on the environment is well known. Despite international divergence in opinion on which country should reduce its CO_2 emission more rapidly, India has pursued a green agenda. However, the CO_2 emitted by India has risen rapidly with the growing economy. To reduce CO_2 emissions without having an adverse impact on growth requires all contributors be managed, including aviation. The aviation industry policies in India offer a good example of a multi-pronged response by the Indian government.

The aviation industry in India is growing fast and is likely to be the third largest industry in passenger transport in the world by 2020 (DGCA, 2013). In the supply chain of the aviation industry, airports play a vital role. Figure 9.3 shows the multiple stakeholders in the aviation industry.

To minimise the environmental damage from the aviation industry, different stakeholders need to address this challenge. In 2013, airlines operating from India and foreign airlines with destinations in and from India contributed about 15 million tonnes of CO_2 (ibid.).

In the past decade, the government of India has liberalised the entry of the private sector in airport development through the public-private partnership (PPP) mechanism. One such PPP project was to develop Cochin International Airport in southern India. The unique feature of this airport is its zero carbon footprint. The airport operates on solar power only.

In August 2015, the Cochin International Airport became the first airport to operate on solar power only. Some 46,150 photovoltaic panels spread over 45 acres near the airport produce 50,000–60,000 kwh of electricity every day and annually 18 million units of electricity using solar power. The excess electricity after daily use is given to the state's electricity board. Built at a cost of US$10 million, the project will recover its cost in about five years after which the electricity will be virtually free. The expected life of the solar panels is 25 years, during which period this green source of power for the airport will avoid carbon dioxide emissions from coal-fired power plants by more than 300,000 metric tonnes, which is equivalent to planting three million trees. This is an excellent example of multiple private and public entities coming together to create a financially and environmentally sustainable infrastructure project.

FIGURE 9.3 Stakeholder map to understand aviation carbon footprint in India

Useful websites

DIPP http://dipp.nic.in/ An official Government of India site that provides information on formal policies, procedures, formalities, information about property rights, and ease of doing business in India.

IBEF www.ibef.org is an information centre for global investors, international policy-makers and the world media, seeking updated, accurate and comprehensive information on the Indian economy, states and sectors. Provides macroeconomic overview and specific industry overviews.

Infrastructure in India https://infrastructureindia.gov.in/home An important portal dedicated to infrastructure opportunities in India.

Make in India www.makeinindia.com/ Provides overview of investment opportunities in all sectors and is one-stop reference for high-level description of policies, investors and logistics.

Public-private partnerships www.pppinindia.gov.in/ A useful portal that contains all the information required for public-private partnership contracts in infrastructure industry. In addition to details about institutional frameworks and databases, the portal provides detailed guidance on PPP agreements and an online toolkit to help understand the requirements and take informed decisions.

Notes

1 See www.worldbank.org/en/news/press-release/2017/10/31/india-jumps-doing-bus
   iness-rankings-with-sustained-reform-focus (accessed 24 December 2017).
2 See http://powermin.nic.in/en/content/overview-0 (accessed 24 December 2017).
3 See http://powermin.nic.in/en/content/power-sector-glance-all-india (accessed 26 May
   2018).
4 See www.pppinindia.gov.in/documents/20181/33749/PPP+Guide+for+Practitioners/
   e3853cb9-ac07-4092-b8ac-60a8c4d4ed35
5 See https://economictimes.indiatimes.com/industry/transportation/railways/indias-1st-ra
   ilway-university-to-come-up-in-gujarat/toshibafornextindia_show/50802404.cms (accessed 25 December 2017).

References

DGCA (2013) Carbon footprint of Indian aviation. New Delhi: Director General of Civil Aviation. Available at: http://dgca.nic.in/env/Carbon%20Footprint2013.pdf (accessed 2 February 2018).

Government of India (2007) National electricity policy. New Delhi: Government of India. Available at: http://cea.nic.in/planning/national_Electricity_policy.htm (accessed 6 August 2009).

Government of India (2008) Opportunities in the world's largest democracy: Investment Commission Report. New Delhi: Government of India.

Government of India (2015) Report. New Delhi: Ministry of Shipping. Available at: http://shipmin.nic.in/showfile.php?lid=1959 (accessed 16 April 2017).

Government of India (2016) Circular. New Delhi: Ministry of Commerce, Government of India. Available at: http://dipp.gov.in/English/Policies/FDI_Circular_2016.pdf (accessed 11 April 2017).

Government of India (2017a) Annual report, 2016–2017. New Delhi: Ministry of Power, Government of India.

Government of India (2017b) Report. New Delhi: Ministry of Petroleum, Government of India. Available at: www.ibef.org/download/Oil-Gas-March-2017.pdf (accessed 11 April 2017).

Government of India (2017c) Report. New Delhi: Department of Industrial Policy and Promotion, Government of India. Available at: www.ibef.org/industry/indian-aviation. aspx (accessed 16 April 2017).

Haque, I. (2016) Infrastructure development and access to basic amenities in Class-I Cities of West Bengal, India: Insights from census data. *Journal of Infrastructure Development*, 8(1): 36–84.

India Brand Equity Foundation (IBEF) (2017a) Telecom industry in India. Available at: www.ibef.org/industry/telecommunications.aspx (accessed 17 April 2017).

India Brand Equity Foundation (IBEF) (2017b) Indian aviation. Available at: www.ibef.org/industry/indian-aviation.aspx (accessed 16 April 2017).

India Brand Equity Foundation (IBEF) (2017c) Summary of infrastructure projects completed. Available at: www.ibef.org/industry (accessed 19 November 2017).

Kelkar, V. (2015) Report on revisiting and revitalizing public private partnership model of infrastructure. New Delhi: Department of Economic Affairs, Government of India. Available at: http://finmin.nic.in/reports/ReportRevisitingRevitalisingPPPModel.pdf (accessed 1 April 2017).

Make in India (2016a) Roads and highways. Available at: www.makeinindia.com/sector/roads-and-highways (accessed 16 April 2017).

Make in India (2016b) Railways. Available at: www.makeinindia.com/sector/railways (accessed 16 April 2017).

Mishra, A.K., Rao, G., Monga, A. and Vishwanath, B. (2016) Assessing competitiveness in emerging Asian economies: Role of governance and infrastructure and lessons for India. *Emerging Economy Studies*, 2(1): 72–90.

Niti Ayog (2017) http://iess2047.gov.in (accessed 11 April 2017).

Olivier, J.G.J.*et al.* (2017) Trends in global CO_2 and total greenhouse gas emissions: 2017 report. The Hague: PBL Netherlands Environmental Assessment Agency. Available at: www.pbl.nl/sites/default/files/cms/publicaties/pbl-2017-trends-in-global-co2-and-total-greenhouse-gas-emissions-2017-report_2674.pdf (accessed 2 February 2018).

Planning Commission (2009) Private participation in infrastructure. New Delhi: Government of India. Available at: http://infrastructure.gov.in/pdf/Infrastructure.pdf (accessed 1 August 2009).

TRAI (2016) Report. New Delhi: Telecom Regulatory Authority of India. Available at: www.trai.gov.in/sites/default/files/PR_No_117_Eng_09_Dec_2016_0.pdf (accessed 11 April 2017).

10

ENTRY MODES AND DYNAMICS

Surender Munjal

Aims of this chapter are to:

- Analyse key entry modes for foreign enterprises entering the Indian market
- Present a framework for selection of entry modes
- Provide key contact details useful to foreign investors

Introduction

The regulations governing the entry modes for foreign enterprises into India have seen some changes since the liberalisation policies began in 1991. The era prior to 1991 was highly regulated with industries reserved for public sector and small-scale enterprises, with high tariffs, quotas and licence raj. Foreign enterprises in most industries were a rarity. Moreover, most import transactions attracted heavy custom duties. Indeed, the aim of this policy was to make the Indian economy self-reliant by protecting domestic firms and minimising the outflow of foreign exchange reserves out of India. However, since 1991, many changes have taken place in the Indian institutional environment that directly affect how foreign enterprises enter and operate in India. Primarily the changes have eased the entry requirements for foreign enterprises by lifting the restrictions on foreign direct investments (FDI), lowering the tariffs on imports and exports, and allowing remittances of profits by foreign enterprises.

Indeed, the changes are welcomed by foreign enterprises, which is reflected in the ever-growing volumes of FDI into India. According to the Foreign Investment Promotion Board, the stock of FDI was over US$518 billion in September 2017, growing at an average rate of over 25 per cent since 2000–2001. However, challenges exist as foreign enterprises are still asking for transparency and further liberalisation of the entry rules in India. Vodafone challenged the Income Tax department's tax demand of Rs 37 billion as a result of its entry into India by acquiring Hutchison Essar in 2007. The tax demand was disputed by Vodafone and finally nullified by the Supreme Court of India because the tax was made effective by making a retrospective amendment of the tax law in 2012. Retail giants such as Wal-Mart, Tesco and Carrefour are still asking for 100 per cent FDI in the multi-brand retail sector.

With a view to facilitating a quick understanding of the subject, this chapter discusses and critically evaluates different modes of entry available to foreign enterprises entering the Indian market. It begins by defining the key concepts of the market entry modes. Next, it describes the different forms of entry modes, both *equity-based* and *non-equity-based*, along with the advantages and disadvantages and the key regulations in India associated with each entry mode. The chapter also provides key contact details useful to foreign investors. It finally discusses the criteria for selection of entry mode by briefly drawing on the key academic literature on the subject.

Entry modes

An enterprise intending to do international business faces a decision crunch time when it needs to decide how to enter a given foreign market. This question usually arises after finalising the market it wants to serve. Entry modes are specific forms of participation an enterprise uses to enter a foreign market. The extant literature in international business classifies foreign market entry modes into equity-based and non-equity-based entry modes. Equity-based entry modes include all forms of foreign market entry where FDI is incurred by the enterprise. This primarily includes setting up a joint venture or a wholly owned subsidiary. In contrast, non-equity-based entry modes include all forms of foreign market entry where FDI is not required, for instance, exporting and licensing.

Exporting

Exporting means the selling of goods and services by an enterprise, that are produced in its home country to a foreign market. The enterprise can undertake exporting directly or indirectly through an agent. Exporting is a non-investment-based entry mode as the enterprise does not undertake any FDI in the host countries. It is also regarded as a non-contractual entry mode as exporting is usually based on orders received from buyers in the host countries.

Exporting is generally more useful for the small and young enterprises which are in the early stages of internationalisation because such enterprises usually lack the finance and managerial resources required to undertake high commitment entry modes in host markets. Exporting, in contrast, requires less commitment, with no capital investment made and no contract signed in the foreign markets. Moreover, at the early stages of internationalisation, the firm has little knowledge of the host market characteristics and exporting allows the firm to gradually gain this valuable market knowledge (Barkema et al., 1996). Thus, exporting is considered a strategy to gain host market knowledge (learning-by-exporting) while lowering risk by avoiding capital investment (Cassiman and Golovko, 2011; Yang and Mallick, 2010). However, this is accompanied by lower profit margins in comparison to other modes of market entry.

India offers a significant market to exporters around the world, partly because of its size, sustainable growth rate (Mallick and Marques, 2017) and partly because of continuing economic and institutional reforms undertaken over the last few decades (for details, see Reddy, 2017). In addition, the recent reform in terms of replacing multiple state-level taxes by a single value-added regime is expected to boost international and international trade. Moreover, India has an advantageous geographic location (Buckley et al., 2013) with a long coastline and close proximity to the African, Asian and Pacific economies. The Indian Ocean sits between the Pacific Ocean (in the east) and the South Atlantic Ocean (in the west), providing clear connectivity with countries around all six continents of the world.

However, exporting to India requires certain formalities and registration with the Director General of Foreign Trade (DGFT), in the Ministry of Commerce. The DGFT issues a licence with a ten-digit Importer Exporter Code (IEC), which needs to be cited on every international trade transaction made by firms exporting to India. An online application can be made for the IEC at http://dgft.gov.in. In addition, exporters also require a certificate from the Bureau of Indian Standards (BIS) which vouches for the labelling requirements. Exports are subject to prevailing customs duties prescribed by the Central Board of Excise and Customs, Ministry of Finance. More details about the tariff rates can be found at www.cbec.gov.in.

Licensing and franchising

Licensing is an agreement whereby a licensor (the parent firm) gives a permit to a licensee to use intangible assets, such as technology, brand, and design, for a fee. The fee can be a lump sum or a per centage of revenue (called royalties), or a mix of both. The licence is usually granted for a limited time period and for a specific geographical area. This means the licensee is not allowed to use the rights after a certain time and beyond the specific geographic area allowed under licence.

Franchising is a special form of licensing in which a franchisor (the parent firm) gives a right to a franchisee to do business in a specific manner. It often involves the transfer of a functional business model and the transfer of some tangible product, for instance, a special ingredient used in production, along with a right to use intangible assets. Like licensing, the franchisor charges a fee that can be a lump sum or a per centage of revenues or a mix of both.

Licensing and franchising are non-equity-based entry modes because the licensor or franchisee does not buy an equity stake in the licensee's or franchisee's business. In contrast, licensing and franchising involve contractual obligations and transfer of rights to use propriety assets. Hence, these modes are often referred as *contract-based* or *transfer-based* entry modes (Shenkar and Luo, 2008).

Licensing and franchising allow the parent firm to rapidly expand internationally. Primarily because the parent firm need not undertake FDI while the local firms in the host market take the burden of capital investment and local management. However, both the parent and the local firms are tied into formal agreements which indicate a commitment by both parties. It is important to note that commitment in franchising is usually higher than other forms of licensing because franchising involves the transfer of a whole business model and the knowledge needed for proper functioning of the business.

Licensing and franchising are quite popular modes of entry in India, primarily in the industries that requires local adaptation, for example, media, publishing, hotel and fast food chains. McDonald's, Starbucks, Burger King, Marks and Spencer, Radisson, Hyatt, Best Western and Hilton Hotels are good examples of successful market entry through licensing and franchising by foreign enterprises in India. Franchising is becoming increasingly popular among Indian entrepreneurs, as using established foreign brands, generally popular among the young Indian population, provide a safe route for business investment in India.

It is interesting to note that despite the popularity of licensing and franchising in the Indian market, India does not offer any specific law to regulate licensing and franchising modes of entry. Licensing and franchising agreements are governed under the umbrella of the Indian Contract Act, 1972, which is a general law for regulating all kinds of contractual agreements. Given the universal application, the Indian Contract Act, 1972 allows a great deal of flexibility in drafting the contractual obligations between the licensor/franchisor and the licensee/franchisee. The agreement may or may not be in writing and if it is written, it may be written in any language.

Payment of royalties and a lump sum fee as a consideration to the licensor/franchisor is covered in accordance with the Foreign Exchange Management Act, 1999 and the Indian Income Tax Act, 1961. Over time, foreign exchange regulations in India have eased. For instance, now remittances can be made without any monetary caps; however, the licensee/franchisee is obliged to deduct tax, as per the prescribed rates of income tax, before making the payments to the licensor/franchisor. Deduction of tax by the licensee/franchisee is mandatory as it ensures the recovery of tax at the source of income (called Tax Deducted at Source or TDS) before income is transferred out of India to the foreign enterprise acting as the licensor/franchisor. The current rate for deducting tax can be found at www.incometaxindia.gov.in.

Joint ventures

A joint venture is an equity-based entry mode. It means a partnership agreement between two or more parent firms that come together to start a new business entity. In the international business context, a cross-border entity is formed by a partnership between two or more parents from different national backgrounds. For instance, Reliance Aerostructure Limited (an Indian company) has entered into an agreement with Dassault Aviation (a French company) to form Dassault Reliance Aerospace Limited (a joint venture).

As a new venture is started under the joint ownership, capital is contributed by the parent firms, which represents their equity shareholding in the joint venture. In the above example of Dassault Reliance Aerospace Limited, Reliance Aerostructure Limited holds 51 per cent and Dassault Aviation holds 49 per cent equity ownership.

Theoretically, there are many advantages to entering a foreign market through a joint venture. It allows the sharing of capital and risk among the partner firms, while exchanging their resources and capabilities. Establishing a joint venture in a host market with local firms further allows access to local market knowledge and political connection. The main drawback of a joint venture is sharing control and ownership with the partner firms. In a cross-border setting, it also involves managing cultural differences between the partner firms.

Foreign firms can set up their operations in India by forming a joint venture with Indian partners. Joint ventures are quite popular in India as many Indian firms see establishing joint venture as a strategy to access sophisticated advanced technology and management processes. Foreign firms that can contribute such resources can gain through joint venture with Indian firms. In return, joint ventures are popular among foreign firms because it can provide them with gains, especially in terms of access to market knowledge, political contacts and exploiting local skills and talent which a foreign investor would not easily find on its own.

The processes and formalities for establishing a joint venture in India are relatively simple. A joint venture can be established through the incorporation of the joint entity. The incorporation can take the form of a joint stock company or a limited liability partnership (LLP). A joint stock company is established under the Indian Companies Act, 2013, while the LLP is established under the Limited Liability Partnership Act 2008. The joint stock company is considered better in terms of governance of the joint venture, as the Indian Companies Act is very comprehensive and it requires the establishment of a better management structure and various internal checks and procedures for the proper conduct of the company's affairs. Moreover, incorporation in the Companies Act provides an independent legal identity to the joint venture. This means that joint venture remains in existence even if the parent firms change or cease to exist. Finally, incorporation of a joint stock company also ensures that the parent's liability is limited by the amount of capital contributed.

As mentioned above, the Limited Liability Partnership Act 2008 also allows incorporation of a joint venture. It provides flexibility to the parent firms in terms of organisation and governance of the joint venture through amendments to the partnership agreement. Flexibility in the partnership agreement is very important. The extant literature in the international business field suggests that joint ventures are often unstable and there are several reasons why, ranging from country-level factors, such as changes in institutional environment and macro-economic conditions, to firm-level and manager-level factors, such as lack of synergy between partner firms and cultural differences between managers (see Yan and Luo, 2016, for a detailed discussion). Citing the case of India, Kale and Anand (2006) suggest that in the broader context of emerging economies, joint ventures are in decline and this can be largely attributed to the instability, which is an inherent character-istic of joint ventures. It is worth mentioning that the issue of instability is largely addressable as joint ventures can be turned into subsidiaries.

In India, the LLP joint venture can be converted into a joint stock company, if all the parent firms wish. Foreign direct investment is allowed in the formation of both LLP and JSC types of joint ventures, subject to regulations framed by the government of India.

Strategic alliances

A strategic alliance is a cooperative agreement between two or more firms. It can be in the form of equity-based joint ventures or non-equity-based contractual agreements. When no formal investment is made in a partnership, no new entity is formed. Partner firms merely form an agreement to cooperate where the rights and obligations of the partner firms are mutually decided. Non-equity-based strategic alliances are formed when the partner firms do not need a separate identity for their partnership and they do not intend to be bound by the formalities of incor-poration. Business enterprises often use strategic alliances for knowledge and tech-nology transfers, and joint product development, buying, promotion and distribution, where combined efforts are mutually beneficial.

When no new entity is formed in a strategic alliance, the agreement between firms to form an alliance is governed by the Indian Contract Act 1972. The partner firms are not treated as partners in the legal sense and therefore the Partnership Act, 1935 is not applicable. It is important to note that non-equity-based strategic alli-ances are not favourably treated in the Indian Income Tax Act 1961. Such alliances are treated as an 'association of person' under Section 2(31) and it attracts the higher tax rate, as prescribed in the Act.

In comparison to a joint venture, where equity shareholding indicates ownership and the commitment of the partner firm, a non-equity-based strategic alliance lacks an adequate measure for partners' commitment (Beamish and Lupton, 2009). However, both joint ventures and strategic alliances have the advantage of risk sharing among partners and relatively quick access to the market and local knowl-edge. Recently, the German automobile manufacturer Volkswagen and Tata Motors announced a plan to form a strategic alliance in the Indian subcontinent. These competing automobile manufacturing giants aim to develop concept cars for the technology-driven automobile market in the near future.

Wholly owned subsidiary

A firm can also enter a foreign market by establishing a wholly owned subsidiary. This mode allows the firm to internalise its foreign operations. There are primarily two ways of establishing a subsidiary: (1) starting a business from scratch which is often referred to as a *greenfield venture*; and (2) acquiring an existing firm in the host country. Establishing a subsidiary in a host market, either way, allows the foreign enterprise to internalise operations instead of outsourcing to third parties. Indeed, establishing wholly owned subsidiaries requires more investment and bears the full risk but it also allows the foreign enterprise to exercise full control and gives the protection of proprietary knowledge.

Foreign enterprises are allowed to open a wholly owned subsidiary in India by undertaking 100 per cent FDI in many sectors, notably in pharmaceuticals, civil aviation and food products manufactured or produced in India. However, certain sectors, such as multi-brand retailing, are still considered politically sensitive where deliberations are going on to allow 100 per cent FDI.

As discussed above, a subsidiary can be established by incorporating a joint stock company under the Indian Companies Act, 2013. This incorporation makes the subsidiary an independent legal identity, separate from its parent firm. The Companies Act allows the subsidiary to be incorporated as a private limited company or as a public limited company. A private limited company is considered a closely held company and it allows certain privileges to the promoters. In contrast, a public limited company is widely held and is subject to more regulations.

There are two routes for undertaking FDI in India:

- *the automatic route:* In the automatic route, FDI is allowed without prior approval from the government. A list of activities/sectors where 100 per cent FDI is allowed by the automatic route is specified by the Reserve Bank of India (RBI) in Annex B of Schedule 1 to Notification No. FEMA 20.
- *the approval route*: In the approval route, all activities/sectors not covered under the automatic route require the prior approval of the government. FDI requests under the approval route are considered by the Foreign Investment Promotion Board (FIPB), the Department of Economic Affairs, in the Ministry of Finance. Applications can be made using the Form FC-IL, which can be downloaded from www.dipp.gov.in

In addition to establishing a subsidiary, foreign enterprises can also open up a Branch Office (BO), a Liaison Office (LO) and a Project Office (PO) in India, as per the guidelines issued by the Reserve Bank of India under the provisions of the Foreign Exchange Management Act, 1999. The BO, LO and PO can represent a foreign enterprise in India. It can engage in exporting and importing activities, carrying out research, collecting information or rendering professional and technical services, and promoting collaborations on the behalf of the parent enterprise. However, the foreign enterprise opening a BO, LO and PO needs to appoint an authorised representative, who is responsible for the local management in India. The manager is required to submit an annual activity report to the RBI as the BO, LO and PO are not allowed to undertake any other activities which are not authorised by the RBI. It is important to note that unlike a subsidiary, the BO, LO and PO do not have limited liability and a separate legal identity.

Selection criteria

After identifying the possible entry modes available, a foreign enterprise needs to decide which entry mode is the best for the given location. Theoretically speaking, there is no perfect entry mode. Each mode of entry has advantages and disadvantages associated with it. In fact, entry modes are not mutually exclusive, they are interdependent. Very often more than one entry mode is used by firms to be successful. The selection of entry mode depends upon a range of factors, which are explained below.

Cost, control, risk and return (CCRR)

The main criterion for selection of entry modes revolves around cost, control, risk and return (CCRR). Based on the internalisation theory (Buckley and Casson, 1976), the CCRR criterion captures the firm's need to minimise cost and risk while maximising control and return in host markets. However, there is a direct relationship between cost and control as well as between risk and return. For instance, by establishing a wholly owned subsidiary, the foreign enterprise can exercise full control over the subsidiary, as a result of full ownership of it. In contrast, by establishing a joint venture, the control is shared with partner firms. Moreover, having a wholly owned subsidiary entitles the foreign enterprise to get full returns but it has to bear the risk alone in comparison to a joint venture where the risk and returns are shared among the partner firms.

In the Indian context, it is important to note that while India provides a large growing market with lower costs of production, especially in comparison to western economies, making it an attractive location to many western enterprises, managing risk and uncertainty is a challenge here. Consequently, foreign enterprises often seek to maximise control by establishing a subsidiary unless the need to have a local partner is necessary due to regulations or to seek local market knowledge and political connections. Marks and Spencer is a good example here which has established a joint venture with Reliance specifically to address the above challenges.

Nature of the product and the industry

Besides the CCRR criterion, the choice of entry mode depends upon the nature of the product and the industry norms. Exporting is more popular in industries where standardisation of the product and centralisation of production are possible. However, other modes of entry are usually helpful when adaptation of the product and decentralisation of production are required. For instance, garments and consumer electronic devices, such as mobile phones, are pretty standard products and therefore firms producing such products are usually clustered in particular geographic regions in the world, usually South Asia for garment production and East Asia for consumer electronics. Producers in these regions export garments and consumer electronics to the other parts of the world.

It should be acknowledged that the clustering of producers in South Asian and East Asian countries is primarily driven by cost advantages offered by the region. Foreign enterprises wishing to exploit the cost advantages undertake FDI in this region to set up production and procurement facilities.

At the same time the nature of the product also equally influences entry mode. Products that are less bulky and therefore easy to transport, for instance, medical drugs and shoes, are usually exported by producing at a few central locations. For example, Pfizer exports medicines from India, Nike exports shoes from its production facilities in Vietnam. On the other hand, products that are bulkier, and therefore difficult to transport, are produced near to the market to be served. For instance, Toyota, the Japanese multinational, has established its production facilities in every continent so as to serve the neighbouring markets, while minimising transportation costs.

Country-specific factors

Host country characteristics are equally important in the choice of entry modes. Prior research has examined a number of location attributes that can affect the firm's entry mode decision.

Distance between home and host country

First, geographic distance between the home and the host countries influences the market entry decision. Greater physical distance adds to transportation costs and makes it difficult to control activities in the host country. *Ceteris paribus*, firms like to avoid undertaking FDI in a physically distant market (Ragozzino, 2009). Second, similar to the geographic distance, the cultural distance between the home and the host countries also deters FDI as it adds to the transaction costs of managing operations in a foreign market (Kogut and Singh, 1988). The Uppsala model of internationalisation suggests that firms mitigate the impact of cultural distance by venturing into countries that are psychologically close to their home country (Johanson and Vahlne, 1977; 2009).

Recent research suggests that the impact of physical and cultural distance can be mitigated by cooperation and alliance between the home and the host country. For instance, sporting events, trade fairs, cultural exchange programmes, free movement of people and opening of new routes and ports as a way to promote trade and investment relationships, under the label of cooperation between home and host countries, positively influence the firm's decision to undertake FDI (Buckley et al., 2017). Cultural distance can also be mitigated by the existence of diaspora (Buckley et al., 2013).

Government policy and the institutional framework

Government policies and the institutional framework further affect the entry mode choice of foreign enterprises in a number of ways. JCB's entry into India is a great example to illustrate how government policy influences entry mode.

JCB, the construction machinery manufacturer from Rochester, UK, served the Indian market by exporting until 1979 as FDI then was not allowed in India. Later in 1979, when FDI rules were relaxed, JCB entered into a 40:60 joint venture with Escorts, a tractor manufacturing firm from India. JCB held 40 per cent shares, the maximum share allowed to a foreign company in India allowed under the Foreign Exchange Regulation Act, 1979. Subsequently, when FDI norms were further relaxed in 1999 with the introduction of the Foreign Exchange Management Act, 1999, JCB acquired an extra 20 per cent equity shares, raising its shareholding to 60 per cent and leaving a 40 per cent stake for Escorts. In 2002, when 100 per cent FDI was allowed, JCB acquired 100 per cent of shares, making the joint venture as a wholly owned subsidiary.

The government's restriction on the import of foreign goods, for instance, by levying tariffs, also affects foreign enterprises' entry mode decision. In order to overcome trade tariffs, foreign enterprises often start local production in host markets instead of servicing through exporting. This is technically referred to as a *tariff jumping strategy* of foreign enterprises (Asiedu, 2002; Buckley et al., 2012). The establishment of Hindustan Lever in India in 1956 is a great example in this respect.

Finally, protection of property rights and the quality of other legal frameworks, for instance, the enforcement of contracts, are also considered very relevant for the firm's entry mode decision. Host countries, where the institutional framework is weak and therefore protection of the firm's brand, technology, trademark and copyrights is inadequate are usually served through wholly owned subsidiaries because the internalisation of the operations allows more control over the firm's proprietary knowledge. On the contrary, if the legal framework is strong, the firm can serve the market using contractual entry modes, such as licensing and franchising.

Host country resources

The availability of resources, the market and a pool of skills and talent are regarded as the firm's motivation for internationalisation (Dunning, 1988; 1993). These factors also influence the firm's entry mode decisions. India offers a significant market and various types of skills and talent to foreign enterprises. Given its large and growing market, it offers a significant incentive to foreign enterprises to open their wholly owned subsidiaries. Buckley and Casson (1981) suggest that over time the economies of scale make FDI more rewarding than other modes of entry. This argument especially applies in a growing market like India.

Availability of skills and talent has also been a significant attraction for foreign enterprises in India. Given visa restrictions on the movement of labour, firms seeking skills and talent needs to go to the source of resources. Many foreign enterprises, such as Cisco and Microsoft, have opened their R&D centres in India, while other foreign enterprises have exploited the availability of skills by operating back office centres from India. Indeed, these research centres and back offices primarily require FDI.

Recent research suggests that, over time, besides economies of scale and opportunities in terms of availability of resources, the experience of foreign enterprises in India and institutional development have reduced the challenges of doing business in India. All these have enhanced FDI inflows to India (Munjal and Pereira, 2015).

Conclusion

The choice of mode for market entry constitutes an important decision in international business. The various modes for entering foreign markets are exporting, licensing or franchising, strategic alliance, joint venture and wholly owned subsidiary. Although the magnitude of advantages and disadvantages of each entry mode can be measured in terms of cost, control, risk and reward, the choice of entry mode depends upon an array of factors ranging from the nature of firm, the product and the industry characteristics and the host market's attributes.

India as a host market is quite popular among foreign enterprises primarily because of its large market and sustainable growth over the last few decades. However, the availability of skills and talent has also attracted foreign enterprises to India. Liberalisation of the Indian government policies towards international trade and foreign direct investment, and the institutional framework with a mature set of legislations, such as the Contract Act 1972, the Companies Act 2013, the Limited Liability Partnership Act 2008 and the Foreign Exchange Management Act 1999, provides a comprehensive institutional environment, covering all entry modes, to foreign enterprises wishing to enter the India market.

This chapter has provided a holistic view, however, it could not discuss the idiosyncrasies applicable to individual industries and which remain a limitation. However, this chapter provides a fundamental understanding that can facilitate an in-depth study of any industry and firm specifics.

CASE STUDY: MARKS AND SPENCER

Marks and Spencer (M&S), headquartered in the City of Westminster, London, is a leading global retailer. It employs around 85,000 people and generates an overall revenue of £10.6 billion, 60 per cent of which comes from food and 40 per cent from clothing and home. M&S has over 450 international stores in 55 countries, generating a revenue of £1.2 billion (M&S, 2017).

To boost its international growth M&S has started to focus on emerging economies, such as India and China. However, the international journey of M&S has been full of ups and down. Its entry into India was in 2001 through a franchising agreement with Planet Sports (BBC, 2001). Realising its initial success in India, M&S increased its commitment, in 2008, by starting a joint venture with Reliance Retail, a subsidiary of the Reliance group, the second largest conglomerate in India owned by the business tycoon Mr Mukesh Ambani. In 2008, M&S also entered mainland China by opening a wholly owned subsidiary (M&S, 2015). However, despite having full control, M&S faced many challenges in China and in April 2017, M&S announced that it was closing all of its stores in China. One of the major reasons for this decision was the lack of market knowledge and the inability to set up an efficient supply chain (*Telegraph*, 2017).

Although M&S's contrasting performance in India and China can be attributed to many factors, the role of entry modes stands out and the success of M&S in India is largely attributable to having a local partner, which is vouched for by the following quote by Marc Bolland, the former Chief Executive Officer of M&S:

> India is a priority market for M&S and working closely together with our partner Reliance Retail we have set a clear plan to build a leadership position here. As the nation's leading retail operator, Reliance Retail is the perfect partner for us in India with extensive local expertise and experience, with strengths in infrastructure, logistics, technology and property.
>
> *(M&S, 2013)*

Useful websites

Central Board of Excise and Customs www.cbec.gov.in
Department of Income Tax www.incometaxindia.gov.in
Department of Industrial Planning and Promotion www.dipp.gov.in
Director General of Foreign Trade http://dgft.gov.in
National Portal of India www.india.gov.in

References

Asiedu, E. (2002) On the determinants of foreign direct investment to developing countries: Is Africa different? *World Development*, 30(1): 107–119.

Barkema, H.G., Bell, J.H.J. and Pennings, J.M. (1996) Foreign entry, cultural barriers, and learning. *Strategic Management Journal*, 17(2): 151–166.

BBC (2001) Marks & Spencer enters Indian market. 12 December. Available at: http://news.bbc.co.uk/2/hi/south_asia/1706256.stm

Beamish, P.W. and Lupton, N.C. (2009) Managing joint ventures. *The Academy of Management Perspectives*, 23(2): 75–94.

Buckley, P.J. and Casson, M.C. (1976) *The Future of the Multinational Enterprise*. London: Macmillan.

Buckley, P.J. and Casson, M.C. (1981) The optimal timing of a foreign direct investment. *Economic Journal*, 91(1): 75–87.

Buckley, P.J., Enderwick, P., Forsans, N. and Munjal, S. (2013) Country linkages and firm internationalisation: Indian MNEs within economic-political alliances of nations. In G. Cook and J. Johns (eds), *The Changing Geography of International Business*. Basingstoke: Palgrave Macmillan.

Buckley, P.J., Forsans, N. and Munjal, S. (2012) Host–home country linkages and host–home country specific advantages as determinants of foreign acquisitions by Indian firms. *International Business Review*, 21(5): 878–890.

Buckley, P.J., Munjal, S., Enderwick, P. and Forsans, N. (2017) The role of country alliances in reducing the transaction costs of internationalisation: Evidence from Indian multinational enterprises. *Cambridge Journal of Economics*, 41(3): 807–828.

Cassiman, B. and Golovko, E. (2011) Innovation and internationalization through exports. *Journal of International Business Studies*, 42(1): 56–75.

Dunning, J.H. (1988) The eclectic paradigm of international production: A restatement and some possible extensions. *Journal of International Business Studies*, 19(1): 1–31.

Dunning, J.H. (1993) *Multinational Enterprises and the Global Economy*. Wokingham: Addison-Wesley.

Johanson, J. and Vahlne, J.E. (1977) The internationalization process of the firm: A model of knowledge development and increasing foreign market commitments. *Journal of International Business Studies*, 8(1): 23–32.

Johanson, J. and Vahlne, J.E. (2009) The Uppsala internationalization process model revisited: From liability of foreignness to liability of outsidership. *Journal of International Business Studies*, 40: 1411–1431.

Kale, P. and Anand, J. (2006) The decline of emerging economy joint ventures: The case of India. *California Management Review*, 48(3): 62–76.

Kogut, B. and Singh, H. (1988) The effect of national culture on the choice of entry mode. *Journal of International Business Studies*, 19(3): 411–432.

Mallick, S. and Marques, H. (2017) Export prices, selection into exporting and market size: Evidence from China and India. *International Business Review*, 26(6): 1034–1050.

M&S (2013) Marks & Spencer to build a leadership position in India. 11 November. Available at: http://corporate.marksandspencer.com/media/press-releases/2013/marks-and-spencer-to-build-a-leadership-position-in-india

M&S (2015) Marks & Spencer investment into greater China. 2 March. Available at: http://corporate.marksandspencer.com/media/press-releases/2015/marks-and-spencer-investment-into-greater-china

M&S (2017) Marks & Spencer: Key facts. 30 December. Available at; http://corporate.marksandspencer.com/aboutus/key-facts

Munjal, S. and Pereira, P. (2015) Opportunities and challenges for multiple-embeddedness through mergers and acquisitions in emerging economies. *Journal of Organizational Change Management*, 28(5): 817–831.

Ragozzino, R. (2009) The effects of geographic distance on the foreign acquisition activity of U.S. firms. *Management International Review*, 49(4): 509–535.

Reddy, Y.V. (2017) Understanding economic reforms for India: A book review. In K. Krishna, V. Pandit, K. Sundaram and P. Dua (eds) *Perspectives on Economic Development and Policy in India*. Singapore: Springer, pp. 33–38.

Shenkar, O. and Luo, Y. (2008) *International Business*. London: Sage.

Telegraph (2017) Marks and Spencer pulls out of China's high street, the world's biggest retail market. 14 March. Available at: www.telegraph.co.uk/business/2017/03/14/marks-spencer-pulls-chinas-high-street-worlds-biggest-retail

Yan, A. and Luo, Y. (2016) *International Joint Ventures: Theory and Practice*. London: Routledge.

Yang, Y. and Mallick, S. (2010) Export premium, self-selection and learning-by-exporting: Evidence from Chinese matched firms. *The World Economy*, 33(10): 1218–1240.

11

MARKETING AND DISTRIBUTION STRATEGIES FOR INDIA

Ravi Shanker and C.K. Sharma

Aims of this chapter are to:

- Describe the evolving consumer markets in India
- Show why diverse country and complex consumer behaviour requires unique customization
- Decode the culture to know the consumer
- Present the dilemma of distribution channels
- Understand the Indian rural market
- Present pricing and advertising in India

Introduction

This chapter contains information pertaining to marketing activities in India. It evaluates consumer behaviour in India as a function of socio-cultural and economic diversity and iterates the need for effective product branding highlighting the success of anglicized brand names in India. Distribution and channel marketing are discussed with respect to rural and urban India, reflecting the key role played by the convenience stores. Consumer sensitivity to pricing is also discussed, and various pricing techniques used by brands are explained.

The evolving consumer markets in India

The first phase of the development of the consumer market in the 1980s and the 1990s was characterized by increased product availability and basic services related to the delivery of goods. Prior to the 1980s, the success of companies was dependent on reach and availability of their products. For example, Hindustan Unilever, the country's largest consumer packaged goods company, was essentially dependent on its distribution network. The company followed a disciplined routine of the bullock cart leaving the redistribution stockist at 9 a.m. every day to make the products available. After the 1991 economic reforms, India had little choice but to make the hyper-leap into the modern world, and marketing teams in companies set the stage for improved processes, cost advantages and high impact innovations, both in packaging and products, to be the best in class. Markets today are changing fast, with price-sensitive customers, new competitors, new distribution channels, new communication channels, the Internet, wireless commerce, globalization, deregulation, privatization … the list goes on. And it is not only markets that are changing, but the technologies that support them. As a result, it is imperative that companies think through the revolutionary impact of these new technologies. Accordingly, the successful marketer is today, like never before, continually engaged in upgrading the brand values of the offer. Responding to such circumstances, the role of the salesperson is expanding to include participation in marketing activities, such as product development, market development, and the segmentation of markets.

Approach to marketing

As per the Accenture Report (Accenture Institute of High Performance, 2012), the major consumer markets in India include automobiles, banking and insurance, cement, chemicals, consumer durables, fast-moving consumer goods (FMCG), industrial equipment, pharmaceuticals and telecommunications. The report further describes the marketers in three categories irrespective of industry: (1) consumer masters; (2) consumer performers; and (3) consumer voyagers.

1. Consumer masters' markets are profitable companies that have significant market share. They excel at execution and they apply rigour to governance and control to make sure their strategies translate into improved sales performance. The masters have developed novel strategies to serve consumers and draw on an intimate understanding of consumers' cultures and needs to enter markets. The market is typified by the discovery and collective synchronization of different elements that differentiate them from their two peers: performers and voyagers' markets.
2. Consumer performers' markets are typified by profitable firms that have established a strong foothold by using conventional approaches or by emulating the success of the masters. However, the performers' markets often lack an innovative streak. They tend to focus on existing product portfolios and try to mitigate risk through aggressive product marketing to strengthen sales performance position. These companies have been successful in the past. However, in the future, they may struggle in a changing and more competitive landscape to achieve the desired sales performance.
3. Consumer voyagers' market is typified by companies that have adopted disruptive approaches to serve India's markets. Entities in voyagers' market create

unique products and services, customize pricing or packaging, or develop new
channels to achieve the desired sales performance. However, they have to
wait to make profits. Though voyagers often understand consumers better
than their competitors do, they usually take a more cautious approach
towards expansion.

In India, indicative performance in the end market at the consumer level and in
terms of market growth is characterized as: ITC, Hindustan Lever and DS Group
will fall under the Consumer Masters; Hamdard and Emami can be termed Consumer Performers, and Paperboat of Hector Beverages and Dant Kanti Toothpaste
of Patanjali are examples of Consumer Voyagers.

Consumer behaviour

Marketing activities such as market segmentation, pricing, positioning, packaging,
advertising and promotions, are heavily dependent on understanding consumer
behaviour. In India, the complexity of consumer behaviour lies in the country's
diversity. There is great complexity of class, both social and economic. Therefore, a
straitjacketed global metric cannot be a meaningful template for India. Further-
more, India has a complex demography, as there are differing linguistic, regional
and cultural groups. At a sociological level, India has been seen as stratified into
ethnicity, caste, religion, food habits, class and gender. Consumer buying behaviour
is not driven by an economic utility alone, but also by social and psychological
concepts of perceived utility. Perceived utility in turn depends solely on consumer
behaviour.

- *Case 1 Kellogg*: This has been seen in the case of Kellogg when they first came
  to India in 1994. Even with only 2 per cent of the market share, Kellogg
  attracted as many as 18 million customers. When introduced in India, in September 1994, the offerings were cornflakes, wheat flakes and basmati rice
  flakes. The products failed to attract re-purchase or gain loyalty. It generated a
  disguised demand probably based on a bull-whip effect (i.e., increasing swings
  in inventory in response to shifts in customer demand as one moves further up
  the supply chain). The reason for the initial failure was simple – the consumer
  habit was to have hot milk with sugar. Flakes with hot milk lead to a soggy
  mess, and flakes in cold milk would not dissolve the sugar. It is a case of
  expecting different consumer behaviour in future and committing disproportionate resources. While it is commonly accepted that disproportionate
  expenditure and investment in a brand are critical to create awareness and
  generate substantial volume, this did not happen in the case of Kellogg. Certainly the marketers in Kellogg misread the breakfast eating habits in India.
- *Case 2 McDonald's*: McDonald's faced a similar challenge. The latter made an
  entry in a phased manner ensuring they had 'tested the waters' and then
  quickly shifted to Aloo-Tikki Burger to customize their offering to the Indian

palate. But, as in the case of Kellogg, they seemed to be aiming for a break-through success on the back of their investment of US$65 million in the first year of the launch. While the consumers are globally aware and demand the best of products, they are also proud of their identity and value their deep-rooted culture. Multinational organizations tend to have a global outlook and even the Indian consumer is influenced by global trends but with a touch of their own societal values. Many McDonald's outlets in India ensure vegetarian items are prepared with dedicated equipment and utensils and sometimes by a separate work force. All of McDonald's food is cooked in vegetable oil and their mayonnaise does not contain eggs.

- *Case 3 Maggi Noodles:* Take the case of the brand Maggi of Nestlé. While Maggi is known as a soup and sauce brand in most parts of the world, in India, Maggi is known more for noodles and their accompanying Masala flavour. This shows how culturally sensitive the food category can be. While the fundamentals of consumer behaviour and positioning of brands remain the same (Shimp and Andrews, 2012), marketers tend to follow different strategic routes in different markets within India.

To understand consumers in any society, it is important to decode the culture in a given market. While India may be a diverse country, sets of people. either based on caste, religion or ethnicity, tend to congregate in their respective groups. While there are multiple groups in any society, the numbers are large in India due to a variety of reasons. Diversity within India reflects groups with different castes, colours, creeds, religions, food habits, languages, societal norms, political beliefs and rituals, and the list can go on. However, the point being made here is the enormity of the challenge facing marketers. While 'Make in India' (an initiative by the present government) is fine as a macroeconomic goal, goods have to be made for India. It implies not only use of multiple languages for marketing communications but also the treatment and even the celebrity endorsements. Companies like Hindustan Lever, P&G and ITC tend to capture consumer insights at the regional level to customize their regional language TVCs. For the marketer, it suggests the use of celebrity for consumer connect but at the same time customization of the product as per the need of different local consumers. In other words, while the communication has to be based on the emotional anchor through celebrity, diverse communications have to be dovetailed. The aim is to deal with different cultures for which a deep understanding of values and norms is critical. Consumers are born and brought up with a set of beliefs, and research in broadly segmented clusters can help in understanding the articulated and unarticulated needs of the consumer to make a successful offering.

Consumer behaviour is not a simple, constant process, but it is determined by an integrated effect of cognition and environmental influences. The trick clearly is to tap into the irrational influences and idiosyncrasies. Marketers often try and create an association of value to the consumer through quality, convenience, emotional anchor, scarcity, prestige, pride and product experience. Essentially the aim is to deliver functional value, which is product-related, and emotional value, which is a sense of affiliation. If we look at the consumption process of any product, it starts with a want or need followed by a cost-benefit analysis and, post purchase, a relationship emerges. Over time the confidence in the brand leads to expressions like 'My brand'. The ultimate aim of any brand is to provide unending hedonistic delight. Statements like 'I like the brand …', 'I love the brand' are common but there are brands which command an expression like 'I cannot live without it'. One brand that evokes this statement is Google.

Product/branding

Quality as a brand attribute has been purely about the 'perception' of quality. Brands need to establish their products as superior through advertising and marketing communications. Trust in brand quality has been influenced greatly by perception. In India, a large population is not fully literate, thus is not as rational and therefore dependent on flagship brands. They would rather follow urban trends to be a part of the mainstream. In such an environment, word of mouth acts as a social fact, and permeates the societal fabric.

A product can be branded on the basis of the gratification/utility that is being taken from it. In India, the beauty cream market is an example of brands satisfying a psychological/social need. A leading FMCG company conducted focus group discussions across the country to ascertain if young females preferred the herbal creams more than the synthetic ones. The findings were along the expected lines and a conclusive statement indicated overwhelmingly a strong preference for the herbal creams. Of the mavericks, as some of them are known, a marketing manager wanted to do the research all over again. This time they asked the young females to reveal the contents of their handbags and, shockingly, not one of them was carrying any herbal product. Further probing revealed that while the young females would prefer a herbal product, they were indeed preparing for marriage and they have to look beautiful soon. They expect herbal creams to take longer to improve the glow and therefore they largely depend on synthetic beauty creams for faster results. The company is reported to have lowered their investments in the development of herbal-based creams.

This is not to say that brands of Indian origin have not succeeded in the Indian market. But there is a key demarcation line between indigenous brands like Vicco Vajradanti, a toothpaste, and Himalaya, cosmetics, on the one hand and L'Oréal from Paris, on the other. Brands like Amul have done well by virtue of their indigenous 'Indianness'. The latter is, however, promoted at a central level and the brand Amul has done well due to its competitive advantage of low cost and distribution.

Most of the brands, however, are anglicized names to lure customers into an 'international' brand perception. Some examples of this are HiDesign, a goods manufacturer based in Pondicherry; Damilano, totally Indian despite Italian undertones, Monte Carlo, a Ludhiana-based group, and Havells Electricals, which is also a Delhi-based company. All the brands have taken foreign brand names to reach their customers. It has been argued that the preference for foreign names has been a result of Orientalism and will continue to impact branding decisions for a few decades. At the other extreme, India has been inundated by huge brands like Lufthansa, where brand communication portrays it as a down-to-earth friendly experience. India has two national languages (Hindi and English) and 22 official languages. However, branding activities cannot vary, and brand dilution is to be avoided. The challenge posed by the linguistic richness has to be resolved through marketing communications and advertising.

While marketers tend to customize their brands for the Indian consumer, this is increasingly becoming more demanding. As the literacy rates grow, the consumer tends to exercise rational thinking. It is therefore important that marketers ensure their products remain contemporary. It goes without saying that changes have to be communicated to the owner (consumer) of the brand. The consumer needs to be assured that the manufacturer cares for them and is continuously improving. This is what technology-driven products like Airtel and Paytm have done well.

The dilemma of distribution channels

A distribution channel is designed to set up a process to deliver core and value-added service to customers. The conventional sales management has been rede-fined, as organizations' quest for competitive advantage in the sales management function gains importance. Changing markets require a change in approach and a greater understanding of the customer being serviced. Brand portfolios and custo-mer portfolios may need equal weight in the future (Ramcharan, 2007). Compa-nies tend to look at competitive advantage in everything they do to be successful. In the context of the distribution channel, the approach has to be holistic and cover all the dimensions of sales, marketing and more.

Multinational companies have learnt to do business the Indian way by investing in infrastructure for rural coverage. Looking at mass distribution consumer goods, companies are often faced with the decision to partner with wholesalers, dis-tributors, or middlemen to facilitate market penetration. FMCGs generally include a wide range of frequently purchased consumer products, such as toiletries, soap, cosmetics, tooth cleaning products, shaving products and detergents, as well as other non-durables such as glassware, bulbs, batteries, paper products, and plastic goods. In the Indian context, often there is a one-stop village shop which main-tains an inventory for almost all consumer products, including the subsets like consumer electronics, mobile phones, digital cameras, etc. Success in the Indian market can be possible due to quick adaptation to the local market way of reaching and ensuring availability rather than imposing global business models. With the change in type of outlets, the competencies required for the sales personnel have to be adapted to the changing market environment. The Indian market is fragmented and therefore a multi-skilled approach is an imperative to succeed. Moreover, with developing markets and viability standards changing with higher demands, the mode of distribution which started with the bullock cart has moved on to motor-ized three-wheelers and a combination of motorized two-wheelers and pedal bicycles. The objective is clearly to increase the reach and availability in the hitherto uncovered remote lanes and by-ways and thus realize market potential. In most cases, FMCG companies have contracted with entrepreneurs as sales agents or distributors to cut costs and raise market penetration. Companies have to factor regional languages and geographic knowledge in their recruitment when managing their sales agents and distributors. The role of the frontline salesman is crucial and more and more companies are realizing that locals should be recruited. It is then safe to state that companies with better sales capabilities will grow faster.

In the Indian context, interaction with the distributors/small-scale businessmen is culture-sensitive. In an Indian context, retail sales are driven through distribution margins. The unsophisticated infrastructure is another daunting hindrance, espe-cially for temperature-sensitive products. With increased uncertainty, distribution can make or break businesses. The multi-layered complex distribution has led to great success for companies like Hindustan Unilever. In India, the outlet numbers are invariably large and their coverage necessarily involves dependence on the wholesale trade, unlike in the West where modern distribution systems were developed to cater to the organized trade both through direct coverage or cash and carry stores. As the markets evolve, trade partners come up with ingenious ways for the last mile. Indians are entrepreneurial and tend to come up with the best solu-tions at the grass-roots level. One of the most unique examples of a locally devel-oped distribution system in India has been recorded as the *dabbawala* network in Mumbai (a person carrying a tiffin box of home-cooked food, which is delivered from the home to a person in an office or a school). In a case study at Harvard Business School in 2010, an attempt was made to delayer the simplicity of the *dabbawala* operational system. The case study entitled 'The Dabbawala System: On-Time Delivery, Every Time' (Thomke and Sinha, 2010) described the Dabbawala organization in Mumbai and how it achieves very high service performance at a low cost and with a very simple operating system. The *dabbawalas* are unsophisti-cated and illiterate, but yet they function with remarkable Six Sigma efficiency. For the Western world, such a labour-intensive service may not be commercially viable but the learning is that non-technology-based services can be as accurate.

The Indian rural market

Of India's total population of 1.30 billion, almost 830 million live in the villages which number more than 600,000. The rural population is aspirational and embracing new services and products. As per a Nielsen study, the fast-moving consumer goods sector in rural and semi-urban India is expected to cross the US $20 billion mark by 2018 and reach US$100 billion in 2025. To be able to tap the vast potential of this market, companies have to acquire a deep understanding of the market in addition to establishing the infrastructure to reach the rural markets. The rural market is changing fast and it requires agility on the part of the marketer to adapt to changing conditions and understand specific end market nuances. It is often necessary that one has to look beyond traditional selling approaches and get away from the competitive spirit to a more accommodative and collaborative spirit. Joining hands with the competition to share resources has become commonplace, especially where vans have to drive long distances with lower sales proceeds for the day. But there is always the cost of piggy-backing. Either the smaller player has to offer higher margins to the trade partner or share the distribution expenditure proportionately to their respective volumes.

Approximately 70 per cent of Indians live in rural areas. While this detail is detrimental to FMCG, there are verticals like retail that cater only to urban areas. Spending in the rural segment of the market is growing and there is a thin line between the type of goods consumed in the urban market and those consumed in the rural market. With increased awareness levels and the advent of electronic media and the internet, the rural consumer is more aware today. Increased literacy levels also enable them to exercise value judgement. Given the staggering numbers involved, it is not sensible to ignore the rural market as it is a significant portion of the Indian consumer market. FMCG market leader HUL had embarked upon a major outreach project named 'Shakti' and the aim was to create opportunities for rural women by providing them with a small-scale distribution opportunity. It involved working with rural self-help groups and engaging them in the distribution network. Local rural women under the Shakti project ensured direct-to-home delivery. Another innovative initiative was ITC's 'eChoupal' where the company built a platform that others can use. The aim was to help farmers with information and also companies to market their products. The eChoupal infrastructure consists of a kiosk with the internet and a warehouse hub typically managed by a former middleman who was engaged to ensure that his income is assured.

Pricing in India

In India, due to cheaper manufacturing and labour costs, pricing is lower and more competitive. A small success can mean millions of pieces sold in the end market. Based on the relative success of their brands, companies plan higher manufacturing capacities and with multiple increases in their volumes, it is natural for them to establish themselves in the premium segment of the market. Here, the key focus for companies is to create a differentiation that can be sustained at higher prices. Segmenting customers is a prerequisite for any strategic brand plan. A higher-paying customer has to be separated from the value customer. While using the Pareto principle is a no brainer, the key is to have different product offerings that can command different pricing. Both types of companies, ones who represent the premium segment and the others serving the popular segment, have a common task of having a presence across the pricing range. For a premium brand leader, it becomes imperative because they have to introduce lower-priced offerings under a different brand name to act as a net for the losses of the premium product after every price increase. Rajnigandha Pan Masala, a premium mouth freshener in the

Indian market, had a unique problem. The brand has dominated the premium segment over the last three decades. The company always focused on quality and innovation to provide the best possible product and an emotional hook of unparalleled success. Both the product and its integrated communication have worked well for the brand with its price gap with competitive brands widening over the years. Today the brand has a monopolistic dominant market share of over 95 per cent and its price at least three times higher than its nearest rival. However, with a progressive excise tax regime, the majority of the mouth freshener category volume was concentrated in the popular segment. It was therefore considered prudent to launch a new brand, Tansen, in the popular segment. The company had the twin objectives of having representation in the popular segment and creating a net for the value for money-seeking consumer who may consider switching from their premium offering to a popular segment brand.

Another phenomenon that has emerged is the organized modern retail store providing affordable alternatives under their own brand name. Retail stores like Reliance have developed in-house brands priced just below the multinational competitors. These brands have been selling due to better placement and point of sales strategy adopted by the modern store. Such stores have the advantage of being able to influence the customers through sense of sight, hearing, smell, taste and touch. There can be free tastings and demos as well, often resulting in impulse purchases. This is a competitive advantage over the FMCG companies who normally have to budget as much as 2 per cent of their revenue on marketing activities. As per a Nielsen survey, perceptions about private labels are becoming popular without the corresponding gains in value share (Nielsen, 2014).. Consumer preference for private labels is largely concentrated in commodities which are also bought in bulk. In some cases, the consumer is more rational and exercises his choice on products where consumers perceive little differentiation. While marginal brands get wiped out, the modern store is able to generate sufficient consumer loyalty if the product offering lives up to expectations.

In the Indian context, it is difficult for any manufacturer to have adequate direct coverage of retail grocery convenience stores or indeed the pan-plus outlets, i.e., the unorganized sector consisting of next door neighbourly grocery and convenience stores is huge in India. It is estimated that there are a total of over 10 million outlets and yet the top two companies, namely, HUL and P&G cover just about 7.5 and 6 million outlets respectively. Wal-Mart and Metro are therefore trying the cash and carry model where retailers are enlisted as members and all their purchasing can be done under one roof. Also, the manufacturer and the intermediaries benefit from the economies of scale and are able to generate huge volumes. Barring toiletries, China seems to have entered the Indian market in a big way through the market skimming strategy, essentially to exploit the potential among India's consuming classes. The trading community converts the price using the exchange rate, adds the custom duty and taxes and then makes the product available. With this strategy, products reach the customers through select wholesale markets like Gaffar Market in Delhi. Previously, most customers would wait and buy an Apple product through a friend travelling overseas. But now they have access to all Apple products whether formally launched in India or not. On the other hand, a new trend of 'Make in India' is emerging with Indian companies like Tata offering Nano and HCL offering the world's cheapest laptop at US$350. Multiple consumer segments are served by different channels competing against each other in the category and price levels.

India is just as price-sensitive as any other market and lower prices can lead to an increase in demand. HLL (Hindustan Lever Ltd.) was quick to bring in cheaper products to cater to the mass market. They brought in a cheaper detergent, Wheel, at 30 per cent lower than the local competitor prices. The objective was to counter the Nirma detergent powder from taking the market share from Surf. Wheel was made for the Indian market, at an affordable lower price and it led to customer loyalty and repeat purchases. For companies with multiple brands, it is always a trade-off decision in favour of economies of scale and large volumes, on the one hand, and presence in the premium segment which actually funds their R&D to make future business sustainable. The challenge clearly is to assess the premium paying ability of a set of products to fund future investments in the same brand and indeed associated brands.

The Indian market is also full of look-alikes and counterfeit products. While Euro Monitor estimates counterfeits are 5–7 per cent of world trade, accounting for about US$600 billion, the Indian market is affected by counterfeits in almost all sectors. As per a report by Thorton (2016), almost all product categories, including FMCGs, tobacco, technology, alcohol and automobiles, etc., are plagued by the threat of counterfeiting. Table 11.1 highlights the scale of the problem in India.

Advertising/promotions

India's advertising industry has been regularly growing by over 10 per cent per annum in the past few years and this trend is expected to continue. This reflects the increase in demand for advertising and promotions in the country and the confidence that marketers have in India. With an increase in digital marketing,

TABLE 11.1 Loss of sales to the industry through counterfeiting (in Indian rupees)

Industry sector	2013–2014	2011–2012
Alcoholic beverages	14,140	5,626
Auto components	10,501	9,198
Computer hardware	7,344	4,725
FMCG (packaged goods)	21,957	20,378
FMCG (personal goods)	19,243	15,035
Mobile phones	19,066	9,042
Tobacco	13,130	8,965
Total losses	105,381	72,969

advertising efforts are relatively cost-effective. Digital marketing has thrived due to its capability to engage with the consumer and India's demographic dividend of a young and learning nation quick to adopt technology. Better networks, cheaper devices and driven content have facilitated effective marketing communication. In a country as diverse as India, multiple mediums of communication and their choice are the key to make it cost-effective. The risk is that often companies tend to get swayed by a trend without considering which medium is the best for their set of products. Hoardings in towns and wall paintings in India are an old method of reaching the masses. Wall sites are also preferred in villages because it is difficult for vendors to maintain display value. While at a certain level it may be true that the medium has to be in line with the stature and nature of the product advertised. It is not recommended to put an up-market brand like L'Oréal on wall paintings in the villages, not because the demand is low but because the medium will pull the image down. This notion is, however, overcome by the soft-drink category where Coke and Pepsi do depend on wall paintings but may not use the same for Coke Zero. The advertising industry has still to come to terms with the possibility of ensuring maintenance and using acrylic materials on plain walls and adding imagery by creating wooden border frames.

While 'promotion' in the Indian context is heavily driven towards wholesalers and distributors, who in turn influence product distribution and placement, there are other strategies at play as well. Promotions in shopping malls, college campuses, etc. are effective for new product introduction like cars, where the feel and sense of the product create awe. Below the line promotions are also equally relevant for intangible products like food ordering apps like Food Panda, Zomato and Swiggy, etc.

Due to the excessive competition in price, promotions play an important role in the Indian market. BOGOF (buy one, get one free) has been adopted by brands to increase immediate circulation and get rid of stock. More commonly seen is cheaper pricing for bigger packages, thereby warranting the sign, 'Save Rs. –'. Pricing with labels that state 'saving' are psychologically effective even if the amount saved is small. Brands have also opted to increase the packaging size without changing the prices. They add 10 per cent more of the product to entice customers.

When a brand is becoming less pocket-friendly, an incentive is offered to the consumer to make the transition smooth. Charm pricing is also used as a tool where a product is priced at Rs 9 instead of Rs 10. This is done for a variety of reasons, the foremost being to counter the psychological impact of a price increase to a double-digit figure. Sometimes, in a fast-moving consumer product, it is done to offer a higher trade margin to the retailer. At the local grocer, more often than not, the one rupee exchange is done in the form of a toffee priced at Rs 1. At retail stores like Reliance, pricing of Rs 199 is quite common.

A more recent trend has been seen in brands like P&G who associate the purchase of the product with donating for a cause. If you buy a P&G product, you can 'feel good' about having educated a child. This form of promotion helps brand image association with good corporate social responsibility (see Chapter 22), thereby, creating a win–win for both customer and the brand. These more modern forms of promoting the product are now aimed at long-term differentiation.

CASE STUDY: GILLETTE

Realizing that the Indian context is unique and extremely diverse, Gillette set aside its global strategy in India to succeed. Realizing there is a strong difference in the shaving habits of Indians, Gillette aimed at changing the consumer's attitude, leading to some creative marketing campaigns (*Business Today*, 2014). In 2009, it launched the Gillette Mach3 and supported it with the 'Shave India Movement 2009' campaign. This included initiatives like the creation of the platform 'India Votes… to shave or not', which asked three controversial questions: (1) are clean-shaven men more successful?; (2) did the nation prefer clean-shaven celebrities?; and the big one: (3) do women prefer clean-shaven men? For two months, various media channels picked up on the campaign and ran interviews, discussions, editorials and news stories, which triggered popular interest. The main aim was to create a debate on shaving. This innovative way of marketing proved to be effective and as awareness grew, sales and market share increased by 38 per cent and 35 per cent respectively.

Conclusion

Marketing in India is constantly evolving, and the challenge is to establish basic facts that form a consistent pattern. Despite predictions, marketing activities in India have coloured outside the lines, and achieved unprecedented success. A key guiding force is the element of trust in a brand which is guided by celebrity endorsement, religious affiliation or regional distribution. Marketing techniques are becoming more complex, as companies are diversifying products and services. A trend that is globally seen, the transition from product to service, can be seen in India as well. With the advent of the experience economy, new dimensions are sprouting, thereby creating a cacophony. The future of marketing lies in what is perceived to be modern, contemporary and relevant. It is also advantageous for brands to be used with more frequency, thereby facilitating repeat purchase and brand loyalty.

Useful websites

Academy of Indian Marketing www.aoim.in/index.html
Digital Marketing Association of India www.direct-marketing-association-india.org/
Government eMarketplace https://gem.gov.in/
Market Research Society of India www.mrsi.in/
MICA www.mica.ac.in/
Rural Marketing Association of India www.rmai.in/

References

Accenture Institute of High Performance (2012) Masters of rural markets: Profitably selling to India's rural consumers. Available at: www.accenture.com/in-en/~/media/Accenture/Conversion-Assets/LandingPage/Documents/4/Accenture-Masters-of-Rural-Markets-Selling-Profitably-Rural-Consumers.pdf (accessed 11 November 2015).

Business Today (2014) How Gillette innovated and improved its market share in India. 13 April.Available at: www.businesstoday.in/magazine/lbs-case-study/gillette-innovated-improved-its-market-share-in-india/story/204517.html

Delmulle, B., Grehan, B. and Sagar, V. (2015) Building marketing and sales capabilities to beat the market. Available at: www.mckinsey.com/insights/marketing_sales/building_marketing_and_sales_capabilities_to_beat_the_market (accessed April 2015).

IBEF (2017) Report on the Indian rural market. Available at: www.ibef.org/industry/india n-rural-market.aspx

Nielsen (2014) Around the globe, private label's appeal goes beyond price. 18 November. Available at: www.nielsen.com/us/en/insights/news/2014/around-the-globe-private-la bels-appeal-goes-beyond-price.html

Perner, L. (2010) Segmentation, targeting and positioning. Available at: www.consumerp sychologist.com/cb_Segmentation.html

Ramcharan (2007) What the customer wants you to know. Harmondsworth: Penguin Portfolio, cover page.

Shimp, T.A. and Andrews, J.C. (2012) *Advertising Promotion and Other Aspects of Integrated Marketing Communications*. Mason, OH: Cengage.

Shukla, P. and Dangarwala, U.R. (2016) *Rural Marketing Strategies for FMCG Products*. Solapur: Laxmi Book Publication.

Thomke, S.H. and Sinha, M. (2010) The Dabbawala system: On-time delivery every time. Harvard Business School Case 610–059. Boston: Harvard Business School.

Thorton, G. (2016) *Emerging Challenges to Legitimate Business in the Borderless World*. New Delhi: FICCI Cascade.

12

IMPROVING ACCESS TO FINANCE IN INDIA

Three recommendations

Soumen De

Aims of this chapter are to:

- Discuss issues with accessing finance in India
- Make recommendations to access finance in India

Introduction

Since the economic reforms were enacted in 1991, there has been a gradual and yet considerable improvement in the modes and channels of access to finance by companies, domestic and foreign alike, in India. In 2017, India moved up 30 notches to the global rank of 100 in World Bank's annual rankings of ease of doing business in general. This is a commendable achievement. However, a lot still needs to be done to improve access to finance in India. In this chapter, three factors that need to be immediately addressed administratively in India are identified, their current problematic attributes and gradually evolving features are critically analysed and recommendations are offered to improve access to financing for established and nascent companies operating in India.

Specifically, it is posited that:

1. Problematic domestic banking issues prevalent in India need to be redressed in order to enable Indian banks to become more efficient and provide seam-less and cost-effective finance to both domestic and foreign firms.
2. India should streamline the protocol for foreign investments in India in view of the growing interest of foreign investors and should also take steps to internationalize its capital markets, especially its bond markets.
3. India should invest in its human resource potential in order to develop, enable and empower entrepreneurs to innovate in all spheres of life, and to success-fully access financial resources on a global scale.

At present, the Indian banking structure is undergoing some significant changes and there are problematic issues related in particular to the public sector banks that need to be addressed, if Indian banks are to make positive strides towards being globally competitive and meet the capital needs of foreign entities entering the Indian markets. On the other hand, if Indian borrowers are to win the best deals in the present era when foreign, private banks are expressing an interest in the Indian market, borrowers in India will have to be free to choose among global borrowing opportunities and Indian banks will have to be truly competitive with global banks.[1]

Second, India should streamline the protocol for foreign investments flowing into India and implement measures to internationalize its capital markets, especially its bond markets. If India is to attract long-term investments from abroad, its bond markets have to rise to global standards.

Third, India's concerns and policy decisions targeted exclusively to the entrepreneurial class, that is slowly but assuredly emerging in India, are important not only for India's organic growth but are also vital for international collaborations that are the hallmark of global growth at the moment. Several global institutions and agencies consider India's entrepreneurial potential to be much higher than that of China. Indian entrepreneurs should be encouraged to work outside the bounds of dominant promoters and family-dominated businesses.

Banking and related issues

It has been repeatedly observed from country to country that developing nations rely initially on bank financing, then on equity, and finally on financing via bonds for their economic growth. A country's financial sophistication has often been gauged by the range and flexibility of its bond market. Indian firms, for a variety of reasons, continue to rely primarily on banks, in particular, the public sector banks, for their financing needs. As such, to realize the full potential of economic reforms, much will depend on how efficiently the banks are run in India and how competitive they are with regard to their lending practices. But there are serious obstacles to Indian banks operating efficiently. Since the largest of the Indian banks are nationalized, they are likely to enjoy an accommodative policy stance and forbearance from India's central bank, the Reserve Bank of India (RBI).

According to the World Bank, India has the highest ratio of non-performing loans to total assets.[2] Estimates of the targeted reduction vary from $100 billion to $150 billion. India's ratio of non-performing loans to total loans, according to Bloomberg, is four times that of China's. As of 31 March 2016, the proportion of stressed assets surged to a 16-year high of 11.5 per cent. The RBI provisionally set March 2017 as a deadline for banks to clean up their levels of distressed assets. RBI's insistence on speedy bad debt recognition and clean-up bodes well for the long-term future of the banking sector but more needs to be done in the immediate term. India now is committed to the Basel III rules and banks are taking steps to comply with the Tier 1 capital requirements.[3] Regulations require that

Indian banks have to hold by March 2017 capital to the extent of 9.625 per cent of their risk-weighted assets.[4] This is termed the capital adequacy ratio (CAR). This requirement rises to 11.5 per cent by March 2019. A study of 27 Indian banks by the ratings agency Fitch found that the CAR for 11 banks was at or below the 11.5 per cent level. Of these, six were below the 9.25 per cent target. Clearly, Indian banks face a capital shortage in the near term and in hindsight the target date of March 2017 for several remedial measures was optimistic.

Presently, the RBI is committed to a policy shift that purports to deal with high inflation and the weak balance sheets of banks, and the central bank has met with some success in lowering inflation rates in India. The RBI would like at the same time to lower deposit and loan rates further and energize policies to reduce a substantial amount of bad loans in the banking sector. There is, however, an in-built resistance to lowering rates and the reluctance does not rest only with the bankers. Depositors too expect deposit rates to be high and to accommodate this wish, banks themselves are willing to live with this scenario with resultant higher loan rates for borrowers, as wider margins are something the banks would prefer to continue to have.

This is the fundamental problem with the Indian banking system. Indian banks are out of sync with what is happening in rest of the world. It is not only the public sector banks but also the relatively newer private banks, who are not open to an environment of market-determined low interest rates, which might indeed be necessary for India's growth strategy. As foreign firms continue to increase their investment outlays into India, they will want to borrow more from banks in India to rid themselves of exchange rate concerns and Indian banks have to offer them competitive terms. Hence, it is important that Indian banks become more efficient in the future.

Of course, the authorities will eventually transfer control of the public sector banks to private ownership but how long that will take is anybody's guess. In the meantime, changes in the banking structure should be permitted to foster more competition within the banking industry. Global trends are portending a limited shelf life for sheltered banking environments. Even in China, the authorities are contemplating ways to reduce the subsidies to state-controlled banks dealing with increasing levels of non-performing loans. Banks in developed nations are aggressively moving into the domestic turf of developing nations in search of higher yields since rates in developed nations have fallen substantially after the financial crisis of 2007–2008. So, borrowers in India might find themselves in an advantageous position to contract favourable loan terms from international lenders. If India is to capture some of the welfare gains from foreign banks making inroads into protected banking markets around the world, state-owned banks in India will have to be weaned from the unquestioned support from the government and be required to offer competitive terms to their borrowers. On the other hand, Indian borrowers – individuals, corporations and institutions alike – will have to be freed to explore borrowing options globally and not be constrained to borrow from inefficient domestic banks.

Requiring Indian banks to face competition from foreign banks will have beneficial effects since exposure to foreign capital markets will not only subject the Indian banks to global scrutiny and lead to a speedier clean-up of their balance sheets but also will provide on the other hand an opportunity for the global investors to gauge the depth and breadth of the Indian financial markets. The RBI's recent proposal to allow banks to issue 'masala bonds' – rupee-denominated bonds issued in offshore capital markets – could also help widen the investor pool and ultimately deepen the market for AT1 bond issuance. Masala bonds will have far-reaching beneficial effects for both corporates and investors even though at the moment only financial institutions have been permitted to raise funds in offshore rupee-denominated bond markets.

Promoting foreign investments in India and internationalizing India's capital markets

Since the economic reforms of 1991 when India removed several governmental obstacles and opened its gates to foreign investment, the Indian government has implemented a series of new regulations to promote cross-border mergers and financing, foreign institutional investments and a seamless cross-border payments system. On 4 July 2013, the RBI issued new revised guidelines pertaining to foreign investments in Indian companies, the calculation of the proportion of foreign investment, the transfer of ownership and control of Indian companies and downstream investment by Indian companies.[5] The aim of the guidelines has been to impart more clarity to the provisions that guide foreign entities in initiating and expanding their investments in India. Like China, India has maintained a two-track approach to foreign investments: one automatic and the other requiring approval from governmental authorities. Foreign investments in activities not covered under the automatic route require prior government approval and investment proposals have to be submitted to the Foreign Investment Promotion Board (FIPB) for review and approval.

In addition to foreign direct investment (FDI), foreign financial institutions (FII) are permitted to invest in India. Once again, like China, India has followed the practice of gradually increasing the quotas for FIIs, both in terms of total investment and the extent of holdings in a single company. Also, the FIIs were not permitted to invest in India's debt markets when they were granted permission to invest in India's equity markets. The FIIs' investments in the Indian capital market began in January 1993. Until December 1998, only equity investments were permitted for FIIs, but beginning in January 1999, FIIs were allowed to participate in India's debt markets as well. The limits on equity and debt investments have been progressively increased over the years. The FIIs' predominant investments, however, continue to in the Indian equity securities market.

The process of obtaining dual approvals from both the RBI and the Securities Exchange Board of India (SEBI[6]) for FIIs registering in India was changed to a single approval process from the SEBI only in December 2003. This streamlined the registration process and reduced the time taken for registration. On 7 January 2014, the SEBI overhauled the regulations to put in place a new framework for registration and procedures with regard to foreign investors who proposed to make portfolio investments in India.

With regard to international financing, Indian companies are allowed to raise equity capital in the international markets through the issue of Global Depositary Receipts (GDRs)/American Depositary Receipts (ADRs)/Foreign Currency Convertible Bonds (FCCBs). These are not subject to any ceilings on investment but there are restrictions on the plough-back of funds raised overseas into India and the purposes for which these funds can be used. For example, a company engaged in the manufacture of items covered under the automatic route whose direct foreign investment after a proposed GDRs/ADRs/FCCBs issue is likely to exceed the prescribed per centage for automatic approval, or a company which is implementing a project not contained in the list of projects falling under the government approval route, would have to obtain prior government approval for such fund raising. Any company seeking the government's approval with regard to issuing GDRS/ADRs/FCCBs should have a consistent track record for good performance for a minimum period of three years.[7] There are no restrictions on the number of GDRs/ADRs/FCCBs that a company or a group of companies can issue in a financial year.

2016 was a banner year for India's bond market. In a report released in January 2017 by the renowned Japanese financial services firm, Nomura Securities, Indian sovereign bonds outperformed those of all the other Asian nations, excluding Japan, even though Indian government bonds are rated one notch higher than junk.[8] Canadian investment and pension funds along with other American and European investment funds are increasingly investing in the Indian bond markets.[9] The perpetual bonds floated by the State Bank of India have been well received in Asian bond markets.[10] India's good fortune coincides with Asia's pre-eminence in the global bond markets. It appears the Asian bond market has surpassed its critical size and is less dependent on European and Middle Eastern investors for success.

By allowing foreign financial institutions to invest 100 per cent of their investable funds in debt securities and announcing its intent to implement a uniform set of policies for investment funds, insurance companies and pension funds, the SEBI is sending out the right signals with regard to its future policies pertaining to India's bond markets. Financing emanating from these three sources is crucial for long-term growth and India needs global financial partners for its long-term investments in technology, process and infrastructure. Of course, a lot more needs to be done to make India's secondary bond markets more liquid and self-sustaining.[11] Foreign investments in India's debt markets will depend critically on the developments in the secondary markets.

The Indian government's decision to lower its borrowings from Rest. 5.80 lakh crores to Rest. 3.48 lakh crores during the 2017–2018 fiscal year bodes well for India's domestic corporate bond markets, which perpetually suffer from the crowding out effect on account of government borrowing excessive amounts. Reduced borrowings by the central government not only will open up viable opportunities for corporations in India but also will make available larger amounts of loans for non-government borrowers. Indian banks have to allocate a fifth of their deposits to buying government bonds. With reduced bond issuance by the central government, banks can redirect the deposits into loans for non-government borrowers.

The Indian government has also implemented some positive policies to enhance the growth potential of the Masala bond market. Effective in October, 2017, masala bonds have been removed from the Foreign Portfolio Investment quota system. This will permit more issuances by foreign borrowers and more purchases by foreign investors. The tax on interest on such bonds has been cut from 20 per cent to 5 per cent. However, the Indian government has imposed some conditions. The minimum tenure of masala bonds will have to be at least five years for deals over $50 million and issuers can offer a maximum of 300 basis points premium over the Indian government bonds of comparable maturity. Nevertheless, despite all the positive moves by the Indian government, ultimately, it is India's growth prospects that will eventually drive up demand in this offshore segment of India's bond market. Rising economic growth will imply an appreciating Indian rupee and bondholders always prefer to hold bonds denominated in appreciating currencies.[12]

Policies targeted toward financing of start-ups

Economic growth in the twenty-first century will be defined by innovation and entrepreneurship, and the government has to provide a realistic infrastructure to promote scalable entrepreneurial activity in India. The introduction of the Start-up India initiative in 2015 is a move in the right direction.

Viewed broadly, nations can adopt a government-centred paradigm or a community-based approach wherein clusters of entrepreneurial hubs are concentrated in locations preferred by the entrepreneurs without much government intervention. In the former, the government directs the funding for the start-ups whereas, in the latter, the government funds the start-ups via angel investors and venture capital funds. India appears to favour the government-centred approach and has formed a special committee, under the auspices of the Department of Industrial Policy and Promotion (DIPP), to simplify regulations and ease of doing business in India. A remarkable sum of Rs 20,000 crores has been allocated to the formation of a Micro Units Development Refinance Agency (MUDRA) Bank, which was launched in April 2015. Additional funds have been allocated to support and fund start-ups. But, since the government has also committed Rs 10,000 crores to go alongside private funding of venture capital funds, it would appear that India is adopting an eclectic approach to developing and funding start-ups in India. This is welcome news. Funding is a major concern for Indian entrepreneurs, and enlisting angel and venture capital funds to identify and promote viable start-ups has the potential of allocating resources more efficiently.

Joining hands with private equity to enable venture capital funds is perhaps a better strategy for India if it wants to monitor the start-ups effectively. Knowledge is as important as funding needs and the government's decision to fund start-ups via angel and venture capital funds would involve professionals who have experience with start-ups and will insist upon review and assessment at various stages of the funding, relieving the government of the pressure of exerting the necessary controls with inadequate knowledge of the start-ups' operations. India presently has around 3,100 start-ups and close to 750/800 start-ups are being added to that list annually. Concurrently, foreign investors – mutual funds, pension funds and other asset managers – are increasingly viewing India as a destination for their investments. The famous Asian finance magazine, *The Asset*, opined in November 2017 that India may be 'one of the most investible emerging markets in the world, seeing increased digitalization of its banking system, tax reforms, and increased activity in its capital markets, including an uptick in IPO activity'. [13] It is to be seen whether the Indian government will offer foreign angel and venture capital funds comparable privileges that it has extended to foreign institutions so far with regard to their investments in the equity, bond, private equity and real estate markets.

Permitting Indian entrepreneurs to collaborate with foreign entrepreneurs is one channel India should actively support. Denmark and Portugal have achieved substantial success in integrating experienced and knowledgeable foreigners into their entrepreneurial initiatives at multiple levels.[14] India should consider following a similar strategy. Of course, corporate rules regarding bankruptcies will have to be modified to entice foreigners to India and India has done this to a large extent. In fact, the World Bank's upgrade for India in the Ease of Doing Business Global rankings was influenced in great part by the introduction of the Insolvency and Bankruptcy Code (IBC) in late 2016. India's remarkable success in information technologies (IT) and IT-based consulting needs to be extended to other vital sectors of the economy. Partnering with foreign investors will facilitate speedier transfer of knowledge and expertise, usher in more foreign capital, promote efficient channelling of entrepreneurial effort and ensure timely and more efficient assessment of entrepreneurial efforts and outcomes. There is lot to be gained from allowing Indian entrepreneurs to collaborate with their foreign counterparts; regulatory burdens should not be permitted to diminish India's chances of joining the global community of innovative and prosperous nations.

CASE STUDY: AEON CORPORATION

In October 2017, Shekhar Gupta, the treasurer of Aeon Corporation, headquartered in Jodhpur, India, had reason to rejoice. Aeon's common stock had doubled in price in the past year despite Aeon having acquired two mid-size companies in the two years preceding 2016. Even though the market had voiced some initial doubts about the direction the company was taking with two large acquisitions, recent movements in the price of the company's common stock led Shekhar Gupta to conclude that the capital market was finally expressing its utmost confidence in the management of the company and its future prospects.

Integrating the two newly-acquired companies successfully with the parent would be a daunting task for the management. The process would require additional capital to the tune of Rs 45–50 crores because Aeon, in acquiring the two companies, had essentially acquired only the core technology to success-fully produce a new product which was still at the prototype stage, requiring thorough testing prior to full-scale launch in 2020 at the earliest. Given the high current price of its common stock, Aeon could opt for a secondary equity offering. But Shekhar Gupta felt confident that Aeon could instead launch an inaugural bond issue since investors appear to be confident about Aeon's long-run prospects and, more importantly, market conditions were propitious enough in the Indian and global corporate bond markets for Aeon to venture into uncharted territory.

Beginning with the Patil Committee Report in 2005, the government of India has identified significant measures and necessary action plans to jump-start the Indian bond market which lags far behind the equity and derivatives markets in terms of market size, trading volume and liquidity. Unlike other nations, Indian corporates rely mainly on bank and equity financing for their funding needs. In June 2013, the Securities Exchange Board of India (SEBI) relaxed the rules for issuing corporate bonds in India. No longer is it necessary for companies to issue investment grade bonds; companies can now have their bonds rated by one agency instead of two; and restrictions on terms have been lifted for all practical purposes.

Even though Aeon has never sought a rating from the ratings agencies in India, Shekhar Gupta is confident that the bonds of Aeon will be rated as investment grade and that Aeon would be able to issue a five-year domestic bond at a fixed interest rate of 6.5 per cent.

It has been estimated that even after maintaining the current pay-out ratio on its expanded equity base after the acquisitions, the free cash flow for Aeon would amount to Rs 5.2 crores in 2018 and will grow by 5 per cent for the next five years.

In view of Aeon's predominant name recognition in global capital markets, Aeon could also be able to issue a US dollar-denominated floating rate five-year note in the Eurodollar bond markets. As part of the phased-in economic reforms that began in 1991, Indian corporates can now issue bonds in the international bond markets. Since 2013, several Indian companies have suc-cessfully issued bonds in the international bond markets. The interest on such bonds is often payable in US dollars and the current rates were hovering around LIBOR (London Interbank Offer Rate) plus 2 per centage points. With current LIBOR at 2.5 per cent, the resultant floating rate is preferable compared to the fixed 6.5 per cent domestic rate in India.

But Mr Gupta is aware of the risks involved in borrowing in Eurodollar mar-kets. The dollar has been lower this time around compared to other years and the sporadic increases in the dollar have not led to the typical capital outflows from Asian nations, as in previous years. Increases in the US interest rates traditionally are transmitted to the Asian capital markets via the exchange rate. Large-scale capital outflows occur first before interest rates in Asian economies rise in tandem. But this time the situation appears to be taking a different turn. Large-scale capital outflows do not seem likely and the increases in interest rates, even if they are transmitted to Asian economies, might not be preceded by large-scale capital outflows from Asian economies. So, even though the risk of rising global interest rates still persists for floating rate notes, the risk of having to incur large-scale losses in buying dollars to pay the interest on the bonds is minimal.

Mr Gupta is also aware that a third option might open up in the near future. Presently, the financial institutions in India are able to issue rupee-denominated bonds in the international bond markets. Labelled Masala bonds, these bonds entail slightly higher rates but are devoid of the exchange rate risks which invariably accompany dollar-denominated bonds. It is only a matter of time before Indian corporates begin following in the footsteps of Indian financial institutions.

Mr Shekhar Gupta sat back in his reclining swivel chair and wondered what additional information he needed to decide which path he should take.

Useful websites

Asset Finance Association of India www.assetfinanceindia.com/
Association of Indian Economic and Financial Studies (AIEFS) www.aiefs.org/
Finance India http://financeindia.org/
Financial Intermediaries Association of India www.fiai-india.org/
Indian Commerce Association www.icaindia.info
Indian Economic Association http://indianeconomicassociation.com/

Notes

1 See the May 2017 report from McKinsey & Company with regard to suggestions for transforming Indian banking. Available at: www.mckinsey.com
2 As of May 30, 2017, non-performing assets of public banks amounted to Rs. 6.46 Lakh crores comprising 11.6 per cent of aggregate loans (*Business World*, 30 May 2017).
3 Ratings agency Fitch has estimated that when the final phase of Basel III is in force, nearly half of India's banks may be in danger of breaching capital triggers.
4 Bank capital comprises Tier 1 and Tier 2 capital. Tier 1 capital includes share capital, share premium and other reserves. Tier II capital is supplementary capital. As per Basel norms, banks need to maintain Tier 1 capital of 7 per cent apart from a total capital of 9.625 per cent.
5 Details of the current regulation for entry into India can be found at http://investindia. gov.in/entry-and-investment-routes/
6 The Securities and Exchange Board of India was established on 12 April 1992 in accordance with the provisions of the Securities and Exchange Board of India Act, 1992.

It is now the primary regulatory agency dealing with securities laws, and listing of securities in India's major exchanges and foreign investments in India.

7 In this regard, India is following the lead of China by insisting on performance beyond veracity. In the United States, performance is not insisted upon by the Securities Exchange Commission as long as the prospectus is accurate and complete.

8 Indian government bonds are rated BBB-.

9 The Indian press has reported that Franklin Templeton Investments bought $1.2 billion of Indian government bonds in two days during March 2017.

10 It is interesting to note that the perpetual bonds of the State Bank of India (SBI) have been greatly in demand because the markets expect SBI to repurchase them as the SBI has too much cash after households deposited cash following the government's decision in November 2016 to demonetize high-value notes.

11 SEBI reported in April 2017 that trading in the secondary corporate bond market grew to Rs 14.7 lakh crore in the 2015–2016 financial year from just Rs 1.48 lakh crore in the 2008–2009 period.

12 Much of the rising demand for China's offshore Dim Sum bonds in Hong Kong followed the market expectation that the Renminbi will continue to rise. The demand fell when the People's Bank of China actively changed that expectation.

13 *The Asset*, 16 November 2017.

14 See http://tech.eu/features/190/

13

THE ACCOUNTING SYSTEM IN INDIA

Rajiv M. Srivastava and Vivek Shabi

Aims of this chapter are to:

- Discuss changes taking place in the Indian accounting standards
- Provide background information on Indian accounting systems
- Explain convergence of Indian accounting standards with global standards

Introduction

Since 1 April 2016, accounting practices in India have undergone a paradigm shift as Indian corporates now are required to adopt a new set of Indian Accounting Standards, called Ind AS, which are driven by the conventions and principles of the International Financial Reporting Standards (IFRS). All listed companies with a net worth of more than Rs 500 crore are required to report their financial statements as per Ind AS, along with a comparison of the corresponding period, and recasting as per the mentioned new accounting standards. Other companies would be required to adopt the same practice subsequently, as per the programme shown in Figure 13.1.

This is perhaps the most important milestone in accounting systems in India, indicating the willingness of the Indian government and business enterprises alike to converge to international practices in accounting. The convergence to global practices in accounting makes Indian corporates more competitive and acceptable in the world with high standards of corporate governance and transparency comparable to those of FORTUNE 500 companies.

This has become a necessity because, increasingly, Indian companies are mobilising capital from global markets, involving stakeholders of various nationalities. The worry is that the adoption of international accounting practices, as laid out in Ind AS, perhaps would make the loopholes in Indian accounting practices too wide and visible, and

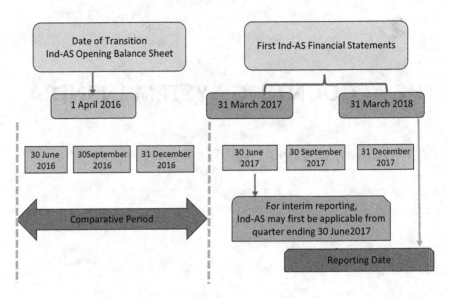

FIGURE 13.1 Migrating to international accounting practices

that would make others judge the Indian accounting practices and systems negatively. From the initial reports, however, it does not seem to be so, as evidenced from the outcome of some of the studies carried out by PwC and others (see case study below).

CASE STUDY: IND AS CUTS BOTH WAYS

At the end of the first quarter on 30 June 2016, a study by Pricewaterhouse-Coopers (PwC) comparing the performance with the corresponding quarter ended 30 June 2015 reported the following:

- 41 companies (55 per cent) reported an increase of income by Rs 3,918 crore equivalent to 5.2 per cent, while 45 per cent of the firms showed a decline in income of Rs 3,621 crore (4.8 per cent).
- Reduction in tax expenses by 0.7 per cent.
- 85 per cent of firms had an impact due to fair valuation of financial instruments, including derivatives. On account of financial instruments, the net income decreased by Rs 1,179 crore, while 52 per cent of firms reported a loss of about Rs 2,330 crore.
- 84 per cent of firms had an adjustment of revenue, with 44 per cent reporting an increase while 56 per cent reported a decrease. The overall revenue of these firm increased by 2.5 per cent.
- 67 per cent of firms had to make an adjustment to the retirement benefit obligations.

Source: *Indian Express*, 27 September 2016.

The adoption of Ind AS would predominantly influence accounting in the following areas: (1) revenue recognition; (2) accounting for financial instruments; (3) valuation of investments; (4) employee benefits; (5) translation of foreign currency-denominated assets and liabilities; and (6) consolidation of subsidiaries, joint ventures, and associates abroad, for both Indian corporates with a presence abroad and multinational corporations with business interests in India. Besides recording and presenting transactions according to internationally accepted practices, the disclosure requirement too would be extremely onerous.

The case study of Tech Mahindra highlights some of the areas that affect the financial reporting under Ind AS.

CASE STUDY: TRANSITION TO IFRS THROUGH IND AS: TECH MAHINDRA LIMITED

Tech Mahindra Limited, a large listed and respected software firm in India, published its results of the first quarter ended 30 June 2016. The company was required to adopt the Ind AS and recast the corresponding period performance as per Ind AS. The firm had a net profit after tax at Rs 67,607 lakhs in the period ended 30 June 2015, as per the earlier accounting standards. This was required to be recast according to Ind AS. The net profit after tax was reduced to Rs 52,488 lakhs and reconciled as shown in Table 13.1.

The case analysis of Tech Mahindra may make one think that earlier accounting standards permitted an overstatement of income and therefore higher valuations of firms in India. It must be borne in mind that the huge variation in profit under the two different sets of accounting standards, the earlier standards referred to as the Indian GAAP and the Ind AS, is a one-off exercise. The wide difference represents the cumulative effects on valuation and the resultant impact on profit or loss as at the date of transition. It is expected that levels of income, profit, and values of assets and liabilities would stabilise as per the new standards, and reduce the volatility that has been witnessed in the transition year.

History and background

Accounting is as old as civilisation and trade. The Indian civilisation is extremely old, as are those of Greece, Egypt, China, and the Romans. 'Arthshastra', written by Kautilya during the Chandragupta Maurya dynasty around 500 BCE, is perhaps the first recognisable reference to systematic accounting in India.

In modern times, the accounting environment in India is controlled by the Institute of Chartered Accountants of India (ICAI), established in July 1949 and which is modelled on the lines of the Institute of Chartered Accountants of

TABLE 13.1 Impact of convergence of Indian accounting practices as per IFRS through Ind AS

As per Indian GAAP	Rs in Lakhs	Reason for adjustment
Net profit	67759	
Of which owners	67607	
Non-controlling interest	152	
Adjustment required under Ind AS		
Stock compensation cost	-1051	Earlier valuation based on intrinsic value, and Ind AS requires valuation based on fair value using model, increasing the cost of compensation
Reversal of provision of non-current investment	-2435	Previous standards allowed reduction in value of investment in provisions. Ind AS permits valuation on fair value and hence no provision required.
Loss on fair valuation of investment in current investment (Mutual Fund)	-91	Earlier standard allowed valuation of investment based on lower of (1) cost and (2) net realisable value. Under Ind AS, these investments are measured at fair value.
Actuarial gain on defined benefits recognised in Other Comprehensive Income (OCI)	-260	Earlier standard did not mandate presentation of OCI separately. Under Ind AS, OCI is a separate head.
Currency translation reserve on foreign operations	-1244	Fixed assets for integral foreign operation were valued at historical cost but now are valued at closing rate and are now routed through OCI as per Ind AS
Adjustment of tax	-435	Due to undistributed earnings of subsidiaries
Impact of business combinations	10	
Others	-9	
Net profit as per Ind AS	62244	
Other Comprehensive Income	-9756	Includes amounts on (1) on account of measurement of long-term investment was on cost basis while Ind AS requires measurement of fair value, and through OCI affecting the carrying amount of investment; (2) reversal of provision; and (3) foreign currency translation
Total comprehensive income as per Ind AS	52488	
Of which owners	52453	
Non-controlling interest	35	

Source: Published results of Tech Mahindra Limited.

England and Wales, established in 1880, a pioneering body setting and influencing accounting practices around the world. These practices containing conventions, rules and procedures, commonly referred as Generally Accepted Accounting Principles (GAAP), were meant to present information to owners and to all those interested in the functioning of the enterprise. Naturally these practices are extremely diverse as they varied from region to region, and from time to time, so each country has its own GAAP: Indian GAAP in India, in Britain, it is the UK GAAP or in America, it is the US GAAP. The US GAAP is considered the oldest and most comprehensive.

Since independence in 1947 and until the early 1980s, corporate India practised a range of different policies for accounting and the preparation of financial statements – partly because of the non-existence of a mandatory set of accounting standards and partly due to laxity in the monitoring of financial reporting by the regulatory authorities. It was common to have divergent accounting practices for the same set of transactions. The divergent accounting practices resulted in ambiguity of comparability, and difficulty in benchmarking.

ICAI was the first accounting standard setter in India. It started releasing accounting standards which can be termed the Indian GAAP. The Indian GAAP comprised 32 Accounting Standards, numbered AS 1 to AS 32, relating to various aspects of measurement, treatment and disclosure of accounting transactions and events. Of these 32 accounting standards, AS 1 to AS 29 were mandatory in nature, while AS 30 to AS 32 remained voluntary for a long time.

International Financial Reporting Standards (IFRS)

In the globalised environment today and with the dominance of multinational corporations in business, it has become imperative to remove diverse accounting practices around the world and converge for a uniform understanding of business. Global sourcing of capital, the varied nationalities of shareholders and stakeholders, and the diverse economic environments where the businesses operate make presentation of accounts complex, divergent, and this can perhaps lead to misinterpretation. The IFRS, emerging as most widely acceptable global framework of accounting, are attempting to remove such discrepancies by developing consistent, transparent and comparable reporting standards of accounting. With the same objective, the International Accounting Standard Committee (IASC) was constituted in June 1973 and later was converted into the International Accounting Standard Board (IASB) in 1999. The aim was to develop a single set of high quality accounting standards to be effective from 1 April 2001. The first IFRS was published in June 2003.

Convergence to global standards

As mentioned earlier, accounting in India has evolved from diverse accounting practices to principle-based standards. Accounting standards are issued by the Institute of Chartered Accountants of India (ICAI) from time to time to achieve uniformity of practices. These standards sometimes clashed with other regulatory authorities. As India was a member country of the IASB, it was bound to adopt global standards. A few Indian companies that sought capital from international investors in the capital markets world-wide voluntarily presented their accounts not only under Indian GAAP but other standards as well, such as UK GAAP and US GAAP, for better credibility and ease of mobilisation of resources.

However, accounting practices and the standards of various nations are not consistent with each other, hindering comparability. They depart from IFRS, in considering the local economic environment and accounting practices. Since any changes in IFRS would have an impact on Indian companies, it would be hard for the companies to adopt IFRS, as and when amended. To bridge the gap, India developed a new set of standards called the Indian Accounting Standards (Ind AS for short), which are composed only of IFRS and are made applicable to Indian companies through a roadmap presented in Figure 13.1. The Ind AS is prescribed under Section 133 of the Indian Companies Act, 2013, as notified under the Companies (Indian Accounting Standard) Rules, 2015. India's set of Ind AS conforms so closely to the IFRS that the Ind As standards are numbered exactly the same as those of the corresponding IFRS. Each Ind AS has an Appendix to bring out the major differences, if any, between the Ind AS and its corresponding International Accounting Standard (IAS) or IFRS. It is a case of convergence rather than adoption of IFRS. The benefit of convergence is that if there is any subsequent change in IFRS (that too is evolving), it would not impact Ind AS directly. However, Ind AS can be modified according to changes in IFRS, if deemed fit and necessary. Having a set of its own accounting standards provides India with much-needed flexibility in following the international standards of accounting, as happened in the case of the deferment of the effective date of IFRS 15 to 1 January 2018.

The Indian government has implemented legislation that enables reporting as per the IFRS. The Ind AS marks a paradigm shift in the financial reporting scenario in India. It is expected to provide not just a much-needed comparability of financial statements between nations but also provide the globally accepted norms for companies to report to and approach the capital markets. Reforms in taxation are on the anvil with the Goods and Services Tax (GST) regime rolled out recently. Income Computation and Disclosure Standards (ICDS), another set of accounting standards, provide a framework for the computation of taxable income. These standards will be applicable from 1 April 2017.

All these regulations affect: (1) reported income; (2) reported profits; and (3) the financial position and net worth, as well as the quantum of disclosures warranting involvement of time and cost for additional data requirements and disclosure levels. The Ind AS take accounting in India to a higher level with greater transparency and a high quality of disclosures, and it is hoped that the requirement of various bodies and regulatory authorities for disclosure and the reporting of financial performance would be consistent with one another.

Convergence to IFRS: first-time adoption of Ind AS

Indian firms are required to adopt the Ind AS and achieve convergence with global standards of accounting, as per the schedule provided in Table 13.2. The exemptions available at the time of first adoption/transition to IFRS are not mentioned in the corresponding Ind AS, but instead a separate standard, Ind AS 101, First-Time Adoption of Indian Accounting, Standards, corresponding to its equivalent IFRS 1 relates to all provisions of transition to IFRS. There are certain exemptions provided at the time of making the transition from Indian GAAP to Ind AS for a smoother and quicker adoption but without sacrificing the sanctity of international accounting practices and standards. These are mentioned in Table 13.2.

The carve-outs

The reason that India decided on the convergence to international accounting standards and did not adopt them as they are, by prescribing its own set of accounting standards, is the recognition of the divergent economic and legal environments prevailing in India. Indian businesses are subject to many regulations. Though not at loggerheads with each other, they remain divergent and perhaps sometimes are inconsistent with one other. Indian businesses are subject to: (1) the

TABLE 13.2 First-time adoption of Ind AS conforming to IFRS

Item	As per Ind AS	As per IFRS
Basis of transition	Only the Indian GAAP can form the basis of transition to Ind AS	Any GAAP can form the basis of transition to IFRS
Carrying value of PPE, intangible assets and investment property	Carrying value of the PPE, intangible assets and investment property as per the previous Indian GAAP can be used as fair value	Carrying value cannot be used but instead fair value model needs to be applied since the date of acquisition of assets
Leases	Facts prevailing in the date of transition can be used to classify the lease as an operating or a financial lease. If any land lease is classified as a financial lease, then the difference in the fair values can be recognised in the retained earnings.	No such exemption is available in IFRS
Unrealised foreign exchange rate differences on long-term monetary assets and liabilities	Exchange rate differences arising out of translation of long-term monetary items can be recognised in equity. Any differences after the date of transition would have to be routed through profit and loss.	All differences arising out of translation of assets and liabilities due to foreign exchange rate need to be recognised only in profit or loss.

Indian Companies Act for shareholders; (2) the Income Tax Act for tax purposes; (3) the Securities Exchange Board of India (SEBI) regulations for investors; and (4) the RBI for foreign exchange transactions, etc. The divergences with IFRS are termed carve-outs as incorporated in Ind AS. Some of the important carve-outs are elaborated below.

Ind AS 1: Presentation of financial statements

IFRS allows a single statement, or a two-statement approach in the presentation of financial statements. In the single-statement form, all items are shown on the profit and loss account. In the two-statement approach, a separate income statement is made followed by a statement of Other Comprehensive Income (OCI). The Ind AS provides for the presentation of all expenses in a single statement only in the profit and loss account.

Under IFRS, a separate statement showing changes in equity has to be prepared. Under Ind AS 1, changes in equity are to be shown in the balance sheet.

IFRS allows the classification of expenses by nature or by function while Ind AS allows only classification of expenses by nature. Function-wise classification would require the apportionment of expenses into different functions.

Ind AS 7: Statement of cash flow

IFRS allows an option to include interest paid or received and dividend received as part of the cash flow from the operating activities. The Ind AS does not permit this and instead interest and dividend received or paid are required to be shown as part of cash flow from investing activities and/or cash flow from financing activities.

Ind AS 21: Effect of changes in foreign exchange rates

IFRS specifies the recognition of exchange rate differences arising out of the translation of foreign currency-denominated assets and the liabilities must be routed through the profit and loss account/Other Comprehensive Income (OCI). Ind AS 21 permits exchange rate differences on certain long-term monetary items to be routed through directly into equity. Such accumulated exchange rate differences can be amortised in the profit and loss account. The reasons for doing so in India are: (1) entities may have large foreign currency borrowings; (2) that are of a long-term nature; (3) hedging may not be possible in the long term; (4) entities do not have the option of prepaying the amount borrowed; and (5) the Indian currency (the rupee) is a non-convertible currency.

Ind AS 28: Investment in associates

The IFRS require that the difference in the reporting period of the entity and its associates should not exceed three months. Ind AS 28 has provided an exception by adding a phrase 'unless impracticable to do so', implying that it may not be possible for an entity to have control over its associates, so as to enforce the change its reporting period. It merely receives interest from the associate but not control. Further, if an associate had received interest from partners with different reporting periods, it might not be possible to adhere to the common reporting period with each interested party insisting on its own reporting date.

Similarly, the IFRS require that while applying the equity method of accounting in associates, uniform accounting policies must be used, and if they are different, then the entity must recast the accounts, using uniform accounting policies. Ind AS 28 again has provided a carve-out 'unless impracticable to do so', recognising that although the entity has a significant influence, it does not enjoy control over the associates, so as to force the changes in their accounting policies to make them conform to those of the entity.

Ind AS 39: Financial instruments: recognition and measurement

Any changes in the fair value of liabilities initially designated as Fair Value through Other Comprehensive Income (FVTOCI) must be routed through OCI. Ind AS 39 agrees with the initial recognition and subsequent measurement with the exception that if changes in fair value are due to changes in the credit rating of the entity itself, this must be ignored. The reason for such an exception is that any loss in the fair value of the liability would increase the Other Comprehensive Income while a deterioration in credit rating perhaps would happen because of the entity making a loss. This would inflate profits.

IFRS and Ind AS: a comparison

A list of major differences between the IFRS and the Ind AS, which are replicas of IFRS, is presented in Table 13.3. These do not include different guidelines that may be issued by different regulatory authorities from time to time and may come in conflict with the implementation of accounting standards.

Implications

A cursory look at Table 13.2 of the differences in the IFRS and the corresponding Ind AS would reveal that most aspects differ in the presentation of financial statements. Whether financial statements are drawn under the IFRS or under the Ind AS, the analytical aspects of profitability, liquidity, capital structure or valuation of firms remain almost the same. However, the transition from the existing Indian GAAP to Ind AS can be a painful exercise, whether for an Indian company or the Indian subsidiaries of multinational corporations. The major challenges in the transition from the Indian GAAP to the IFRS through the Ind AS remain in the areas of: (1) revenue recognition; (2) valuation of financial assets and liabilities; (3) hedge accounting; (4) translation of foreign currency-denominated transactions; (5) disclosure requirements; and (6) the consolidation of accounts. It would be far easier for

TABLE 13.3 Differences between the IFRS and Ind AS

Item	IFRS	Ind AS
Presentation of financial statements		
Breach of a long-term loan agreement: classification of current and non-current	When a breach of a long-term loan agreement results in liability payable on demand, such loans must be classified as current and not as non-current	When a breach of a long-term loan agreement results in liability payable on demand, and if the lender becomes agreeable not to demand payment before approval of accounts, such loans can continue to be classified as non-current
Breach of a long-term loan agreement, events after reporting period	The event of breach of long-term loan agreement cannot be classified as adjusting event	Action of lender is termed as an adjusting event
Income statement, or statement of Other Comprehensive Income (OCI)	An analysis of expenses is presented using the classification based on either the nature of the expense or their function. If classified by function, the nature of the expenses is provided in the notes.	The only admissible classification is based on the nature of expenses. Classification based on the function is not permitted.
	All items of income and expenses can be presented either in a single statement or in two separate statements – one for items of profit and loss and the other for items of OCI	Only a single statement is permitted, including all items of profit and loss and OCI
	Periodicity of 52 weeks is allowed	Only annual statements are allowed
Excise duty		Excise duty that forms the part of revenue to be shown separately
Inventory	Can be classified based on function	Only classification based on nature allowed
Cash flow statement	Interest/dividend paid/received may be classified as cash flow from operating activities	For non-finance companies, interest and dividend received are classified as cash flow from investing activities, and interest and dividend paid as cash from financing activities. These cannot be a part of the cash flow from operating activities.
Revenue recognition		
Revenue recognition		Where a penalty is inherent in the determination of price ,it would be part of a variable consideration
Related party disclosures		
Definition of related party	Related parties do not include parents and siblings	Related parties include parents and siblings and transactions entered with them need to be disclosed

Item	IFRS	Ind AS
Transactions to be included	Management contracts are not required to be disclosed for related parties	Management contracts, including deputation of employees, are covered in related parties disclosures
	Minimum disclosures are required in respect of government-related parties	Disclosures that conflict with the confidentiality requirements are not required to be made
Leases		
Leases (leasehold land)	Recognised as operating or finance lease as per definitions. Land has an indefinite economic life. An interest in an operating lease may be classified as investment property, accounted for as a financial lease and measured with fair value model.	Property interest in operating lease cannot be measured using the fair value model
Operating lease rentals	Recognised as expense on straight line basis over lease term	A carve-out is made to allow for the escalation of the operating lease rental in line with inflation
Employee benefits		
Post-employment employee benefits – discount rate	Post-employment benefit obligations are discounted using the market yield prevailing in high quality corporate bonds, and in countries where the markets for corporate bonds are not deep enough, yield on government bonds may be used as the discount rate	Post-employment benefit obligations are discounted using the market yield prevailing in the government bonds market. Subsidiaries, joint ventures, associates outside India can use yields in the high quality corporate bonds.
Government grants		
Non-monetary grants	May be recognised at fair value or nominal value	To be recognised only at fair value
Grant-related assets	Can be presented as setting grants as deferred income or by deducting the amount of grant from the carrying value of the asset	Are presented only by setting grants as deferred income
Translation of foreign currency-denominated items		
Effect of changes in foreign exchange rates	Exchange rate differences on translation of monetary items to be recognised in profit and loss account or in OCI if it relates to net investment in the foreign operation, and is reclassified from to profit and loss upon disposal	In respect of the translation of long-term monetary items recognised as part of capital assets
Investment in associates		
Differences in fair value	Excess of investor's share of net fair value of associates over cost of investment is shown as income	Excess of investor's share of net fair value of associates over cost of investment is recognised directly in equity as capital reserve

Item	IFRS	Ind AS
Accounting policies	Uniform accounting policies must be followed	Uniform accounting policies must be followed, unless impracticable to do so
Reporting date	The difference between the reporting dates of the associate and investor should be no more than three months	The difference between the reporting dates of the associate and investor should be no more than three months, unless impracticable to do so
Separate financial statements	Either at cost or using equity method	Equity method of accounting not permitted in separate financial statements
Financial instruments		
Conversion in FCCBs	Conversion embedded in FCCBs is treated as embedded derivative and hence to be measured at fair value at each reporting date	Conversion option to acquire fixed number of shares at fixed amount is treated as equity and hence need not be re-measured at fair value at each reporting date
Earnings per share (EPS)		
Disclosure of EPS	EPS is required to be disclosed only in consolidated financial statements and it is voluntary to disclose EPS in separate financial statements	EPS must be presented both in consolidated and separate financial statements
Items of expenses		Where an item of income or expense required to be disclosed in profit or loss is routed through reserves, it must be adjusted to reflect in computing EPS
Investment property		
Measurement	Initially, investment property is measured at cost including the transaction cost	Investment property is measured at cost and use of fair value model is not permitted. Fair value, however, needs to be disclosed.
Changes in value	Subsequently they are measured at cost or fair value with changes in fair value recognised in the profit of loss	
Business combinations		
Measurement method	Use of purchase method is permitted while pooling of interest method is not permitted	Entities under common control must be accounted for using the pooling of interest method
Changes in value	Gain on bargain purchase to be routed through profit and loss	Gain on bargain purchase can be recognised in capital reserve under equity

multinational corporations to adjust to these changes because they already have systems and procedures in place in their homelands.

CASE STUDY: SATYAM COMPUTERS FRAUD

The Satyam example of fraud is an interesting one as it falls under the category of a 'creative-accounting' scandal, which brought to light the importance of ethics and corporate governance. Nevertheless, it confirms that the conduct of the owners was swayed in large by human greed, ambition, and hunger for power, money, fame and glory. Unlike other global frauds, Satyam was brought to its knees due to the 'tunnelling' effect. The Satyam scandal highlights the importance of securities laws and corporate governance in India. It forced the government of India to tighten the corporate governance norms to prevent the recurrence of similar frauds. The key messages from the case are along the themes of major flaws in financial reporting, what lessons can be learnt and what strategies should be adopted to reduce the chance of such incidents in future reoccurring in future.

(Adapted from: http://file.scirp.org/Html/2-2670015_30220.htm)

Useful websites

Indian Accounting www.indianaccounting.in/
Indian Accounting Association http://indianaccounting.org/
Indian Accounting Association Research Foundation www.iaarf.in/
Indian Commerce Association www.icaindia.info/

14

MANAGING THE CHALLENGES OF PROJECT MANAGEMENT

A case study of the oil industry

Prasanta Kumar Dey, Debashree De and Vivek Soni

Aims of this chapter are to:

- Explain risk analysis
- Detail project planning covering scope, schedule, budget, quality, human resources, procurement, communication, and risk
- Present the relationship management across the supply chain
- State the advantages of keeping the project plan flexible
- Present how to integrate the decisions at the strategic, tactical and operational levels in both the project implementation and operation stages
- Show why the dynamic evaluation of projects is an absolute necessity

Introduction

The success parameters for any project are time completion, within a specific budget and with the requisite performance. The main barriers to their achievement are the changes in the project environment which include customers' demand, political scenarios, technological developments, and suppliers' businesses. The problem multiplies with the size of the project as uncertainty of the outcome increases with the size of the project. For example, large-scale construction projects are exposed to an uncertain environment because of such factors as planning and design complexity, the presence of various interest groups (project owner, owner's project group, consultants, contractors, vendors, etc.), resources (materials, equipment, funds, etc.), availability, climatic environment, the economic and political environment and statutory regulations. Although risk and uncertainty affect all projects, size can be a major cause of risk. Other risk factors include the complexity of the project, the speed of its construction, the location of the project, and its degree of unfamiliarity. Projects are risky as they are planned with many assumptions.

In the above context, industrial projects in India are characterized by technical complexity, and the environmentally and socially sensitive, capital-intensive, involvement of many stakeholders (clients, consultants, contractors, suppliers, etc.). Therefore, achievement of projects on time and within budget is never assured. There are many instances of project failure due to time, cost and quality non-achievement. Projects are complex to implement with respect to lack of experience in relation to certain design conditions being exceeded (water depth, ground condition, pipeline size, etc.), the influence of external factors that are beyond human control, external causes which limit the resource availability (of techniques and technology), various environmental impacts, government laws and regulations, and changes in the economic and political environment. Both factors of cost and time overrun and the unsatisfactory quality of a project are the general sources of disappointment to the management of organizations. In such circumstances, a conventional approach to project management is not sufficient, because it does not do the following:

- enable the project management team to establish an adequate relationship among all the phases of a project;
- forecast the completion of the project and build confidence in the project team;
- make decisions objectively with the help of an available database;
- provide adequate information for effective project management;
- establish close co-operation among the project team members.

In the literature, project failures have been looked at from the government (Damoah and Akwei, 2017) and the engineering sector perspectives. The reason for failure has been investigated from the project and stakeholders' perspective (Sutterfield et al., 2006). The strategies are designed to avoid failure, maximize success (Kealey et al., 2006) and suggest some solution to the project management failures. Projects in India suffer from an accurate prediction of demand that calls for an increase in facilities soon after the project completion. Such challenges include design optimization with the consideration of all technical, economic, as well as environmental factors throughout the project life, poor performance of contractors, suppliers, or lack of management ability of client and consultants. The foreign investment projects in India suffer from an additional complexity as along with the project variables, as stated above, cultural differences also play a major role. These projects also suffer from issues related to supply chain integration, relationship management, project planning, dealing with economic and political challenges, environmental regulations, and social needs. Of critical concern in Indian project management are the following: inaccurate assessment of project risks, lack of management to manage projects' complexity, inability to correctly estimate and monitor the ineffective use of best practices and benchmark difficulty to involve multiple and diverse stakeholders, and an inability to synchronize project plan and its evaluation. Therefore, in the Indian oil and gas sector, it is imperative to implement an effective project management method to optimize investment in the project, specifically those which are foreign-funded. Therefore, the main aim of this chapter is to analyse the project management maturity of an organization in the Indian oil industry and suggest improvements, and also to depict issues in and challenges of managing projects in India and the means of achieving success. The second section describes the methodology, while the next section demonstrates reasons for project failure, as reported in the literature. Some examples of issues and challenges of project management of the organization under study are given and a root cause analysis of non-achievement is provided. The project management maturity of the organization under study is then discussed, while the penultimate section suggests improvement measures and, finally, the dos and don'ts of managing projects in India are presented.

Methodology

This analysis is based on a critical review of the literature on reasons for project failure in general, along with the risk factors essential to achieve project success in the Indian oil industry in particular. An organization in the Indian oil industry has been identified to highlight project management maturity. Further, a few examples have been captured from the organization under study on project failure, using informal discussions with the relevant staff, followed by root cause analysis. Subsequently, a questionnaire survey quantitatively captures the perceptions of the project executives of the organization under study. Moreover, a review of project documents and informal interviews with the project executives validate the findings from this exercise. Finally, a benchmarking exercise determines the relative project management performance of the participating organizations, which identifies the improvement measures and their priorities for the organization under study.

The organization under study

Born from the vision of achieving self-reliance in oil refining and marketing for the nation, the organization under study has gathered a luminous legacy of more than 100 years of accumulated experiences in all areas of petroleum refining from 1901. At present, it controls 10 of India's 20 refineries, with a total refining capacity of 60.2 million metric tons per annum (MMTPA) or 1.2 million barrels per day, the largest share among refining companies in India. It accounts for a 33.8 per cent share of the national refining capacity. It operates more than 10,000 km of pipeline network (69.60 MMTPA) across the country. It has one of the largest petroleum marketing and distribution networks in Asia, with over 34,000 marketing touch points. Its world-class R&D Centre, established in 1972, has state-of-the-art facilities and has delivered pioneering results in lubricants technology, refining processes, pipeline transportation, bio-fuels and fuel-efficient appliances.

Reasons for project failure

Both academics and industry-based practitioners have extensively researched the reasons for project failure. They have discovered many risk events that might have a negative impact on projects (e.g., Belout and Gauvreau, 2004; Dey et al. 2009, Dey, 2010; 2012; Dey et al. 2013). There are instances of project failure due to operational risks, such as technical complexities, contractors' and suppliers' inabilities, government red tape, etc., which remain unidentified till they occur. Dey et al. (1994) reported cost and time overruns respectively due to implementation issues of cross-country oil pipelines in India.

Empirical studies covering 20 countries across the five continents by Flyvbjerg, Holm and Buhl (2004) have shown that infrastructure projects often suffer from cost problems. Ogunlana et al. (1996) reported costs overrun in high-rise building projects in Thailand due to the contractor's failure. Social and environmental issues caused prolonged postponement of the Chad-Cameroon oil pipelines (Ndumbe, 2002). Several projects in the oil industry in Vietnam were delayed as they had to wait for government approval (Thuyet et al., 2007). A thorough review of such research reveals a few generic risk events. These are valid for the Indian context as well as for foreign companies investing in India. Table 14.1 shows the risk events across phases (planning, implementation and evaluation) and risk categories (project management processes, organizational transformation, and technology management).

The occurrence of any one of the above events may cause the failure of a project to achieve time, cost and quality targets. The following examples show reasons for project failure in the Indian oil industry.

Project management challenges and issues: the Indian oil industry

The following incidents demonstrate the project management problems experienced by the oil pipeline operators of the organization under study while managing oil refinery and related construction projects.

Laying a pipe across a river

In 1995, a 60-km-long pipeline (with diameter 12 inches) was planned to replace the mode of transporting crude oil and petroleum products via vessels in the eastern part of India. The project duration was 18 months. The project consisted of laying pipe across the River Ganges (river width was 2 km at the point of crossing) along with other work packages (laying mainline pipes, station construction, cathodic protection, and telecommunications). The river crossing work package was planned to be executed by a turnkey contractor to be selected through the global tendering method. As the owner had previous experience of laying a pipe across rivers/canals (width max. 1 km) using Horizontal Direction Drilling through turnkey contractors, no study was made either during the feasibility analysis or during the planning phase to check whether laying a pipe across a river of 2 km width is technically feasible or not for some experienced turnkey contractors. From previous experience, the bid document was prepared to engage a turnkey contractor to lay the pipe across the river and floated to receive offers globally. However, no offer was received within the due dates and subsequent checking on the prospective contractors revealed that they did not have experience in laying pipe across a river of 2 km width. The case was referred to a

TABLE 14.1 Risk events in project management

Project phases	Risk categories		
	Project management processes	Organizational transformation	Technology management
Planning	Inaccurate business case Unclear objectives Weak implementation team Inappropriate supplier, contractor and consultant selection	Lack of management/ executive commitment and leadership Lack of synergy between technology strategy and organizational competitive strategy Unclear change strategy	Inappropriate technology selection Sub-optimal design Lack of communication with the end users Inadequate training plan for the users
Implementation	Inappropriate management of scope Lack of communication between implementation team, designers, supplier, contractor and consultant Poor contract management Not meeting statutory requirements (e.g., environment and safety, etc.)	Inappropriate change management Inappropriate management of culture and structure	Business process reengineering incompetence for use of new technology Inappropriate system integration Inaccurate performance data Inappropriate users' training
Hand-over, evaluation and operations	Inappropriate contract close-out Inappropriate disbanding of team Lack of knowledge management	Inadequate organizational readiness Resistance to change Lack of user training	Inappropriate system testing and commissioning Lack of clarity on inspection and maintenance Inaccurate performance measurement and management framework

global consultant to identify a suitable contractor for the project. They reported that there were only two contractors with experience of laying a pipe across river of 1.8 km width. They recommended selecting one of them and checked with them the applicability of using their technology to lay the pipe across a 2-km-wide river. However, they cautioned that the owner had to take the risk of failure. Alternately, they suggested constructing a bridge across the river and laying the pipe along the piers of the bridge. This option was not acceptable to the owner, as constructing a bridge across the river did not come under the scope of their business and would involve huge extra expenditure. The owner decided to abandon the project in its current form and decided to look into alternative techno-economically feasible solutions. The project had been commissioned in 1999 to lay a branch pipeline from an existing pipeline, by suitably augmenting the capacity of the existing pipeline through a river crossing upstream, where the river width was within the limits of the available contractors who had experience of laying a pipe across river.

The above issues highlight the pitfalls of the project management practices of the organization understudy. The technical feasibility analysis was poor as the implementation methodology selection and procurement plans were not developed by a thorough analysis. They were mainly experience-based. Project management practices are more reactive than proactive as crisis management approach was adopted in order to resolve the issues.

Delayed delivery of vertical turbine pumps

Another example includes that of an oil refinery project in central India, which was commissioned in 2002, with substantial time overrun because of delayed delivery of a few vertical turbine pumps by a supplier in the Indian public sector. The bid for supplying the pumping units was awarded to them on a competitive basis, considering their past performance, including the delivery schedule. Although the financial performance of the company had been deteriorating in the past few years, this was ignored when evaluating their offer. During the manufacturing of the referred order, the management of the supplier decided to reduce the production capacity so as to minimize losses. This caused the disruption of the delivery schedule of all of their orders, including the vertical turbine pumps under consideration. However, the project owner could not anticipate the delayed delivery until the due date was reached, as they did not establish many follow-ups with the supplier. Later, they improved the follow-up with the supplier and took delivery of the pumping units five months after the scheduled delivery. This caused the overall delay in completing the project by more than a year.

This shows that procurement management is one of the important issues of managing projects in India. The organization under study lacks procurement planning for all project materials and implementation activities. A strong synergy between design and detailed engineering and procurement planning needs to be adopted in order to strengthen project management practices. The above examples show clear evidence of a lack of appropriate project management practices of the organization under study.

The root causes of project non-achievement

The root causes for project failure of the organization were analysed with the involvement of a few relevant project executives through informal discussions, which revealed that project non-achievement in the Indian oil industry is mainly due to two reasons: sub-optimal design and poor project management. Inappropriate site selection, poor technology selection and implementation methodology selection are the evidence of sub-optimal design. Improper project planning (scoping, scheduling, budgeting and specification), inefficient project organization, and ineffective supply chain management are the evidence of poor project management. The broader picture of root causes for project failure are depicted in Figure 14.1.

The logical framework for reduction in project failure

The reviewed literature indicates that there is great scope for improvement in the reduction of project failure in the Indian oil industry. A logical framework can be used to understand an issue by using the hierarchical approach. One hierarchy turns to be the objective for the next hierarchy calculation of the solution in the Quality Deployment Function (Baccarini, 1999). A logical framework has been developed in Table 14.2 to reduce project failures. The purpose, output and activities are derived from the critical literature review. A detailed demonstration of the logical framework is available in Buttigieg et al. (2016).

Project management maturity of the organization

Project management maturity of the organization under study was carried out using the protocol, as shown in Figure 14.2. The project management maturity self-assessment questionnaire (Grant and Pennypacker, 2006) was used in Stage 1. The questionnaire is based on the Project Management Institute's (PMI) nine Project Management Knowledge areas (PMI, 2004).

The aim of this study is to analyse the project management maturity of the organization under study and to provide recommendations in order to achieve 'World Class Capital Project Delivery'. The below overview depicts the following:

- Feedback on the Project Management Maturity Questionnaire from Stage 1.
- Feedback on the follow-up interviews and documentary analysis conducted in Stage 2.
- New practices and knowledge transfer opportunities identified by Stage 3.

Stage 1 Quantitative analysis

The self-assessment questionnaire contains nine subject areas and an 'overview', with each subject area containing multiple questions. Each question is rated from Level 1 (lowest rating) through to Level 5 (highest rating). The nine subject areas consisted of:

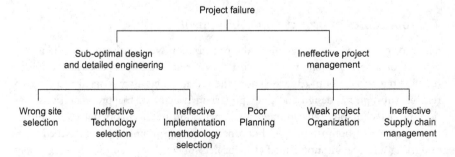

FIGURE 14.1 Root causes for project failure

TABLE 14.2 Logical framework to reduce the incidence of project failure

	Verifiable indicators	*Means of verification*	*Important assumptions*
Goal	Reduction in project failure	Time, budget, risk	
Purpose	Sub-optimal design and detailed engineering Ineffective project management	Project failure due to design and engineering decisions Issues in project due to project management efficiency	Delay in project delivery, increase in project cause and risk failure in a project
Outputs	Wrong site selection Ineffective technology selection Ineffective implementation methodology section Poor planning Weak project organization Ineffective supply chain management	Site chosen is infeasible for the project Technology is not compatible with the project requirements Issues occurring due to problems in implementation strategies Project faces challenges in planning and execution Issues in project scope, cost and time Issues due to lack of coordination between supplier and organization	
Activities	Ability to make current decision on site selection	Get the key decision-makers on search parameters, ensure the necessities of the requirement are relevant to the sites	There is scope for improve- ment and a similarity between projects
	Ability to make technol- ogy selection	Deciding the compatibility of the technology with the project	
	Project integration management	Continuous improvement of pro- ject management process, custo- mizing projects	
	Project risk management Poor communication management	Developing an integrated risk management framework, training the project personnel to practise it Developing an integrated planning, monitoring and controlling framework	
	Project human resource management Project time management Project cost management Project quality management	Developing project governance structure for each project with clear roles or responsibilities for each stakeholder. Objective selection of project people and assigning them responsibilities Customized project management with training Developing robust quality manage- ment plan for each project by link- ing material specification and activity specifications	
	Project procurement management	Developing procurement portfolio for each project	

Stage One

- Select stakeholder sample and send them a project management maturity self-assessment questionnaire

The questionnaire is based on the following models & takes max. 30 mins to complete:

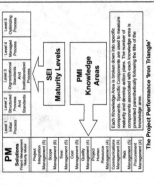

Stage Two

- Gather data on the match between different self-assessments & self-assessment and actual practice

Data gathered through:

- Interviews with a subset of stakeholders
- Collection of project management documentation
- Observation of project meetings

Typical interview questions:

- *Are differences in PM practice an issue?*
- *What knowledge areas are causing real problems in project perfomance?*

Researcher in the organisation for ~2 days

Stage Three

- Benchmark project management maturity with other organisations
- Identify where new project management practice could improve project performance

This stage is undertaken using data from all the Impact Assessments carried out by the CPMP, and a database of a further 120 cross-sectoral organisations who have used this tool.

Stage Four

- Feedback findings to the organisation
- Get the organisation's viewpoint on the effectiveness of the project maturity evaluation process

Deliverables to the Organisation

A report and a presentation benchmarking Project Management practice in the organisation and identifying how practice could be improved

FIGURE 14.2 Protocol for project management maturity

Source: Grant and Pennypacker (2006).

TABLE 14.3 Project management maturity level of the organization under study

Project management knowledge areas	Average maturity level	Prioritized problem areas
Project integration management	2.13	Absence of customized project management processes, change control
Project scope management	2.06	Change control
Project time management	1.97	Schedule control
Project cost management	1.53	Cost control
Project quality management	2.50	Suppliers' and contractors' quality improvement
Project human resource management	2.00	Organization planning and team development
Project communications management	1.88	Performance reporting and issues Tracking and management
Project risk management	1.63	All sub-areas need attention
Project procurement management	2.29	Selection of stakeholders on the basis of quality

- project integration management
- project scope management
- project time management
- project cost management
- project quality management
- project human resource management
- project communications management
- project risk management
- project procurement management.

Six senior staff were invited to participate in the self-assessment questionnaire from all functions of the business involved in capital project delivery. This was a sufficiently representative cross-section of the organization's business. The average maturity levels against each knowledge area are shown in Table 14.3.

Table 14.3 reveals that the organization under study has gross average maturity very close to the factor of 2. Project quality management and project procurement are relatively strong areas, whereas project cost management and project risk management are the weakest areas. Overall, the organization is lacking in managing project risks, controlling scope, time and cost, and organization planning and team development.

Stage 2: Interview outcomes

Two project executives were interviewed (semi-structured interviews) together to understand the project management maturity of the organization. The discussion was limited to the nine knowledge areas of the project management body of knowledge. Along with the discussion, various project management documents were reviewed. There was no major disagreement on the organization's project management practices or its maturity as revealed in the questionnaire survey. Both of them agreed on the following points with respect to each knowledge area:

Integration management

Although the organization under study has ISO 9000 certification, project management practices are experience-based. There are project plans (business case, activity network, budget, specification, design and drawings, etc.), but there are no customized documented project management processes for each strategic project. Project planning and implementation are managed through individual project management skills, using meetings and other communication methods.

Project changes are not formally documented if these do not have time and cost implications. Project changes that do have time and cost implications are hierarchically approved through the organization's governance. There is project management office (PMO), which is manned by experienced staff with functional (mechanical, electrical, civil, telecommunications, human resource management, finance and information) expertise. Each project forms a matrix organization to manage projects. Formal contract closings are done for all the projects. However, there is no formal project evaluation report covering lessons learned.

> *Key takeaway:* Develop a project management office and establish standardized project management practices across the various phases of a project. Customize the standard project management practices as per requirements.

Scope management

Project scope is developed from the business case with the involvement of the relevant stakeholders. There is no protocol for project scope change control. Currently, project review meetings address the issues of scope management. Anything beyond the control of the project manager goes to the organizational hierarchy to address. There is no formal procedure.

> *Key takeaway:* There should be a scope management plan in place, which will enable the project management team to make decisions on scope change quickly.

Time management

Project activities are based on project scope (work breakdown structure). An activity duration estimation is deterministic and mainly based on planners' past experience. Suppliers and contractors are also involved in many cases to provide valued information on activity duration. Therefore, development of an accurate project schedule is an issue. An activity network is developed using Microsoft Software project. However, the major challenge in time management is schedule control.

> *Key takeaway:* A realistic schedule development for every project activity is the key. Schedule implications of any scope change decision should be appropriately evaluated.

Cost management

The business case for specific projects indicates the resource requirements and forms the basis for the cost estimate. There is no cost database. Both past data and supplier budgetary quotations help develop the project cost estimate. The cost estimates are not linked to the activity network in the MS project. The project budget is controlled by the finance department and they produce a report on a regular basis. There is no earned value management practice in the organization. Cost control is one of the major issues in the organization's project management. Both time and cost management are directly related to scope management. An integrated approach to change management is absent in the current project management practice.

> *Key takeaway:* Appropriate contingency planning is vital for the project. Cost and schedule control along with scope management help achieve success.

Quality management

Specifications for every project are incorporated in the business case. Depending on the type of project, detailed specifications are developed by the relevant stakeholders (e.g., suppliers, designers, contractors, etc.) and approved by the project manager or appropriate competent authority in the organizational hierarchy. Inspections are carried out as planned either on-site or at the supplier's premises. However, there is no standardized process for managing project quality. Involving quality suppliers and contractors is the major issue as the contemporary approach to supplier and contractor selection is governed by least cost criteria.

> *Key takeaway:* Developing a quality plan for each project activity and material, selection of quality suppliers and contractors, and monitoring of quality/specifications of every project activity will help achieve the desired project quality and ultimate customer satisfaction.

Human resource management

There is no formal process for project organizational planning, forming a responsibility matrix and team development activities. However, a project-specific organization breakdown structure is developed. There is no formal project personnel selection and work package authorization process in place. Although the project personnel are technically/functionally qualified, they may not have project management experience. In many projects, basic project management skill gaps are quite visible.

> *Key takeaway:* Identifying the appropriate project manager and the right personnel, and fostering a project management culture across the project supply chain are critical to the organizational leadership in order to achieve success.

Communication management

Although there are a few report formats, mainly to monitor and control project progress, the communication between project stakeholders is mostly informal. Although information technology-based communication systems (MS project, MS Office, email, etc.) do exist, there is no formal protocol for inter- and intra-organization communication. The minutes of project review meetings work as authentic documents for project control.

> *Key takeaway:* Identifying appropriate project stakeholders, understanding their requirements from the project and making the right information available in time will not only help to make the right decisions on time, but also will keep those who are affected by delays in the project aware of the situation.

Risk management

A risk management culture exists within the organization. In fact, many projects are initiated to mitigate business and technical risks. However, there is no formal risk management practice (e.g., logging risks using a risk register, planning, monitoring and controlling risks) in managing projects. However, informal risk identification and analysis are carried out and suitable mitigating measures are suggested, mainly using past experience. The project management approach is more reactive than proactive.

> *Key takeaway:* As a foreign investment project is always risky, the overall project plan must consider the risks that are involved in the project. Identifying them at the early stages of the project, analysing their impact and developing responses to mitigate them are the key to success of many foreign projects.

Procurement management

Project procurement planning is undertaken in the early stage of a project along with activity planning. Normal tendering processes are adopted to engage suppliers and contractors. Major suppliers and contractors are selected on the basis of their technical attributes along with their price offer. There is no long-term relationship among the project stakeholders (suppliers and contractors).

> *Key takeaway:* Long-term partnerships, relationship development, selecting suppliers/contractors on the basis of total cost ownership will certainly be an added advantage to manage projects in India.

The stakeholder interviews have revealed that the overall project management maturity of the organization under study is medium to low. Although projects are planned/scheduled using leading project management software, monitored and controlled through a number of project review meetings throughout the project phase, they still lack effective project management approaches. The interviewees agreed that standardized project management processes with project-specific customization will help practise better project management throughout the organization.

Stage 3: Benchmarking

The project management practices of the organization under study were benchmarked against six other organizations in various industries (e.g., manufacturing, services, retail, etc.) across the world, and the results of the project maturity self-assessments of all the participating organizations are summarized in Figure 14.3.

Figure 14.3 shows the level of maturity of the project management practices of the organization under study in the nine project management knowledge areas compared to other participating organizations. This demonstrates that the

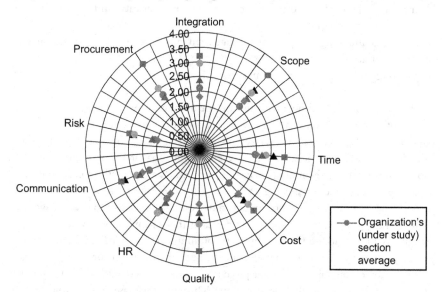

FIGURE 14.3 Comparative project management maturity levels

concerned organization has a low level of maturity in all nine areas compared to the participating organization. Therefore, there is room for improvement across all the project management knowledge areas.

Improvement measures

On the basis of the project management analysis (self-assessment questionnaire survey, focused interviews and benchmarking), the following recommendations are made. Table 14.4 shows the suggested improvement measures along with the relevant project management references for the best practices.

Conclusion

This chapter has focused on a selected Indian case study of an oil and gas project and presents a method to analyse the project management maturity of any organization using a triangulation approach. The case study aimed to capture real-life project experiences, using a questionnaire survey to statistically observe project management maturity, personal interviews and also the project document reviews to validate the maturity. The proposed method highlights five steps:

Step 1: Developing a study of issues and challenges of project management practices of the organization and analysing their root causes.
Step 2: Pursuing a questionnaire survey among the key executives of the organization under study, which is followed by statistical computation of their responses.
Step 3: Interviewing a few selected senior project executives informally in order to capture their perceptions on project management maturity and to validate the outcomes of the earlier step.
Step 4: Benchmarking the project management maturity of the organization with other organizations.
Step 5: Suggesting improvement measures.

The proposed method helps to measure the absolute project management performance of any organization and as well as benchmark its performance with other organizations. The chapter further reveals that the organization under study suffers from low project management maturity and argues that it needs improvement in project site selection, technology selection, implementation methodology selection, project planning, and organizing and managing project supply chain. The study recommends that the organization under study could improve its project management by fostering a project management culture across the organization, developing a project governance structure for each project, continuous improvement of standard project management processes, customizing project management processes for each strategic project, organizing relevant project management training, and managing the project portfolio across the organization. Through the case study, this analysis demonstrates issues and challenges of managing projects in India. It also suggests that

TABLE 14.4 Recommendation for improving project management practices

Knowledge areas	Problem areas	Recommendations	Relevant best practices theories
Project Integration Management	Absence of customized project management processes, Change control	Fostering project management culture across the organization, developing project governance structure for each project, continuous improvement of standard project management processes, customizing project management processes for each strategic project, organizing relevant project management training, managing project portfolio across the organization	Dey (2006); Ibbs, et al. (2001)
Project Scope Management	Change control	Practising customized project management through appropriate training	Ibbs et al. (2001)
Project Time Management	Schedule control	Practising customized project management through appropriate training	Ibbs et al. (2001)
Project Cost Management	Cost control	Practising customized project management through appropriate training	Ibbs et al. (2001)
Project Quality Management	Standardized processes for project quality management are absent	Developing a robust quality management plan for each project by linking material specifications and activity specifications	Winch et al. (1998)
Project Human Resource Management	Organization planning and team development	Developing a project governance structure for each project with clear roles and responsibility of each stakeholder, Objective selection of project people and assigning responsibilities	Belout and Gauvreau (2004)
Project Communications Management	Performance reporting and issues on tracking and management	Developing an integrated planning, monitoring and controlling framework with clear links with the concerned stakeholders	Charoenngam et al. (2004)
Project Risk Management	All sub-areas need attention	Developing an integrated project risk management framework, training the project personnel to practise it	Dey (2002)
Project Procurement Management	Supplier and contractor relationship management	Developing procurement portfolio for each project, establishing desired relationship with all the stakeholders	Vrijhoef and Koskela (2000)

organizations planning major projects in India should emphasize the following in order to be successful in implementing and operating major projects.

- A detailed project feasibility analysis covering the market, technical, financial, environmental and social needs to be carried out before making an investment decision. Moreover, the best project alternatives in terms of technology, the market, etc. should be analysed using multiple criteria, such as complexity, flexibility, adaptability, return on investment, cost, environment friendliness, and employability.
- A risk analysis should be carried out by identifying risk factors, analysing their effect (probability and impact) and developing risk responses in order to justify the investment.
- A detailed project planning, covering scope, schedule, budget, quality, human resources, procurement, communication, and risk, should be done before implementation. Project organizing and procurement must be emphasized in the overall planning. Appropriate leadership, project governance and communication among the project stakeholders need proper attention.
- Relationship management across the supply chain (upstream suppliers and downstream customers) could be the key to success not only during the implementation stage of the project but also in operations.
- Keeping the project plan flexible would be an added advantage to adopt the necessary changes in projects as they proceed. There should be a scope management plan in place.
- Integrating the decisions at the strategic, tactical and operational levels in both the project implementation and operation stages could help achieve the desired goals of the projects.
- Dynamic evaluation of projects is an absolute necessity to track the project progress and make quicker decisions in order to remain on time and within budget.

Useful websites

L & T Institute of Project Management www.lntipm.org/
Project Management Associates http://pma-india.org/

References

Baccarini, D. (1999) The logical framework method for defining project success. *Project Management Journal*, 30: 25–32.

Belout, A. and Gauvreau, C. (2004) Factors influencing project success: The impact of human resource management. *International Journal of Project Management*, 22(1): 1–11.

Buttigieg, S., Dey, P.K. and Rose, M. (2016) Combined quality function deployment and the logical framework analysis to improve quality of emergency care in Malta. *International Journal of Healthcare Quality Assurance*, 29(2): 123–140.

Charoenngam, C., Ogunlana, S.O., Ning-Fu, K. and Dey, P.K. (2004) Reengineering construction communication in distance management framework. *Business Process Management Journal*, 10(6): 645–672.

Damoah, I.S. and Akwei, C. (2017) Government project failure in Ghana: A multi-dimensional approach. *International Journal of Managing Projects in Business*, 10(1): 32–59.

Dey, P.K. (2002) Project risk management: A combined analytic hierarchy process and decision tree analysis approach. *Cost Engineering*, 44(3): 13–26.

Dey, P.K. (2006) Integrated approach to project selection using multiple attribute decision-making techniques. *International Journal of Production Economics*, 103: 90–103.

Dey, P.K. (2010) Project risk management using the analytic hierarchy process and risk map. *Applied Soft Computing*, 10: 990–1000.

Dey, P.K. (2012) Project risk management using multiple criteria decision-making technique and decision tree analysis: A case study of Indian oil refinery. *Production Planning and Control*, 23(12): 903–921.

Dey, P.K., Charoenngam, C., Ogunlana, S.O. and Kajornkiat, D. (2009) Multi-party risk management helps manage cement plant construction. *International Journal of Service Technology Management*, 11(4): 411–435.

Dey, P.K., Clegg, B.T. and Cheffi, W. (2013) Risk management in enterprise resource planning implementation: A new risk assessment framework. *Production Planning and Control*, 24(1): 1–14.

Dey, P.K., Tabucanon, M.T. and Ogunlana, S.O. (1994) Planning for project control through risk analysis: A case of petroleum pipeline laying project. *International Journal of Project Management*, 12(1): 23–33.

Flyvbjerg, B., Holm, M.K.S. and Buhl, S.L. (2004) What causes cost overrun in transport infrastructure projects? *Transport Reviews*, 24(1): 3–18.

Grant, R.R. and Pennypacker, J.S. (2006) Project management maturity: An assessment of project management capabilities across and between selected industries. *IEEE Transactions on Engineering Management*, 53(1): 59–68.

Ibbs, C.W., Wong, C.K. and Kwak, Y.H. (2001) Project change management system. *Journal of Management in Engineering*, 17(3): 159–165.

Kealey, D.J., Protheroe, D.R., MacDonald, D. and Vulpe, T. (2006) International projects: Some lessons on avoiding failure and maximizing success. *Performance Improvement*, 45(3): 38–46.

Ndumbe, J.A. (2002) The Chad-Cameroon oil pipeline: Hope for poverty reduction? *Mediterranean Quarterly*, 13(4): 74–87.

Ogunlana, S.O., Promkuntong, H. and Jearkjirn, V. (1996) Construction delays in a fast growing economy: Comparing Thailand with other economies. *International Journal of Project Management*, 14(1): 37–45.

PMI (Project Management Institute) (2004) *A Guide to Project Management: Body of Knowledge Guide*. Upper Darby, PA: PMI.

Sutterfield, J.S., Friday-Stroud, S.S. and Shivers-Blackwell, S.L. (2006) A case study of project and stakeholder management failures: Lessons learned. *Project Management Journal*, 37(5): 26–35.

Thuyet, N.V., Ogunlana, S.O. and Dey, P.K. (2007) Risk management in oil and gas construction projects in Vietnam. *International Journal of Energy Sector Management*, 1(2): 175–194.

Vrijhoef, R. and Koskela, L. (2000) The four roles of supply chain management in construction. *European Journal of Purchasing & Supply Management*, 6(3–4): 169–178.

Winch, G., Usmani, A. and Edkins, A. (1998) Towards total project quality: A gap analysis approach. *Construction Management and Economics*, 16(2): 193–207.

15

MANAGEMENT OF HR IN INDIA

Pawan S. Budhwar, Arup Varma, Indu Rao and Sudeshna Bhattacharya

Aims of this chapter are to:

- Describe dynamics of human resource management in India
- Present the factors influencing HRM in India
- Reveal the patterns of HRM in foreign firms operating in India

Introduction

The Indian Human Resources Management (HRM) function has a long tradition where a number of key milestones over the course of a century have been responsible for its growth and development. The first formal beginning can be attributed to a collective action in the 1920s when several groups expressed concern about the welfare of factory labour. This led to the Trade Union Act of 1926, which gave formal recognition to workers' unions. Consequently, through time, a number of labour and industrial laws were initiated, along with the unionisation of large nationalised sectors, such as the railways, coal, oil and gas, among others. This meant that the personnel managers within organisations performed industrial relations (IR) functions as a significant part of their role. The IR role of personnel managers formed such an important part of their work that they came to be known as children of the Industrial Disputes Act 1947 (IDA).

A few years after India's independence, two professional bodies emerged: the Indian Institute of Personnel Management (IIPM), and the National Institute of Labour Management (NILM). In the 1960s, the personnel function began to expand beyond the welfare aspect with three distinct areas of specialisation: labour welfare, industrial relations and personnel administration. In the 1970s, the thrust of the personnel function shifted towards greater organisational 'efficiency', and by the 1980s it began to shift focus to issues such as HRM and human resource development (HRD). The two professional bodies (i.e., the IIPM and the NILM) merged in 1980 to form the National Institute of Personnel Management (NIPM), based in Bombay. Table 15.1 provides a summary of the evolution of the personnel function in India.

After the liberalisation of economic policies in the early 1990s, Indian firms came under great pressure to change from indigenous, cheap and probably less effective technology to a high, more effective and costly technology. The challenge was to balance infrastructural issues of increasing productivity and reducing costs while generating employment, improving efficiency, and reducing voluntary and involuntary absenteeism at the individual level (Budhwar and Bhatnagar, 2009). As a result, from the early 1990s onwards, HRD in India became the most dominant topic in the broad area of personnel function (Saini and Budhwar, 2014).

This period saw an elevation in the status of personnel managers to the board level, though only in a few professionally managed organisations. The term HRD then began to denote the personnel function more than HRM in India in the late 1990s. It has been seen as a continuous process to ensure the planned development of employee competencies and capabilities, the motivation and exploitation of inner capabilities for an organisational development purposes, and the pursuit of dynamism and effectiveness. Further, there are indications of movement towards performance-related pay and promotions. Overall, it would be appropriate to say that the HR function in India is in a phase of rapid transition.

Determinants of HRM in India

An analysis of the existing literature reveals the existence of both 'culture-bound' (such as national culture and national institutions) and 'culture-free'

TABLE 15.1 The evolution of the Indian HR function

Period	Development status	Outlook	Emphasis	Status
1920s–1930s	Emerging	Pragmatism of capitalists	Statutory, welfare, paternalism	Clerical
1940s–1960s	Establishing	Technical legalistic	Introduction of techniques	Administrative
1970s–1980s	Impressing with sophistication	Professional, legalistic, impersonal	Regulatory conformance, imposition of standards on other functions	Managerial
1990s	Promising	Philosophical	Human development, productivity through people	Executive
2000–	Rationalisation and formalisation	Strategic and change agent	Organisational performance	Strategic and change partner

Source: Venkataratnam and Srivastava (1991); authors' own analysis.

(such as age, size and nature of the firm) determinants of HRM (e.g., Budhwar and Sparrow, 2002a). For the convenience of both researchers and practitioners, these can be classified into three levels: (1) the national factors (i.e., national culture, national institutions, business sectors and dynamic business environment); (2) the contingent variables (such as age, size, nature, ownership, lifecycle stage of the organisation, the presence of trade unions and HR strategies and interests of different stakeholders); and (3) organisational strategies (such as those proposed by organisation gurus, like Raymond Miles and Charles Snow, and Michael Porter) and policies (related to primary HR functions, internal labour markets, levels of strategic integration and devolvement of HRM, and the nature of work). It is beyond the scope of this chapter to provide empirical evidence regarding how the different factors and variables impact HRM systems in India. Given that the national-level factors tend to vary significantly for foreign investors and also are known to play a significant role in determining relevant HRM practices for a specific set-up, we will illustrate how different national factors influence HRM in the India.

National culture and HRM

Research (e.g., Budhwar and Sparrow, 2002b) shows that, on average, Indian HR managers give high priority to the importance of cultural assumptions that shape the way employees perceive and think about the organisation, as well as common Indian values, norms of behaviour and customs and the way in which managers are socialised in India. Indian managers believe that social relations play an important role in managing human resources. Indeed, managers' actions are often dictated by these values and norms of behaviour. To contextualise the findings in the Indian cultural environment, we draw upon Hofstede's (1991) five standardised dimensions (power distance, uncertainty avoidance, individualism/collectivism, masculinity/femininity and long-term/short-term orientation) as an illustration on how they impact Indian HRM.

India scores high on the power distance dimension and accordingly Indian HR managers tend to rely on the use of power in superior-subordinate relationships, and, thus, are not actively inclined towards consultative or participative styles. Indeed, such barriers are slowly being overcome in the new sectors like IT and business process outsourcing (BPO) (see Budhwar et al., 2009) – though managers are often observed misusing their power, due to different pressures (such as political, caste, and bureaucratic processes). They operate within a logic of 'power myopia', which has created a culture of sycophancy, inequality, apathy, triggered by a feudalistic outlook of employers and the strong backing of political parties by unions. One possible explanation for such behaviour can be traced to the long imperialist history of India and the traditional hierarchical social structure of India that has always emphasised respect for superiors – they can be elders, teachers or superiors at work.

The analysis of existing empirical evidence also reveals less importance is given to the dimension of uncertainty avoidance, indicating that, for Indians, uncertainty is inherent in life and they are well prepared to take each day as it comes. Such an attitude towards uncertainty is congruent with the living conditions in the country with high rates of poverty, unemployment, institutionalised corruption practices in government offices, political instability, the caste system, low per capita income, a country prone to natural and man-made disasters and an increasing gap between rich and poor. Accordingly, the personnel function places more emphasis on training and development and career development to reduce uncertainty in the workplace. The element of uncertainty forces Indian managers to take calculated risks, which means that people value job security and stability.

On the third cultural element of individualism-collectivism, traditionally, the Indian national culture shows a strong emphasis on collectivism. There is an increased emphasis on individualism at the managerial level and collectivism at the shop-floor level. The emphasis on collectivism for the lower level of employees is also dictated by the strong trade unions. A strong interference of social relations, caste and religion dynamics in the workplace is still observable in Indian organisations (Sparrow and Budhwar, 1997).

As per Hofstede's (1991) masculinity and femininity dimension, masculinity indicates the extent to which society within a country is driven by competition, achievement and success, while femininity refers to the societal values of caring for others and quality of life. India scores 56 on this dimension, implying a comparatively high masculinity score and this has implications for recruitment, pay and benefit packages, and promotions and career progression in general.

Traditionally, India has been a long-term-oriented country (ibid.). However, in the ever-increasing uncertain and competitive business environment, Indian HR managers feel that the question is that of immediate survival, hence it seems that there is now more emphasis on short-termism. This pattern of short-termism is particularly found in the turnover rates within the BPO sector, especially where employment is within the routine service roles such as customer services. Empirical studies by Sparrow and Budhwar (1997) report similar trends of short-term attitudes and behaviours within the emerging new forms of work and organisations in India. Accordingly, this is contributing to the development of performance-based systems and the gradual demise of life-long stable employment and tenure-based compensation, especially within the private sector.

National institutions and HRM

Regarding the influence of national institutions on HRM, Indian HR managers prioritise national labour laws, trade unions and the educational and vocational training set-up, when designing and executing HRM policies and practices. There is an underlying tension between the HR practitioner perception and the country's labour laws and unions. Indian labour laws have a strong focus on employee protection and enabling collective action. HR managers, particularly in modern corporations, find these laws archaic and ill equipped to handle the labour flexibility that they need to strategically adopt in their HR policies and practices.

Indian managers also feel that trade unions and the educational vocational training set-up of India are important influencers of their HRM policies and practices. The presence of the latter is helpful in increasing employees' efficiency, contributes to the process of up-dating their skills and facilitates better stress management.

The high priority attached to the influence of national labour laws on their HRM policies and practices is understandable as, at present, there are over 150 state and central laws in India which govern various aspects of HRM at the enterprise level. Unions still significantly influence HRM policies in India. In many places, they still have a conflictual nature, which is mainly due to the strong political support they have and the existence of pro-labour laws. A number of institutes, such as Indian Society for Training and Development, Management Associations (at both the local and national levels) and the HRD Academy are now well established. These and many similar bodies emphasise vocational training in India, especially to combat the pressures posed by foreign competition, which at the moment are working hard towards the regular upgrade of skills.

Dynamic business environment and HRM

An analysis of the existing empirical evidence highlights that, on average, Indian managers give a relatively high priority to customer satisfaction and increased competition/globalisation of business structure regarding their influence on HRM policies and practices. The managers also believe that their personnel function is under severe pressure to improve productivity by developing an efficient and responsible workforce. The emphasis is on the need for teamwork, enhanced training programmes, HRD, skills improvement and retraining of employees by providing technical skills. HR managers feel that the personnel should contribute more actively to the restructuring of the business, i.e., facilitating delayering, downsizing, decentralisation and cost reduction. The managers also feel that competitive pressures have resulted in enhanced levels of manpower planning to ensure that the right person is in the right place at the right time, and a need to attract and retain scarce-skilled labour and improve the efficiency and quality of their work. In the new economic environment, Indian managers perceive the aim of the Indian HRM function is to increase productivity, costs reduction and over-manning while generating employment, improvement in quality, and a reduction in voluntary and involuntary absenteeism.

Patterns of HRM in foreign firms operating in India

The information in this section is based on in-depth interviews in 103 multinational companies (MNCs) operating in India, one top HR specialist in each of these foreign firms was interviewed (see Budhwar, 2012). The views presented here are those of a minimum of 40 per cent of the interviewees.

HR department

Most of the top HR managers recruited to head the India operations are from within India (recruited from the Indian partner in the joint venture, from an Indian company, or from another Indian unit of the MNC). The HR managers are helping to establish the HR function, both as a 'business partner' and a 'change agent' in their Indian operations. Recruiting an Indian as the HR manager in India has a number of advantages, such as they have a better understanding of the local social, cultural, political and legal environment; they can be recruited for a relatively small compensation package in comparison to an expatriate; they know the ways of working in the local system; they can easily become part of relevant networks (not only related to HRM but also related to customers, suppliers, and distributors); and they can easily be moved between different units of the MNC (not only between joint ventures but also to wholly owned subsidiaries). Similarly, all the other HR people in the operations units are local.

Most MNCs in India have established HR departments and HR is represented at the board level and there are specialisation heads within the HR department such as for HRM, industrial relations (IR), administration and HRD. In the majority of firms, the HR department is actively involved in the strategic planning processes and it is viewed as a partner in the management of the business and as an agent of change by people outside the HR function. Further, most firms make an explicit effort to align business and HR strategies. Generally, someone in the position of vice president or director heads the HR department. He or she is followed by senior manager, manager, senior executives, executives and staff. Perhaps an important challenge to HR in foreign firms operating in India is to eliminate some hierarchies from their HR departments as this has been found to be affecting their efficiency. Moreover, there is also a need to further devolve routine HR activities to line managers, something which is not usual in the Indian context (Budhwar and Sparrow, 1997).

HR functions

Many firms in our sample have been successful in adopting the MNCs' global HR policies related to recruitment, employee development, performance appraisals and compensation of local employees, to a great extent with some local adjustments. For example, most MNCs are able to use global recruitment and selection policies with minor local adjustments. All the MNCs adopt a formal, structured and systematic approach to recruit new employees. Interestingly, this is not so in the case of many Indian national companies (especially in the private sector) which adopt an informal and unstructured approach to recruitment function (for details, see Sparrow and Budhwar, 1997). A number of methods have been adopted by MNCs to find new recruits, such as using consultants, employee referrals, via the net, campus interviews, and through advertisements. When it comes to adopting different criteria and methods to select new candidates, the global HR polices of the MNC are seriously considered. For example, at Motorola, 'skills as per Motorola specification', integrity, honesty and ethics are looked for in all candidates. A strong emphasis is also given to the attitude of the person, along with different skills, educational qualifications and the institute from which the candidate has graduated. Many MNCs conduct different general tests to evaluate the general ability, technical competency, behavioural competency, and aptitude of the candidates. Due to the existence of many educational institutions and the wide variation in the nature and quality of education standards, most MNCs deliberately look for graduates from the premier institutions to fill various positions. In the Indian context, where social relations are important, most MNCs use this to their advantage to attract good candidates via techniques like word of mouth and employee referrals and then by using structured and formal approaches to bring objectivity into the recruitment process.

All employee development is also clearly structured, formal in nature and most of the time linked to the performance system of the MNC (this is another strong deviation from local firms). The training programmes used in India are to a great extent a reflection of the global training set-up of the MNCs. For example, companies like Max New York Life Insurance, Honda, Motorola, GE, Siemens, Hyundai and Hughes Software Systems have established their own 'management training centres' in India, where the courses offered are similar to those offered in other parts of the world in their affiliates or HQs. Apart from in-house training facilities, external training consultants are also employed. A variety of area-specific training programmes are provided by MNCs in their Indian operations. These include both soft (such as behavioural, supervisory, management, leadership, communication, ethics, culture, team building) and hard skills (such as operational, technical, quality).

A formal and structured approach to a performance appraisal system is common in most MNCs operating in India. To a great extent, the majority of firms have introduced a periodic appraisal or assessment system, generally developed in their HQs, which forms part of their global policies concerning performance appraisal in India. The majority of firms have an annual appraisal system. Some firms have it on a six-monthly basis and some even on a quarterly basis tied to the yearly cycle. All the firms have a structured format and a clear set of parameters for appraisals. In many cases the appraisal starts with a self-appraisal, in which the individual writes about himself or herself and then he or she is appraised by an immediate supervisor. However, the general trend is that the immediate supervisor appraises the employee and gives their report to the person. They then read it and have to counter-sign before it is submitted to the section head. If required, the section head may make adjustments. A number of issues related to future moves, cross-function moves, training needs identification, key performance areas and possible targets are analysed. The above-discussed appraisal system, which is quite comprehensive, has some drawbacks. For example, in the present system, there is relatively low participation of individual employees regarding their goal setting (though some companies claim to be doing this). This reflects the hierarchical nature of Indian society.

Perhaps, a more participative approach could be beneficial (as experienced by some Japanese firms operating in India).

It seems that by far what is most different among the global HR policies is the compensation of local employees in the Indian units. The main reasons in this regard are the low labour costs and the availability of large number of skilled human resources in India. However, in comparison to Indian national companies, the compensation packages of MNCs are far more attractive. Many MNCs adopt a grading system to compensate their employees. Others, on top of this also practise performance-related compensation – a mixture of company and individual-based performance. Almost all the firms pay a bonus to their employees. A significant number of MNCs do not have a formal career planning system for their Indian operations. However, well-educated Indian employees expect a clear career progression and with the increasing level of competition both from national and international firms, it soon is expected to become an important tool to retain the best employees.

The problem of attrition

Attrition refers to the reduction in the number of employees, especially when attrition is caused by the resignation of new recruits it means a loss both of talent and the resources spent on training (Mehta et al., 2006). While there are a multitude of factors that can lead to this attrition, the particular factors of perceived growth and organisational culture emerge as salient. Interestingly, recent research on organisational socialisation (Cable et al., 2013) conducted in a call centre in India, found that socialisation tactics that encouraged authentic self-expression of newcomers' personal identities and signature strengths had the best organisational and employee outcomes.

However, unlike the suggestions made in the research that alludes to providing individuals within the organisation with more agency, the leadership/ management style found in Indian organisations is strongly tied to high power distance and authoritarian styles. Evidence supports this as Budhwar et al. (2006) found a tightly controlled structure, cost-efficient, bureaucratic and customer-oriented philosophy as the driving management motivation in modern Indian workplaces. Further, research found middle managers insufficiently trained to retain, motivate and keep employees happy within the workplace (Mehta et al., 2006). Given this evidence of poor organisational leadership and management practices, there is an urgent need to realign the traditional power distance orientations to a more democratic and open leadership/management style within the firm to recruit and retain talent. Practitioners need to pay close attention to the problems of rigidity, power and control endemic in the wider cultural context in India being mirrored within organisations, that deal more and more with younger millennials, who are challenging these socio-cultural norms.

Globalisation versus localisation

Despite clear differences in national, regional and organisational systems, most MNCs are able to adopt many global HR practices in Indian units with minor adjustments. Perhaps the key reason for this is the awareness of Indian employees about the ways of doing things in different parts of the world (due to their management training system). Still, the importance given to social networks can be a big hindrance in further reducing the gap. Many MNCs send their senior managers for training in the HQs, also working with expatriates in India is helping to minimise such gaps significantly. However, many global HR policies are being modified to fit Indian conditions. Many MNCs also localise recruitment practices as per the qualifications and the graduating institution.

Nevertheless, it is important to keep in mind that India is a large country with massive regional differences – cultural, economic and political. Accordingly, the employment conditions (such as the availability of labour, the cost of living, state taxes, etc.) vary significantly. Also, there are opportunities for MNCs to learn from and teach local partners in India. Further, a number of established HR-related networks do exist in India. These networks form part of many forums (such as the Delhi or Mumbai chapters of the HRD network), professional bodies, national and regional HRD networks, local and national management associations (such as the All India Management Association), the Confederation of Indian Industries (CII), and the Indian Society for Training and Development. Information related to different HR trends such as compensation, recruitment practices, retrenchment, work environment, new developments in the area, staff welfare, competition, etc. are shared via such networks.

Conclusion

Below are the main takeaways from the above analysis:

- The developments in Indian HRM have been significant, however, they vary between public, private, local/national-owned and foreign-owned firms and from traditional manufacturing to modern service-based sectors. Thus, it is possible to develop and successfully practise formal, rationalised and structured HRM systems in India.
- A combination of both national and organisational level factors and variables significantly influence HRM in India. HR managers need to have a good understanding of such determinants of HRM in order to develop relevant HRM policies and practices for the Indian context.
- The social, political, legal and economic context of India needs to be clearly understood in order to be successful there and avoid any detrimental effects.
- India has a long list of labour legislations, whose provisions in many cases are outdated and they lack clear implementation. Nevertheless, foreign firms are expected to fully adhere to such provisions.

- A number of HR-related professional bodies and networks exist in India. Membership of such bodies is useful when learning, networking and sharing best HR practices.
- It seems that with minor modifications, foreign firms are able to adopt their global HRM systems in India.
- Given the drastic variations in the skills inculcated in new graduates by different institutions; training needs to stay a priority in order to raise the level of Indian employees to the required standards and also to inculcate the philosophy of a given MNC.
- It is important to have a clear and authentic approach to organisational socialisation where the new entrant can explore how their skills and knowledge fit in with the organisation and what their progression within the firm will look like within a realistic timeline. Indian graduates are full of enthusiasm, energy and exciting ideas – the right kind of support and encouragement can help lead to the desired results.

CASE STUDY: HRM AT NAVSAR INDUSTRIES

Mr Seth was confused – he had expected that the various unit heads would be overjoyed at his new proposal, called 'Move and Groove'. Seth had recently come back to India after obtaining his MBA in HRM from one of the top business schools in the USA. His thesis was on the subject of 'job rotation' and he was keen to implement that in his new employment. Before going abroad for further studies, Seth had worked for almost eight years in India and had noted that most people stayed in the same job and the same department for years. He had concluded that people often get bored performing the same jobs, and want to try and learn new things. He was excited as he now had the opportunity to try out this theory.

However, when he put forward his proposal at the monthly divisional meeting, most attendees seemed disinterested and quite reluctant to discuss his proposal. He tried again at the next meeting and was met with the same response. He was also surprised that the department/divisional heads dominated the meetings, and that the rest of the officers and executives only spoke up when they were called upon.

During his stay and studies abroad, he had become convinced that job rotation was the way to go – that individuals would significantly enhance their skillsets through his programme, by learning additional skills, and this would lead to job satisfaction and increased levels of motivation. Indeed, he had seen this first-hand at his internship in one of the top diversified conglomerates. In addition to the benefits of job rotation, the one other thing that had really struck him during his MBA studies was that everyone should be treated equally, and that any new programme or initiative should be implemented across all departments and all levels.

On his return to India, he was looking to join a progressive organization that was willing to try out different things. He had heard about Navsar through his sister's friend, Miss Kohli, who worked at Navsar. She had told him about the progressive culture at Navsar and the fact that many of the top executives had studied in the USA, and that many of them had attended training in the USA, ever since Navsar had tied up with the leading US-based global manufacturer in their field. However, Seth was not so sure that he had made the right choice, and wondered if he had misunderstood what he had been told. He decided to approach Miss Kohli and ask her what he should do. Miss Kohli calmly told him not to try and rock the boat, and to take it slow. She further explained that while his ideas were clearly cutting-edge and represented the latest trends, he should recognise that people-related practices and policies do not transfer easily across cultures. Seth did respect Miss Kohli a lot, so he agreed to hold off on pushing his job rotation programme but decided to start looking for another job.

1. What was wrong with Seth's job rotation proposal? Why was it rejected by all the department and division heads at Navsar?
2. If Seth asked you to help him implement his proposal, what would you recommend to him?
3. What role does national culture play in transferring successful HR policies from one culture to another?

Useful websites

HR Association India http://hrd.online/
HR InfoTech http://hrinfotech.org/
HR Katha www.hrkatha.com/
HR Sangam https://hrsangam.in/
Indian Society for Training and Development www.istd.co.in/
National HRD Network www.nationalhrd.org/
National Institute of Personnel Management https://nipm.in/

References

Budhwar, P. (2012) Management of human resources in foreign firms operating in India: The role of HR in country-specific headquarters. *International Journal of Human Resource Management*, 23(12): 2514–2531.
Budhwar, P. and Bhatnagar, J. (2009) *The Changing Face of People Management in India.* London: Routledge.
Budhwar, P. and Sparrow, P. (1997) Evaluating levels of strategic integration and devolvement of human resource management in India. *The International Journal of Human Resource Management*, 8(4): 476–494.

Budhwar, P. and Sparrow, P. (2002a) An integrative framework for determining cross-national human resource management practices. *Human Resource Management Review*, 12(3): 377–403.

Budhwar, P. and Sparrow, P. (2002b) Strategic HRM through the cultural looking glass: Mapping cognitions of British and Indian HRM managers. *Organization Studies*, 23(4): 599–638.

Budhwar, P. and Sparrow, P. (1997) Evaluating levels of strategic integration and devolvement of human resource management in India. *The International Journal of Human Resource Management*, 8: 476–494. Budhwar, P., Varma, A., Malhotra, N. and Mukherjee, A. (2009) Insights into the Indian call centre industry: Can internal marketing help tackle high employee turnover? *Journal of Services Marketing*, 23(5): 351–362.

Budhwar, P., Varma, A. and Patel, C. (2016) Convergence-divergence of HRM in Asia: Context-specific analysis and future research agenda. *Human Resource Management Review*, 26: 311–326.

Budhwar, P., Varma, A., Singh, V. and Dhar, R. (2006) HRM systems of Indian call centres: An exploratory study. *The International Journal of Human Resource Management*, 17(5): 881–897.

Cable, D., Gino, F. and Staats, B. (2013) Breaking them in or revealing their best? Reframing socialization around newcomer self-expression. *Administrative Science Quarterly*, 58: 1–36.

Hofstede, G. (1991) *Culture's Consequences: Software of the Mind*. London: McGraw-Hill.

Mehta, A., Armenakis, A., Mehta, N. and Irani, F. (2006) Challenges and opportunities of business process outsourcing in India. *Journal of Labor Research*, 27(3): 323–338.

Saini, D. and Budhwar, P. (2014) Human resource management in India. In A. Varma and P. Budhwar (eds) *Managing Human Resources in Asia-Pacific*. London: Routledge, pp. 126–149.

Sparrow, P.R. and Budhwar, P. (1997) Competition and change: Mapping the Indian HRM recipe against world-wide patterns. *Journal of World Business*, 32(3): 224–242.

Venkataratnam, C.S. and Srivastava, B.K. (1991) *Personnel Management and Human Resources*. New Delhi: Tata McGraw-Hill Publishing Company Limited.

16

HRM PRACTICES IN THE INDIAN CONTEXT

A mixture of modern and traditional perspectives

Rajesh Chandwani and Upam Pushpak Makhecha

Aims of this chapter are to:

- Reveal why HRM practices in Indian context indicate a confluence of modern and traditional perspectives
- Present the modern perspective and the traditional perspective on HR management
- Explain the sources of confluence and how to leverage it in the design and implementation of HRM systems

Introduction

As one of the fastest-growing economies in the world, India is positioned to become the fourth largest economy by 2020. With economic liberalization post 1991, and major foreign operators entering the Indian market, HRM in India has rapidly evolved into a specialized function (Budhwar, 2009). However, there is a *critical scarcity of empirical research that could help researchers, practitioners, and policy-makers understand the emerging patterns of HRM in the new Indian economy* (Budhwar and Varma, 2010: 345). In this chapter we partially address this gap by exploring what determines the success of HRM practices in the Indian context. In our view, the overarching answer lies in the appropriate confluence of traditional and modern HRM practices in Indian context. Through an analysis of case studies and interviews with managers across organizations in India, we explain the sources of traditional and modern HRM practices and how their confluence makes Indian HRM practices unique and successful. We consider the modern western perspective as derived from organizational theories developed largely in a western context and the traditional perspective as rooted in local contextual and cultural factors. Our analysis of cases highlights that, though the formal written and codified content of HRM systems, as evident in the HR policies, may derive from a modern western perspective, the implementation of HRM, which is determined by the understanding of line managers, predominantly draws on the traditional aspects. We attempt to explore two questions: (1) are the design of HRM contents and the implementation process of HRM systems in the Indian context unique?; and (2) if so, how and why are these systems different?

An investigation into these questions is critical to understand the nuanced functioning of HRM systems in the Indian context. For firms operating in India or foreign multinational companies (MNCs) planning to enter India, an increased awareness and understanding of the confluence of modern and traditional perspectives would help them design and implement appropriate HRM systems for the Indian context. The organization can gain insights about leveraging contextual understandings from the descriptions of how this confluence plays out in the case organizations considered in this chapter.

We provide inputs on successful HRM practices in an Indian context by unravelling the uniqueness of HRM systems in its diverse contexts, captured by context-embedded analysis and exploration of new variables, rather than applying existing frameworks (Hofstede, 1993). We adopt a qualitative approach based on the multiple case studies method (Yin, 2003) to analyse the phenomenon.

Indian HR practices: modern and/or traditional

The term 'modern' denotes HRM practices that are contemporary, progressive and recent. The 'modernity' in Indian HRM practices can be attributed to the external influence from West. It has often been argued that HRM in Asia is imported from the West: through American or European multinational corporations (MNCs), Western business media, and through learning in business schools where the curriculum is based on theories derived from research in a western context, through consulting firms, expatriates and repatriates (Pio, 2007; Yeung, Warner and Rowley, 2008; Budhwar et al., 2017; Malik et al., 2017). The term 'traditional' denotes HRM practices that are long-established, customary and conventional. The 'tradition' in Indian HRM practices can be attributed to the national context. Several scholars posit that HRM practices instituted by firms are determined by contextual nuances such as national culture dimensions; norms about employee–employer relationships, socio-economic dimensions, and local education and training facilities (Jain et al., 2012). These local contextual dimensions play an important role in shaping not only the HRM practices adopted by firms but also the available talent pool.

Confluence of traditional and modern HR practices in India

The coexistence of traditional and western value systems may lead to ambiguous and sometimes conflicting situations in which the HR manager and employees develop their own repertoire of responses (Saher and Mayrhofer, 2014). Further, as well as actual HR practices adopted by organizations, the perception and interpretations of HR practices, i.e., how employees make sense of the HR practices implemented by organizations, are important in establishing the link between HR practices and performance (Nishii and Wright, 2008; Wright and Nishii, 2013). Therefore, though there may be isomorphism in intended HR practices, the implemented or actual HR practices and perception and behaviour of employees will depend on contextual nuances.

In the subsequent sections we highlight the confluence of modern and Indian traditional HR practices through the case study examples, focusing on four aspects of HRM: staffing, training, performance management and diversity. However, before we discuss the specifics of the HR practices, a brief overview of the Indian context would help to put our analysis in perspective.

The contextual aspects of Indian HRM

India has a distinct demographic advantage over many developed countries in terms of a young population with a mean age of 27.9 years (Index Mundi, 2016). With 65 per cent of population in the productive working-age group (15–65 years), the overall productivity of the country can be very high in the coming years. However, while the country can boast of a huge educated workforce, a large per centage of that population is 'unemployable'. According to a study conducted by Aspiring Minds National Employability, out of 150,000 engineers graduating from 650 colleges in 2015, about 80 per cent were lacking employable skills (*The Times of India*, 2016). The above aspects present an opportunity as well as a challenge for the organizations. While the pool of employment-ready candidates could be restricted, the organizations that can invest in converting qualified candidates into employable candidates can have access to, and benefit from, a large talent pool.

Another important feature of the Indian workforce is the inherent diversity across the nation. India has about 10,000 ethnic groups, representing every existing religious group. With 29 states and 7 Union Territories, each with a unique socio-cultural milieu, diversity in the Indian context can only be termed 'extreme'. This diversity spans multiple dimensions including language, food habits, clothing, mannerisms, social orientation, and so on. Even the states and Union Territories are extremely heterogeneous with unique socio-cultural dimensions varying every few kilometres. There are more than 780 languages and 66 scripts spoken across the nation.[1] It is interesting to note that in the Indian context diversity has not culminated in a 'melting pot' where these differences are dissolved. Rather the nation has sustained these differences as a 'salad pot' with the coexistence of diverse socio-cultural groups. Moreover, recently, organizations are facing the increasing challenge of managing a multigenerational (Srinivasan, 2012) and a gender-diverse workforce (Donnelly, 2015).

The contextual aspects described above pose both a challenge and an opportunity for the HR function in India. In the following sections, we describe how these contextual and cultural aspects are reflected in the Indian organizations' HRM strategy, policy and practices. Specifically, we describe these manifestations across four HRM aspects: recruitment and staffing, training and development, performance management processes, and diversity. The three cases belong to diverse sectors, namely, health care Narayana Hrudayalaya (Chandwani et al., 2012) and Aravind Eye Care System[2] (Chandwani et al., 2014), and a retail organization (Makhecha, 2016). These case organizations are successful organizations and, in our view, part of this success comes from their innovative way of blending modern and traditional HR practices.

Recruitment and staffing

The availability of the talent pool, which is qualified, but lacks employable skills can be an opportunity for organizations to tap into, especially if they design their recruitment and training systems appropriately (Srinivasan and Chandwani, 2014). Organizations investing heavily in employer branding strategy can especially take advantage of this huge *potential* talent pool. For example, Narayana Hrudayalaya (now Narayana Health or NH) built a strong brand as a 'training institute' for fresh pass-outs from nursing colleges. These young nurses then aspire to get a job in the Middle Eastern countries or in the western developed world as these jobs are financially much more rewarding. The fact that they have been trained in NH enables them to seek these career opportunities. Further, intentionally targeting fresh untrained nurses from colleges rather than nurses who have experience in hospitals enables the organization to mould incoming nurses into the NH work culture. The nursing superintendent at NH specifically maintains a close association with prominent nursing colleges in the region (Karnataka state), which enables the organization to tap into this talent pool. On a similar note, Aravind Eye Care System (AECS) builds its paramedical force, which accounts for about 70 per cent of the workforce, from the pool of girls who have just completed their senior level schooling, belonging to nearby local areas. The criterion for recruitment at AECS focuses solely on a respectful attitude towards teachers and elders rather than on technical skills and intelligence.

To cite an example from the retail organization on the staffing front, the sales force is hired based on the available local talent pool, which varies in their gender composition from one region to another (Makhecha et al., 2016). Though at the corporate level the organization has a prescribed gender composition suiting the retail context in general (70:30, male: female), it varies across stores as in certain regions of India, joining a sales force or being a customer service representative is not seen as an appropriate job for women, whereas in other regions women are encouraged to be independent and seek out employment in various sectors.

The above examples from the case organizations reflect that though the modern perspective of hiring would focus on selecting the best candidate (employment-ready candidate), these candidates are scarce and hence this creates challenges when hiring in the Indian context. The case organizations instead used the traditional perspective to make do with the available local talent pool and mould them based on their organization-specific requirements.

Training and development

Prior literature on the 'Indian way' highlights the importance of training and development initiatives in Indian organizations (Cappelli et al., 2010). The authors posit that organizations emphasize investing in training and development to ensure that employees have the tools to do their best work, but it is also designed to strengthen their commitment to the company. We extend the argument by positing that the 'qualified but unemployable' talent pool and 'extreme diversity' in the workforce act as an imperative for organizations to focus on training and development which also facilitates acculturation. The organizations that target fresh pass-outs as the talent pool, especially need to focus extensively on training.

In the case of NH and AECS, which provide subsidized health care services to lower socio-economic strata of India, a high volume of patients creates an opportunity for on-the job training for fresh pass-out doctors to hone their skills. This acts in favour of the organization as it is then regarded as a tertiary care hospital where the number and variety of cases, including complicated ones, enable doctors to sharpen their 'surgical and clinical acumen'. Both organizations created the brand of being an important training ground for medical professionals, who want to develop and sharpen their skills and knowledge.

In the retail organization, stores have high levels of training and this resonates positively with the employees. However, many training sessions are informal in nature. For example, several training sessions on soft skills, customer relations, and product-based training are carried out on the department floor without being part of the formal training calendar and without being accounted for. The supervisors and department managers feel that it is their duty to undertake various training sessions relevant to their categories as that will help improve the employees' knowledge and skill base, which in turn is expected to lead to better sales and higher customer service rankings and helping the employee to perform better. The line managers invest their time and energy in training-related activities even though training per se had a low KRA (Key Result Area) component in the line managers' performance appraisal. Clearly, the traditional Indian value of patronage is evident in stores as department or division managers tend to take on the mantle of mentoring and training employees in a 'Guru-Shisya' (i.e., teacher-disciple) relationship, as evident in the process of top-down training in which the manager-trainer takes on the mentor role and guides the employee through various nuances of the work, leading to a strong bonding between manager and employee.

Therefore, we argue that though the modern perspective focuses on formal aspects of training to play an instrumental role in increasing the firm's performance, the traditional Indian perspective focuses on the informal aspects of training where the managers feel a sense of duty to train, not just to hone, the subordinates' technical skills but also to bring them into alignment with the organizational culture and ethos, thus creating a sense of bonding, belonging and commitment to the organization.

Performance management

The organizations' performance management systems reflect a mixture of modern and traditional aspects with a focus on attitude rather than technical skills and a sense of duty and commitment.

In both AECS and NH, performance management systems prioritize softer attitudinal aspects over technical skills. The managers reiterate that though technical skills are considered important, as health care delivery requires professionals to be knowledgeable and skilled, the lack of efficient performance in the technical domains is tolerated more than the attitudinal issues. The organizations give a long rope to the concerned employee to take corresponding corrective measures to upgrade their technical and professional skills, by providing extra training and mentoring. However, attitudinal problems and behavioural issues such as mishandling financial matters, misbehaving with the patients or with colleagues, involvement in corruption, and so on, which are not aligned with the value systems and culture of the organization, are dealt with strictly.

In retail stores, the corporate rhetoric of formal performance appraisal systems does not materialize at the ground level. The corporate designs an elaborate process for appraisal and feedback of employees by managers, and there is close to 100 per centage compliance on paper. However, in reality, several employees are unaware of their KRAs and many do not receive year-end performance feedback. Reasons cited by the managers for the deviations from the formal performance appraisals include:

- an extremely tight work schedule;
- extended work hours of 14–16 hours per day;
- a high attrition rate, which increases their workload.

Hence the need to focus on core operational duties makes them default on their non-core duties such as performance appraisal and scheduled training of employees. An analysis of the KRAs of supervisors and managers indicates that their performance evaluation on HR-related activities, such as training, performance appraisal, hiring, etc., ranges between 0 to 5 per cent and hence under time constraints, they do not mind foregoing this. However, there is a sufficient amount of informal appraisal that line managers keep doing to make the employees perform well on a regular basis. Thus, in our view, though the modern western perspective of focus on strict compliance with performance management systems and dominance of ratings based on technical skills would hold good for organizations, the traditional Indian value of paternalism finds its way into the performance management system scenarios. Unlike in the West, employees judged weak in performance are not shown the door easily in Indian organizations. The supervisors and managers adopt the paternalistic roles of taking care of employees working in their departments, irrespective of their competencies and merits. They are tolerant of weak performance and to certain extent even take the onus of improvement on themselves.

Diversity

An important aspect of the Indian context is the extreme diversity in terms of local and regional cultures, which are distinctively different from each other. As indicated earlier, diversity is multidimensional, in terms of language, food preferences, societal influences, interpersonal relationships, and so on, which can drastically affect an individual's attitude towards work. In addition, organizations have to increasingly manage a multigenerational workforce and also gender diversity.

Organizations in India therefore face a challenge in terms of aligning an extremely diverse workforce to common organizational values, vision or mission. The key aspects of leading the 'Indian way' as explained by Cappelli et al. (2010), are emphasizing and highlighting the social mission or cause pursued by the organization and prioritizing the organizational culture over shareholder value. Further, while the literature on organizational culture has moved from considering a 'strong organizational culture being an important determinant of organizational performance' to 'organizational culture as a repertoire', thus undermining the importance of links between a strong organizational culture and performance, most of these studies (e.g., Bertels et al., 2016) are rooted in the western individualistic societies. Given the importance of aligning an extremely diverse workforce, an emphasis on the organizational culture might carry a very different and imperative meaning in Indian context.

Prior research has reiterated the involvement of Indian organizations in a social mission and their substantial investment in building an organizational culture. A strong organizational culture, we believe, facilitates the alignment of HR practices across levels and across geographies. In the retail organization, stores spread across diverse geographic regions tend to inadvertently or advertently create their own systems and practices based on the regional context that are distinct from the corporate mandates. However, at the organizational level, this kind of differentiation creates issues of integration as each store has a distinct look and feel for customers and this hampers the brand image of the retail chain. This is where overall organizational culture plays a critical role in bringing back the desired consistency in organizational systems and processes. The retail organization focuses on a strong culture of customer-centricity through the Indian values of '*atithi devo bhava*' which means the guest (customer) is equivalent to God. Other symbols and artefacts that convey a strong sense of belonging to the organization are: the uniform dress code worn by employees, the standardized layout of stores and their language and ways of greeting and treating customers as a guest. Thus, in our view, a strong organizational culture can be an aid in handling the diversity in Indian context.

Table 16.1 summarizes the unique aspects of HRM relevant to the Indian context and their organizational implications.

TABLE 16.1 Unique aspects of HR systems in India and their implications

Sub-system	Unique aspects of HRM prevalent in the Indian context	Implications for the design and implementation of HR system
Recruitment and selection	Local subsystems have their own ecosystems of socio-cultural norms and competitive environment Lack of availability of readily 'employable' talent	Understand the local socio-cultural nuances and design the recruitment practices accordingly, for example, focusing on specific criteria and/or local norms Focus on potential talent Focus on informal aspects of recruitment and selection, for example, employee referrals
Training and development	Availability of huge 'potential' talent who are high on qualification but low on employability. Guru-Shishya relationship between the managers and subordinates Extremely diverse workforce	Design training and development systems to convert potential talent into a highly productive workforce Manifestation of training as 'patronage', creates mentor-mentee relationships beyond formal arrangements Training and development systems for acculturation Balancing power relationships
Performance management	Paternalistic relationship between the supervisor and the employee Low emphasis on non-core KRAs, such as training performance appraisals, and feedback	High tolerance for weak performance The supervisors take the onus of improvement Though on paper compliance with prescribed formats is there, feedback and appraisals largely occur informally, over work
Managing diversity	Extremely diverse workforce with multiple dimensions of diversity	Strong emphasis on 'organizational culture' Emphasis on unifying social cause and purpose

Conclusion

The chapter highlights the contextual nature of HRM practices in Indian organizations. We proffer that unique HR practices relate to a mix of modern HR practices and traditional ones. Further, we relate contextual aspects of HR practices to distinct aspects of the labour market (such as a highly qualified yet unemployable young workforce) and socio-cultural dimensions (extreme regional diversity) existing in the Indian context.

Our analysis of case organizations shows that HR practices are successful in the Indian context, when the isomorphic western-dominated aspects of HR practices are appropriately supplemented and complemented by traditional Indian aspects based on the contextual specificity of organizations. This is required due to the uniqueness of the diverse context in which the organizations operate in India. The traditional Indian values, which are the basis of actions at the implementation level, could sometimes conflict with western values, which dominate at the design level.

The formal approach of planning, analysis and standardization at the design level is amalgamated with the informal improvisations of formal practices based on time constraints, resource constraints and convenience of the implementers. We conclude that a broad conceptualization of uniqueness in the HR practices in the Indian context can best be captured by the confluence of the westernization of the HRM content, driven by strategy, market orientation and a global mind-set, overlaid by the Indianization of the HRM process, driven by diversity in context, a welfare-paternalistic orientation and a local mindset. The dominant narrative in the existing literature (e.g. Virmani, 2007) projects the confluence of western and Indian HR practices as a source of confusion and disorder and hence a deterrent to organizational performance. On the other hand, our analysis of limited case studies makes us believe that this middle path (as advocated by Buddhism) could actually be beneficial to organizations as it satisfies the pluralist interests of multiple stakeholders.

CASE STUDY: DILEMMAS FOR JULIA (HEAD, HUMAN RESOURCES)

Early on the morning of 6 September 2017, Julia is planning for a meeting with her team members. Julia heads the Human Resources function of APL (Adelard Pvt. Ltd.), a German MNC that manufactures valves. Though APL ventured into India two years ago with big plans, unfortunately the firm performance had been extremely poor. In order to identify and address the issues, the Head Office in Germany has asked for reports from all the function heads of their Indian subsidiary. Julia is planning to discuss the HR-related issues in the meeting today. As the manufacturing facility in India had to be made functional at a short notice, Julia had replicated the HRM systems designed for their manufacturing facility in Germany in the Indian subsidiary. The four top issues that have been bothering her and the HR team are:

- filling the vacant positions at the manufacturing facility in a timely manner;
- ensuring that training sessions are conducted by line managers as per the training calendar sent by the head office;
- training the underperforming employees at the facility;
- resolving the constant conflicts between the older and younger generations of employees.

Help Julia resolve these issues.

What could be the sources of the above challenges that Julia and her team are facing at the Indian subsidiary?
What are some of the key points regarding the Indian context that she should specially be aware of?

Useful websites

Ministry of Labour and Employment http://labour.gov.in/
Replacing the existing 44 labour laws with limited five laws to increase the ease of doing business www.livemint.com/Politics/DsIHskpoSUU4DpbdpkReFM/Govt-seeks-to-replace-44-labour-laws-with-just-five.html)
Retail industry trends www.ibef.org/industry/retail-india.aspx
Retailers Association of India www.rai.net.in/
Siemens' analysis of its Indian workforce www.livemint.com/Companies/cJa 60w10WHrQiEBWnLIqNN/India-is-among-the-top-5-in-terms-of-Siemenss-people -and-gr.html

Notes

1 See www.thehindu.com/news/national/language-survey-reveals-diversity/article4938 865. ece
2 See www.narayanahealth.org/ and www.aravind.org/

References

Bertels, S., Howard-Grenville, J. and Pek, S. (2016) Cultural molding, shielding, and shoring at oilco: The role of culture in the integration of routines. *Organization Science*, 27(3): 573–593.
Budhwar, P. (2009) Managing human resources in India. In J. Storey, P.M. Wright and D. O. Ulrich (eds) *The Routledge Companion to Strategic Human Resource Management*. London: Routledge, pp. 435–446.
Budhwar, P., Tung, R.L., Varma, A. and Do, H. (2017) Developments in human resource management in MNCs from BRICS nations: A review and future research agenda. *Journal of International Management*, 23(2): 111–123.
Budhwar, P. and Varma, A. (2010) Guest editors' introduction: Emerging patterns of HRM in the new Indian economic environment. *Human Resource Management*, 49(3): 345–351.
Cappelli, P., Singh, H., Singh, J.V. and Useem, M. (2010) Leadership lessons from India. *Harvard Business Review*, 88(3): 90–97.
Chandwani, R., Jha, M., Nagadevara, V. and Srinivasan, V. (2012) Narayana Hrudayalaya – How the HR practices and policies enable organizational strategy implementation. In J. Bhatnagar, G. Bajaj and S. Ghosh (eds) *Innovations in People Management: Cases in Organizational Behaviour, HR, and Communication*. New Delhi: Macmillan Publishers.
Chandwani, R., Jha, M. and Nagadevara, V. (2014) Aravind Eye Care System: Time to shift gears. IIMA Case (CMHS0037). Ahmedabad: IIMA. Donnelly, R. (2015) Tensions and challenges in the management of diversity and inclusion in IT services multinationals in India. *Human Resource Management*, 54(2): 199–215.
Hofstede, G. (1993) Cultural constraints in management theories. *Academy of Management Executive*, 7(1): 81–94.
Index Mundi (2016) India Demographics Profile 2016. Available at: www.indexmundi. com/india/demographics_profile.html (accessed 8 November 2017).
Jain, H., Mathew, M. and Bedi, A. (2012) HRM innovations by Indian and foreign MNCs operating in India: A survey of HR professionals. *The International Journal of Human Resource Management*, 23(5): 1006–1018.

Makhecha, U.P. (2016) Multi-level gaps in HR practices: A study of intended, actual and experienced HR practices in a multi-unit Indian retail chain. Doctoral dissertation. Bangalore: Indian Institute of Management Bangalore.

Makhecha, U.P., Srinivasan, V., Prabhu, G.N. and Mukherji, S. (2016) Multi-level gaps: A study of intended, actual and experienced human resource practices in a hypermarket chain in India. *The International Journal of Human Resource Management*, 27: 1–39.

Malik, A., Pereira, V. and Tarba, S. (2017) The role of HRM practices in product development: Contextual ambidexterity in a US MNC's subsidiary in India. *The International Journal of Human Resource Management*, 28: 1–29.

Nishii, L.H. and Wright, P. (2008) Variability at multiple levels of analysis: Implications for strategic human resource management. Available at: www.cornell.edu

Pio, E. (2007) HRM and Indian epistemologies: A review and avenues for future research. *Human Resource Management Review*, 17: 319–335.

Saher, N. and Mayrhofer, W. (2014) The role of Vartan Bhanji in implementing HRM practices in Pakistan. *The International Journal of Human Resource Management*, 25(13): 1881–1903.

Srinivasan, V. (2012) Multi-generations in the workforce: Building collaboration. *IIMB Management Review*, 24(1): 48–66.

Srinivasan, V. and Chandwani, R. (2014) HRM innovations in rapid growth contexts: The healthcare sector in India. *The International Journal of Human Resource Management*, 25(10): 1505–1525.

The Times of India (2016) Over 80% of engineering graduates in India unemployable: Study. 11 July. Available at: http://timesofindia.indiatimes.com/tech/tech-news/Over-80-of-engineering-graduates-in-India-unemployable-Study/articleshow/50704157.cms

Virmani, B.R. (2007) *The Challenges of Indian Management*. London: Sage.

Wright, P.M. and Nishii, L.H. (2013) Strategic HRM and organizational behaviour: Integrating multiple levels of analysis. In J. Paauwe, D. Guest and P. Wright (eds) *HRM and Performance: Achievements and Challenges*. Chichester: Wiley, pp. 97–110.

Yeung, A., Warner, M., and Rowley, C. (2008) 'Guest editors' introduction: Growth and globalization: evolution of human resource management practices in Asia. *Human Resource Management*, 47: 1–13.

Yin, R.K. (2003) *Case Study Research: Design and Methods*. 3rd edn. London: Sage.

PART III

Emerging practices

17

MANAGING BUSINESS ALLIANCES

Experiences of a European company in India

Claudia Müller and Rajesh Kumar

Aims of this chapter are to:

- Understand the different types of ambiguity that an alliance is subject to
- Highlight the significant cultural gap between the mindset of the foreign investor and the potential Indian partner
- Show the significance of effective communication between the partners
- Reveal that flexibility is critical if the foreign investor and the local partner are to overcome the challenges posed by ambiguity

Introduction

Strategic alliances are increasingly becoming important in today's globalized economy. Alliances are formed for a variety of reasons. such as to enter new markets, cut costs, share risks, or develop new technology (Lasserre, 2007). However, such partnerships and alliances are challenging to manage. This arises from the fact that they bring together two – or more – partners with divergent history, culture or even business objectives. This implies that the partners rarely have a deep understanding of each other's needs, and given that there is often not a lot of time to get to know each other's organizations well, partnerships are always characterized by a high degree of ambiguity and uncertainty. Ambiguity implies that a given event can be interpreted in more than one way (Kumar, 2014). Differences in national cultures exacerbate ambiguity as the partners operate with different mental frames in mind (Kumar, 2004).

Kumar (2014) proposes three types of ambiguity: (1) partner ambiguity; (2) interaction ambiguity; and (3) evaluation ambiguity. Partner ambiguity deals with the appropriateness of the partner. Is the partner capable, committed, and offering complementary assets? The potential partner is likely to present himself or herself in the best possible light and this may or may not be an accurate representation of reality. Interaction ambiguity arises when the alliance is underway and the alliance is experiencing a performance shortfall. The question then is: Why has the performance shortfall arisen? Is it due to the external environment or due to the failings of the partner? Evaluative ambiguity pertains to assessing the alliance performance. If the alliance is underperforming, is it time to pull the plug on the alliance? In particular, at what stage should such a decision be made?

Alliances are an important vehicle through which firms implement their strategy (Yoshino and Rangan, 1995). Foreign investors form alliances to obtain easier and faster market access with the help of local know-how and contacts. This allows them to test the market before making a more substantial and firm commitment. In this chapter we examine how a European company – Pima (name altered) – used a distribution alliance to enter the Indian market. When foreign firms choose to enter alliances, they need to learn the art of managing ambiguity. The case study presented in this chapter (although somewhat dated) demonstrates how a lack of competence in this art can be detrimental to the business and provides useful insights that we believe continue to be still relevant today. The challenges of ambiguity that are presented in this chapter are not unique to India but the sources of ambiguity are and while it might be the case that there may be some cultural shifts underway in India, these shifts may still be at an early stage and the impact unevenly diffused.

CASE STUDY: PIMA

Company background

Pima had an annual turnover of approximately US$1 billion per year. It sold electrical household items and electrical personal care and grooming products. Pima's identity was grounded in the superior design, high functionality, quality and reliability of their products and they protected these fiercely by keeping close control of production. As part of an initiative by Pima's parent company to enter emerging markets aggressively, Pima was asked to enter the Indian market in the late 1990s. Pima's CEO himself was hesitant about India, given their prior experience in other emerging markets, and was therefore personally not strongly committed to the initiative.

The Indian market and Pima's strategic approach

At the time Pima entered India, the market for their products was largely non-existent and there was no data other than gut feeling from people in the industry and in the trade. Despite Pima's efforts to understand the market, it remained very hard to estimate its potential. The absence of reliable data is a typical feature of starting a business in emerging markets and India was no exception. The size of the middle class in India could not be determined precisely. There were still many market entry barriers in place, one of which was a law that constrained Pima to local production for most of their products. Given Pima's focus on quality control, they wanted to avoid such local production arrangements, particularly in this first phase, and the CEO wanted to keep investment and risk to a minimum.

This had major implications for their product deployment strategy: They decided, after several visits to India and long internal deliberations, to initially launch one product only, an epilator which is a device to remove body hair. This product seemed the best candidate: it sold well in other countries in the region; it received worldwide marketing support as it was one of the key strategic products; it received favourable reactions during focus groups and, very importantly, it did not have to be all locally produced but could be assembled from imported parts, protecting Pima's quality control requirements. Local retailers felt that the product had some, albeit not huge, potential in the market and hoped that Pima would follow up with household products rapidly. Pima's CEO saw the success of this product as a test of the market viability.

Distribution for Pima's products was also underdeveloped, both in quantity and quality in India. There was a huge number of pots and pans and general stores that could potentially sell electrical household items but mostly did not do so. As for electrical personal care products, such as the epilator, only very few of these stores seemed up to the challenge. The epilator might be sold through – newly developing – cosmetic stores or even pharmacies. Given this difficult retail environment and the huge distances and logistics involved in distributing goods in India, Pima estimated that it would take too long to build their own distribution and therefore looked for a suitable partner.

They eventually settled on a southern Indian, privately held company with its own production facilities for some – non-competitive – household products as well as pharmaceuticals. This company had a big distribution network in several retail segments and seemed very enthusiastic to represent a European consumer goods company which was one of the reasons for Pima's choice.

Formation of the distribution partnership

It is at the stage of the negotiation that it is most important to invest time in learning about the partner's background, underlying goals and vision for the business, establishing a common perspective. Companies frequently underestimate this need, seeing a distribution partner merely as an implementer of strategy. When this happens, ambiguity and misunderstandings can impact the relationship and make collaboration difficult and results hard to achieve.

This was also Pima's case. To them, the distributor's role was a logistical one, they saw him as an implementer of their strategy, not as a partner with whom they would jointly develop it. Therefore, Pima built their strategy and their actual sales estimates for the first five years – 200,000 pieces in year one, gradually increasing to 1 million pieces annually after five years – with minimal input from the distributor. They based their assumptions on experience in other markets, data on hair removal habits in India and by conducting local focus groups. The distributor, in line with the retailers, stated his belief that household products were the way to go in India but did not strongly oppose the epilator as a first entry. No attempt was made on either side to jointly estimate sales for this product. They did not realize it at the time but this lack of clarity dramatically increased the ambiguity between the partners and led to the distributor not feeling committed to any numbers. Neither of the partners investigated the other side's deeper ambitions and perspectives.

On the surface, negotiations were easy. Both sides wanted to introduce Pima's products to the Indian market and saw many opportunities. The financial arrangement was sorted out quickly. The distributor seemed to care about adding high quality products to his assortment. He was also interested in producing household products for Pima in the longer run but did not communicate this as essential. Pima had reservations about this as they did not consider the production facilities of the distributor adequate, but they also had not finally decided against the possibility. These things were left 'hanging in mid-air'. It served both sides not to be overly clear because this way they could both continue to hope and therefore would keep doing their best. In the meantime Pima thought that the distributor's slight resistance to the epilator was a reflection of them favouring household products so as to obtain the production rights. In the end, there was no explicit, strong, shared agreement and ambiguity remained, but neither side realized it.

For Pima, the most important aspect of the negotiations focused around the elements necessary to build the distribution. They wanted a Pima-dedicated manager at the distributor to be the contact person for all Pima-related issues, whom the distributor agreed to nominate. They also wanted their own staff to train and guide the distributor's sales people but failed to share their views about organizational culture and sales processes. Finally, and most importantly, they expected the distributor to use his existing sales force to introduce the epilator into whatever existing distribution was appropriate but at the same time hire and develop new sales staff who would sell into outlets the distributor did not yet cover, such as cosmetic stores. The distributor again agreed to this. These things were discussed in rather informal settings between Pima's regional marketing manager and a person reporting to the distributor's CEO. The CEO himself kept dropping in and out of the meetings. What Pima did not realize at the time were the cultural implications of India's hierarchical orientation: The distributor's CEO and owner, a man of superior standing in his community and of Brahmin origin, would have been prepared to discuss and share more deeply had Pima produced a negotiation partner of similar rank, that is Pima's CEO himself. However, Pima's CEO never went to India at that stage.

In retrospect, both sides did not do enough to eliminate partner-related ambiguity. Many important issues remained untouched, such as the issue of long-term ambitions, the need to reconcile different organizational cultures, and, most importantly, the sales projections for the epilator. There were many reasons for ignoring these issues. Both sides were happy to do their own thing, which is what they had always done before. Also, several cultural differences played a role here, exacerbating the ambiguity between the partners: Europeans make detailed quantitative plans for several years basing their investment decisions on them. Asians tend to start slowly, evaluating and then adapting strategy and plans. Thus the distributor naturally would not give the numbers the same importance, so why challenge them (Kumar and Nti, 2004)? Indians also tend to communicate less directly and more subtly than European cultures, particularly when criticizing the other (Kumar and Sethi, 2005).

Indians require a strong personal relationship to develop sufficient trust in the other side to speak up. It takes time and effort to build that personal relationship. Europeans in large part focus on negotiating the contract. Pima did not make a lot of time to get to know their business partners on a personal level and did not produce a negotiation partner of acceptable standing to the distributor. The distributor misjudged the importance of plans to the Pima team and the definite nature of agreements given to people of a lower rank than himself to whom decision power had been delegated.

The distributor's visit to Europe

The distributor was eager to get a long-term commitment from Pima having lost distributorships of European companies before, a fact he again concealed from Pima. Pima's intention was indeed a long-term relationship, as they had with many other distributors.

A written long-term commitment had not been discussed explicitly during the various meetings in India though. The distributor's CEO decided to come to Europe to finally establish personal contact with the CEO and get his explicit commitment to a ten-year contract. He arrived at short notice without communicating his intentions clearly to Pima. Pima thought he was paying a courtesy visit and, being busy in their annual planning phase did not particularly prepare for this meeting. The visit did not go as the distributor's CEO had expected. In India, someone of his rank would have been picked up from the airport, taken to a lavish lunch and given full attention from top management. Nobody was aware of the difference this would have made to the relationship. Pima's culture was task-oriented and egalitarian. He had to take a taxi all by himself. When he arrived at the office, the Sales Director and his team had allocated a limited amount of time to meet him. The CEO himself was not available, so he met the Vice President for Sales and Marketing. Nobody had time for a prolonged lunch in a special place.

He then presented his request to enter a clause into the contract that specified a ten-year duration and specific stiff penalties for early termination. Pima's team was taken aback. This represented a serious lack of trust in their eyes.

Both sides had not worked together yet and while the intention of a long-term arrangement was there, they wanted to be able to judge the merit of the alliance based on the distributor's performance. In their evaluation the distributor had very limited risk and their cost was more than covered through their margin, therefore Pima's managers felt that the penalties the distributor desired in the contract were unacceptable.

The Vice President felt awkward at getting involved in what he clearly saw as an issue for regional management. He certainly made no special efforts to develop the relationship with this man. A compromise was reached in the form of a letter of intent, giving the distributor his word that, if the duties spelled out in the contract were fulfilled, Pima was definitely intending to build a long-term relationship with the distributor. These duties included the extra sales force for new distribution. Penalties were then dropped from the contract and it was finally signed.

In this episode, we can see clearly how the cultural differences between the two parties and their lack of mutual understanding actually reinforced the ambiguity between them. Both sides had a very different understanding about how to develop trust. For the Indian CEO, trust was developed through building a strong relationship with somebody of equal status and being treated accordingly. For Pima, trust was to be developed through fulfilling the previously discussed contractual obligations and achieving the plan. The manner in which the distributor showed up at their office and confronted them with previously unstated requests, wanting to finalize the contract not with the relevant team but with the top bosses, really was an affront to the Pima team. This did not help to develop trust at all. Pima recognized that the distributor was actually annoyed but could not understand why.

Collaboration with the distributor in preparation of the launch

As the collaboration is implemented, an alliance is potentially subject to experiencing interactional ambiguity (Kumar, 2014). Interactional ambiguity reflects the presence of unfavourable process discrepancies (Kumar and Nti, 1998) where the interaction between the partners falls short of what it should be because of differences in approach. As Pima started to gear up to the launch, they became increasingly aware that there were significant differences in the selling approach and overall organizational culture of the two entities that they had not envisaged.

Pima had planned and communicated to launch within three to four months from signing the contract. Apparently, the distributor had not reckoned for Pima to move fast enough to keep these dates. Pima was ready to train the sales force in product knowledge and sales process. The additional sales force for the important cosmetics store distribution, however, was not in place. At the distributor's end, a manager had been dedicated to oversee the Pima business, but it soon became clear that this manager was not able to take any decisions. All decisions were taken by the CEO of the distribution company himself. This is consistent with how decision-making and leadership are exercised in India (Kumar and Sethi, 2005). It was next to impossible for the Pima India Management or even the Pima Regional Director to get in touch with the distributor's CEO who travelled frequently. As the launch approached, Pima was getting increasingly nervous about the missing sales force. Assurances they were given about imminent hire did not materialize and Pima did not understand why. The distributor, however, not having been involved in the planning, did not worry so much about the speed of introduction. This was a consequence of not jointly developing, sharing and committing to concrete objectives.

As the launch approached ...

The Pima team found that the distributor's sales people needed a lot of handholding and lacked many sales management practices that the Pima team considered basic. They helped them with the sell-in and managed to achieve more or less the planned numbers in the first two weeks. Then came week three and not a single order. What had happened? The distributor's team had gone back to selling pots and pans! There was no sales force to assure performance continuity. As the Pima team tried to push the distributor to put at least a few salesmen on their business permanently, they found that the owner of the company was again on a business trip to the USA and could not be reached. The distributor pretended that there were salesmen visiting customers for Pima, but that no orders were forthcoming. However, when Pima's sales managers visited the retailers, they heard a different story. This situation was further aggravated once the advertising kicked in. There were on average only three pieces in each store and these were hardly visible in the shelves. As advertising kicked in, Pima risked customer frustration if their customers could not find the product to buy.

The Pima team felt increasingly disorientated, annoyed and somewhat helpless while at the same time being under pressure from their own company to achieve results. The distributor's actions simply did not match their words and it seemed to be impossible to achieve clarity in the short term, a truly ambiguous situation. Pima did the only thing they could do: they diverted some of their advertising funds to hire several salesmen 'to support' the business themselves. The distributor, surprisingly, had nothing against this. Pima continued to hire more salesmen and after several months ran almost the entire sales force. Running the sales force had been part of the distributor's contract and so Pima felt let down early on. During the next 12 months, several meetings at the distributor's office remained inconclusive and ineffective.

Interactional ambiguity needs to be minimised for the alliance partnership to develop well. Unfavourable process discrepancies should be avoided in the first place by discussing all the elements of collaboration openly. Second, even if these problems do emerge, they need to be tackled in a timely and a forthright way, otherwise negative emotions will develop and trust will be eroded. A negative vicious cycle may emerge, making it difficult for the partners to stabilize their interaction. Negative emotions should not be allowed to dominate the interaction (Anderson and Kumar, 2006; Kumar et al., 2016).

Lack of success in the marketplace

The Pima India team worked hard to compensate for the challenges they faced. Despite their efforts and many campaigns, the epilator never sold anywhere close to the numbers that had been forecast by Pima. In year one they sold 65,000 pieces, and these numbers stayed more or less stable over the next couple of years, a far cry from Pima's forecast. This leads us to the third stage of partnership ambiguity, which is evaluative ambiguity.

Evaluating progress with the distributor

When Pima sat down with the distributor to evaluate the sales results after year one, the distributor surprisingly did not seem to be unsettled by the shortfall. For the Pima team, the dramatic shortfall was a major disaster. The head office blamed them for not having worked hard enough. Rather than generating a profit, the business had incurred a loss. That made it that much more difficult to convince the CEO to introduce other products to the Indian market. Part of this shortfall was due to a lack of consumer understanding but another part was also due to the distributor's lack of effort and underperformance in the trade, even though Pima worked so hard to compensate for this. As they sat down with the distributor, the distributor's reaction was: 'Well, we only ever expected to sell 20,000 pieces, so 65,000 is great and this is certainly also due to our efforts.' The Pima team was absolutely stunned at the gap in perception between the parties.

In retrospect, we can now see how during the three stages of that partnership, the ambiguity was never adequately dealt with by the partners and it continued to impact the business.

Starting to question the relationship

At this point in time, Pima's India team started to question the viability of the distribution arrangement. They ran the sales force anyway and had already found possible alternative logistics to operate their own distribution system. Pima's top leadership felt bound to the commitment they gave, however. It was in this context that Pima's CEO could finally be convinced to take the trip to India. By the time he made it there, more than one and a half years had elapsed since first starting the business. The Pima India team and their CEO sat down for a meeting with the distributor's CEO and this time he finally gave a complete presentation on his company. It became clear that his company's goal was to run each business they were involved in completely, including the production. Pima's distribution was an oddity that did not match the rest of the company. He had tried distributorships with other western companies before and they had failed for similar reasons.

He had obviously never taken Pima's strategy seriously. Rather than telling Pima upfront, he expected them to find out by themselves. He reiterated that he had only ever expected to sell around 20,000 epilators a year, a tenth of the official Pima plan, but had never mentioned this during the formation stage of their agreement. He had hoped that once Pima came to the right conclusions, they would then introduce household products, which his company would produce. Or so he thought. His intention was not bad or devious, just a lot more indirect and less time-bound than Pima could understand. It was also subject to his own cultural understanding of hierarchy and status considerations.

When put under pressure about not complying with the agreed sales force for Pima, he, in turn, voiced his discontent with the product line-up. The India team finally understood that in fact pushing the epilator sales had not been in the distributor's interest at all. The faster Pima recognized the limited potential of the epilator, the faster they would introduce household products. So why push it ...?

This attitude tragically misjudged the way Pima functioned. Pima needed to make this first product a success, and that meant achieving the sales numbers that had been planned. Pima's CEO, who had been sceptical about India in the first place, saw his doubts confirmed., He now became fully aware of the distributor's part in the unfolding of events. The indirect approach, the lack of straightforwardness substantially decreased his trust in the distributor and in fact removed the last chance of ever considering him for a larger partnership, including production. He threatened to withdraw the business if things did not change significantly over the next six months. At the same time, he did agree to move into some local production of a hairdryer and later even a mixer/blender, but in a separate legal set-up that allowed Pima to have a fairly strong control over the production site. No longer was any production seriously considered with the distributor.

Severing the relationship

The Indian distributor did not take the threat to withdraw the business seriously, as tempers easily flare up in India and threats are easily made but not necessarily carried out. Over the course of the next half-year, nothing much changed. Pima introduced the first new product, the hairdryer, and the distributor saw that he was not getting to produce it. So even though there was more clarity now over the ambitions and ways of proceeding for both parties, it was too late to improve the relationship. Too much trust had been destroyed already. Half a year later Pima's CEO gave the consent to terminate the relationship with the distributor.

Relaying the message was the task of the regional director and the country manager. They travelled to the distributor's office with a heavy heart, expecting a fight. They had not written beforehand about the decision as they felt that conveying it personally was the only acceptable way. To their dismay, as they arrived at the airport, the distributor's CEO actually came to pick them up, taking them to his place to have drinks. This had never happened before and was definitely intended as a sign of trust and developing relationships. When over dinner, they finally announced the decision, the CEO turned red, jumped up so quickly that his chair fell over and exclaimed: 'I have invited you into my house, but you have treated me like a *kuli* [porter]. I will never talk to you again.'

They never did see him again. Lawyers handled the severance arrangement and the communication. The distributor tried to obtain the severance payment that he had originally wanted to be in the contract. In fact, he did not believe that the termination was definite until he managed to phone Pima's CEO and hear it directly from his mouth. Even though it had never been in writing, Pima needed to come to a compromise as the distributor could seriously harm their business in India. They eventually settled on a part of the requested sum and took over the distribution, but the business suffered for several months and in the end, it still cost Pima a lot of money. On the positive side, it turned out that it was not as difficult to establish their own distribution as they had imagined. They probably could have done it right from the beginning.

Conclusion

What can we learn from this case?

1. An important partnership needs top management support. It is important to involve senior management as early as possible in the negotiation process so that the other side feels respected and will open up early on.
2. It is also essential to build the relationship beyond the task at hand and beyond the professional contact. It is essential to learn about the cultural imprint of your potential partner and take this learning into consideration while developing the relationship.
3. This needs to be complemented by a mindset and attitude of open inquiry and interest in the partner. Before starting to negotiate, take time to find out your potential partner's deep ambitions and vision for his business. And share your own.
4. Only when the fundamental objectives of both partners can be integrated towards a common goal and when there is a complementarity of strengths and principles, will the partnership be a successful one. This was clearly not the case with Pima. In fact, at a deeper level, their objectives were in contradiction with each other.

5. A partnership is a joint effort to achieve certain objectives. Therefore, you must jointly develop these objectives, whatever they may be. If partners can get their objectives fulfilled under the same overall business goals, this can work. But they need to talk this through to make sure of it.

6. While some of the processes will probably always be emergent in a partnership, it helps to look early at the culture of each partner and those processes and principles that will have an impact on the collaboration. Be very clear about the roles each partner has to play in the partnership. Do not leave any ambiguity on roles and responsibilities.

7. Do not be afraid to turn down a partnership proposal when you feel that there is no compatibility in objectives and principles. You may be better off going it alone.

8. As the partnerships develop, create a structure to check in regularly and frequently with your partner so that you can detect friction early. Develop routines to address points of conflict early and find solutions that satisfy both parties. This will probably involve speaking about the way you communicate with each other.

9. Make sure that you agree on how to measure and assess the success of your partnership. And make sure you do celebrate your successes together and spread them!

References

Anderson, P.H. and Kumar, R. (2006) Emotions, trust and relationship development in buyer seller dyads: A conceptual model. *Industrial Marketing Management*, 35: 522–535.

Kumar, R. (2014) Managing ambiguity in strategic alliances. *California Management Review*, 56: 82–102.

Kumar, R. and Nti, K.O. (1998) Differential learning and alliance dynamics: A process and outcome discrepancy model. *Organization Science*, 9: 358–367.

Kumar, R. and Nti, K.O. (2004) National cultural values and the evolution of process and outcome discrepancies in international strategic alliances. *Journal of Applied Behavioral Science*, 40: 344–361.

Kumar, R. and Sethi, A. (2005) *Doing Business in India*. New York: Macmillan.

Kumar, R., Van Kleef, G. and Higgins, E.T. (2016) How emotions influence alliance relationships: A multi-level model. Unpublished manuscript.

Lasserre, P. (2007) *Global Strategic Management*. New York: Macmillan.

Yoshino, M.Y. and Rangan, S. (1995) Strategic Alliances: An Entrepreneurial Approach to Globalization. Boston: Harvard Business School Press.

18

RISK MANAGEMENT AND GOVERNANCE IN OUTSOURCING AND OFFSHORING TO INDIA

Sanjoy Sen

Aims of this chapter are to:

- Highlight how risk management and (corporate) governance around outsourcing initiatives can help achieve the wider strategic benefits, not just mitigate the risk of 'bad things happening'
- Highlight the changing perceptions about risk management and governance and the emergence of risk management as a 'matter of choice' rather than a 'matter of chance'
- Show how good governance and risk management require a chain of related areas to be addressed with equal rigour
- Showcase how the new breed of global organizations is taking calculated risks by outsourcing critical processes

Introduction

The Information Technology (IT) and Business Process Outsourcing (BPO) sector in India has developed as one of the most dominant industries in India's interactions with the rest of the world. In such global interactions with India, concerns continue to be raised by potential investors (or those planning to engage with Indian organizations in any capacity, for instance, as customers or technology partners of these organizations) over the quality of corporate governance and the risk management practices in India that would affect the realization of their ultimate objectives for such engagement.

This chapter discusses the growth of the IT-BPO sector in India, specifically addressing the evolution of strategic governance and risk management. It highlights the significance of this sector in India, together with the current and future challenges and opportunities that impinge upon issues related to both governance and risk management. In this connection, 'outsourcing' refers to contracting out to an agency external to the organization, while offshoring specifically includes scenarios where the outsourcee (service provider or vendor) uses a delivery location that is geographically different from that of the users of these services (i.e., mainly overseas).

Global trends around outsourcing and offshoring continue to emerge, just as the related perceptions and practices around risk, risk management and governance continue to evolve. These changing trends and perceptions are examined below to set the context for understanding the related impact on governance of outsourcing arrangements. Assessing the quality of governance and risk management around outsourcing is often an initial checkpoint for overseas clients prior to outsourcing IT or business processes to India or even establishing their Indian subsidiaries to provide back office/support services to their global organization.

Rise of IT-BPO in India and global trends in outsourcing/offshoring

Various global market research agencies, including Forrester and Gartner, continue to predict a significant growth in outsourcing and offshoring of IT and supporting business processes such as Finance, Human Resource Management, Procurement, Legal Compliance, Decision Support and Analytics over the next five years. According to a report by Forrester Research, the IT Services market (including related consulting and systems integration services) grew by 7.5 per cent year on year between 2009 and 2013 and is expected to grow at a compound annual growth rate (CAGR) of more than 5 per cent during 2013–2017 with a market forecast to exceed US$1000 billion by the end of 2017. Similarly, Gartner forecasts a CAGR of 5.6 per cent in BPO from 2012 through 2017 to a market size estimated in the region of US$400 billion. These exponential growth predictions are reflective of their recognized potential for enhancing organizational value in the aftermath of the recent global financial crisis.

The Deloitte Global Outsourcing Survey 2016 recognizes three key emerging trends with regard to outsourcing IT and business processes. These are:

- Companies are broadening their approach in outsourcing as they begin to view it as more than a simple cost-cutting exercise. In other words, while cost savings continue to remain an important motivator for outsourcing or offshoring IT and business processes, global organizations are now starting to take a broader strategic view of the opportunities that this opens up for them, such as access to scarce skills and resources, agility and flexibility in operations, bringing in innovation to their business processes and enabling the transformation of their business. This also opens up a new strategic dimension, enhancing the earlier operational focus driven by the need to reduce organizational costs through outsourcing and offshoring.
- Organizations are redefining the ways they enter into outsourcing relationships and manage the ensuing risks. For instance, a number of organizations are now

clearly articulating performance measures related to benefits achieved, including measuring the degree of innovation brought into the business through outsourcing and offshoring, to be able to reward the provider for good performance. In addition, innovative arrangements such as 'pay-as-you-go' contracts are minimizing the upfront investment in an outsourcing arrangement by remunerating the provider, based on the actual volume of transactions. All these mechanisms are intended to maximize the strategic opportunities enabled through the outsourcing or offshoring arrangement.

- In keeping with the above changes, organizations are also changing the way in which they are managing their relationships with outsourcing providers to maximize the value of these relationships. For instance, the average contract duration has now significantly reduced from 7–10 years to 3–5 years, enabling an ongoing opportunity to incorporate the learning in subsequent versions of outsourcing and offshoring arrangements. In addition, contract scope renegotiations are increasingly taking place as and when business circumstances change, often well in advance of contract expiry timelines, to proactively ensure benefit maximization from the arrangement.

According to the India Brand Equity Foundation (IBEF), India is the world's largest sourcing destination for the information technology (IT) industry, accounting for approximately 67 per cent of the US$124–130 billion offshore market for IT and BPO. The industry employs about 10 million individuals. The National Association for Software and Service Companies (NASSCOM) estimates that India's technology and BPO sector (also referred to as Business Process Management or BPM in these estimates), including hardware, currently generates annual revenues of US$160–175 billion with an expected growth rate in the region of 7–9 per cent, contributing to around 10 per cent of India's Gross Domestic Product (GDP). NASSCOM expects this sector to reach US$350 billion by 2025. Despite this continued growth of the IT–BPO sector in India, the vendor organizations constituting this sector have to continually reinvent themselves to be able to address these changing client expectations as well as embrace the new ways of client engagement/management. All these create new opportunities but also bring new risks. This in turn reiterates the need to continually review and revisit the adequacy of governance and risk management mechanisms, so that all the relevant stakeholder requirements are addressed and all compliance requirements are met under the changing circumstances.

To be able to gain an understanding of risk management and governance considerations relevant to the Indian IT-BPO, it is important to understand the impact of the three key emerging global trends described above. These are discussed below.

Emergence of global delivery models

Historically, Indian IT and BPO providers have operated with an India-centric model, staffed primarily by Indian residents in India and have delivered services to global clients out of their delivery centres located in India. This operating model had been key to offering the cost savings to their global clients, given that the average salaries paid to these staff was one-third to one-quarter of the salaries paid to their American or European counterparts. However, with the client view of outsourcing broadening beyond just cost savings, it is now becoming more and more important to deliver services from the client location ('onshore') or from a location that has a reasonable geographic proximity ('near-shore') to the client. This would enable the Indian providers to build stronger relationships with clients, understand their business better and provide end-to-end solutions to clients (competing against local players in the marketplace) that would fully address their complex business problems rather than just providing a technology solution. Also, Indian IT-BPO providers realized that the development of a management consulting services business, that would enable the provision of strategic and operations consulting services to clients, could be built only with a higher investment in onshore staff. As a result, the traditional India-centric model has now evolved into a global delivery model-based approach, and consequently Indian IT companies have established overseas subsidiaries in major clients' locations around the world. These delivery centres are staffed not just by Indian nationals but also by individuals who reside in and are members of the local community, which also helps in addressing immigration pushbacks and concerns against the movement of jobs from locals to immigrant workers. For instance, the 'Big4' Indian IT companies – TCS, Infosys, Wipro and HCL technologies – are currently focused on increasing the headcount in their overseas delivery locations faster than in India, together with a continuous stream of international staff secondments. As a result, overseas organizations who plan to outsource IT or Business Processes to India are likely to find themselves in the comfort zone of being served by some members of their own community or nationality, who are based in India, speak their language and understand their culture – thus, allaying their initial fears of outsourcing to an alien country.

Delivering value and innovation to global clients amid increasing risk and regulation

In addition to delivering services from global delivery centres located around the world, the broader focus on the pursuit of value and innovation by clients has resulted in Indian IT companies continually enhancing their capability in areas such as cloud technologies, data and analytics, cognitive and robotics process automation, blockchain, etc. to be able to diversify their offerings and showcase leading ideas in order to create differentiated offerings. Indian IT-BPO providers have also made a number of global acquisitions over the past few years to be able to enhance these capabilities as well as rebuild their organizational brand as global solution providers rather than only Indian IT providers who merely do business on a cross-border basis. Indian IT-BPO providers are also bringing in innovation by offering pricing models based on 'pay-as-you-go' as well as pricing linked to project outcomes. These new developments also bring in new risks (e.g., cyber-threats) that need to be managed through appropriate governance mechanisms. In addition, increasing regulation and legislation in areas such as data privacy, anti-bribery and corruption, operational resilience in outsourced/offshored processes, immigration, etc. are all emerging as new areas requiring attention and investment by Indian IT-BPO providers. For instance, overseas clients who are planning to outsource IT and Business Processes to India must recognize and address the potential corruption risks they may face in the course of their dealings. While India is taking strong legislative and enforcement action to combat bribery and corruption, these efforts will likely not result in quick fixes to endemic problems. Assessing these risks is key to establishing a proper foundation for the related governance practices, and involve: (1) an understanding of local practices and customs; (2) training relevant personnel who will be in a position to identify the 'red flags'; and (3) implementing internal controls that will serve to prevent, monitor and detect potential violations can help the client organization establish an effective and defensible position to protect themselves against risks inherent in doing business with India.

Addressing the challenges of shorter contract duration and frequent contract scope renegotiation

Traditionally, IT outsourcing contracts have typically spanned 7–10 years with limited interim scope renegotiation, enabling the provider organization to reap profits progressively over the life of the contract. However, following the last global financial crisis, the world has become far more volatile and uncertain. Recent developments, such as Brexit in Europe and the lack of clarity associated with the government policies of the new US administration, have significantly increased the overall atmosphere of uncertainty. This has resulted in large global organizations spending cautiously on IT-BPO-related initiatives, reducing the average contract duration to 3–5 years, together with a similar reduction in the scope and scale of these contracts. Existing contracts now have clauses to enable frequent scope renegotiation to retain the agility of the client organization and the ability to adapt to changing external circumstances and profit pressures. All these factors increase the strategic and operating risks of the IT-BPO provider that would need to be addressed through investments in enhancing the maturity of its governance and risk management mechanisms. For instance, most of the Indian IT companies have now established a centralized organizational engine for risk management and compliance, typically headed by the Head of Governance and Risk Management (also referred to as the Chief Risk Officer) who reports to the Board or to the Chief Executive Officer. The role of this centralized organizational engine is to evolve, standardize and innovate good governance and risk management practices that can quickly be replicated across all key client project teams, with devolved accountability in the form of a 'hub and spoke' model to the designated accountable official within the client project delivery team. In this way, each client team is able to benefit from the centralized investment in scanning for future risks to the specific project, measuring client satisfaction on an ongoing basis and building in follow-up mechanisms to promptly address any issues arising. Any risks impacting all projects (such as the recent spate of Wannacry/Ransomware cyber attacks) can also be centrally assessed and common guidance disseminated across all relevant project teams.

Position of corporate governance in India

As India heralded in a phase of market-oriented liberation of its economic policies in 1991, corporate governance as a critical prerequisite for attracting private and foreign investment started gaining prominence. Initially introduced by the Confederation of Indian Industry (CII), as a voluntary measure to be adopted by Indian companies, it soon became mandatory for the larger listed companies through Clause 49 of the Listing Agreement. In late 2009, the Ministry of Corporate Affairs (MCA) released a set of guidelines for corporate governance, addressing a number of corporate governance issues. Although the MCA guidelines were voluntary, it triggered a parallel process of key corporate governance norms being consolidated into the new Companies Act, 2012. The key focus of corporate governance in India has traditionally been that of disciplining the dominant shareholder and protecting the interests of the minority shareholders and other stakeholders. This is different from the main focus of corporate governance in Western Europe and Northern America, where the key emphasis is on disciplining management that has ceased to be effectively accountable to the owners who are dispersed shareholders. This change in focus, which addresses the expectations of foreign investors to India, has triggered a set of mixed reactions in India with regard to the rigour of enforcement of corporate governance, together with lack of appropriate support in enforcement from the Indian legal system. As a result, form often prevails over substance by companies 'ticking the box' on governance, risk management and compliance without actually implementing the spirit of the expected norms in their organizations. However, most of these challenges do not apply to an outsourcing or offshoring arrangement where governance and compliance requirements are primarily driven by the overseas customer rather than by the prevailing corporate governance framework in India.

CASE STUDY: IMPLEMENTING STRATEGIC GOVERNANCE AND RISK MANAGEMENT BY A EUROPEAN CLIENT OUTSOURCING IT AND BUSINESS PROCESSES TO AN INDIAN IT-BPO PROVIDER

Internet Bank[1] has been one of the prime movers in European direct banking. The bank offers the Internet as its key sales and delivery channel and does not have any physical branches. It, however, provides to its customers access to a call centre as a back-up channel for unresolved service enquiries only. The main target customers of the bank are well-educated people with a high income who do not need financial advice and who are also not dependent on any specific geographic location for banking services. The bank differentiates itself as a 'price and quality leader' providing a free current account and higher-than-average terms for savings accounts and consumer loans. The bank's strategic business model to enable this differentiation is: (1) to make as much of its costs variable by outsourcing as many of its operational activities as feasible, with a strong preference for pay-as-you-go pricing which significantly reduces the total number of staff employed and retains profitability in the event of a lower volume of business; and (2) to enhance cost-effectiveness by saving costs through outsourcing and offshoring while also bringing in specialized knowledge and skills relevant to specific tasks. This outsourcing strategy is discussed in further detail based on four functional areas: (1) Sales and Product Development; (2) Customer Acquisition and Service Delivery; (3) Transaction Processing; and (4) Strategic Governance and Risk Management.

Sales and Product Development are intertwined processes at Internet Bank where the business strategy is to develop and sell simple and standardized products, such as the current account and consumer loans which do not require personal advisory online. Standardization and simplicity of the product are critical to cost-effectively control the volume of sales enquiries as well as minimize additional costs of IT delivery that may have been required to process complex offerings. Sales efforts include Internet-based marketing to customers by placing them on the bank's website as well as on price-comparison portals. Internet Bank has chosen to keep these activities in-house rather than outsourcing them, in view of the strategic knowledge required on customer preferences, competitive forces and service provider capabilities, who process the transactions related to the product.

Customer Acquisition and Service Delivery processes, including the call centre that provides a second (back-up) channel for resolving customer queries beyond the information available through the bank's website, are primarily automated or outsourced at Internet Bank. Given the relatively small number of simple and standardized products offered to customers, the bank was able to codify the customer service processes to enable this automation and outsourcing. However, given that some of these processes involve direct customer interactions and are extremely strategic to its business, the bank's Board and senior leadership ensure a significant focus on strategic governance and risk management of the related service providers with the full support of the top leadership and Boards of the provider organizations. This is discussed in greater detail in the section on Strategic Governance and Risk Management below.

Transaction Processing is expected to be the back-office operations of most of the other key activities, having been outsourced to multiple outsourced providers, with the exception of lending operations where the credit decision has been retained in-house, given the higher extent of objectivity as well as tacit knowledge required to determine the creditworthiness of potential borrowers. However, other routine activities around loan processing have been outsourced. The service provider organization responsible for transaction processing-related services is different from the provider responsible for operating the call centre, given the difference in the related skill-sets (low-cost staff with capability to ensure a minimal error-rate for transaction processing, as against slightly higher-cost staff based in-country with communication skills and cultural orientation for customer-facing tasks). Additionally, the process of addressing customer complaints is currently carried out in-house, although the bank recognizes that future ability to codify these processes may make the same amenable to automation or outsourcing.

With regard to Strategic Governance and Risk Management processes, the need for a formal Governance, Risk Management and Compliance function is a mandatory regulatory requirement and although the bank is driven by the need to compulsorily comply with such requirements, its focus on leveraging the value of outsourcing, particularly for customer-facing activities discussed above, has led the bank's Board to recognize the strategic benefits this brings about. As a result, the bank has been working to closely align strategic discussions with the relevant risks and start to see such risk-taking through its outsourced business model as a 'matter of choice rather than a matter of chance'.

As mentioned earlier, the bank's senior leadership (with the ultimate accountability of the Board) has established a governance and risk management framework. This framework has been implemented in conjunction with the Indian provider organization and has the following elements.

Working with the vendor to establish robust governance structures

First and foremost, global organizations like Internet Bank, who are outsourcing or offshoring IT and business processes to India, must ensure that a robust governance structure that guarantees an appropriate level of governance and risk management is placed both in the client organization as well as in the provider organization. Strong governance and risk management structures should typically be led by the Board and have dedicated teams in place at a senior management level, who are empowered to drive organization-wide behaviours. This is critical to ensure that a broader range of risks across the entire organization, covering the entire set of internal and external stakeholders within the client and provider organizations, are considered for risk management, covering not just threats but also focused on identifying and leveraging the potential opportunities that risks present to the organization, This, in turn, will enable evolving objectives around strategic dimensions to be met. Similarly, from a provider perspective, the involvement of senior management will ensure that governance and risk management mechanisms are implemented to a uniform standard across all the geographies in which the provider organization operates, with a buy-in from all relevant stakeholders.

Removing any ambiguities on ownership (clarity of roles and responsibilities)

Both the client organization as well as the provider organization must ensure that complete clarity over the ownership of activities for strategic governance and risk management is the case for those tasked with performance and oversight of the governance and risk management framework. Activity ownership must be kept up to date to avoid an inability to manage risk when individuals either leave the organization or move to different roles. Given the increasing focus on achieving the strategic objectives of outsourcing and offshoring, including delivering value and innovation, it is important to ensure that nothing 'falls between the gaps' between the client and the provider organization as well as with the individuals responsible for risk management and governance in each of the operating geographies as well as the business units or functional teams within both these organizations.

Ensuring stakeholder engagement (awareness and commitment)

The extent to which the client, as well as the delivery organization's, key internal and external stakeholders, are aware of and committed to the relevant outsourcing governance and risk management processes is critical for these processes being able to deliver the intended results around strategic objectives, delivering innovation and value and in making the related investments. This also covers the quality of 'back-end monitoring' that is carried out to determine internal compliance with outsourcing governance and risk management policies. This includes both those current stakeholders as well as those who may become so in the future.

Developing strategic governance and risk management capability

This relates to allocating governance and risk management activity ownership to appropriate individuals. Given the increasing uncertainty and volatility of the external environment in which both client and delivery organizations currently operate (as discussed in the earlier section), it is also critical to assign decision-making authority at both a transactional and at the governance framework level to individuals with the competencies and skills to apply judgement on a timely basis in line with business requirements and risk management needs.

Addressing people and skillset issues

Both the client and delivery organizations need to ensure that the outsourcing governance and risk management structures are appropriately resourced. Individuals responsible for making decisions and setting the approach to outsourcing governance and risk management across the organizations must have the skills, experience and seniority to do so.

Establishing appropriate governance and risk management processes

Appropriate governance and risk management processes must be in place for the management of outsourcing risks. These processes must be robust, clear and achievable. Good processes are in line with the organizations' risk appetite and provide a positive experience for business unit and functional stakeholders, as well as for the provider organization.

Addressing technology issues

Both the client as well as the provider organization must have appropriate tools and technology in place, across their operations, to facilitate the performance of the outsourcing risk management and governance framework seamlessly, from inception to exit of a provider relationship. At the very highest level, this would include the ability not just to manage the provider organization at both an engagement and relationship level, but also to be able to leverage the full potential of the provider and the outsourcing arrangement. These systems should be readily available and usable for those tasked with outsourcing governance and risk management activities.

The Bank's Board and senior management, working collaboratively with the leadership of the provider organization, have ensured that governance and risk efforts are *proportionate to the related risks*, which is another critical element of the outsourcing strategy. To ensure the fulfilment of this objective, almost all the bank's key staff are required to possess the following management skills:

- Awareness of the bank's strategy.
- Functional knowledge of the services provided by Internet Bank.
- Have a 'service mentality'.
- Ability to think like an entrepreneur, particularly with regard to managing costs.
- Ability to manage and steer different services, recognizing the linkage between them.
- Knowledge of regulatory requirements.

Key governance processes include a high level of due diligence for new outsourcing projects and ongoing review and monitoring for existing outsourced services. The evaluations are discussed at the Board level, supported by structured questionnaires to determine the operational risks and assess the ability of the service provider to comply with the bank's requirements and on-site visits. Further, depending on the relative importance of the contract, governance and risk management processes are reinforced through weekly or monthly status meetings. It is interesting to know that certain regulatory compliance activities that require specialized knowledge and experience are also outsourced at

Internet Bank, as is some of the internal auditing activity where specialized contractors are used. However, Internet Bank recognizes strategic governance and risk management as a core competency and the need to retain overall in-house responsibility, although specific sub-processes have been outsourced.

This case study demonstrates how Internet Bank successfully supports and leverages its competitive advantage through outsourcing a variety of services, although the steering of the providers through strategic governance and risk management mechanisms has to work flawlessly in order to guarantee customer satisfaction and compliance with all regulatory requirements. Internet Bank belongs to a group of emerging companies termed 'born digital' which can make better predictions and smarter decisions and are able to measure and therefore manage and govern more strategically than ever before. This ability makes a significant contribution to the bank's competitive advantage.

Also, as indicated earlier, the case study demonstrates how governance and compliance requirements are primarily driven by the customer (Internet Bank in the above example) rather than by the prevailing legal framework related to corporate governance in India, the limitations of which do not necessarily act as a barrier to benefits realization. The case study also indicates how investments in enabling clients achieve a high level of strategic governance and risk management by the Indian IT-BPO provider can also help them differentiate themselves and win more work from overseas clients across multiple geographies, amid pay-as-you-go arrangements, reducing contract size and duration and increasing strategic expectations of customers.

Useful websites

India Brand Equity Foundation (IBEF) www.ibef.org
NASSCOM www.nasscom.in

Note

1 Real name withheld in keeping with confidentiality arrangements.

19

LIVING IN INDIA

Arup Varma, Bhaskar Dasgupta, Pawan S. Budhwar and Peter Norlander

Aims of this chapter are to:

- Learn about Indian food habits and availability of global cuisine
- Explore housing, transport, and health care options
- Understand the importance of religion in the daily lives of Indians
- Learn about the unique cultural and contextual practices of India

Introduction

Over the last two decades, the Indian economy has been growing at a tremendous pace (e.g., Budhwar and Varma, 2011) and is now tipped to be the world's second largest economy by 2050.[1] Indeed, India has been a part of an extremely important and critical bloc called BRICS (Brazil, Russia, India, China, South Africa) that has been guiding, and will continue to guide, global economies for the foreseeable future (Budhwar et al., 2017). As a result of this growth, multinationals from around the globe have been setting up shop in India, while Indian companies have steadily expanded their footprints around the globe. While the opening up of the Indian economy began in the early 1990s, it was given a real fillip by the election of Mr Narendra Modi of the Bharatiya Janata Party (BJP) as Prime Minister in 2014. The BJP and Mr Modi's forward-looking policies have resulted in a sharp increase in foreign direct investment (FDI) with investments worth billions of dollars from countries like Japan, China and the USA as well as from such companies as Boeing, IBM, General Electric, Pepsico, Amazon and Facebook.

A recent survey[2] notes that India has sharply moved up as a preferred location for inbound expatriates and is now ranked 14th, with expatriates earning the highest average salaries among expatriates in any country (US$176,000). It has often been argued that India's diversity is its strength, and no matter how one describes India, the opposite is also likely to be true! In this chapter, we present useful information that can help expatriates on assignment to India, as they navigate their way through this complex and compelling country. Accordingly, we cover key topics such as transport, health, and food, etc., making sure to highlight the unique Indian angle to each of these topics. At the end of the chapter, there is a case study of a first-person account by Peter Norlander, one of the co-authors, who lived and worked in India for over two years.

Food availability and habits

There are Indian restaurants almost everywhere in the world, so the chances are that the expatriate has tried Indian cuisine. While Indian families have traditionally prided themselves on eating their meals at home, this practice is slowly evolving and adapting to new realities, such as the rise in mobile nuclear families. With many families now seeing both husband and wife work outside their home, eating out, or ordering in is not seen as such a foreign concept any more. Almost all major chain restaurants are now operating in India, and most have adapted their menus out of respect for religious sensibilities. The good news is that most restaurants will happily deliver food to individuals' homes within a reasonable period of time.

In terms of meal timings, the typical Indian family consumes four meals a day – a hearty breakfast followed by lunch, a high tea and then a big dinner. The breakfast composition varies widely between regions, and can comprise a wide variety of items including toast, eggs, cornflakes, fruits, chapatti, and regional delicacies, such as *poha, dosa, idli,* and so on. In addition, *chai* (black tea infused with ginger and cardamom, and topped off with milk and sugar) is an important part of breakfast (in the four southern states, tea is often replaced with filter coffee). Indeed, tea and coffee are drunk throughout the day, and no guest will be allowed to leave without consuming one of these drinks along with snacks.

While the general view is that Indians are vegetarians, truth is that in several parts of the country meat is consumed liberally, with fish often replacing meat or accompanying it in cities and states that are situated along India's long coast. It is important to note that Hindus typically do not consume beef. As such, lamb/goat or chicken are the most common meat items on the dinner table.

Clothing

An old Indian saying goes that everyone must have the three basic necessities of life – *roti* (food), *kapda* (clothes), and *makaan* (house). After discussing food, we now turn our attention to clothing, as this is an important part of successfully settling in to, and blending in with, the local customs. Any visitor to India will find that the dress habits of Indians are as diverse as the people themselves. While most men in the cities prefer western attire, including suits and ties, women will often be seen in Indian clothing, including saris and *salwar-kameez*, for both formal and informal events. In the rural areas, most men would be seen wearing the long shirt known as *kurta* paired with a pyjama, which can be fashioned tight or loose. Of course, Indians tend to be fairly conservatively when it comes to social mores, so the best way to handle the issue of dress is to dress conservatively, comfortably, and similar to the local people.

Housing

In Indian cities, one can find the whole range of housing options – from stand-alone single-family homes, to townhouses, and large apartment complexes. Ironically, housing tends to be expensive in most Indian cities, due to demand far exceeding supply. This imbalance, combined with the lack of space and increasing willingness of Indians to move within the country, leads to significant pressures on rents, with some cities (e.g., Mumbai) boasting some of the highest rents anywhere in the world. The best way to approach this issue is to hire a knowledgeable and reliable real estate broker. In addition, it would be a good idea to call upon friends/ colleagues for help with identifying the right neighborhoods and getting the best deals. In general, expatriates are viewed as good tenants, due to their willingness to sign long-term leases and pay in foreign currencies.

The weather

A common misperception held in many parts of the world is that India is "hot." Ironically, this leads to many inaccurate generalizations about the country. In terms of topography, India is a vast country boasting some of the tallest mountains in the world, alongside large deserts, seven major rivers and over 7,500 kilometers of coastline. As such, the country experiences all weather patterns – with each region experiencing unique weather patterns. So, in the north, India experiences significant amounts of snowfall, while the north-east receives some of the highest rainfall in the world. In general, the country experiences four distinct seasons – winter (December to February), summer (March to May), rainy season (June to September), and the post-monsoon period (October to November), though based on its location, it can be said that the bulk of the country experiences a tropical climate.

Transport

Often, the first thing that visitors to India remark about is the chaotic traffic that seems to follow no apparent rules or guidelines. And, yet, somehow the traffic keeps moving. It is indeed a fact that Indian roads are full of all manner of vehicle: cars, scooters, motor-cycles, auto rickshaws, cycle-rickshaws, buses, trucks, and so on, with almost everyone's horn blaring constantly. In addition, in many cities, animals can also be found peacefully sharing the roads with vehicles and pedestrians. Given the resultant chaos, it is indeed a wonder that traffic moves at all! The lack of sufficient roads, the constantly increasing number of vehicles on the roads, combined with a general lack of traffic sense, lead to almost utter chaos. For those not adventurous enough to want to own and operate their own vehicles, most cities have state-run or controlled public transit systems. Of course, these are usually crowded, since the majority of the population continues to rely on these systems for their needs. Kolkata was the first city in India to build and operate the underground metro, though New Delhi has built and operates an extremely efficient and extensive network of the metro. Several other cities are in the process of building metro lines, indeed, Bengaluru and Lucknow already have parts of their proposed networks operational.

The Indian railways have one of the largest networks in the world, reaching almost every corner of the country. The long-haul trains typically offer two classes of travel: a first class, air-conditioned class with comfortable sleeper berths, and a second class, which is typically not air-conditioned and may offer wooden sleeper berths or seats. The typical business traveler will find that air travel is very convenient, and comfortable, and serves his/her purpose extremely well.

Shopping

Over the last two decades or so, India has seen substantial changes in the availability and range of consumer products. One result of the policy changes at the national level is the growth in the number of malls and shopping complexes across the nation, especially in the larger cities. While people did most of their shopping at neighborhood markets and grocery stores in the past, these are now complemented by the larger chain stores such as Spencer's, Metro, and Reliance Fresh etc. Interestingly, most middle-class and lower-income families still rely on their local market to procure their daily needs in terms of fish, meats, vegetables and fruits, etc.

Security

In general, India is a very safe place to live, especially for expatriates, for any number of reasons. First, expatriates are considered guests, and guests are considered the equivalent of deity. Next, the laws in India prohibit ordinary citizens from procuring or carrying weapons of any kind, leading to fairly safe cities and towns. Of course, like any other country with a large population and a good percentage of disenfranchised people, there are cases of petty crime – purse snatching, pick pocketing, and so on. For the most part though, Indian cities have prided themselves on being safe for everyone. Indeed, the strong neighborhood concept led to the practice whereby people look out for each other. While this is sometimes seen as infringing on others' privacy, the flipside was that everyone in a neighborhood knew each other and outsiders stood out. Ironically, one outcome of the economic growth has been that many neighborhoods have changed dramatically, with old two-storeyed homes being replaced by high-rise apartments, where most people may not know their neighbor.

While foreigners are rarely targeted in crimes, taking precautions is best advised for everyone. Thus, for example, it is best to avoid being out at night in poorly lit areas specially if one is alone. Many of the new apartment complexes attract potential tenants by offering round-the-clock security guards, who are often supported by numerous CCTVs and other electronic gadgets.

Health care and medical insurance

The Indian health care system is characterized by a vast public health care system topped by an equally large private health care system. Most expatriates, and middle-class families, as well as the rich, primarily rely on private medical health care provided by a huge array of doctors, clinics and hospitals. Compared to the western world, health care is much cheaper, and more accessible, although the process of medical insurance, claims and reimbursements can be challenging. Medicines and drugs produced in India are extraordinarily cheap compared to western prices and imported medicines can be very expensive. However, it is important to find your local pharmacy as soon as possible, and establish good links with them. In most case, pharmacies will deliver required medicines to your doorstep, and many have even introduced frequent-purchaser discounts.

Religion

One recurring theme throughout this chapter has been the diversity of India, which extends to its religious practices. Not surprisingly, religion plays a major role in the day-to-day lives of Indians. While there are numerous historical places of worship of each religion, there are literally thousands of small shrines established all over the country. If one were to travel across India, either by train or road, one would be amazed at the ubiquitous presence of the various religious shrines, often next to each other.

The majority of the population practices some form of Hinduism, though other world religions, such as Christianity and Islam, have been present in India for a very long time. In addition, other major religions, such as Buddhism, Sikhism, and Jainism were born in India. Among the major Hindu festivals are "Holi" which marks the beginning of Spring, and Diwali, also known as the Festival of Lights, which is celebrated as the Hindu New Year. During Holi, people can be seen dowsing each other with dry colours (called *abeer*) and also with water balloons and jet-sprays (*pichkarees*). These water games usually end by mid to early afternoon, after which people visit friends and relatives with boxes of sweets and exchange gifts. During Diwali, which is also celebrated as the victory of good over evil, people decorate their houses with lights to welcome Laxmi, the goddess of wealth. In addition to these Pan-Indian festivals, there are several regional festivals that are celebrated with equal fervor. For example, West Bengal is known for celebrating Durga Puja and Kali Puja during the autumn months, while Mumbai, in the state of Maharashtra, is known for celebrating Ganesh Chaturthi. It is recommended that expatriates participate in the Indian festivals, as Indians generally welcome newcomers into their "family" and this would be a great way to learn more about the country and its people, and also partake in some amazing food that is associated with each celebration.

The softer side

A sense of humor is an absolute essential while living in India: "It's the ability to take a joke, not make one that proves you have a sense of humour." The ability to laugh off the challenges due to bureaucracy, people saying yes when they do not know, transportation gridlock, linguistic issues, etc. will be a godsend for people moving to India. One would also find that Indians love a joke (but not a personal one). Cultural jokes aimed at religious or cultural minorities are a dime a dozen, but at worst, casual discrimination exists and is particularly evident to nationalities with dark/darker skin, and this will be reflected in the level of politeness, cost of goods, availability of housing, etc. This may be personally uncomfortable for you and the level of acceptance will differ greatly from situation to situation. To be on the safe side when faced with an uncomfortable joke, a smile goes a long way and it is best to discreetly move on to some other subject.

Services such as household maids, servants and drivers, hairdressing saloons, plumbers, electricians and telecommunications are considerably cheap and plentiful. These days, there are agencies who can help with these domestic services and, yes, there are apps for it. Again, asking your neighbors over a cup of tea or leaning over the fence will give you the real deal. There is an art to dealing with household servants, which can be learnt quite easily, although the language may be a challenge.

Generally, one will find neighbors very helpful, if a bit nosy. Be prepared for the lack of personal space and some rather strange and perhaps surprising personal questions. If you feel a bit disconcerted, a gentle but firm negative goes a long way in clearing the air.

Another potential jarring experience is the concept of time. Working in the West would generally mean that times and dates are rather sacrosanct. In India, an agreed date and time are usually indicative, one would not be surprised if even the date is moved. People start work late and work till late. Breakfast meetings at 9 a. m. or even later should not come as a surprise. Dinner invitation times are loose and one might find that guests appear anything between one or two hours later than specified.

Recommendations

1. Create a clear transparent set of guiding business principles, which will drive the relationship. Too many commercial relationships begin by trying to create legal contracts and very detailed master service agreements. Cultural factors and the speed of business change mean that the relationship should be

governed under a light touch governance framework. Flexibility and the ability to review and renew are critical.

2. Be very clear about the reasons for operating in India or operating in/with an Indian MNC. Are you operating to take advantage of lower costs? Or for higher capacity? Or are you operating to access new markets? Or market share? Or a combination of the above? Given the nature of Indian business and the long-term culture, clarity and consistency are key.

3. Recognize the cultural challenges and work with them. There are different angles and dimensions of culture. There are many sub-cultures emanating from differences in religion, language, region, gender, and so on – indeed, there are no hard and fast rules except for one – recognize the cultural factor and incorporate it in your plans.

4. Apply the "trust but verify" principle. Micromanagement rarely works in the Indian environment or in Indian MNCs. High-level strategy, direction and guidance supported by good governance, tracking and reporting form a good starting point to establish a relationship or a business.

5. It is important to be knowledgeable about, and devote resources (time, funding, employees) to regulatory and government requirements. Non-compliance with stated and unstated regulatory, government (central, state, local and institutional) requirements can be problematic.

6. Political involvement can and does play a part in business and it is critical that managers are cognisant of that fact. While this may not be a huge issue on the operating level, at the strategic level, there is frequently a close and important linkage with local, state and central political institutions.

7. Learn as much as you can about India before you set out – while the country is too diverse and complex for anyone, including Indians, to claim they know all, it is essential to have a basic understanding of the country and its systems and people.

CASE STUDY: LIVING IN INDIA: A FIRST-HAND ACCOUNT, BY PETER NORLANDER

I moved to India as a young college graduate. After living and working in India for nearly two years, I left as an adult.

My experience living in India began while I was a college student in 2003. I spent a summer as an unpaid intern in Mumbai, working as a journalist for the *Financial Express* while also taking Sanskrit classes at *Somaiya Vidyavihar*. As a journalist, I wrote solo bylined publications to add to my portfolio as an aspiring journalist while covering the shareholder meetings of major corporations such as Tata Motors and Hindustan Lever. As a student, I practiced speaking Hindi while reading classic Indian literature in the original under the guidance of an expert.

India's business community is incredibly clever, entrepreneurial, and thrifty. The press covers the business news closely and freely. Both the popular and business press in India are gossipy and relevant, boasting some of the world's largest circulations. While living in India, I read the paper almost every day, and recommend it for speeding up acclimation. You'll probably need a local friend to help you understand the idioms, political machinations, and rules of cricket, but each is a vital part of the culture.

One thing about getting things done in India is that the best resources aren't on the web or in a book. The best resources are the people you know. Ask them for help, and you will get further, faster, than any other way. Research helps, but people know things, and can open doors. You'll also have a much better experience this way. While this may seem obvious and true for life in general and is not strictly applicable to India, it's a lesson that my time in India drilled deeply into me.

I lived in a dorm room in the International Guest House of the University of Mumbai. I had a small room with a cot and a view of the Arabian Sea, just next to Churchgate station. I paid 100 Rupees (<$2) a day to live there, and was surrounded by students from Africa, Arab countries, Nepal and a number of Indians. The metro regions in India are busy, crowded "vast seas of humanity," and they represent opportunity for many migrants from around India and all over the world. My daily routine was packed full. From my home base, I took the packed local trains every morning north to Vidyavihar for Sanskrit classes, and then traveled by train south to Chinchpokli, to the offices of the *Financial Express* in the afternoon, staying there until late evening.

During my time in Mumbai, I walked daily past shuttered cloth mills and present-day markets and spice-grinding facilities. I would fall asleep easily at night after packed and sweaty days. I often cold-called sources for my journalist work, but people are much more likely to pick up the phone if someone they know introduces you to them. While being a foreigner gives you some cachet as you are possibly a bit exotic, to speed up your acclimation, start introducing yourself and drink tea with as many people as you can. Moreover, once you know a person, they are much more likely to want to work with you if you get to know them a bit before discussing business. I think this lesson is translatable to the US, but our business and social culture are often so transactional that before living in India, I had not adequately considered the important role relationships play in getting things done. Americans also don't appreciate how efficient and equitable many of our institutions are; you don't notice the power of relationships until you experience living in a context where bureaucracies and markets are often less efficient than having relationships to help get things done.

After that summer in Mumbai, I caught a bug – and not just the famed Delhi belly. After returning to my senior year in college, I knew that after I graduated, I wanted to go back to live in India to work full-time. I felt I was growing at a faster rate in India, where things were different, puzzling, and vibrant, than I was in the comfort of home. I told everyone who could possibly help that I was seeking a job in India, and I asked for help. A friend found a job advertisement seeking Americans for work in India. The position I applied for was in the HR department of an Indian IT company, and while I had journalism aspirations at that point, I decided I would go back to India as long as I could find a job that would pay me to live there. Thus, this is a very idiosyncratic narrative.

I was one of 10 American college graduates hired to work at Infosys Technologies Ltd., in Bangalore, full-time in 2005. When I lived in India as an expat, I was never on a luxurious expat package. Many of my expat friends and acquaintances were, but the post-graduate job of my dreams was one that paid my airfare and living expenses.

Another key lesson of trying to accomplish things in India is that relationships can get you to the right door, but then you need to walk through it yourself and talk with someone who can get things done. Many people think that India is chaotic, and certainly that description fits the traffic. I think a common mistake I saw among expats was feeling powerless and that efforts to do something about a problem (say, trash in the alley next door) were futile. But enter a home, live in a neighborhood, study in a university, or work in a business in India, and you'll find that someone is either in an authority position and firmly running the show or is actively seeking to change the status quo, usually creatively and impressively under resource constraints that we would struggle with. Elders are respected at home, there are leaders and factions in the community, the boss is "yes-sir'd" and feared at work. If you're in a bureaucratic jam, there's probably an individual who knows the issue far better and can help you, but, first, you need to find the right person, which is the person with authority. A lot of efforts will not pay off and only lead to frustration if you don't learn to identify who just talks and who has the power to change things. This lesson is also transferable to life in general.

While in India, you will have to negotiate prices. If you want to shop for a gift in a bazaar or get in a taxi or a rickshaw, or do anything except in the Western-style malls and hip, modern stores, you have to negotiate. A common, but mistaken and irrational, assumption among foreigners is that everyone who tries to sell you something is out to cheat you on the "real price." In this telling, the "real price" is what locals pay. If you think you're being discriminated against because you are an American or other foreign national, you are quite possibly correct in a narrow sense. However, field research shows that when foreigners buy from artisanal crafts workers directly, they may pay less than locals because the craft worker is proud to have their work displayed in a home abroad. In contrast, merchants often take pride in charging the maximum they can, and may try to charge foreigners more than locals. Go shopping with a local or check a few prices against multiple vendors if you're worried about being ripped off.

In my job at Infosys in HR, I wound up playing a minor yet important role establishing the acculturation program for what I believe was the largest expat program for Americans in India since the Peace Corps was expelled in the 1970s. After 10 of us arrived in 2005, I helped set up processes to help hundreds arrive, for 6, 12 and more months.

I was often puzzled by the behavior of expats, often far richer than me, who negotiate completely irrationally. I have seen Americans let rickshaw after rickshaw go by, adding to their frustration and waiting time, in order to find a rickshaw who would take the "meter rate." Never mind that locals I encounter face the same hassle, but ultimately rational people decide what a trip is worth and negotiate deals up to their willingness to pay, which they decide in advance. I met an American whose sense of justice was so offended by an "unfair" rate that he lacerated his arm while trying to make an emphatic point by smacking the glass on a rickshaw. An Indian colleague also once got in a fight with a driver. These incidents occurred over price differences of under $2. As any rational negotiator knows, before you enter a negotiation, you should answer one question: What is your willingness to pay? As I matured, I started asking myself and others what it was worth to them not to wait for the "fair" price. This really decreased frustration.

Despite the meager pay mentioned above, that same salary paid me to live in India. It paid my monthly rent in a giant apartment in a desirable neighborhood (which to be fair, was subsidized by the company) with balconies that monkeys would enter to get food. Be forewarned that if your neighbors are vegetarians, the smell of cooking meat might be offensive to them. Be sensitive, but also consider dining out for those meals if you must.

As a final note, that meager salary (which did increase over time) paid me to travel all over India. I have been back many times since, for both work and pleasure. While living in Bangalore, I would venture into Karnataka, Tamil Nadu, and Kerala on long weekends, and to explore Nepal and northern parts of India on longer week-long excursions. That salary paid for a private yoga tutor, and for many gifts and wonderful adventures.

For travel, I recommend finding a good travel agent. Leave the cities and spend time in the country, even for short weekends. Trains, overnight (sleeper) buses, private cars with drivers, and air fare all offer affordable and comfortable ways to get around. A travel agent can usually help get tickets faster than I could, and can advise on appropriate options. Find a good one and focus your travel research on what it is you'd like to do and see, instead of the transactional frustrations of booking tickets and doing a price comparison for each service.

In the news

India and Japan have launched work on the Bullet Train project in India. See www.reuters.com/article/india-japan/india-to-get-japans-bullet-train-deepens-defence-and-nuclear-ties-idUSKBN0TV07D20151212

The "Make in India" initiative of the Indian government has resulted in a major boost to manufacturing operations in India. See www.makeinindia.com/home

In November 2016, the Indian government launched a major demonetization scheme, aimed at weeding out illicit monetary transactions and so-called "black money," further strengthening this government's continuing efforts to provide a clean, corruption-free, administration.

Useful weblinks[3]

Adoption www.india.gov.in/outerwin.php?id=http://www.adoptionindia.nic.in/
Air tickets online www.india.gov.in/howdo/otherservice_details.php?service=4
Applying for a PAN card (Permanent Account Number) www.india.gov.in/howdo/otherservice_details.php?service=15
Applying for a TAN card (Tax Deduction Account Number) www.india.gov.in/howdo/otherservice_details.php?service=3
Birth certificate www.india.gov.in/howdo/howdoi.php?service=1
Checking status of stolen vehicles www.india.gov.in/howdo/otherservice_details.php?service=1
Death certificate www.india.gov.in/howdo/howdoi.php?service=2
Domicile certificate www.india.gov.in/howdo/howdoi.php?service=5
Driving license www.india.gov.in/howdo/howdoi.php?service=6
Income tax returns www.india.gov.in/howdo/otherservice_details.php?service=12
Marriage certificate www.india.gov.in/howdo/howdoi.php?service=3
Registering a company www.india.gov.in/howdo/otherservice_details.php?service=19
Registering a vehicle www.india.gov.in/howdo/howdoi.php?service=13
Registering as employer www.india.gov.in/howdo/otherservice_details.php?service=17
Registering land/property www.india.gov.in/howdo/howdoi.php?service=9
Registering the IN domain for online use www.india.gov.in/howdo/otherservice_details.php?service=18
Registering with the State Employment Exchange www.india.gov.in/howdo/howdoi.php?service=12
Train tickets online
www.india.gov.in/howdo/otherservice_details.php?service=5

Notes

1 See www.pwc.com/gx/en/issues/the-economy/assets/world-in-2050-february-2015.pdf
2 See http://money.cnn.com/2017/09/26/pf/expats-best-places-britain-brexit-uk/index.html
3 While we have provided several important links, clearly there would be other links that the reader would need. Also, many of these links may have been updated or moved to different platforms, so please search the relevant domains for the most current links.

References

Budhwar, P., Tung, R., Varma, A. and Do, H. (2017) Human resource management in MNCs from BRICS nations. *Journal of International Management*, 23: 111–123.
Budhwar, P. and Varma, A. (eds) (2011) *Doing Business in India*. London: Routledge.

20

ENTREPRENEURIAL GLOBALIZATION

Lessons from the "new" Indian global firm

Sam Hariharan and U. Srinivasa Rangan

Aims of this chapter are to:

- Learn from the "new" Indian global firm (NIGF)
- Explain features of the NIGF
- Present the framework of entrepreneurial globalization and the challenges and opportunities highlighted by the NIGFs for foreign investors

Introduction

Consider the following stylized facts on the Indian economy in recent years:

- Between 1995 and 2015, Indian firms' outward foreign direct investment (FDI) went up from 0.03 per cent to 0.47 per cent of global net outward FDI outflow, a sixteen-fold rise (World Bank, 2015).
- During that period (1995–2015), the number of Indian firms in the Fortune Global 500 list went up from 1 to 7 (*Fortune*, 2017).
- In the same 20 years (1995–2015), India's trade as a share of its GDP doubled from 22.47 per cent to 44.99 per cent (World Bank, 2015).
- In those 20 years (1995–2015), India's share of global GDP more than doubled from 1.2 per cent to 2.82 per cent (ibid.).

As the Indian economy integrates into a globalized world, Indian firms are seeking scale, scope, and opportunities globally. This chapter explains the context, process, and strategic approach of how Indian firms have sought to globalize and the implications of this transformation. It also highlights the opportunities and challenges they pose to foreign firms entering India.

The new Indian global firm

Since the 1980s, the academic framework explaining the rise of multinational corporations (MNCs) from emerging economies has been based on the literature on Third World multinationals (Lall, 1983; Wells, 1983). Its arguments stem from the expansion of Third World firms into other Third World markets, such as Indian bicycle firms exporting/assembling low-end bikes in Africa and Indian producers of ethnic food setting up factories in Africa/the Middle East to make and sell it to the Indian diaspora. It argues that Third World MNCs had specific advantages in other Third World markets due to the use of appropriate technology and applicability and ease of transfer of their products and services to economies similar in infrastructure, market needs, and institutions.

The current wave of Indian MNCs is different from the Third World MNCs of the past. For one thing, this expansion is focused on developed, not emerging, economies. Good examples are the global expansion of firms such as Tata Motors (TM), Tata Steel, Bharti Airtel, Bharat Forge (BF), and Sundram Fasteners. The NIGFs span a wide range of industries (see Table 20.1). A second characteristic is their mode of entry into developed economies is mainly through acquisitions. The industries entered were often mature with established incumbents and large entry barriers.

Another characteristic is the potential of NIGFs to transform the competitive landscape. It is partly because they have entered with some scale or with creative and entrepreneurial strategies to take advantage of their unique capabilities while overcoming their resource disadvantages.

These entrepreneurially globalized firms pose a major challenge to entrants into India. To meet the challenge, entrants should understand the phenomenon of NIGF. The attributes of the NIGFs persuade us that this is not the same phenomenon as the earlier waves of globalization. We argue that changing Indian institutional context may best explain the emergence of the NIGF.

Non-globalization of Indian firms prior to 1990s

Until the early 1990s, the Indian environment was detrimental to the globalization of Indian firms. Government policies since independence were largely responsible

TABLE 20.1 The new Indian global firms and industries

Sector	Companies
Mining, minerals and materials	ONGC, Tata Steel, Vedanta, Balco
Engineering	Tata Motors, Sundram Fasteners, Bharat Forge, Amtek, Samvadhana Motherson, CUMI
Pharmaceuticals	Dr. Reddy's Labs, Cipla, Biocon
Services	TCS, Infosys, MindTree Consulting, Bharti Airtel, Apollo Group, Fortis

for this state of affairs. First, Indian policy-makers were biased against trade due to their export pessimism that held that developing nations could not export their way to prosperity (Hughes, 1992). Therefore, trade policy was driven by the goals of autarchy and import substitution. By 1993, India's share of world exports (Porter, 1995) was less than 2 per cent. Second, India's protectionism entrenched incumbents and blunted incentives for innovation. For example, for more than 40 years, Hindustan Motors dominated the Indian auto market with a 1953 Morris model, with little change in the design. The policy of capacity licensing barred the entry of new firms, reduced competition, and made Indian firms globally uncompetitive in terms of cost structures, technology, and products. In 1991, Indian bicycle firms, for example, held a paltry 3 per cent share of the world market (ibid.). Third, India's policy of reserving some sectors for small-scale industries lowered the incentives for successful firms to ever attain global scale and global competitiveness. For example, the Indian footwear and garment industries were able to achieve less than a 5 per cent share of global exports (ibid.) largely concentrated in low value-added items. Fourth, India's central planning ossified the industrial sector. The hurdles faced by entrepreneurs, in terms of the regulations, approvals and permits, along with challenging access to capital, led to the dominance of family-owned conglomerates, such as the Tatas, Birlas, Goenkas, Thapars, and Modis. The policy of capacity licensing and the rent-seeking actions of conglomerates led to unwieldy diversification, often lacking any depth of core competences needed to be competitive. In early 1990s, through a fortuitous set of circumstances, Indian economic policies became more market-oriented and that, in turn, led to the globalization of Indian firms.

Globalization of Indian firms: macro factors and micro drivers

The impetus for the new wave of globalization can be traced to the India's economic crisis in 1991. The crisis manifested itself in three ways: (1) Indian economic growth, which rose above, the anemic rate of about 3 per cent per annum (derisively dubbed the Hindu rate of growth) in the mid-1980s began to falter (Panagariya, 2004); (2) inflation that fell in the mid-1980s began to rise again (Shah, 1998); and (3) India's exports began to fall even as its import bill began to balloon. By 1991, India's foreign exchange reserves could barely finance three weeks of imports. The confluence of these problems forced the government to pursue macro-economic reforms, which triggered a series of micro-economic changes that strongly pushed Indian firms to go abroad.

The main policy changes were directed at opening up the economy to FDI and imports, thus ditching a model of import restrictions, industry protection, and autarchy. At the micro level, as MNCs began to enter India, Indian firms began to recognize the need to compete with agility. The second set of changes involved the dismantling of restraints on firms put in place as part of central planning. Out went the policy of capacity licensing, imports through permits and quotas, and restrictions on foreign firms that had made incumbents severely uncompetitive. As

MNCs started coming in, it became critical for India to loosen the restrictions on domestic firms to enable them to compete on a more level playing field.

The third change was the move away from a *dirigiste* model of development as the government started disinvestment and privatization of state-owned enterprises (SOEs). The withdrawal of the state from running business entities meant more room for the private sector. SOEs operating in a business-like manner also meant the non-availability of subsidized inputs of energy, transportation, and communications. This forced Indian firms to compete more efficiently. The policy changes enacted since (and due to) the 1991 crisis have energized the Indian business landscape. The micro-economic revolution has led to four key developments as listed below.

First, and perhaps the most important development, is the arrival of entrepreneurs in a range of industries, such as Bharti Airtel in telecommunications, and Havells in electrical goods. They have not only been entrepreneurial within India but have sought to build a global presence. Second, some of the big business groups have adapted to the new environment. The Tatas undertook a restructuring effort to become competitive both locally and to create a platform for global expansion. The TVS group began an effort to improve competitiveness. The Aditya Birla Group and the Reliance Group adapted their business scope and focus to cope with the new opportunities created by the changes in the policy environment. Third, some business groups have faded following these policy changes. Some attempted, but unsuccessfully, to enter new businesses while others ceded leadership positions to new entrants. For example, the Modi group's planned venture with Lufthansa never took off, and the Thapar group's Crompton-Greaves lost its old luster and is now a mere shadow of its old stature. Fourth, the entry of MNCs has provided the impetus for some local firms to "up their game." When the new entrant, Pepsi, changed the rules of the game in the soft drink industry, Parle's had to become competitive eventually being acquired by Coca-Cola. Faced with the entry of McDonald's, Nirula's in New Delhi greatly upgraded the quality of their offerings and customer service.

These developments in India pose formidable challenges for entrants into India. The newly energized Indian firms have lessons for entrants on how to compete in India of today. None of these developments, though, is as challenging as the "new" Indian global firm (NIGF).

Entrepreneurial globalization and the "new" Indian global firm

The net effect of macro policy changes which opened up the economy to foreign investors and firms, and the micro-economic changes that pushed local firms to become competitive, was that, for the first time since India's independence, Indian firms began to think in global terms. With the loss of the soft option of being globally weak but domestically dominant behind protectionist walls, Indian companies began to recognize the need to specialize, focus, and compete globally.

We found both family firms (Bharat Forge or BF and Havells) and business groups (Tatas, Birlas, and Mahindras) evolving into professionally managed firms before globalizing. New entrepreneurial firms – Bharti Airtel, Infosys, and Dr. Reddy's Labs – chose to globalize early in their life cycle. In all cases, globalization was driven by either the opportunities global markets presented for revenue growth (e.g., TCS, Havells, Bharti Airtel) or the opportunity to leverage domestic advantages globally for profit growth (e.g., Tata Steel, Dr. Reddy's, BF).

After the 1990s, Indian firms were forced to fend for themselves against MNCs within India and simultaneously pushed to go abroad. After decades of protection, Indian firms realized that they lacked competitive advantages often associated with MNCs, such as brand reputations, customer relationships, advanced technologies, patents, process capabilities, and so on. Lacking such specific assets and encountering incumbents with strong competitive advantages, Indian firms have had to craft creative globalization strategies to overcome resource constraints. It is best to view the globalization of these firms as a phenomenon of "entrepreneurial globalization," i.e., globalization through entrepreneurial thinking and action (Hariharan and Rangan, 2012).

An entrepreneurial orientation is best seen as one driven by the desire to capitalize on opportunities without being constrained by the resources owned (Stevenson, 1983; Hamel and Prahalad, 1993). "Entrepreneurial globalization" is the process by which Indian firms have, through creative entrepreneurial choices, globalized in spite of the constraints they faced in terms of the resources they owned, the lack of global brand reputations, inadequate internal sources of capital and cash flow to fund expansion, while facing significant barriers to entry. Such entrepreneurial globalization has allowed Indian firms to overcome significant resource constraints and scale relatively high barriers to entry and mobility to take on established competitors globally.

Based on the framework of entrepreneurial globalization, we formulated a series of themes or propositions and sought evidence to see if they were supported when the strategies of Indian firms were examined in detail. In general, we found that while each firm used not every theme, as each faced its own unique situation, the themes were in evidence across many situations. For new entrants into India, entrepreneurial globalization offers both a challenge and an opportunity. It challenges traditional ways of competing and provides an opportunity to learn from India's successful global players.

Disaggregating, redefining and reconfiguring the global value chain

An important way in which entrepreneurs compete against incumbents is by creatively disaggregating the value chain, redefining the way value activities are executed, and reconfiguring the activities to leverage the entrepreneur's competences (Rangan and Schumacher, 2012). Many of the NIGFs have resorted to such an entrepreneurial strategy. For example, Bharti Airtel (BA) adopted a different configuration of value activities from its global rivals like Vodafone. It decided to focus primarily on the marketing, collaborating with different players such as IBM, Nokia, Ericsson, Tech Mahindra, and Spanco to manage its IT systems and support, and management of its network infrastructure. Unlike its rivals, BA chose to "outsource" non-core activities to partners, thus changing its cost structure relative to rivals (lower fixed costs as a component of its total costs). This model was tied to BA's "factory model" of pricing, which was the most aggressive of the global mobile operators, focusing on volume rather than the standard ARPU (Average Revenue per User) focus of most operators. BA replicated the strategy as it expanded into Bangladesh and Sri Lanka and in Africa with its acquisition of Zain.

In addition to having a different value chain from their rivals in developed economies, these Indian players have also expanded abroad in creative and selective ways. While extending their footprint into developed economies, they have not always chosen to replicate the entire domestic value chain in these markets. Often, they have chosen to expand only some value activities in the new markets. In others, they have actually chosen to deconstruct the value activities into smaller components and chosen to perform them differently and in dispersed locations.

Dispersing globally the locus of activities

Globalization opens up the whole world to perform value activities. The NIGFs are free, unlike incumbents that are wedded to legacy commitments (Ghemawat, 1991), to disperse the activities differently and globally. They reconfigure their value chain by choosing alternative locations, different from their established rivals, in which to perform value activities, and in some cases, choosing collaborators/ partners to perform these activities (Kogut, 1985).

The logic behind the choices reflects the specific sources of competitive advantage enjoyed by the Indian firm, and regarding "what" and "where" capabilities needed to be built. For example, in many cases, the Indian firm chose to locate (or relocate in cases where acquisitions were the vehicles used to expand globally) value activities differently from incumbents: performing some engineering and product development in their domestic operations, while choosing to build in the developed economy markets customer-focused design capabilities by blending talent from their domestic operations with local engineering talent, and enhancing local marketing capabilities and customer relationships by retaining and strengthening local management and marketing talent.

Again, companies such as Tata Motors (TM) expanded aggressively using such a strategy. Tata Motors' acquisition of Jaguar Land Rover (JLR) allowed it to leverage India both as a low-cost manufacturing location for components and sub-systems and as a growing market for higher-end cars, a segment where TM needed an offering. TM had taken advantage of its access to low-cost skilled labour in India by shifting part of the new car design effort to India, thus marrying access to leading-edge customers in the developed markets with low-cost but highly skilled engineers in India. It allowed TM to be a better competitor globally.

Choosing modes of globalization to overcome barriers to entry

Emerging Indian multinationals recognized that they were latecomers and did not have the luxury of time or resources to follow the globalization path of early movers. Often, Indian firms were expanding globally in mature industries and markets with entry barriers and entrenched rivals. The barriers ranged from capital requirements and brand reputation to customer relationships, and capabilities in R&D and marketing. Moreover, given the maturity of these industries and markets, it was uneconomical to add additional capacity in industries facing low growth and, often, excess capacity. Consequently, India's emerging MNCs often globalized through acquisitions, a convenient and quick way to vault over entry barriers. Indeed, acquiring an existing business often provided valuable assets such as a list of customers, a distribution and marketing infrastructure and capabilities, market-tested product offerings, manufacturing facilities and capabilities, R&D capabilities, and finally local management and local knowledge.

All of the Indian companies we examined in this study used acquisitions to globalize. Some notable examples of these acquisitions and the role they have played in enabling these firms realize their global ambitions are: Tata Motors' acquisition of JLR, Bharti Airtel's acquisition of Zain, BF's series of medium-sized acquisitions in the USA, Germany, England, and Sweden, Tata Steel's acquisition of Corus in Europe, and Havells' acquisition of Sylvania's operations in Europe and Latin America. The companies used these acquisitions to significantly increase their global footprint and to vault into becoming a major global player.

Through acquisitions, BF overcame the significant barriers that new suppliers face when serving global automobile industry manufacturers, such as lacking established customer relationships and delivery reputations. To avoid being left behind in a weak competitive position, Tata Motors arguably had no option in a scale-intensive and brand-dominant global auto industry other than to acquire JLR and leverage it to enter geographical markets ranging from Europe to North America and Asia.

Tapping diverse sources of capital and other resources

The new Indian MNCs often face stiff resource constraints, primary among which is access to capital for funding their global expansion through acquisitions. However, acquisitions need either access to funding or stock that the target firms will accept as payment. This implies that Indian MNCs have to tap into diverse sources of capital. Again, it was clear from the case studies that the Indian companies have been creative in raising funds to complete their acquisitions.

Indian MNCs, largely from the private sector, lack the advantage of government support in funding that MNCs from a country like China seem to take for granted. So, they have largely depended on global capital markets to facilitate their acquisition transactions. While the greater transparency of their financial condition as revealed in their financial statements (relative to Chinese companies) probably worked to their benefit when raising funds in global capital markets, the increased availability of global capital, at attractive rates, was probably equally as important in obtaining funding for global expansion (Rangan and Hariharan, 2012). Every major Indian company we looked at in this study – TM, Tata Steel, Aditya Birla Group, BF, Havells, and so on – tapped into global capital markets to fund their acquisitions. Luckily for them, the global expansion of these Indian multinationals coincided with the increasing availability of capital in global markets, and slowing growth in developed economies.

Deepening customer relationships to drive growth

As Indian firms globalized, they needed to drive growth to make their global expansion pay off. In this, they faced formidable challenges both in the relatively weak market positions of acquisitions and in the acquisition premiums they paid. Thus, while the acquisition in the developed economies gave them access to an existing set of customers, they used it to grow revenues well beyond the acquired firm's growth trajectory. Again, this proposition was supported by the case studies of firms such as Infosys and Bharat Forge.

Can entrepreneurial globalization survive the world of Trump and Brexit?

Perhaps no other question comes quickly on the heels of any mention of globalization today than whether globalization will survive the economic direction in which United States is being pushed by the newly elected president Donald Trump. Add to this the unease created by the vote in favour of Great Britain's exit from the European Union. Since both the USA and EU have historically been seen as promoters of globalization and the attendant benefits for all nations, the rise of Trump and the impending Brexit are seen as challenging the hegemony of such a consensus (Chikermane, 2017). Naturally, this has given rise to even more calls for pulling back from globalization by politicians in countries, such as France and the Netherlands. Moreover, since many politicians hailing from poorer countries in Africa and Latin America have historically been skeptical of globalization, it is worth asking the question: Can the entrepreneurial globalization pursued by Indian firms survive the coming global economic order where autarchy rather than globalization seems to be gaining intellectual ascendance?

We believe that the entrepreneurial globalization route pursued by the Indian firms may be able to withstand the pressures to move to less globalization relatively easily. We base this assessment on three related arguments; (1) the pull-back from globalization is not likely to be complete and so Indian firms may find it easier to adapt; (2) entrepreneurial globalization has allowed Indian firms to acquire new capabilities that may allow them to adapt to the new global reality of more autarchic national economies; and (3) as a latecomer to globalization and coming from an economy that has a lot of domestic potential to exploit, Indian firms would be able to survive relatively easily as they are less reliant on global markets.

In the first place, despite the talk about renegotiating NAFTA and bringing jobs back home, the Trump administration does not seem to be moving toward a total break with the post-war consensus of promoting global trade. Trump's main complaint seems to be that, in the past three decades, the USA had been too generous when it negotiated trade agreements, multilateral and bilateral, with others. This grievance is coupled with the perception that other countries were not playing by the tenets of trade agreements thereby benefiting more from trade than the USA did. Trump believes he is merely seeking a level playing field. Moreover, in both the USA and the UK, there are enough sane economic voices that will counter any efforts to take the world too far down the path to autarchy. In other words, Trump and Brexit will call for some modification of the pace, processes, and plans of global economic integration but not a complete halt or reversing of it.

Second, the globalization moves have given NIGFs the opportunity to build globally competitive capabilities. The capabilities come from the realization of scale economies, in manufacturing (e.g., Tata Steel), in R&D (at pharmaceutical firms such as Dr. Reddy's Labs or Ranbaxy), or in purchasing and marketing (Tata/Tetley tea). Globalization has enabled Indian firms to achieve lower costs or leverage through economies of scope, in distribution (as in the case of Dr. Reddy's Labs or Sun/Ranbaxy with product families), in operations (as at Infosys using global delivery models), or in marketing (as in Tata Motors with its product line). Globalization has also given them access to global resources, such as a global talent pool (for TCS and Infosys), raw materials (CUMI India), or access to specialized knowledge (Dr. Reddy's Labs and TCS) because of their participation in global markets. Such an accumulation of new capabilities, which are more process-based, and asset-light rather than through investments in fixed assets, has the benefit of allowing Indian firms to easily adapt to new demands by host countries. Thus, the fortuitous circumstances that led to the late globalization of Indian firms have also meant that their globalization strategy is much more flexible and adaptable to changing circumstances due to Trump and Brexit.

Finally, globalization has led to Indian firms linking their domestic and global strategies more closely. The NIGFs have recognized that globalization calls for a more integrated global perspective as well as a more tightly focused competitive effort. This strategic realization has forced the Indian business houses to become more focused, especially compared to the unwieldy conglomerates that they once were. The Tata group has withdrawn from some of its non-core businesses by divesting Tata Oil and ACC, while building a stronger presence in its core business such as tea, chemicals, steel, and automobiles. The Aditya Birla group has restructured its non-competitive businesses such as Grasim (in textiles) and Indo-Gulf (fertilizer), while entering new growth businesses with Birla-Sun Life (insurance), Idea (cellular), and Minacs Worldwide (BPO services). The Mahindra group has restructured its non-core businesses in logistics, retail, and trading and moved its chemicals business into Mahindra Partners, while entering into the growth area of IT services through the acquisition of Satyam. Such clear business focus and the linkage between domestic and global markets also mean that Indian firms can leverage their market knowledge, global presence, and capabilities to win domestically as well as globally. This ability, in turn, has meant that, as India outpaces the rest of the world in economic growth rate, drawing on its latent demand premised on its large and young population, Indian firms can easily survive the temporary slowing, if any, of global opportunities.

To summarize, the NIGF, entrepreneurial in thought and action, has globalized in a highly flexible way. Being a latecomer to the global arena has partly helped it. Instead of an export-based model that earlier globalizers adopted and aided by its low-cost, highly skilled labour pool, Indian firms have pursued strategies that relied right from the beginning on a disaggregated value chain-based model of globalization. In that pursuit, the NIGF has been aided by the steady accumulation of global capabilities that has enhanced its flexibility that should allow it to adapt smoothly to changing global economic circumstances. In many ways, the NIGF is anti-fragile as it incorporates investments in assets and capabilities that simultaneously serve a domestic as well as a global strategy, thus allowing it to actually benefit from volatility in the global arena (Taleb, 2012).

CASE STUDY: BHARAT FORGE (BF)

One of the companies we studied, Bharat Forge (BF), serves as a good illustrative example of the NIGF we discussed above.

BF chose to expand overseas through acquisitions, allowing it to overcome significant entry barriers presented by these mature markets. The acquisitions by BF took advantage of a downturn in developed countries when a number of firms were in financial distress due to the global recession in 2008. It would have been challenging for BF to initiate a de novo entry into these markets in terms of time and funds, especially in the face of an industry downturn.

BF did not have the internally generated funds to undertake these acquisitions, but fortuitously funds were available on the global capital markets. The global savings glut allowed BF to tap capital at very attractive interest rates. Access to low cost financing through global capital markets facilitated the globalization of NIGFs, such as BF.

After the acquisition, BF still had to find ways to "turn around" the acquired firms and make them competitive. BF chose to do this by reconfiguring its value chain activities to create and exploit sources of competitive advantage that were uniquely available after the acquisition. This was primarily achieved by changing the locus of activities after the acquisition. BF broke down the usual manufacturing operations into micro-steps and chose to reconfigure the value chain differently from its established rivals. BF located "finishing" manufacturing in the developed economy, close to the customer, while the "basic manufacturing" and "preparation" were done in India, We have labelled this a strategy of "micro-splitting" of value activities. This strategy of "micro-splitting" and "dual-shoring" had the dual benefit of lower costs and better customer responsiveness through customization and timely deliveries. See Figure 20.1 for a visual depiction of this reconfiguration.

BF also used these acquisitions to build a set of capabilities that were dispersed globally, e.g., frugal innovation and R&D were based in India, building local marketing, and advanced customer-focused product conceptualization was initiated in the overseas markets. This had the desired outcome of making the company more globally competitive.

Finally, BF went beyond using the acquisition merely as an additional sales channel. BF used the entry into the new markets to drive innovation and growth. Combining the local marketing resources and their customer relationships with engineering talent relocated from India, BF was able to initiate conversations with existing customers to significantly enlarge the portfolio of products that BF could develop and supply for their existing customers. These were products that were outside the scope of the acquired firm and only possible for BF to develop, given the engineering resources that it could command from its home business. BF used such innovation and growth efforts to deepen its relationships with existing customers and attract new ones.

Lessons from the NIGF for firms choosing to enter the Indian market

The development of the Indian industrial scene since 1991 has some important lessons for foreign firms seeking to enter India. These range from changes in the policies that the government has pursued through the reinvigoration of local firms in terms of their willingness and ability to compete against foreign firms to the development of the NIGF through entrepreneurial globalization. We summarize them here.

In the first place, with respect to government policies, three irreversible changes are worth noting. First, the governments, at the federal as well as the provincial levels, are more focused on building infrastructure than in creating SOEs to compete against the private sector. This opens up opportunities for new entrants; it also means that entrants cannot expect state-sanctioned largesse in terms of subsidies for inputs. Second, federal and provincial governments are actively striving to improve the ease of doing business, which helps both foreign and local players, a situation different from prior years when being a foreign firm might have led to some advantages in terms of preferential access to the government machinery. Third, with governments at all levels promoting the need for Indian companies to be globally competitive, new entrants are likely to face local players who are not easily discouraged by the entry of foreign companies.

Second, spurred by shifts in government policies, Indian companies have begun to compete more effectively within India. Witness how Havells has steadily expanded its market position in markets ranging from electrical components to

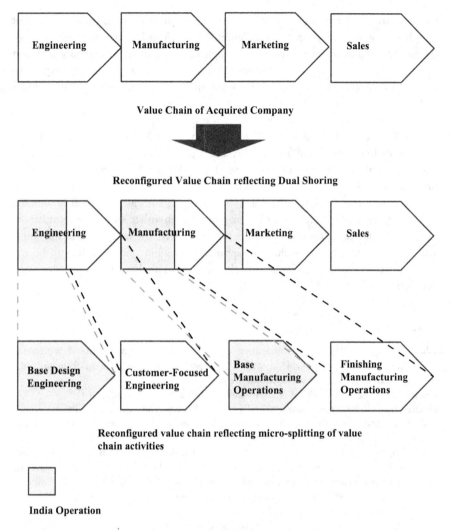

FIGURE 20.1 Bharat Forge's dual shoring and micro-splitting of the value chain

consumer electrical products through systematic investments in brands, quality, and distribution. Similarly, a late arrival in the consumer products market, Patanjali has managed to provide stiff competition to global players like Unilever. New entrants need to recognize that Indian firms are not the easy pushovers they used to be in the last century.

Third, and perhaps, the most formidable challenge to new entrants comes from the NIGF we have described in this chapter. When overseas firms enter the Indian market, they are likely to encounter in many industries the NIGF. The NIGF is likely to be a strong competitor at home. Not only does the NIGF have the advantages of being a local firm with informational advantages and established networks of relationships for marketing and distribution, but it also has low cost operations, supplemented by frugal innovation capabilities. And it has upgraded its capabilities through the transfer of know-how and best practices from its overseas operations. Overseas firms can no longer expect to have significant advantages over the local Indian competition, if that includes NIGFs.

Here three lessons are worth noting. First, in any industry where the new entrant faces the NIGF, it is critical to remember that NIGF is familiar with both sophisticated customers and advanced technologies, two areas where global players have historically been stronger than local players (Porter, 1991). Second, the NIGF brings formidable advantages of its own through entrepreneurial approaches such as the micro-splitting of value chain activities and dual shoring capabilities, which a new entrant would need to either match through other means or emulate to compete on an equal footing with the NIGF. Finally, the late globalization move and the entrepreneurial globalization approach have allowed the NIGF to be not only nimble but also anti-fragile, which a new entrant has to account for when competing against the NIGF.

References

Chikermane, G. (2017) The globalization of autarchy: The return of closed economies. *Swarajya*, 7 February. Available at: https://swarajyamag.com/world/the-globalisation-of-a utarchy-the-return-of-closed-economies

Fortune (2017) Fortune's Global 500. Available at: http://fortune.com/global500/

Ghemawat, P. (1991) *Commitment: The Dynamic of Strategy*. New York: Free Press.

Hamel, G. and Prahalad, C.K. (1993) Strategy as stretch and leverage. *Harvard Business Review*, 71: 75–84.

Hariharan, S. and Rangan, U.S. (2012) Entrepreneurial globalization: emerging multinationals from emerging economies. Paper presented at the 8th European Conference on Management, Leadership, and Governance (ECMLG-12), Paphos, Cyprus, November.

Hughes, H. (ed.) (1992) *The Dangers of Export Pessimism: Developing Countries and Industrial Markets*. San Francisco, CA: ICS Press.

Kogut, B. (1985) Designing global strategies: Comparative and competitive value-added chains. *Sloan Management Review*, 26: 15–28.

Lall, S. (1983) *The New Multinationals*. Chichester: Wiley.

Panagariya, A. (2004) India in the 1980s and 1990s: A triumph of reforms. IMF Working Paper, WP/04/43. Available at: www.imf.org/external/pubs/ft/wp/2004/wp0443.pdf

Porter, M.E. (1991) *The Competitive Advantage of Nations*. New York: Free Press.

Porter, M.E. (1995) Competitive advantage of India. Mimeo. Boston: Harvard Business School.

Rangan, U.S. and Hariharan, S. (2012) Acquisition advantage: how emerging market firms use acquisitions and what incumbent firms can do about it. In A.K. Gupta, T. Wakayama, and U.S. Rangan (eds.) *Global Strategies for Emerging Asia*. San Francisco, CA: Jossey-Bass/Wiley.

Rangan, U.S. and Schumacher, P. (2012) Entrepreneurial globalization: Lessons from European small and medium sized enterprises. In L. Bals, T. Pedersen, and P. Jensen (eds.) *The Offshoring Challenge: Strategic Design and Innovation for Tomorrow's Organization*. London: Springer Verlag.

Shah, K.R. (1998) Inflation and economic growth: The Indian experience. CMDR Monograph Series No. 24. Karnataka, India: Centre for Multi-Disciplinary Development Research. Available at: http://cmdr.ac.in/editor_v51/assets/mono-24.pdf

Stevenson, H. (1983) A perspective on entrepreneurship. Harvard Business School Working Paper #9-384-131.

Taleb, N.N. (2012) *Antifragile: Things that Gain from Disorder*. New York: Random House.

Wells, L.T. (1983) *Third World Multinationals*. Cambridge, MA: MIT Press.

World Bank (2015) Database. Available at: https://data.worldbank.org/indicator/NY.GDP.MKTP.CD?end=2015&locations=BR-CN-IN-RU-ZA&start=1995&view=chart

21

ADHYATMA[1] OR SPIRITUALITY

Indian perspectives on management

Dharm Prakash Sharma Bhawuk[2]

Aims of this chapter are to:

- Discuss the long tradition of spirituality in India and its continuing relevance
- Show how spirituality is an integral part of Indian life
- Explain how international managers can explore various spiritual practices, such as yoga and meditation

Introduction

India has a long tradition of spirituality (Bhawuk, 2003; 2011a; 2012), and the essential characteristics of an indigenous concept of *adhyAtma* or spirituality are derived from the *bhagavadgItA*. It is proposed that *adhyAtma* is an inward-looking process of self-discovery, whereas management is an outward-looking process of managing people and resources. The Indian concept of self is closely related to *adhyAtma*, and people strive to balance the spiritual and the material aspirations, as captured in the indigenous Indian leadership models. The implications of *adhyAtma* for doing business in India are examined by presenting a critical incident.

Spirituality in India: a long tradition

Management is about planning, organizing, commanding, coordinating, and controlling resources with an aim in mind (Fayol, 1949), which is necessarily about effecting some change in the environment by employing the resources procured. Managing, therefore, is about an outward process for the self, which is encompassed by others, organizations, nations, the Earth, and the universe (see Figure 21.1). The contributions of the world's ecosystem to the human economy was estimated to be US\$33 trillion in 1997 when the global gross national product was about US\$18 trillion (Costanza et al., 1997). So, we must include the Earth, and the universe beyond it, in our socio-economic deliberations. Thus, management is an outward-looking process. In contrast, spirituality is an inward-looking process, without neglecting the impact of the outside world on the person as shown in Figure 21.1. The focus on other versus self is captured succinctly in *Daodejing*, Chapter 33, in the following words:

> To know others is wisdom; to know oneself is acuity (*ming*). To conquer others is power; to conquer oneself is strength. To know contentment is to have wealth; to act resolutely is to have purpose. To stay one's ground is to be enduring; to die and yet not be forgotten is to be long-lived.
>
> *(Ames and Hall, 2010, p. 132)*

Though most Indian and Nepali bilinguals translate spirituality as *adhyAtma* and spiritual as *AdhyAtmika* or *dhArmika* in common parlance, the *saMskRta*-English dictionary by Monier-Williams (1899) defines *adhyAtma* as "the Supreme Spirit, own, belonging to self, concerning self or individual personality," and that by Apte (1890) defines *adhyAtma* as ("*Atmana saMbaddhaM, Atmani adhikRtaM vA*") "belonging to self or person, or concerning an individual." Clearly, *adhyAtma* is related to the self, the Supreme Spirit or *bramha*, and the individual being or person that we are. In the *bhagavadgItA*, *adhyAtma* appears eight times in verses 3.30, 7.29, 8.1, 8.3, 10.32, 11.1, 13.11, and 15.5. In verse 3.30, *kRSNa* asks *arjuna* to offer all *karmas* (or actions) to him by being conscious that the self is *bramha*, and to fight in the battle without any hope, sense of self, or sorrow.[3] *Adizankara* explains *adhyAtmacetasA* as "*vivekabuddhayA ahaM kartA IzvarAya bhRtyavat karomi iti anayA buddhayA*" or having the *buddhi* (or discriminating understanding) that one is the servant of God and one always does all actions with that mindset. To act as the servant of God, thus, is one of the definitions

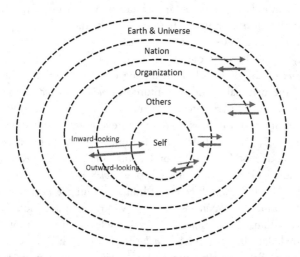

FIGURE 21.1 Managing self and others

of spirituality, as applied to action. *swAmi gambhIrAnand* translates *adhyAtmacetasA* as "mind spiritually imbued."[4] *swAmi prabhupAda* translates it as "with the full knowledge of the self."[5] *swAmi cinmayAnand* translates it as "with a mind soaked with devoted remembrances of the Self" (Chinmayanand, 2005, p. 234) and also as "with the mind centered on the Self" (ibid., p. 61).

In verse 8.1,[6] *arjuna* asks *kRSNa*, "What is *adhyAtmaM*?" But the question itself is embedded in a set of eight questions providing a nomological network for the construct in verses 8.1 and 8.2,[7] such as What is *bramha*?, What is *adhyAtmaM*?, What is *karma*?, What is called *adhibhUtaM*?, What is called *adhidaivaM*?, Who is *adhiyajJaH*?, How is it in the body?, and How do people know it at the end of their life? So, it is important to understand *adhyAtma* in the context that is presented in verses 8.1–8.5 in the dialogue between *arjuna* and *kRSNa*.

Further, *kRSNa* defines *adhyAtma* as *svabhAva* or the intrinsic nature of *bramha*. Some interpret *svabhAva* as the presence of *bramha* in each individual body (ibid.), "that which exists in the context of the body as the enjoyer" (*madhusudan saraswati*, translated by Gambhirananda, 1998, p. 537), or "as the Lord-of-self is that which bears the name Consciousness which never ceases to be in It (*bramha*) and which is nothing but the *bramha*" (*abhinavagupta*, translated by Sankaranarayananan, 1985). Thus, *adhyAtma* is defined and interpreted as the presence of *bramha* in the human body. Therefore, the definition of *adhyAtma*, "working as the servant of God," presented above, is consistent as a method to realize the presence of *bramha* in one's self or to become one with *bramha* in one's daily living. In other words, to be one with God, one has to work as the servant of God, and that is the Indian perspective on spirituality.

Finally, in verse 8.3, *kRSNa* states that *karma* is said to be *bhUtabhAvaudbhava-karaH visargaH* or that sacrifice which is the cause of the creation of all beings. All *yajJas* require sacrifice and are considered the cause of the creation and growth of beings (see Bhawuk, 2011a, p. 192). Therefore, *karma* refers to *yajJa*. Here we can see that even mundane activities are made into non-mundane and spiritual, implying that all *karma* is spiritual. In other words, there is no gap between the secular and the spiritual; everything is spiritual. Thus, we see the Indian emphasis on spirituality in all domains of life. In verse 8.4,[8] *kRSNa* defines *adhibhUta* as *kSaraH bhAvaH* or the perishable or changing entities. Anything that is born and dies, or all of the material world, is captured in *adhibhUta*. *adhidaiva* is defined as *puruSaH* or that which permeates every entity in the world. And *kRSNa* calls himself the *adhiyajJa*. And he says he resides in every being, equating himself with *bramha*. In verse 8.5,[9] *kRSNa* tells *arjuna* that one who leaves the body at the time of death by thinking of *kRSNa*, beyond doubt, merges with *kRSNa* or achieves *kRSNa*'s essence. This has been referred to as *mokSA* (or liberation) or self-realization, which is the ultimate objective of human life in the Indian worldview.

In the tenth canto, *kRSNa* describes his various manifestations, and in verse 10.32,[10] he calls himself *adhyAtmavidyA* or knowledge of self among all kinds of *vidyA* or knowledge. In verse 11.1,[11] *adhyAtma* is used in the same sense as the pious knowledge of the self. In verse 13.11,[12] *adhyAtma* is used in association with *jJAna* or knowledge, and *adhyAtmajJAna* or knowledge of self alone is said to be knowledge, and all else is non-knowledge. This emphasizes spirituality as the foundation of knowledge in the Indian worldview, and all other knowledge as secondary. In verse 15.5,[13] *kRSNa* tells *arjuna* that those who are devoid of pride and delusion, without the faults of attachment, devoted to spirituality or ever immersed in the reflection on self, free from all desires, free of duality, and equi-poised in happiness and sorrow, such wise ones reach the undecaying state of per-fection, or become self-realized. We see that *adhyAtma* or spirituality is included among the many criteria of enlightenment in this verse, emphasizing the role of spirituality in the pursuit of *mokSa* or liberation. Thus, *adhyAtma* or spirituality is an important Indian cultural construct, and it permeates everyday living. Its salience can also be seen in the very definition of Indian concept of self that is discussed in the next section.

The Indian concept of self and spirituality

The concept of self has been studied from multiple perspectives in India. A review of the study of self in India reveals that indeed the core of Indian self is metaphysical, and it has been the focus of study by philosophers as well as by psychologists. Examining the concept of self, Bharati (1985) concluded that, compared to the Western perspective, self is defined in a rather unique per-spective in the Indian worldview. The Indian concept of self consists of both gross and subtle elements, which can be further categorized as physical, social, and metaphysical selves (Bhawuk, 2011a). The internal self that consists of *ahaGkAra, manas* and *buddhi*, is also called *antaHkaraNa* [14] or the internal organ or agent. Beyond all this is *Atman*, which is the most subtle (ibid.). This con-ceptualization of self is captured schematically in Figure 21.2.

There is general agreement that the metaphysical self, *Atman*, is the real self. This metaphysical self is embodied in a biological or physical self, and situated, right at birth, in a social structure as a result of past *karma*. The importance of the metaphysical self is reflected in the belief that of all the living beings, human beings are the only ones who can pursue *mokSa* (or liberation), enlightenment, *jJAna* (or knowledge), or self-realization, which is presented as the highest pursuit of human life. Most Indians, including Hindus, Buddhists, Jains, Sikhs and people of many other religious groups believe that they go through many life forms on their way to ultimate liberation, and the pursuit of self-realization is a common shared belief.

In the traditional Indian worldview, people were assigned social roles according to their phase of life. The first phase was called the *bramhacarya Azrama* in which people received an education and learned life skills. In this phase, the primary focus was on achievement of skills, and traditionally one lived with a *guru* in his *Azrama* and led a frugal life.

Upon the completion of one's education at the age of 25, traditionally people entered the *gRhastha Azrama* or the second phase of life in which they became householders and led a married life, raising children. In this phase of

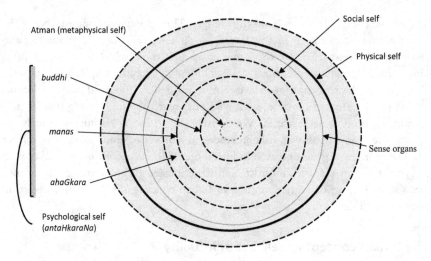

FIGURE 21.2 The Indian concept of self

life the focus was on family and community responsibilities. One lived to find meaning in life by pursuing *dharma* (duty), *artha* (money), *kAma* (pleasure), and *mokSa* (liberation), which is referred to as the four *puruSarthas* or pursuits of life.

At the age of 50, one entered the third phase of life or *vAnaprastha Azrama* and became a forest-dweller, and focused on his or her spiritual life. In this phase of life, people led an austere life much like they did in the first phase as a student. Indeed, people would often live near an *Azrama* to get guidance from a *guru* to pursue a spiritual practice.

Finally, at the age of 75, one entered *sannyAsa Azrama* or the fourth phase of life, and became a *sannyAsin* or a monk, and renounced all pleasures of life to pursue *jJAna* (or knowledge) or self-realization. The third and fourth phases of life are not adopted by most Indians today, who remain *gRhasthas* all their lives. However, many do cultivate spiritual practices after retirement, which was the main characteristic of the third phase of life.

There is little adherence to the stage of life in India today on a mass scale, but the idea still persists. However, it is not unheard of to find some people practicing the normative stage of life principle. Thus, the concept of stages of life, though not popular, is still a relevant concept in India, and thus important for understanding the psychology of Indians.

Balancing material with spirituality

India is the largest democracy in the world, and there is some support that some form of democracy existed in India during the *licchavI* era a little before the time of *buddha* (sixth century BCE), making it the oldest democracy too. According to Indian census data from 2011, India is also one of the most diverse countries with respect to religion, and practitioners of most world religions can be found here. Hindus (79.8 per cent) constitute the largest group with tremendous variability among rituals and much convergence in worldview and practice of spirituality. Sikhs (1.7 per cent), Buddhists (0.7 per cent), and Jains (0.4 per cent) are all indigenous to India, and have traditionally lived harmoniously. Muslims (14.2 per cent) constitute the second largest religious group in India, and there is both an oral tradition and historical evidence that Islam has existed in India from the time of the Prophet Mohammad. Christianity also has been in India for more than two thousand years since the apostle St Thomas came to India in CE 52. Indeed, it can be asserted that religious diversity has flourished in India because of its emphasis on spirituality.

Spirituality and leadership in India

Scanning the Indian environment of leadership, Bhawuk (2011a; 2011b) presented two types of leaders who are unique to India, *sannyasin* and *karmayogin* leaders, who are inspired by spirituality. People who have renounced the world are called *sannyasin*, and it would seem that *sannyasins* would have no reason to be a leader since they are by definition not to own any worldly belongings or be attached to any relationship. A leader who focuses on work without paying attention to the outcomes of the work, which is a concept derived from the *bhagavadgItA*, is called a *karmayogin* leader. A *karmayogin* leader pursues *lokasaGgraha* or social good in all his or her actions. *gAndhI*, *vinobA bhAve*, *gopAl kRSNa gokhale*, and *bAl gaGgAdhara tilak* are exemplars of *karmayogin* leaders.

CASE STUDY: SPIRITUALITY AND TRADITIONAL INDIAN BUSINESS VALUES

This is a family story of a close friend, which has provided me with a deeper understanding of indigenous business practices and how they are rooted in Indian cultural values. This incident happened in *rAjasthAn*, India, in a traditional business family in the *mArawADi* community. Mr Goyal (not his real name) was in trading construction material, particularly steel products. His younger son, Sahadeva (not his real name), worked for a big business company as a chartered accountant. The owner, Mr Agrawal (not his real name) was also from a traditional *mArwADi* family. Mr Agrawal was looking to buy some equipment in a town near the area where Mr Goyal lived. He negotiated the purchase of the equipment for Rs 300,000 (then about US$40,000), and the deal was finalized. As a safety measure, he asked Sahadeva to ask his father to check the equipment to ensure the quality and the price of the equipment. Mr Goyal went to check the equipment and was satisfied with it. The seller knew Mr Goyal's reputation as a business man in the area, and told him that since he had become the middleman, he would only charge Rs 200,000 for the equipment. Mr Goyal told Sahadeva that he was personally satisfied with the equipment and that the seller had lowered the price. Sahadeva reported this to Mr Agrawal.

Mr Agrawal was pleasantly surprised. He came to see Mr Goyal, and told him that Mr Goyal need not have told him about the new price and could have taken the difference as his service fee, since Mr Agrawal was quite willing to pay Rs 300,000 for the equipment. It was still a bargain for him. Mr Goyal told him that he was doing it for his son, and this was not a business deal for him. He was also not in the business of brokering deals. Extremely impressed, as Mr Agrawal talked to Mr Goyal, he realized that Mr Goyal, who was a major distributor of steel construction material, did not sell his products, or carry them in his store. Mr Agrawal asked him to carry his products. Mr Goyal said, "When I buy 1,000 kilograms of your steel rods, they weigh only 950 kilograms. I don't want to do business with people who are not honest with their measurement." Mr Agrawal understood that the problem was with his distributor, not with his production, but appreciated Mr Goyal's forthrightness. He was so impressed by this that he groomed Sahadeva over the years as one of his most trusted executives and included him in all his financial deals. Sahadeva still works for him, and is responsible for all kinds of transactions that are done on trust alone. For example, Sahadeva is trusted to personally deliver ten million rupees cash to a client, and he is the only person who counts the money. Sahadeva feels a bit nervous with such assignments, since the receiving party also does not count the money in front of him. Sahadeva's experience is typical of the Indian business environment as a lot of business in India is done on trust. He hopes to retire with an untarnished record in a few years.

There are many lessons to be learned from this critical incident. The cultural value driving Mr Goyal's behavior is the most important thing to keep in mind. A business person's character is judged in India on the basis of his or her impeccable honesty with *tulA* or balance, the value being, one never gives less than what the customer is paying for; one never rigs the balance; and one never tricks the customer with the balance in any way. This is referred to as *tulA-dharma* in *saMskRta*. *tulAdhar* is the person who holds the balance, and there are families that have done this for generations in many part of India and Nepal. They are paid to weigh tons of grains that are transacted in the bazaar or the marketplace. *tulAdhar* is still a family name in Nepal, and a merchant is also known as *tulAdhAra* in *saMskRta*. I must confess that all the corruption that goes on in India had led me to forget this basic Indian business value, which was brought to my conscious thinking when my friend narrated this incident. Corruption has no place in Indian traditional business culture, since all business is guided by *tulAdharma*. Honesty in business dealings is the *dharma* of the business people. As noted above, *dharma* guides daily behavior, including business behavior in India.

The second lesson to be learned from Mr Goyal's behavior is that not all transactions are to be taken as business transactions. He passed on the benefit (US $13,000 in the 1970s was a lot of money in any part of the world!) to Mr Agrawal, which he could easily have pocketed. Even Mr Agrawal thought that it would have been considered a service fee. Mr Goyal was very clear about when he did business and when he did what could be called family or community work. This was a task he undertook for his son, not for money. The underlying principle is that a business person knows his business, and does not look at every transaction as a business deal. He or she does not make money in all of his or her transactions with people. If Mr Goyal was a broker, and he was brokering for Mr Agrawal, it would have been acceptable for him to accept the money, not otherwise. Again, here we see the concept of *dharma* guiding the behavior of a business person.

Third, Mr Goyal was always careful in his transactions, and firmly walked away from making the quick buck or being greedy. When business people are transacting in the market place, there are many occasions when they can make a "quick buck," but that is not the *dharma* of a business person or anybody in the market. When we fail to do so, the consequences are not favorable to the community as can be seen in various reports from around the world (Anonymous, 2006). Making the quick or fast buck is not only a problem with traders in the financial market but also in other areas of business. We can see that spirituality dampens people's greed and tendency to make a fast buck in India.

Finally, Mr Goyal refused to do business with a dishonest business person. He was very clear that if the distributors were cheating the traders by selling less than what was stamped on the package, the retailers were also going to make up lies by cheating the customers, and he simply did not want to be a part of such an unethical business system. All social transactions are based on trust, and business dealings are no exception. Mr Goyal earned an honest living, and was not going to change it for any network value that Mr Agrawal and his organization might have brought to him. Making an honest living is not only a part of spiritual practice in Hinduism but also one of the key tenets, right livelihood, of the eight-fold path in Buddhism. Also since Jainism values truth, non-violence, not stealing, non-attachment, and control over senses, not stealing would guide their business transactions. Jains are known to be honest tradespeople in India.

We also see how two wise business people interacted following the traditional business values. Mr Goyal's refusal to work with Mr Agrawal was not held against him. Mr Agrawal was more than happy to nurture and promote Sahadeva in his organization because he considered that coming from such a family was an invaluable asset, which Sahadeva has demonstrated in his long career. On the other hand, Mr Goyal did not blame Mr Agrawal for his distributors' wrongdoing, and was comfortable that his son worked for Mr Agrawal. This also shows that people are relational in India, and building relationships is critical to be effective in Indian business environment.

We should also note how cultural values are transmitted from one generation to another through socialization and family stories, and, therefore, are as relevant today in the life of Mr Agrawal and Mr Goyal's families as they were decades ago. The relevance of cultural socialization to organizational performance is supported in organizational literature as Ouchi (1980) defined organizations as the pattern of exchange among individuals and demonstrated that beyond markets and bureaucracies, socialization can be used as a mediator to minimize transaction costs where goal congruency and performance ambiguity exist. Thus, recognition and understanding of traditional business values are likely to be important for managers of MNCs working in India.

Conclusion

India can be called the spiritual capital of the world, considering how many hours are spent by Indians in holy places like *tirupati, haridwAr, RSikeza, vAraNasi, zirdi, rAmezwaram*, and so forth. Spirituality and social entrepreneurship are also merging, as can be seen in the growth of spirituality-based organizations led by spiritual leaders like *ammA, rAmadeva bAbA, sadguru,* and *zri zri ravizankar.* India is a wonderful destination for spirituality-based tourism, and economic reforms have opened up India so that people can travel to India freely, which is likely to help the spiritual aspirants visiting India for their *sAdhanA* or practice. In Prime Minister Modi's absolute majority, ministers are unapologetic about being a Hindu and speaking of their faith in public, and hope it helps nurture spirituality of all traditions, which is India's strength, by utilizing it rather than viewing it as a weakness. In the increasingly stressful world, meditation and yoga may provide relief and help foster well-being, and India could lead the world with its spiritual heritage. And, finally, India also offers a model of anti-terrorism philosophy through the integration of various religious faiths present in India and the teachings of the Sufi saints. India continues to be a model culture of peace for our global village by integrating spirituality and management.

Useful websites

New Indian Express www.newindianexpress.com/lifestyle/spirituality
The Hindu www.thehindu.com/society/faith/
The Times of India https://timesofindia.indiatimes.com/spirituality/articlelist/5106542.cms

Notes

1 The Harvard-Kyoto protocol for transliteration for devanagarI is used for the saMskRta and hindI words and names, and the first letters of names are not capitalized.
अ a आ A इ i ई I उ u ऊ U ए e ऐ ai ओ o औ au ऋ R ॠ RR ऌ IR ॡ IRR अं M अः H क ka ख kha ग ga घ kha ङ Ga च ca छ cha ज ja झ jha ञ Ja ट Ta ठ Tha ड Da ढ Dha ण Na त ta थ tha द da ध dha न na प pa फ pha ब ba भ bha म ma य ya र ra ल la व va श za ष Sa स sa ह ha क्ष kSa त्र tra ज्ञ jJa श्र zra
2 I am grateful to Vijayan Munusami and Pawan Budhwar for their insightful comments that helped me improve this chapter. Parts of this chapter were presented at the NAoP conference at IIT *kharagpur,* 22–24 December 2017.
3 Verse 3.30: *mayi sarvANi karmANi sannyasyAdhyAtmacetasA, nirAzIrnirmamo bhUtvA yudhyasva vigatjvaraH.* "Offering all *karmas* (or actions) to me by being conscious that the

self is *bramha*, fight in the battle without any hope, sense of self, or affliction (or anxiety)."

4 *swAmi gambhIrAnand* translates this verse as follows: "By becoming free from desires, devoid of the idea of 'mine' and devoid of the fever of the soul, engage in battle by dedicating all actions to Me with (your) mind spiritually imbued."

5 Using the meaning presented by *swAmi prabhupAda*, the verse translates as follows: "O *arjuna*, fight without desire for profit, without ownership, and without being lethargic, by surrendering all activities completely unto me (i.e., unto *kRSNa*), with full knowledge of the self in the consciousness."

6 Verse 8.1: *kiM tadbrahma kimadhyAtmaM kiM karma puruSottama, adhibhUtaM ca kiM proktamadhidaivaM kimucyate.* What is *bramha*? What is *adhyAtmaM*? What is *karma*? What is called *adhibhUtaM*? What is called *adhidaivaM*?

7 Verse 8.2: *adhiyajJaH kathaM ko'atra dehe'asminmadhusudana, prayANakAle ca kathaM jJeyo'si niyatAtmabhiH.* Who is *adhiyajJaH*? How is it in the body? And how do people know it at the end of their life?

8 Verse 8.4: *adhibhUtaM kSaro bhAvaH puruSazcAdhidaivatam, adhiyajno'hamevAtra dehe dehabhRtAM vara.*

9 Verse 8.5: *antakAle ca mAmeva smaranmuktvA kalevaram, yaH prayAti sa madbhAvam yAti nAstyatra saMzayaH.*

10 Verse 10.32: *sargANAmAdirantazca madhyaM caivAhamrjuna, adhyAtmavidyA vidyAnAM vAdaH pravadatAmaham.* "O *arjuna*, I am the beginning, middle, and the end of the creation. I am the knowledge of self among all knowledge, and the debate in which truth is sought."

11 Verse 11.1: arjuna *uvAca: madanugrahAya paramaMguhyamadhyAtmasaJjnitam, attvayoktaM vacastena moho'yam vigato mama.* "Arjuna said, 'You have kindly spoken about the secret knowledge of self to me, and your words have cleared my delusion or confusion.'"

12 Verse 13.11: *adhyAtmajJAnanityatvaM tattvajJAnArthadarzanam, etajjJAnamiti proktamajJAnaM adato'nyathA.*

13 Verse 15.5: *nirmAnamohA jitasaGgadoSA adhyAtmanityA vinivRttakAmAH, dvandvairvimuktAH sukhaduHkhasaJjnairgacchantyamUDhAH padamavyayaM tat.*

14 See Bhawuk (2011a), Chapter 4, for a definition and discussion of *manas, buddhi, ahaGkAra,* and *antaHkaraNa.* The closest translation of *ahaGkAra* would be ego, which comes at the cost of much loss of meaning. People often use mind for *manas,* which is simply wrong, since *manas* is the locus of cognition, affect and behavior, whereas mind is only cognitive. And *buddhi* is closest to the super-ego in Freudian parlance, but without ego, which makes the similarity rather superficial. And *antaHkaraNa* is the composite internal organ or agent combining *manas, buddhi,* and *ahaGkAra. Adizankara* also includes *citta* in the definition of *antaHkaraNa* (see Bhawuk, 2014, for a discussion of *citta*).

References

Ames, R. and Hall, D. (2010) *Dao de jing: A Philosophical Translation.* New York: Ballantine Books.

Anonymous (2006) They are traders out to make a fast buck. *Dawn,* 11 September. Available at: www.dawn.com/news/209870/traders-out-to-make-a-fast-buck

Apte, V.S. (ed.) (1890) *The Practical Sanskrit-English Dictionary.* New Delhi: Motilal Banarsidass Publishers Pvt Ltd.

Bharati, A. (1985) The self in Hindu thought and action. In A.J. Marsella, G. DeVos and F. L.K. Hsu (eds.) *Culture and Self: Asian and Western Perspectives.* New York: Tavistock Publications, pp. 185–230.

Bhawuk, D.P.S. (2003) Culture's influence on creativity: The case of Indian spirituality. *International Journal of Intercultural Relations,* 27: 1–22.

Bhawuk, D.P.S. (2011a) *Spirituality and Indian Psychology: Lessons from the Bhagavad-Gita.* New York: Springer.

Bhawuk, D.P.S. (2011b) Beyond conflict, violence, and retaliation: Gandhijee as an exemplar of indigenous approaches to leadership education. In J. Paande, T.N. Sinha and A.K. Sinha (eds.) *Dialogue for Development.* New Delhi: Concept Publisher, pp. 105–141.

Bhawuk, D.P.S. (2012) India and the culture of peace: Beyond ethnic, religious, and other conflicts. In D. Landis and R. Albert (eds.) *Handbook of Ethnic Conflict.* New York: Springer, pp. 137–174.

Bhawuk, D.P.S. (2014) Citta or consciousness: Some perspectives from Indian psychology. *Journal of Indian Psychology,* 28(1): 37–43.

Bhawuk, D.P.S., Mrazek, S. and Munusami, V.P. (2009) From social engineering to community transformation: Amul, Grameen Bank, and Mondragon as exemplar organizations. *Peace & Policy: Ethical Transformations for a Sustainable Future,* 14: 36–63.

Chakraborty, S.K. (1987) *Managerial Effectiveness and Quality of Work Life: Indian Insights.* New Delhi: McGraw-Hill.

Chinmayanand, S. (1992) *The Holy Gita: Commentary by Swami Chinmayananand.* Mumbai: Central Chinmaya Mission Trust.

Chinmayanand, S. (2005) *Holy Gita: Ready Reference/A Compendium of Questions and Answers with an Alphabetical Index of the padas and Gita Astottarasat Namavali.* Mumbai: Central Chinmaya Mission Trust.

Costanza, R., d'Arge, R., de Groot, R., et al. (1997) The value of the world's ecosystem services and natural capital. *Nature,* 387: 253–260.

Fayol, H. (1949) *General and Industrial Management* (trans. C. Storrs). London: Sir Isaac Pitman and Sons. (Original work published in 1916).

GambhIrAnanda, S. (1998) *bhagavadgItA with the annotation guDhArthadIpikA madhusudana saraswati.* Tiruchirappalli, India: zrI rAmakRSNa tapovanam.

Monier-Williams, M. (1899) *A saMskRta-English Dictionary.* Oxford: Oxford University Press. Reprinted in 1960.

Moore, C.A. (1967) Introduction: the comprehensive Indian mind. In C.A. Moore (ed.) *The Indian Mind: Essentials of Indian Philosophy and Culture.* Hawaii, Honolulu: University of Hawai'i Press, pp. 1–18.

Ouchi, W.G. (1980) Markets, bureaucracies, and clans. *Administrative Science Quarterly,* 25: 129–141.

saGkaranArAyaNanan, S. (1985) *zrImadbhagavadgItA with gItArthasaGgraha of abhinavagupta.* Tirupati, India: Sri Venkateswara University.

Williams, M. (1899) *A Sanskrit-English Dictionary Etymologically and Philologically Arranged with Special Reference to Cognate Indo-European Languages.* Oxford: Clarendon Press.

22

CORPORATE SOCIAL RESPONSIBILITY AND VOLUNTARY SUSTAINABILITY STANDARDS

The India story

Bimal Arora and Divya Jyoti

Aims of this chapter are to:

- Discuss developments in corporate social responsibility (CSR) and voluntary sustainability standards (VSS) in India
- Explain how to engage in CSR and VSS in both Indian and western multinational companies (MNCs)

Introduction

Two separate events in India on 14 February 2017 – one in Mumbai and another in New Delhi – testify to the growth, penetration and institutionalization of CSR and sustainability in India. The Amsterdam-based Global Reporting Initiative (GRI)[1] launched the GRI Standards in India (the global launch was in October 2016), and the Bombay Stock Exchange hosted the event in Mumbai. To gain legitimacy and acceptance by Indian institutions, the GRI also developed and launched the linkage document of GRI Standards-Business Responsibility Reporting[2] framework at the same event. KPMG's global Survey of Corporate Responsibility Reporting 2017 highlights that India is leading the top ten countries with the highest rates of corporate responsibility information in annual financial reports, and is ahead of nine other countries surveyed: Denmark, the UK, Sweden, Norway, France, South Africa, the USA, Malaysia, and Taiwan.[3] The prominent presence of India's stock exchange regulator Securities and Exchange Board of India (SEBI) and leading corporates and NGOs at the event is testimony to the growing influence and acceptance of GRI and the corporate responsibility disclosures in India.

In New Delhi, on the same day, a home-grown voluntary watchdog coalition of several civil society organizations, Corporate Responsibility Watch (CRW) launched 'India Responsible Business Index 2016' (the first index was launched in

2015). The India Responsible Business Index (IRBI) measures alignment of company policies with the National Voluntary Guidelines (NVGs) for the Economic, Social and Environmental Responsibilities of Business (issued by the Ministry of Corporate Affairs, Government of India, in July 2011). The CRW report analyses information disclosed by companies on their websites and presents the data of top 100 companies in India, showing how they have performed across five factors: (1) non-discrimination in the workplace; (2) respecting employee dignity and human rights; (3) community development; (4) inclusive supply chain; and (5) the community as business stakeholder. The opening statement of the report reads:

> Ten years ago, it was inconceivable that corporates would disclose aspects of their core business in the public domain. In fact, many have hesitated to even consider aspects like community as business stakeholders or supply chain as part of their core business. That both public and private sector companies, even if only the top 100 listed companies on the Bombay Stock Exchange (which will soon include 500 top listed companies on the National Stock Exchange) are doing so *is a matter of success.*
>
> *(IRBI, 2017, p. 8, emphasis added*[4]*)*

Several CSR and sustainability events are held in India every month now, which indeed indicates wider awareness and acceptance of CSR and sustainability in the country.

India's growing economy, the increasing pace of production and consumption, its vast natural resources and a large supplier base, linked to global businesses, along with democratic and demographic dividends, make it both an attractive market and a destination for international businesses. However, India also faces major environmental and social challenges, such as poverty, pollution, unemployment, unequal resource distribution and growing inequality. All these propositions make India a ripe territory for discussion and diffusion of concepts like CSR and VSS. Also, due to the growing ambitions of the Indian government to secure a global position and role (such as a permanent seat on the UN Security Council and membership of the Nuclear Suppliers Group), the Indian policy-makers are actively and positively participating in global governance institutions and processes. Such processes include the climate change negotiations during the annual Conference of Parties (COP) meetings and the United Nations Sustainable Development Goals (SDGs) (or the Global Goals 2030).[5]

With a legal mandate, introduced through the Companies Act 2013, CSR in India has come of age. Likewise, internationally defined and developed private and voluntary governance standards and frameworks for sustainability too are gaining rapid ground in India. In parallel, the Indian policy-makers are making attempts to improve India's ranking on the World Bank Group's 'Ease of Doing Business Index'. By implication, this also means that businesses are expected not only to grow, prosper and enhance only the shareholder value, but also take ownership and responsibility for their externalities through self-regulation (at the firm and industry level) and make positive contributions to society as well. Hence, success-fully operating a business in India makes engagement with stakeholders beyond shareholders, CSR and VSS an imperative for both Indian-origin businesses and for foreign businesses operating in India or sourcing products and services from India.

This chapter highlights the growing and critical importance of business stake-holders, CSR and VSS for businesses in India in general, and for MNCs in India and for foreign businesses with interests in India in particular. In the first section, the chapter presents CSR and issues in managing CSR by firms. In the second section, the chapter presents issues on VSS for firms and industry sectors.

Deciphering CSR in India

Building on the historical Indian traditions of charity and philanthropy, the per-ceptions and practices of CSR in India predominantly referred to social investments by business (Arora and Puranik, 2004). Such investments mainly included con-tributions to community-related development issues and humanitarian aid – usually following natural disasters. The liberalization and globalization of the Indian economy during the 1990s offered space for more discretion in business decision-making, thereby opening scope for more 'explicit' forms of CSR engagements by businesses (Matten and Moon, 2008). With the diffusion of CSR as a management concept, a shift towards strategically aligned core business initiatives, ostensibly to create societal value, is also evident in some companies in India. The Shakti Amma Project of Unilever's Indian subsidiary, Hindustan Unilever Ltd, (Jaiswal, 2008) and the large Indian company ITC Ltd's e-Choupal are classic examples of such initiatives (Anupindi and Sivakumar, 2007). Nevertheless, the majority of compa-nies in India still believe and treat CSR as a subject related to externally-oriented social development issues. This belief is accentuated by the Indian policy-makers as a clause in the Indian Companies Act 2013, which made CSR a mandatory requirement for businesses in India.

Replacing the Indian Companies Act of 1956, the Companies Act 2013, along with significant corporate governance reforms, also introduced CSR through Section 135. This is now widely known as the 'CSR Mandate', and brings India into the league of very few countries in the world to mandate CSR through legislation.[6] The Section 135 mandates qualify companies to comply with the law. The provisions of this section include spending at least 2 per cent of average net profit in the previous three years on CSR activities. Companies with a net worth of Indian 5 billion rupees or more, or a turnover of 10 billion rupees or more, or a net profit of 50 million rupees or more qualify for compliance under this mandate. The 2 per cent spend is prescribed to be made in predetermined areas (Van Zile, 2011; Karnani, 2013a; 2013b; Afsharipour and Rana, 2014). Schedule VII of the Act identified areas reflecting different facets of inequality in India, which should be addressed by companies through their CSR projects including, among others, eradicating extreme hunger and poverty and promoting education.[7]

To ensure that the earmarked funds for CSR are well managed, the Act also requires the qualifying companies to create a governance system. The board of the company is required to form a CSR Committee, consisting of at least three directors, of whom one member is to be an independent director of the company. This committee is required to do the following:

- formulate the CSR policy, for approval by the board;
- enlist the CSR projects that shall be undertaken in a financial year;
- recommend expenses required for these activities;
- monitor the implementation of the CSR policy.

If a company fails to meet the CSR spending obligations, the directors of the company are required to disclose to the government and also publicly, through the company website and annual reports, the reasons for not doing so. In a sense, the Indian CSR law follows the 'comply or explain' principle (MacNeil and Li, 2006). Failure to explain could lead to legal action similar to that of non-compliance with accounting requirements. One of the key Indian government officials, in a media interview on May 2015 stated, 'eventually the companies will comply with 2% spending, otherwise they will be "named and shamed"'.[8]

Thus, the board members, senior management and executive-level staff in companies are increasingly expected to develop compliance-oriented thinking and also increase the importance and acceptance of CSR across the organization. Apparently, the spirit of the CSR Mandate is to facilitate companies in transitioning from disconnected and unplanned philanthropic giveaways and unstructured community development activities to seeking strategic and integrated business opportunities through CSR projects and initiatives. About 16,000 companies in India are expected to spend $2.5 billion (approximately 15,000 crore Indian rupees) on CSR in the coming years, from the current $0.5 billion, according to a Boston Consultancy Group report in February 2015. The Ministry of Corporate Affairs in India also tracks and reports the CSR spending by companies.

The CSR Mandate in India is also attracting much attention globally among policy-makers, practitioners and academic scholars, and also receiving both praise and critiques. As the CSR Mandate is narrowly focused, heavily prescriptive, and mostly identified with the 2 per cent spend clause, in some circles, this is referred to as a '2% law', and widely debated as promoting philanthropy. The critiques also argue that the CSR Mandate may contribute to the growing inequalities, corruption, political interference, and differentiated spatial development and impacts in India (Karnani, 2013a; 2013b).

However, viewed positively, some of the implications and possibilities of the CSR Mandate in India could be that it is expected to widen the net for companies that engage with CSR (even though with compliance to the law, 16,000+ companies qualify to comply). The mandate introduced the globally prevalent terminology of CSR to companies that possibly might not have heard or thought about it before. In a few years, this may perhaps result in India becoming the country with the largest number of companies engaged in CSR. The CSR Mandate brought CSR from the fringes into the boardrooms and within the realm of corporate thinking, policy, strategy and actions. The CSR Mandate will move companies to undertake certain CSR actions, such as set policy and structures, set aside resources (human and financial, among others), formulate strategies for implementation, in some cases, identify and engage with external partners, monitor, evaluate and disclose actions and compliance. The CSR Mandate has created the avenues for mutual respect, closer engagement and ties of companies with non-governmental organizations (NGOs) and state agencies involved in development work. In the face of increasingly declining international and national financial aid and grants, the CSR Mandate has created new funding avenues and opportunities for NGOs in India. The CSR Mandate, and most of its focus areas, may drive companies to contribute to some of the SDGs and the national development goals of India. The CSR Mandate may, in some cases, support business corporations in developing closer and strategic ties with their local communities, and in return make it relatively easier to acquire the 'social license to operate' (Prno and Slocombe, 2012).

Additionally, the CSR Mandate has been successful in creating mass awareness of CSR in India. Possibly, the Indian CSR Mandate and corporate CSR practices may influence the global definitions, understanding, debates and discourses around CSR, which is currently widely viewed and debated as a voluntary notion (Matten and Moon, 2008; Brammer et al., 2012). It may take a few years before the full impact and implications of compliance with the CSR mandate are fully realized and studied. The government is yet to put all the necessary administrative, monitoring, policies and support structures in place to ensure wider and full compliance.

Importantly, it should be noted that the CSR Mandate is not the only framework and measure related to CSR and sustainability, introduced by the government of India. A few other CSR frameworks and guidelines have been developed by the government or its agencies in recent years. Prior to the introduction of the CSR clause in the Indian Companies Act 2013, different government agencies in India promulgated their own versions of CSR obligations on companies. The Indian Ministry of Corporate Affairs first released a draft Voluntary Guidelines on CSR in 2009, and the final one in 2011 as the NVGs. The role of the board in formulating a CSR policy and ensuring its implementation was mentioned in the NVGs. The Ministry of Petroleum and Natural Gas had taken an independent step in 2007 of reaching an agreement with oil companies to voluntarily spend 2 per cent of their profits on CSR activities. The Department of Public Enterprises (DPE) issued CSR guidelines in 2010 for Central Public Sector Enterprises (CPSE), which made CSR spending mandatory. The DPE guidelines have been revised a few times since, and the latest one is 'Guidelines on Corporate Social Responsibility and Sustainability for CPSEs', issued on 21 October 2014.

While the Indian MNCs have been making big strides in the global markets, they are also very active in their engagement on social development issues, and several of these companies exploit core competencies addressing societal needs and challenges. IT companies like Tata Consultancy Services, Wipro and Infosys use IT as an instrument for social change and development. Dr. Reddy's Lab manufactures affordable pharmaceutical products and provides health care services for the rural poor by organizing health camps, running a mobile dispensary, and offering medical aid, besides actively pursuing employability and a skill development agenda for underprivileged youth in India. Similarly, the traditional MNCs such as Unilever, Proctor & Gamble, Nestlé, Glaxo Smithkline, Lafarge and Microsoft have all developed and been engaging with community-related initiatives in India. All such initiatives are usually categorized under the label of CSR by both Indian companies and the foreign MNCs in India.

The CRW and its IRBI can be seen as demands to companies by local stakeholders for enhanced corporate/business sustainability, transparency and CSR engagement in India. Being relatively new, IRBI may as yet not be a well-known initiative, however, GRI has gained global recognition over the last 20 years, since its inception in 1997. The MNCs from the western countries in particular are usually familiar with GRI standards and may find it comforting that GRI is actively engaged in promoting transparency and disclosures in India, which serve as a mechanism for reducing uncertainties and transaction costs, which are among the major cause of worries for MNCs when investing in emerging and developing economies (Herremans et al., 2016). As CSR continues to gain traction in India, with Section 135's specific definition and interpretation, companies need to be prepared to engage accordingly.

Deciphering voluntary sustainability standards in India

In the past few decades, voluntary sustainability standards (VSS) – as forms of private, self-regulated, multi-stakeholder initiatives (MSIs), codes of conducts – have witnessed a speedy and steady growth (Nadvi and Wältring, 2004; Potts et al., 2014; Wijen, 2014). Thousands of VSS in a variety of forms, sectors and themes have been developed and continue to grow, addressing a wide range of issues --like human and labour rights, working conditions, child rights, environmental protection, water, carbon, transparency and disclosures. Such VSS include, for instance, the Forest Stewardship Council (FSC); Social Accountability 8000 (SA8000); the Alliance for Water Stewardship (AWS); Child Rights and Business Principles (CRBP); Fairtrade; the United Nations Global Compact (UNGC); and the United Nations Guiding Principles on Human Rights (UNGP). A World Bank study on VSS in 2003 had already estimated there were over 1,000 sustainability codes and standards (Smith and Feldman, 2003). VSS are increasingly attaining economic and political salience and significance, and associated products, commodities, services and processes are attaining high absolute volumes and growing market shares[9] (Nadvi and Wältring, 2004; Berliner and Prakash, 2014; Potts et al., 2014; Wijen, 2014). The policy advocates and professionals argue that adoption of and compliance with VSS are a better way for companies to improve their sustainability objectives and performance; VSS have the potential to be a 'game changer', and that the VSS community (comprising of state and non-state actors) and space are growing fast (Pedersen and Gwozdz, 2014). A special UN agency – the United Nations Forum on Sustainability Standards (UNFSS) – was created by the United Nations Conference on Trade and Development (UNCTAD) in 2012. Another UN agency, the International Trade Centre (ITC), created by the World Trade Organisation (WTO) and UNCTAD, developed a web portal www.standardsmap.org in 2011, listing several VSS, addressing sustainability hotspots in global supply chains in particular.

The local social, economic and ecological challenges and institutional complexities in a particular country, along with the increasingly limited capacities/ inadequacies of states and intergovernmental agencies, are creating opportunities for institutional innovations and space for non-state actors to play roles (Hale and Held, 2011). The VSS are a manifestation of such opportunities of institutional entrepreneurship and innovations (Battilana et al., 2009). The standards setters are aggressively engaging and making attempts to promote the uptake of standards in sourcing countries, which usually are developing and emerging economies, such as India.

The social and environmental impacts of business activities and unsustainable production and consumption practices are a growing concern in India. The growth and broader acceptance of the notion of sustainability and sustainable development[10] is also gaining prominence in India, and therefore interest in such notions is growing among companies as well. India has long been a key source destination for MNCs, but is fast becoming an important consumer market of its own. This process can be observed in industries such as palm oil, metals, tea, forestry, agriculture, food & beverages, apparel and textiles and other key sectors of the economy. India's importance as a global consumer market will continue to increase as average household incomes are projected to triple, which is expected to turn the country into the world's fifth largest consumer economy by 2025.

The continuing integration of the global economy through geographically dispersed value creation and capture has been increasingly directing scholarly and policy-makers' attention to the governance of global supply chains (GSCs) and global value chains (GVCs) through MNCs as coordinating and lead firms (Lee and Gereffi, 2015). Participation in GSCs/GVCs is regarded as developmental and an upgrading opportunity for local firms, particularly in developing countries and the emerging economies (Mathews, 2002; Kumaraswamy et al. 2012). The advantages suppliers obtain through engaging with MNCs as part of GSCs/GVCs is evident in the Indian economy as well, and therefore the government of India incentivizes export-oriented small and medium enterprises. The MNCs are increasingly adopting, endorsing or pushing sustainability standards in their supply and value chains, targeted at improving the social and environmental performance of their GSCs/ GVCs. While VSS have been predominantly introduced and supported by western MNEs, increasingly there is a new generation of standards emerging in developing economies (Schouten and Bitzer, 2015; Foley and Havice, 2016). Industries in emerging markets are developing their own standards and certification schemes to satisfy domestic, and in some cases, international market needs and demands. Governments in emerging markets, including in India, are increasingly attempting to create an environment that fosters the development of such standards.

The growth in awareness in India regarding sustainability is also due to the aggressive promotion, marketing and engagement by international organizations like the International Finance Corporation (IFC), IDH, the Sustainable Trade Initiative, the Carbon Disclosure Project (CDP), GRI and UNGC. The demands by foreign financial institutional investors and western business counterparts, and an orientation among several Indian companies to globalize, along with their operations and distribution networks too are playing a part (Kumar and Gaur, 2007, Kumar, 2008). There are now thousands of Indian companies that have business interests beyond India (through export activities, for instance), and several of them are now MNCs. The western MNCs, the traditional supporters of VSS, too are spreading their sustainability practices in India, particularly through supply chains.

A study by IDH and True Price[11] found that the certified farms in India are 52 per cent more profitable on average than non-certified farms and have 35 per cent lower external costs. VSS-driven practices, such as lower water and pesticide use, all contribute to reducing the environmental cost of cultivation and promote higher farm productivity.[12] Another example of the impacts and benefits of VSS is found in the coffee sector in the Indian states of Andhra Pradesh and Telangana, that suggests that the certified coffee farmers earn 52 per cent more than non-certified farmers.[13] Several MNCs in the garment, food & beverages and retailing sectors source cotton and coffee from India and the findings related to benefits and impacts of VSS of these studies would be of great interest to them.

The Tea Board of India partnered in the launch of the Trustea programme in 2014 with tea industry leaders like the Tata Global Beverages Ltd. and Unilever, aimed at transforming the Indian tea market with sustainability-oriented objectives. The NVGs, by the Ministry of Corporate Affairs, are also seeing an uptake at different levels among regulators, businesses and NGOs. The growing acceptance and significance of VSS in India, as tools and processes for risk reduction, market and material access, or for social and environmental value creation, can be seen as valuable. The community, platforms and space for VSS can be leveraged well by everyone in the interest of business and of benefits to society and the economy.

Conclusion

CSR and VSS, as mechanisms for governance and tools to support firms in improving their sustainability performance, are a growing global phenomenon, including in India. The discussions above in two parts demonstrate the increasing importance of CSR and VSS in India. The GRI action on linking its global standard to the Indian standards and regulations, also exemplifies the keenness of international standards-setters to adapt to the local needs in emerging markets, such as India. Enthusiasm by the government and policy-makers in India for CSR, as indicated through the legislative mandate on CSR and the reporting mandate by SEBI, are yet other signs of the changing times for businesses in India and for foreign MNCs doing business in India.

To effectively engage with and leverage the CSR Mandate, sustainability and VSS to the advantage of a company, there are certain challenges. First and foremost, orienting, educating and enabling the board members, senior management and executives to integrate CSR and a sustainability vision, policy and activities into the core processes and business models. Creating a CSR and sustainability vision aligned to the core business with multi-stakeholder perspectives in the short and long run, communicating both tangible and intangible benefits of this vision-based strategy, aligning internal and external processes and structures to this strategy, convincing employees of the relevance of these strategies (for their motivation and organizational citizenship behaviour), and identifying and coordinating with suitable external partners, all this will require appropriate education and skilling and will be some of the major challenges facing companies. MNCs in particular need re-orientation to the very specific notion of a legally mandated CSR. On VSS, some critiques argue that the VSS compete with national public regulations and serve as barriers to trade. These could pose challenges in the adoption and pushing of VSS in supply chains. Perhaps, the case of public-private partnership and collaboration between Tata Global Beverages Ltd. and Unilever (as private entities) and the Tea Board of India (as a public entity) to form Trusttea as a VSS to improve tea sector sustainability in India, including addressing the improved livelihood needs of tea farmers and producers, could be useful in dealing with such VSS-related criticisms and challenges.

Useful websites

Corporate Watch www.corporatewatch.in/reports.html
Government of India www.mca.gov.in/SearchableActs/Section135.htm
Government of India www.mca.gov.in/Ministry/pdf/FAQ_CSR.pdf
Government of India www.mca.gov.in/MinistryV2/csrdatasummary.html
Sustainability standards www.sustainabilitystandards.in/

Notes

1 The GRI is a voluntary multi-stakeholder initiative to develop a *global standard for organizational sustainability reporting (i.e., on social, environmental and economic results and impacts)* and has now become a provider of the most widely-used global standard for sustainability reporting (thousands of companies, including 90+ per cent of the S&P 250 apply it).

2 The Business Responsibility Reporting (BRR) framework is based on the NVGs and SEBI requires the top 500 listed companies in India to submit a BRR framework as part of their Annual Reports at www.sebi.gov.in/legal/circulars/nov-2015/format-for-business-responsibility-report-brr-_30954.html. Failure to provide an annual BRR constitutes an act of non-compliance for listed companies with SEBI's Clause 55 of the Equity Listing Agreement.

3 Page 22 of report at https://assets.kpmg.com/content/dam/kpmg/xx/pdf/2017/10/kpm g-survey-of-corporate-responsibility-reporting-2017.pdf (accessed 3 December 2017).
4 See www.responsiblebiz.org/wp-content/uploads/2017/08/India-Responsible-Business-Ind ex-017-Web-Version-1.pdf (accessed 2 December 2017).
5 The historic global Climate Change Agreement in Paris in December 2015 under the United Nations Framework Convention on Climate Change (UNFCCC) aims at keeping the rise in global temperatures well below 2°C and the UN SDGs set the global development agenda for the next 15 years, till 2030.
6 Other countries that have mandated CSR, though in different ways, include Malaysia and Indonesia (Chatterjee and Mitra, 2016).
7 See www.mca.gov.in/SearchableActs/Schedule7.htm
8 Fear of 'name and shame' will push firms to comply on CSR, e.g., IICA's Chatterjee by Arundhati Ramanathan (4 March 2015), see www.livemint.com/Companies/ EzwvbztSMQsyJ8Y26iaBrL/Fear-of-name-and-shame-will-push-firms-to-comp ly-on-CSR-I.html (accessed 3 December 2017).
9 The *State of Sustainability Initiatives Review 2014* reports on systems and market trends across 16 standards initiatives operating across 10 key commodity sectors, which account for an estimated $31.6 billion in trade value. Also, the report claims that the average annual growth rate of standard-compliant production across all commodity sectors in 2012 was 41 per cent, significantly outpacing the annual average growth of 2 per cent in the corresponding conventional commodity markets (Potts et al., 2014, p. 8).
10 The terms 'sustainability' and 'sustainable development' in practice usually refer to issues related to environmental management systems, including natural resources use, management and conservation.
11 See www.standardsimpacts.org/sites/default/files/True%20Price%20of%20Cotton%20 India.pdf
12 See www.standardsimpacts.org/resources-reports/infographic-india-benefits-and-impa cts-sustainability-standards-2017
13 Ibid.

References

Afsharipour, A. and Rana, S. (2014) The emergence of new corporate social responsibility regimes in China and India. *UC Davis Business Law Journal,* 14: 175–230.

Anupindi, R. and Sivakumar, S. (2007) ITC's e-Choupal: a platform strategy for rural transformation. In V.K. Rangan, J.A. Quelch, G. Herroro and B. Barton (eds) *Business Solutions for the Global Poor: Creating Social and Economic Value.* San Francisco: Jossey-Bass, pp. 173–182.

Arora, B. and Puranik, R. (2004) A review of corporate social responsibility in India. *Development,* 47(3): 93–100.

Battilana, J., Leca, B. and Boxenbaum, E. (2009) How actors change institutions: Towards a theory of institutional entrepreneurship. *The Academy of Management Annals,* 3: 65–107.

Berliner, D. and Prakash, A. (2014) The United Nations Global Compact: An institutionalist perspective. *Journal of Business Ethics,* 122(2): 217–223.

Brammer, S., Jackson, G. and Matten, D. (2012) Corporate social responsibility and institutional theory: New perspectives on private governance. *Socio-Economic Review,* 10(1): 3–28.

Foley, P. and Havice, E. (2016) The rise of territorial eco-certifications: New politics of transnational sustainability governance in the fishery sector. *Geoforum,* 69: 24–33.

Hale, T. and Held, D. (2011) *Handbook of Transnational Governance: Institutions and Innovations.* Cambridge: Polity.

Herremans, I.M., Nazari, J.A. and Mahmoudian, F. (2016) Stakeholder relationships, engagement, and sustainability reporting. *Journal of Business Ethics,* 138(3): 417–435.

IRBI (2017) Responsible business. Available at: www.responsiblebiz.org/wp-content/uploads/2017/08/India-Responsible-Business-Index-2017-Web-Version-1.pdf (accessed 2 December 2017).

Jaiswal, A.K. (2008) The fortune at the bottom or the middle of the pyramid? *Innovations*, 3(1): 85–100.

Karnani, A. (2013a) India makes CSR mandatory: A really bad idea. *The European Financial Review*, 29 October.

Karnani, A. (2013b) Mandatory CSR in India: A bad proposal. *Stanford Social Innovation Review*, 20 May.

Kumar, N. (2008) Internationalization of Indian enterprises: Patterns, strategies, ownership advantages, and implications. *Asian Economic Policy Review*, 3(2): 242–261.

Kumar, V. and Gaur, A.S. (2007) Internationalization of Indian firms: Regionalization patterns and impact on performance. In A. Rugman (ed.) *Regional Aspects of Multinationality and Performance*. Oxford: Elsevier, pp. 201–219.

Kumaraswamy, A., Mudambi, R., Saranga, H. and Tripathy, A. (2012) Catch-up strategies in the Indian auto components industry: Domestic firms' responses to market liberalization. *Journal of International Business Studies*, 43(4): 368–395.

Lee, J. and Gereffi, G. (2015) Global value chains, rising power firms and economic and social upgrading. *Critical Perspectives on International Business*, 11(3/4): 319–339.

MacNeil, I. and Li, X. (2006) 'Comply or explain': Market discipline and non-compliance with the Combined Code. *Corporate Governance: An International Review*, 14(5): 486–496.

Mathews, J.A. (2002) Competitive advantages of the latecomer firm: A resource-based account of industrial catch-up strategies. *Asia Pacific Journal of Management*, 19(4): 467–488.

Matten, D. and Moon, J. (2008) 'Implicit' and 'explicit' CSR: A conceptual framework for a comparative understanding of corporate social responsibility. *Academy of Management Review*, 33(2): 404–424.

Nadvi, K. and Wältring, F. (2004) Making sense of global standards. In H. Schmitz (ed.) *Local Enterprises in the Global Economy: Issues of Governance and Upgrading*. Cheltenham: Edward Elgar, pp. 53–94.

Pedersen, E.R.G. and Gwozdz, W. (2014) From resistance to opportunity-seeking: Strategic responses to institutional pressures for corporate social responsibility in the Nordic fashion industry. *Journal of Business Ethics*, 119(2): 245–264.

Potts, J., Lynch, M., Wilking, A., Huppé, G., Cunningham, M. and Voora, V. (2014) *The State of Sustainability Initiatives Review 2014: Standards and the Green Economy*. London: International Institute for Sustainable Development and the International Institute for Environment and Development.

Prno, J. and Slocombe, D.S. (2012) Exploring the origins of 'social license to operate' in the mining sector: Perspectives from governance and sustainability theories. *Resources Policy*, 37(3): 346–357.

Schouten, G. and Bitzer, V. (2015) The emergence of Southern standards in agricultural value chains: A new trend in sustainability governance? *Ecological Economics*, 120: 175–184.

Smith, G. and Feldman, D. (2003) *Company Codes of Conduct and International Standards: An Analytical Comparison*. Washington, DC: World Bank.

Van Zile, C. (2011) India's mandatory corporate social responsibility proposal: Creative capitalism meets creative regulation in the global market. *Asian-Pacific Law & Policy Journal*, 13: 269–303.

Wijen, F. (2014) Means versus ends in opaque institutional fields: Trading off compliance and achievement in sustainability standard adoption. *Academy of Management Review*, 39(3): 302–323.

INDEX

Page numbers in *italics* denote figures, those in **bold** denote tables.

Printed in the United States
by Baker & Taylor Publisher Services